The Cook's Handbook

The Cook's Handbook

PRUE LEITH

Stewart House

Toronto

Canadian Cataloguing in Publication Data

Leith, Prue.
    The cook's handbook

Bibliography: p.
Includes index.
ISBN 0-7710-5246-4

1. Cookery. 2. Kitchen utensils. 3. Kitchens.
I. Title.

TX651.L45 1989   641.5   C89-093491-6

Published in 1989 by

Sphere Books
A division of LDAP, Inc.
166 Fifth Avenue
New York, NY 10010

Published in Canada in 1989 by

Stewart House
481 University Avenue
Toronto, Ontario
M5G 2E9

By arrangement with Marshall Editions Limited

Library of Congress Catalog Card Number: 80-69128

Printed in the United States of America

Contents

Introduction

This book is not a recipe book. True, it has a few blueprint recipes in it but they are there because they exemplify one or other of the classic cooking methods or techniques. It is, I hope, the book that will make other cookbooks as clear to their readers as they are to their authors. How often has the inexperienced cook come to a full stop on "one boned chicken" or "a cupful of chopped onions, sweated"? Not every poulterer or butcher will bone a chicken for you, and if you do not know your sweated onions you are lost.

The techniques of cooking have always fascinated me. True, a cucumber sliced on a machine tastes as good as one sliced by the hand of an experienced cook, but there is something almost magical, certainly beautiful, about the easy rocking motion of the professional chef's wrist, and the scrape, chop chop chop, scrape, chop chop chop of the knife. There are few sights as satisfying as that of an ordered restaurant kitchen, clean, quiet, dedicated and very busy, with people doing things *right*. Slithery, fresh fish quickly, simply and cleanly gutted and skinned; piles of clean fresh carrots rapidly transformed into bowls of red-gold matchsticks; veal turned from uninteresting lumps into paper-thin scallops under the steady, even whack of the cleaver or mallet.

But it is not the wizardry it looks. At catering schools, students are first taught to hold the tools of their trade correctly. At first they work painfully slowly, but because they are following the right technique, improvement is rapid. A two-finger typist may eventually type moderately well, but will never become really fast, never look good doing it, and never feel any pride in the work done.

So this book is for the cook who really wants to *do it right*. It is also for the reader who is fascinated by cooking; who loves to have a go at some dish never tried before, and who likes to experiment with new combinations of taste and texture.

Of course some of the best cooks in the world have never invented a dish in their lives, never gambled with anything, being content devoutly to follow Escoffier, Julia Child or Elizabeth David. I have no criticism whatever of such careful dedication.

Indeed, I spent much of my life imploring cookery students *not* to run before they can walk, and to trust the great professionals rather than risk the frustration and expense of failure. For, unhappily, cooks with nothing but enthusiasm and a desire to "create" often produce over-complicated dishes confusing to the palate and expensive to the pocket.

However, if cooks understand what they are doing—if they know what makes an emulsion; that Swiss cheese goes into melted strands when heated; that tomatoes and basil are an unbeatable combination; that spicy things benefit from a touch of sweetness, and so on—they are in the perfect position to enjoy cooking. They can be "creative" without much risk of ruining the ingredients, wasting their time, and abandoning the whole thing in despair.

The fact is that inventing something delicious (I say "inventing" but the chances are a dozen cooks will have already stumbled on the same thing) is amazingly satisfying to the inventor. Discovery provides an unrivaled buzz of pleasure.

This is an intensely practical book. I have tried to cram into it everything a good cook should know: how to plan a kitchen; the "whys and wherefores" of kitchen processes like storing, freezing, salting, drying, smoking, bottling and preserving, the "do's and don'ts" of shopping, the pros and cons of available kitchen equipment, gadgets and tools. I have also included the "tricks of the trade"—short cuts, remedies and dodges that really work without impairing the product. It is the sort of book I have wanted for years, and I think it fills a needed gap in the cook's library.

Kitchen planning

Design

As splendid a meal may be produced in the Spartan confines of a ship's galley as may come from any spacious dream kitchen full of the latest in gourmet gadgetry. Fortunately, the size of the kitchen in no way affects the quality of the cooking. In many households, though, the kitchen has also to be used for eating, ironing, doing the laundry, as a playground for children and animals, and for entertaining neighbors. The ancestral status of the kitchen as the heart of the household has been restored and at the same time interest in sophisticated cooking has grown. Home cooks are now ever ready to look to the professionals for ideas, but they have to be cautious in transposing restaurant practices to the home. Some work, but some do not. The chef is like an orchestra conductor; the household cook is usually a one-man band.

In planning a kitchen, think first about who is going to use it and what is going to be done in it.

★ Will there be a single, working person turning out the occasional evening meal, but venturing into ambitious gourmet cooking at weekends?

★ Is it for a couple who like to cook together as a team?

★ Is it a family room where mother cooks three meals a day?

★ Does the cook prefer things visible and constantly at hand, or neatly hidden away?

A roller blind mounted between the two panes of a double-glazed window stays clean and grease-free.

Near the entrance to the kitchen, have a convenient flat surface. Use it to put down heavy garden produce, shopping and trays. This also keeps tracked-in dirt to a minimum.

For low-level storage, deep drawers that glide out on rollers use space efficiently and give easier access.

Have sufficient draining racks directly over the sink (with a tiled wall behind them) so that dishes can be left there for storage. If "invisible" storage is preferred, have a bottomless cabinet, with a fold-away door, built around the racks.

Wherever possible, have recessed handles rather than knobs which may catch sleeves or cause injury if they are fallen against.

Surgical tap handles are a great asset when working with pastry- or grease-covered hands. A high swivelling tap is useful for filling tall pans and helps prevent chipping of glassware.

Use deep, potentially wasted, corner work-surface area to keep appliances permanently set up for use. This ensures that they do get used to the full instead of languishing in a cabinet because it is too much trouble to get them out each time they are needed.

Have the garbage pail directly beneath the sink or the area where most of the preparation takes place. Arrange that its lid lifts automatically as the door opens.

Open shelves are a constant reminder of what is running low and what needs using up. There is also less work involved in getting things to and from them.

The most convenient and safe way to store kitchen knives is in a row of slots in the wooden work-surface. Allow at least 2 in clearance from the back wall for easy access.

An oven door that drops down provides a ready shelf for hot and heavy dishes.

Illuminate work surfaces with small fluorescent strip-lights mounted under the front edge of the under-side of wall cabinets. Have a frame in front of them deep enough to keep the glare out of the eyes of people who are seated.

There are three principal elements in kitchen design: function, aesthetics and comfort. The most important is function. The kitchen must be practical, safe and efficient. A professional kitchen need be nothing more, but in a domestic kitchen the other elements come into play.

The kitchen should be attractive because the cook should be able to enjoy the time spent in it. For the serious cook, handsome is as handsome does—bear this in mind when subjected to promotion about units and fittings.

Too often, symmetry and clean lines are allowed to take precedence over commonsense and practicality. As an example, the tops of sinks are usually brought level with counter-tops, making the sink bottom uncomfortably low to work on. Standardized kitchen units may not always work out to the cook's advantage.

Take the approach of hi-fi enthusiasts: they buy components separately from the many options in the marketplace to create their own ideal. There are many little touches which make a kitchen attractive, so the cook need not suffer taste dictated by someone else's purely practical design.

A revolving corner cabinet unit makes the most efficient use of this awkward space.

Have good-size sections of the work-surface made out of wood (sycamore or maple) for cutting and chopping; and marble for pastry-making. Ideally, have them fitted as an integral part of the surface, rather than just set in. There is then less chance of dirt collecting in the joins. Each section should be about 20 in wide.

Possibly the best way to arrange burners on a stove is to have them in one long line at the back. Each pan can then be given attention without any stretching or lifting of one over the other. Pans can also be pulled straight forward to a heat-resistant work-surface at the front with minimum chance of spillage. The extractor hood above can then be narrower. Have the burner controls set at the front of the work-surface with the oven controls.

A floor covering curved up into the toe gap under floor units keeps this area easier to clean. Support it from behind with a wooden angle fillet to prevent it cracking. A similar curve at the work surface/wall join has the same advantage.

More often than not, the kitchen is the most lived-in room. It should be easy on the eyes, ears, nose, back and feet. The cook needs a place to sit down, and to settle the family and friends who are inevitably drawn to the heart of the house. A functional, beautiful, comfortable kitchen is the ideal incentive to cook often and cook well.

Design/2

The cook's environment
The atmosphere in the kitchen is made up of a variety of environmental factors—heat, light, ventilation, acoustics and visual space. These, in turn, are influenced by structural factors such as floors, doors, walls, ceilings, windows and decor.

Lighting
Cooking requires more utilitarian lighting than any other activity in the house. Two types of lighting are needed: general and work-top.

There should be a steady level of uniform lighting, free from glare and cast shadows. Fluorescent lights are increasingly common in kitchens because they provide this steady, uniform illumination. They also give off very little heat, making them uniquely suited to kitchens. For this reason, too, they last longer and consume less electricity. They can, however, flicker and hum irritatingly, and so it is best to conceal them behind diffusers.

Recessed, adjustable spotlights are an ideal alternative for general lighting, although they are comparatively expensive. They should lie flush with the ceiling when pointing straight down, but they can be angled to pick out a picture, table pinboard or bowl of fruit. They can also be fitted to the tops of cabinets to bounce light off ceilings.

The different areas to be lit—work-tops, eating area—should have separate control switches. Differential lighting can make a dining area in the kitchen seem separate enough for more formal entertaining.

Ventilation
Even the best-equipped kitchen will be unpleasant to work in if not properly ventilated. The short-term benefits are the immediate removal of excess heat, steam and cooking smells; and, in the long term, airborne grease and dirt do not build up on the walls, ceilings and cabinets.

A fan-activated hood over the stove can either clean and recirculate the soiled air by passing it through replaceable filters or, if ducted, can extract fumes to an exterior outlet. A hood should be as low down as possible over the stove—never more than 3 ft above it. Where there is an eye-level broiler, the hood should be installed no more than 18 in above that. If the extractor hood over the stove is well-positioned, extraction need not be mechanical. A simple pipe to the outside wall will be enough. It also helps to have high-level mechanical extraction. A fan high up in the room, close to the sink, dishwasher and stove, is advisable. An extractor fan in the window is cheap, but the window has to be closed while the fan is being used. Another technique for extracting steam at source is to have a ducted fan built at burner level. Make sure that no one fan is too strong—an overhead fan pulling smells away from the hood, for instance. More sophisticated installations can be adjusted to different speeds, according to need. If the kitchen is also the dining area, ventilation must be as quiet as it is effective.

Heat
It is desirable to generate some form of continuous warmth in the kitchen (if it is not already centrally heated), even when the stove is not in use, to discourage condensation and to keep the room always at a pleasant ambient temperature. There are several ways of providing background heat: say, with under-floor heating or tubular chrome heated rails for keeping dishtowels dry. Only rely on the stove alone for heating if it is a solid-fuel range. (Never use gas burners or an open gas oven to warm a kitchen as these exhaust the oxygen in the air.)

Acoustics
A combination of noise-reducing surfaces such as cork, vinyl and softwood, used on floors, walls, furniture and ceilings, plus sound-insulating housings for electrical appliances, can keep noise at acceptable levels.

Visual space
Judicious use of color, line and illumination can make cramped quarters seem more spacious, and may, conversely, make a roomy kitchen cosy.

Use mirrors between the work-tops and the cabinets, or above the wall cabinets to the ceiling to create visual space.

* A kitchen in similar pale colors will look larger than one in contrasting or dark colors.

* Rounded corners and soft shapes make the space look larger, as the eye cannot then easily focus on particular points.

Ceilings
The kitchen ceiling, like the floor, must be treated so that it may be easily cleaned, as this is where most condensation and steam-borne grease will accumulate.

It should also have good acoustic properties.

In establishing visual space, a dark ceiling tends to look lower.

A false or suspended ceiling affords indirect lighting but is unlikely to be sufficiently strong to support, say, a hanging cast-iron pan rack.

Obviously, a very low ceiling will necessitate especially effective ventilation.

A sound tongued-and-grooved softwood ceiling will solve a number of kitchen problems. First, if it is lowered from the main ceiling, it can hide ugly pipes. It can then also allow the space between it and the main ceiling to be used for housing recessed light fittings (4 in to 8 in will be needed, depending on the fitting). Having a warm surface, it will not gather condensation like an ordinary hard plaster ceiling. It will deaden some of the noise in a modern kitchen. It will allow access traps for getting at pipework. It can also be positioned at just the right height to match the kitchen units.

Timber ceilings need not be flat; they can be arched between units in, say, a narrow, galley-type kitchen. For safety they should be backed with $1\frac{1}{2}$ in of fireproof board, such as plaster board or mineral insulating board.

Floors

More demands are made on the floor of the kitchen than of any other room in the house. It is subject to the most traffic, the most mess, the most extended periods of standing and walking. Therefore, although it has a decorative function, practical matters must be considered first.

Kitchen floors should be non-slippery and easy to keep clean. Rough or porous floors with joins will collect dirt, so any porous flooring must be sealed. Waxed wooden floors, however beautiful, are treacherous when wet. It is unlikely that anyone would consider carpeting a kitchen, and even carpet tiles, which can easily be lifted, cleaned and replaced, could prove more trouble than they are worth when subject to a cascade of crumbs, flour and other kitchen debris.

Although ceramic tile, slate and brick are handsome and durable, the cook may pay in leg and back strain for their beauty and in the cost of replacing the many cups and plates which will inevitably break if dropped on such a surface. Such flooring is suitable for under-floor heating and is naturally cool in hot weather. Unglazed tiles give a non-slip surface; quarry tiles and slate are naturally waterproof. None of these needs polishing. Properly sealed cork tiles provide an excellent combination of natural warmth and resilience.

Flexible and resilient floors also have desirable acoustical properties, in helping to deaden culinary clatter, rather than amplifying it as harder surfaces do.

The choice of floor may be limited by the nature of the sub-floor. A concrete sub-floor may have any flooring laid over it, but any ceramic or marble-type flooring would crack if laid over timber joists, which are subject to movement. For any kitchen above ground level, a tiled or brick floor may be too heavy. Also, remember with a solid-fuel or oil-burning stove, flooring must be strong enough to support it.

An old wooden floor must be covered with sealed hardboard before laying vinyl or linoleum. If planning a wooden floor, it would still be advisable to lay an apron of tiles in front of the stove for easier cleaning.

* **Vinyl is virtually impervious to all damage except that caused by extreme heat such as cigarette burns or a heavy iron pan taken straight from the oven or burner. Vinyl asbestos tiles are cheaper than pure vinyl, but they are brittle and have to be replaced more frequently.**

* **Concrete sub-floors may be covered with epoxy resin, a plasticized liquid, laid with a trowel.**

* **Do not cover old floorboards with hardboard; it is a false economy as hardboard is, in fact, too soft, and will eventually assume the uneven form of the boards below. Instead, use resin-bonded plywood to level them.**

Doors

Dutch, or stable-type, outside doors are useful for letting the sun in and keeping animals out. A Dutch door may be used inside with a fold-down serving shelf on the lower half of the door. If a solid door separates the kitchen from the dining room, replace it with a glass door, which permits communication between the two and yet prevents cooking smells from permeating the whole house.

The ideal is a two-way swing door between the kitchen and dining room so trays may be carried easily from one to the other. Such doors should be similar to those used in hospitals which have small windows in them to prevent collisions.

Sliding doors are good for storage areas, especially in narrow kitchens. They should have projecting handles so that one door will catch and push the other along and will also prevent fingers getting caught. Sliding doors must be light, yet rigid enough not to warp, and should be set in plastic or in reinforced nylon tracks that are widely spaced for easy cleaning. Or, better still, they can be top-hung.

Walls and partitions

The chief consideration for kitchen wall finishes is that they should wipe clean. Vinyl and polyurethane paints stand up to cleaning well, as do the many types of plastic or vinyl-coated wallpapers. Wood, cork tiles and fabrics such as burlap must be given a seal of polyurethane varnish. If the wall covering is not readily cleaned (and even if it is) it is good to have a splashback—tiles are excellent—behind both the sink and stove. The splashback should extend sideways at least 1 in beyond the junction of the fitment and the wall.

Walls must also be considered in terms of their load-bearing potential. An internal partition is not the best support for heavily-laden shelves or cabinets.

* **A serving hatch knocked through the wall dividing the kitchen from the dining room will save a lot of journeys. Plan a hatch with two levels, dirty dishes returning to the kitchen by the lower one. Trolleys are another means of transporting food from the cooking to eating area; ideally, store them under work-surfaces.**

* **If the partition is open above the work-top, install roller or venetian blinds, a sliding or concertina door, or a folding louvre door to close off the kitchen when necessary.**

* **If the partition work-top is also to serve as a breakfast bar with tall bar stools, there must be enough overhang to allow knee-room.**

* **Provide an eating area in the kitchen to keep the cook with the diners. A high table can also serve as the cook's office desk or as somewhere for children to do their homework under supervision.**

Design/3

Windows

Opinions vary as to the optimum position for kitchen windows. Often there is no choice, since the sink is generally placed directly beneath a window and sinks and their plumbing are the costliest items to move. This convention would seem to have arisen from the idea that washing up is so boring and time-consuming it would be a relief to have a view. Now that dishwashers are widely used, the relation of the window to the overall kitchen design may be reconsidered. However, it is a good compromise to have the window at right angles to the sink, or by the eating area. Curtains should be hung only if the window is a safe distance from the stove and even then they should be both flame-proof and washable.

★ **Tilting sash windows are convenient to clean and can provide continuous ventilation. Windows substantially affect the temperature, illumination, acoustics and air-flow in the kitchen.**

★ **If the kitchen window has an ugly view, put thick glass shelves across it, supported on aluminium angles. Space them to match the window bars or about 12 in apart. They can be used to support plants and pots of herbs, so pleasantly disguising the view while admitting the light and producing a useful crop just where it is needed.**

Decoration

There are no absolute laws about kitchen colors; the cook is free to use personal favorites. Bearing in mind that the most important thing in the kitchen is the food, try to keep to colors that set off food. It is no accident that among the most popular kitchen colors are the naturals, colors that harmonize with brick, tile, wood chopping boards and food itself, like cream, terracotta and orange. Flooring, work-surfaces and commercially produced kitchen units, which together comprise the most dominant color features in the room, are now available in a prodigious range of colors, as are the many washable paints. The yellows to reds to browns are known as warm colors; greens and blues are cool, as are the neutral and achromatic whites and stainless steel of appliances and fixtures. The choice of colors influences impressions of temperature and dimension. Consider the direction the window faces (cold north light or warm south light) and the room size. Generally, pale means cooler and more distant; dark means warmer and closer.

Coming to some arrangement

The ingredients which make a kitchen are quite simple: a standard combination of sink, stove, refrigerator, work surfaces, storage area and waste disposal with an assortment of handy appliances. The quality of individual components, and the manner in which they are laid out in relation to one another, govern the quality and efficiency of the kitchen as a cook's workshop.

Ergonomics (the study of efficiency in the working environment) can be applied in the kitchen to such problems as the number of steps between sink and stove; how the body must bend or reach to lift a heavy pan from an awkward storage place; the angles and levels at which specific tasks, such as chopping, kneading or washing dishes, are best done. Since strain and pain come from holding the body in an unnatural position over an extended period of time, work areas in a kitchen must be planned to eliminate, or substantially to reduce, static work. A certain amount of built-in exercise in the kitchen is a good thing for the largely housebound cook. However, no cook should have to negotiate an obstacle course from stove to sink in order to drain the spaghetti.

The phrase "work triangle" evolved due to ergonomic studies of kitchens. It refers to the relative positions of sink, stove and refrigerator. It is a neat concept, but it does not comprehensively reflect the realities of cooking. It might be more helpful to think in terms of the "work path" which adds in storage, waste and—most important of all—work-surface to the triangle. A cook might think to take all necessary ingredients from cabinets, refrigerator and storage before cooking, so the action takes place between the stove, sink and work-surface.

The best arrangement for equipment in the kitchen (for a right-handed person) is, working from left to right: storage area (refrigerator and cabinets), preparation area, sink, mixing area, stove, and serving area. The objective in planning the kitchen is to have the minimum of necessary journeys between these areas—by relating them logically.

In a small to medium kitchen the sum of the distances between the refrigerator, sink and stove should not exceed 15 ft, or 25 ft in a large kitchen.

It is also essential, for both convenience and safety, to allow enough elbow room when opening drawers and cupboards, and also space for unrestricted passage when carrying pots and pans, or other heavy and/or hot containers. Through traffic should not cross the work-path—particularly between the sink and stove.

If the kitchen is too small, more space can be gained by annexing part of a hallway, taking out an old closet (if willing to sacrifice that type of storage), opening the kitchen to the living area, changing a solid door for a sliding or folding one, or building an extension. Any large appliance that will not fit into the kitchen could be installed elsewhere. For example, the refrigerator can be fitted into a closet under the stairs.

If the kitchen is too large, put all the work area in one part of it in an L- or U-shape and use the rest for a dining area or utility room. If there is an island or peninsula built in the center to provide some additional storage, or additional work space, be sure the cook does not have to walk round it in the cooking process.

If the kitchen is an L- or U-shape, note the position of the right-angles on the plan. The cooker should not be placed close to a right-angle turn (allow about 12 in elbow room on either side) or next to a door or window because of the risk of fire-catching draughts, curtains or blinds.

Of the different types of kitchen, that in a U-shape arrangement is the most efficient as it allows the work path to be maintained without interruption, but it might have cabinets that are difficult to use.

The galley kitchen with equipment on both sides is also particularly efficient as it has no dead corners. The single line kitchen, along one wall, is usually too long.

Opinions vary as to optimum work-surface heights. Too high a work-top tends to strain the shoulders; too low strains the back. Each country has set standards based on the average height of the adult female. Manufacturers of kitchen units follow these guidelines. Short or tall cooks should take care that heights are adjusted appropriately. Some experts argue that hands are at their best in power and precision when elbows are at the sides, bent at right-angles, in which case the ideal work-top height is determined by measuring from the floor to the bent elbow. This suits activities such as chopping. Heavier manual work, such as kneading or rolling out pastry dough, is more easily carried out on a lower surface, where the palm would rest flat at the end of a fully extended arm.

As tasks like beating or mixing by hand are better done sitting down, a kitchen with no room for a table could have a pull-out work-top at the correct height for a cook sitting on a chair or a stool—or the stool may be adjustable.

The height of the sink work-top is most important because so much time is spent at the sink. Ideally, it should be about 2 in higher than the general work-surface, to accommodate the fact that both hands are at work more at the bottom of the sink than the top. But, if a uniform height is preferred (giving an unbroken run of work-surface), then a compromise must be made, either lowering the sink or raising the work-top height. This is one reason most standardized units are prejudiced in favor of the tall; manufacturers tend to make work-top surfaces smoothly level with the sink-top.

The heights of cabinets and shelves must also take into account the length of the cook's arms and whether the back of the shelf can be reached without strain. On average, heights of 2 ft to 5 ft, and a depth of 2 ft at or below shoulder level, are easy to reach. Above shoulder height, narrow shelves of about 18 in depth are more convenient. The tops of storage cabinets should not be over 6½ ft in height. Over work-tops it is sensible to bring top cabinets above 6½ ft out to line with the front. They will be above head height, useful mainly for items used only occasionally and reached by step-ladder.

Work-surfaces

There are two schools of thought on kitchen work-surfaces. One is that there can never be too much, especially for the cook who entertains a great deal and needs space for prepared dishes; the other is that limited space will suffice and is even desirable, as it obliges the cook to clean up continuously during preparation.

Surfaces and heights vary according to the tasks performed: chopping and cutting, pastry making, kneading, or setting down pans hot from the oven. There is no one ideal work-top surface. Use stainless steel for sinks, sink-tops and around the stove area. Alternatively, use stainless steel sinks and drainers set into a tiled top.

The best surface for a general work-top is one that can be wiped clean with a finish that will not show fingermarks too obviously. Dark tops mark more easily than light ones.

A convenient depth from back to front for a work-top is 2 ft and it is usual to have a ½ in lip overhanging at the front edge, preferably curved.

Avoid joins in a work-top as they will trap dirt. Do not interrupt a run of work-top with a tall unit housing, say, an oven.

The work-surface on either side of the stove should be at the same height as the stove so that there is no danger of pans being tipped over when removed from the heat.

★ Fit a pull-out chopping board under the work-top over a narrow drawer.

★ A fitted cover for a sink can provide an additional work-surface, which would be well suited to a messy job such as cleaning fish.

★ A hinged work-top, raised when needed, saves valuable space in a small kitchen.

The space between the work-surface and the wall cabinets above should be at least 16 in but not more than 20 in. The smaller space will give greater cabinet space within easy reach above, but the larger space is more convenient for handling and storing utensils.

Plastic laminates, such as formica, are the best for all-purpose work-top surfaces, and they come in a wide variety of colors, patterns and textures. They will scratch, so a separate chopping surface should be used.

Polypropylene work-top surfaces resist spills and scratch marks well and are fairly cheap.

Stainless steel (which is only truly stainless when of the highest quality) is heat-resistant and easy to clean. It is available in matt and polished finishes. It is noisy; paint it on the underside to dampen this effect.

Sealed hardwood is attractive for all kitchen surfaces from walls to floors, but the seal must be renewed frequently. Softwood can be stained or painted before sealing.

Tongue-and-groove or sheet timber is a cheap surface material for the walls, cabinet doors, ceilings and floors, and it insulates against heat-loss and noise as well as concealing uneven walls.

Design /4

Storage

Everything kept in the kitchen—cooked food, raw ingredients, utensils, machinery, crockery—needs a storage place, and obviously the things used most often have to be the most accessible.

The two main approaches to storage are the "visible" kitchen, where as much as possible in the way of equipment and ingredients is out there where the cook sees it and has access to it readily; and the "closed" kitchen, where everything is put away in cabinets. Personal preference usually dictates which style is chosen. In a busy kitchen, however, the items stored on open shelves and hanging from walls and ceilings are used so regularly they never have time to gather dust.

Choose a system of kitchen units that is well made and flexible enough to suit all needs. If starting small, with the intention of adding more units later, select a popular range that will be available for years. Examine catalogues with care: Most manufacturers have units which are designed to use every inch of space.

Alternatively, kitchen units may be built by a carpenter or skilled do-it-yourself enthusiast. Or there are factory-made, ready-to-assemble units that are easy for the less experienced. If working on a tight budget, try using cheap furniture not normally associated with kitchens, such as shelves on metal brackets, or discarded shop fittings or dressers.

Most kitchen units are made of timber, plywood or chipboard, sheet plastics or metal. Timber and chipboard are the most adaptable as they can be readily adjusted to fit awkward corners. Metal feels cold and (unless made of stainless steel, which is expensive) can corrode in the humid atmosphere of the kitchen.

Units made of whitewood can be painted (and do *need* to be repainted many times) to change their color; a polyester finish cannot be so readily changed, but stays looking good longer. If an enamel finish is required, coat once or twice with clear polyurethane varnish to prevent any chipping.

For the sake of safety, wherever possible avoid protruding knobs and handles on kitchen furniture. All such handles and catches must be strong and easy to clean.

For the same reasons of safety, wherever possible cupboard and work-top edges and corners should be rounded off.

★ A partition which divides the dining from the cooking area, or the laundry from the food preparation area, could provide extra storage with shelves or closets which are accessible from both sides and/or an extra work-top.

★ Drawers should have heavy-duty plastic or nylon slides. The insides of drawers and cabinets coated with laminated plastic are easy to clean (but more expensive) than those with the more usual coating of impact-resistant paint.

★ Another handle on the inside of a large closet avoids the possibility of anyone being trapped inside.

★ Choose units that have adjustable shelves. Many units have racks or shelves on runners for bottles, glasses or canned goods. The unit should suit the proposed contents rather than the reverse—which is, unfortunately, more usual.

In positioning kitchen units take into account where their contents will be required. Dry goods such as flour and sugar should be kept near to the food preparation area, where appliances such as the food-mixer will be stored. Those utensils used frequently should be within easy reach, and utensils used in combination should be stored together.

Shallow shelves can be much more useful than deep ones. They will often hold more, as the whole vertical space can be used. With deeper shelves, space must be left for reaching over the things in front to get at those at the back.

A relatively narrow (3-in) shelf or ledge just above the work-top makes a useful space for grouping herb jars and other small items in constant use. For general food storage, 4-in-deep shelves take most items.

Ideally, kitchen wall cabinets should have sliding doors or be fitted with a counter-balanced door that is raised up and over the head so there is no danger of banging heads. With ordinary doors, pay attention to the direction of the door swing; most units give a choice of the hinge being either on the left or the right.

As with open shelves, glass-fronted cabinets allow what is inside to be seen—an incentive to tidiness and to using up bits and pieces.

An open carousel on a large central table is extremely useful. It gets rid of all clutter—salt, pepper, mustard, jam, herbs, oil, vinegar—and spinning it saves walking around looking for the right thing.

Wall units can go all the way up to the ceiling or stay just within easy reach, leaving a shelf gap at the top for seldom-used or purely decorative utensils. Have a pair of stepladders to reach the top shelf or shelves—or, better still, a kitchen stool which converts to a set of steps.

Do not install wall cabinets where there is no work-top or shelf below; there is too great a chance of heads hitting corners and protruding surfaces.

If possible, do not install a wall cabinet over the stove as it is dangerous to reach up over the hot burners. If this space must be used for storage, be sure the units are specifically made to be hung over a stove.

Do not hang a wall cabinet within a 12-in range of a radiator: The heat could damage the goods inside. (Also, hanging units over a heating element reduces its efficiency.)

Store goods requiring ventilation, such as fresh fruit and vegetables, away in a "storage cabinet." Ideally, this is an insulated chest-high or floor cabinet with pull-out racks or drawers, installed against a shady outside wall into which an air brick or replaceable cleaning filter has been fitted. For other items, such as jam, cooked meats and cheese, which are ordinarily kept quite cool, install some cold shelves of marble or slate in the storage area.

Store heavy pans and small appliances preferably on a shelf that glides up and out on rollers so the cook need not lift the pan or appliance while stooping or bending.

Allow adequate space (about 48 in) in front of a floor unit to allow easy access to the cabinets and to let two people pass each other in front of it with ease.

A toe space 3 in high and at least 4 in deep should be allowed under floor units.

In a tiny kitchen, open shelves have the advantage over wall cabinets: Far more goods can be placed on shelves, racks and hooks than would ever fit inside a cupboard. Remember, however, that dust will coat everything not in daily use.

Shelves above a work-surface will relieve it of clutter. The less cluttered the work space, the more encouraged a cook is to make full use of it.

Position open shelves where cooking fumes will not reach them to deposit greasy dirt, and be sure these shelves can be easily cleaned.

★ Use any gaps between standing units to fit slide-out towel racks, tray racks or to install bottle shelves.

★ Cover shelves built into a recess with a fireproof roller blind.

★ Hang pans and other utensils on hooks or a butcher's rail fixed to the ceiling if the ceiling is high enough and strong enough. This can make an attractive feature of cooking utensils.

The sink is the most expensive thing in the kitchen to move because of the cost of plumbing it into the main drain and water supply, so if possible plan any kitchen alterations around it in its original position. Arrange other water-using appliances, such as the dishwasher and waste-disposal unit, next to, or in, the sink.

Use a professional plumber with good references. Any mistakes discovered later will be expensive to rectify.

There should be at least one draining surface next to the sink, on the side furthest from the stove. The sink should always be close to the stove, for filling pans and for tipping away hot water. If the main washing-up area has to be far away, put a small extra sink by the stove.

The sink and draining board(s) should, ideally, be in one piece to avoid any dirt-collecting joins.

If there are double drainers, arrange to have one flat and the other ridged. The flat drainer can then be used as an extra work-surface.

Kitchens with no dishwasher, and which are never likely to have one, should have a double sink, perhaps with one smaller bowl for rinsing. If possible, put a waste-disposer in its own small sink so that it will not lock up sinks needed for other purposes. For a right-handed person the main bowl should be on the right. If one bowl is larger than the other, and a waste-disposal unit is installed, set it in the smaller bowl.

The bowl used for washing dishes should be deep (at least 7 in) and wide enough if possible

to take an oven shelf.

The most popular material for sinks is stainless steel because of its durability: It cannot chip, rust or burn. It is not as attractive as other materials such as vitreous enamelled steel. The latter is available in many colors but it chips easily and can become unhygienic (dirt is absorbed into the cracks) as a result. The same is true of glazed fireclay. However, an enamel-finish sink could be fitted with a stainless steel rim to protect the edge.

In professional kitchens, separate hot and cold water taps are considered more economical as less hot water is wasted. However, many people do prefer thermostatically - controlled mixer-taps with a swivel spout that will swing sideways to get it out of the way.

Tall, arched, surgical taps are extremely practical as they allow tall pans to be fitted under them. The tap handles should be inclined toward the body. A spray/brush attachment is useful, especially if there is no dishwasher.

Plastic-covered steel draining racks are more hygienic than the traditional wooden ones. They also hold more dishes and will not warp.

All items for washing dishes should be stored above or below the sink.

The garbage pail can be stored under the sink or under the work-top next to the sink. A slot cut into the work-top will allow the rubbish to drop straight through to the pail beneath; or install a chute (with a lockable trap for security) in an outside wall, leading directly to the garbage cans.

Appliances

The major kitchen appliances are the stove, refrigerator, freezer and dishwasher. These all represent large, long-term investments, and, while a wide range of prices and styles is available, it is advisable to aim for the best the household can afford.

The stove is the cook's most important instrument and of all appliances stoves differ most in character. This has to do with the different fuels used to provide heat—gas, electricity and solid fuel. Each has its advantages and disadvantages.

In selecting the stove, first decide which fuel to use. Not all may be available, depending on location.

Gas is quicker to produce heat and is easier to control. No heat is wasted waiting for a burner to cool down. Gas burners will heat a pan that does not have a flat base. Some gas ovens are hotter at the top, which is preferable for cooks who like to bake several dishes together at slightly different temperatures. It is essential that there be good ventilation in a kitchen where gas is used. Gas is, at the moment, normally cheaper than electricity.

Electricity is cleaner than gas. There is less of a fire risk with a radiant electric coil or plate than with a gas flame, although children will recognize a naked flame more readily than a glowing element. Electricity does not have the minor inconvenience of having to be lit manually. Automatic ignition is a solution, but pilot light channels do get blocked and electrically-operated ignition devices often get short-circuited or the batteries run down.

One definite advantage of electricity over gas is that a gas flame will sometimes go out when turned very low for simmering, whereas an electric burner can be kept hand-hot for long periods. The automatic simmering devices also available on gas stoves work well and are a great convenience.

Electrical convection ovens heat up quicker than the traditional radiant ones, and all electric ovens give a more even heat than most gas ovens.

Gas ovens give a drier heat (as the steam is not trapped), which makes them better for roasting and for baking cakes and meringues. They are also easier to clean.

Solid-fuel stoves, using coke, coal, anthracite or wood, are even cheaper than gas or electricity, and they have the added advantage of acting as a radiator to heat the kitchen (but this can be a distinct disadvantage in hot weather). Most have at least two solid-top burners and two ovens to provide hot and simmer temperatures. Solid-fuel ovens are self-cleaning and the heat is always available for cooking. They never need pre-heating.

It is possible, and to some cooks desirable, to combine fuels, such as a gas stove with an electric oven, or gass or electric stove with a solid-fuel oven, or two ovens—one gas and one electric—or a stove combining two gas burners and two electric ones. This also affords a defence against power-cuts or other failures in fuel supply.

A free-standing stove should have a minimum of 1-in space at each side to allow for air circulation.

Choose a stove with a minimum of dirt traps (hard to clean switches, controls and handles, inaccessible corners, etc.) and look for easy cleaning features such as snap-out coil rings, a lip on the burner surface to hold spills, removable oven linings—especially a removable pan at the bottom to catch spills—and rollers or castors on the stove that facilitate cleaning behind it.

Any arrangement of burners on a stove is possible, and they can be set into a work-surface made of a heat-resistant material such as stainless steel, stone, marble or slate. At least a 6-in space should be allowed between the burners.

Some modern stoves have thermostatically controlled burners and this type feature a spring-loaded disc set in the center of the radiant ring. They heat quickly and keep the temperature of the pan's contents at a fixed, constant level.

Another feature of some electric stoves is the dual ring: one burner made of two coils with separate controls. The smaller central coil can be used alone for small pans, to save fuel and time in heating up.

There is no essential difference in the heat produced by electric spiral burners and solid plates. The plates are slower to heat up and cool down and do not glow, even at high temperatures.

Ceramic stoves, usually made from toughened, heat-resistant opaque glass, have burner areas marked but not raised above the stove surface, which makes them attractive and easy to clean. Pans (which must have flat bases) can be slid around the stove rather than lifted. When not heated for cooking, the stove can be used as a pastry board.

Some ceramic stoves have magnetic control knobs that lift off after use, to be stored in a drawer; others feature touch controls, but these can be brushed against accidentally.

A ceramic stove heats up more slowly than spiral electric plates, and is slow to cool.

A more modern version of the ceramic stove has coils underneath the surface which transfer energy directly to the metal of the steel or iron pans, heating the pan and its contents while leaving the stove cool and safe to touch. Any spills will not burn.

The direction the oven door opens must be considered; there is usually a choice of left- or right-hand opening door that preferably opens a full 180°, or a door that drops down. The latter is useful for setting down hot dishes.

A double oven is better than a single one, as baking or roasting at different temperatures may be done at the same time. The ovens can be placed one on top of the other or side by side. They can be the same size or one larger than the other. One oven may be fitted with the broiler or a motor-driven rotisserie. On some conventional stoves the second oven cannot be used when the main oven is being controlled by the auto-timer. Check this point as it can be inconvenient.

A second oven is also useful as a warming oven for plates and serving dishes and to hold cooked food prior to serving.

As cleaning an oven is an unpleasant job, a self- or stay-clean oven is desirable. An automatic self-clean oven carbonizes splashes and spills during a two-hour cleaning cycle; the resulting fine dust is mopped up easily. Stay-clean ovens are lined with a special coating that combines with heat and oxygen to vaporize splashes while cooking is in progress.

Wider, shallow ovens are easier to clean, and dishes are placed side by side, making their contents easier to inspect.

Fan-circulated ovens, and the less efficient fan-assisted ovens, heat up very quickly and maintain an even temperature throughout the oven. Some models have filters near the fan which eliminate cooking smells.

Split-level stoves are more expensive than ordinary stoves, but the extra cost is justified by their flexibility, convenience and safety. Different fuels can be combined and kitchen space used more effectively. The ovens can also be placed higher to eliminate stooping.

A window in an oven door, or a separate window door, allows food to be inspected without loss of heat.

There should be a light on the controls to indicate that the oven is on, not just that it has reached the correct temperature; and a light inside the oven that is turned on when the door is opened or, preferably, that can be turned on by a switch on the controls.

An automatic oven, which turns itself on and off at pre-set times, is an asset to busy cooks, particularly those out at work all day. A timer alarm is also essential.

Broilers can be above the stove top at eye-level, below it, or inside the oven as is most common in the United States. The latter positioning is awkward: If there is only one oven it cannot be used for any other cooking until the broiling is completed. The siting of the broiler depends on how much it is used.

An eye-level broiler must be positioned high enough to allow the tallest pan to be set on the back of the stove.

Dual-element broilers are economical as half may be used or just the central portion. Double-sided broilers cook food on both sides at once.

A motor-driven rotisserie roasts faster and better than ordinary methods.

★ **A large-capacity oven is important because, aside from cooking the occasional 20-lb turkey, at some time it may be necessary to keep two vegetable dishes and the gravy boat hot as well as the dinner plates. Nobody ever has enough space and few people have a plate-warmer.**

★ **Solid-fuel ovens, always hot, encourage cooking and keep the kitchen cosy.**

★ **There is little advantage in an eye-level oven; there are more important things to be at eye-level, like the broiler.**

The refrigerator

A refrigerator can be positioned under a worktop, built in at chest height or free-standing, and ideally it should be close to the food preparation area for economy of labor. If the refrigerator is built-in, space for air circulation should be allowed behind and underneath it, and holes made in the rear of the shelf above it to let warm air escape.

If a refrigerator is set above floor level, be sure the shelf or bracket supports are strong enough to keep it level (so that its pump works properly).

The refrigerator ought not to be placed next to the stove or any other heat source (such as the central heating boiler) as it will have to work extra hard, and use more fuel, to stay cold. In a small kitchen there is often no choice, so if the refrigerator must go next to the cooker, insulate it with a heat-resistant shield such as a $\frac{3}{4}$-in-thick asbestos board.

Mostly, refrigerators have doors that swing all the way open so that shelves may be pulled out. Bear this in mind in positioning it. Choose a model with a door hinged to open on the most appropriate side.

Slide-out shelves will make it easier to reach things stored at the back, but the shelves must have stops so that they will not tip out. Adjustable shelving is best for maximum storage convenience.

Interior and exterior surfaces must be wipe-clean and door handles should be sturdy and at a suitable height. The door should have a strong seal and good-quality insulation. The thermostat needs to be con-

veniently placed. Downward opening flaps, such as on the dairy compartment, are easier to use than upward-opening ones, which have to be held up while the food is taken out.

For the same reason, a side-opening door on a freezer compartment inside the refrigerator is more convenient than one that drops down.

Automatic defrosting is a great asset. Older refrigerators have to work harder if the ice gets too thick and most need defrosting every two weeks. The semi-automatic defrosting refrigerators switch themselves back on when defrosted. The fully automatic defrosts itself during the normal running cycle. Frost-free or frost-proof refrigerators constantly circulate cold air so frost is never deposited.

Free-standing refrigerators on castors are easy to move for cleaning.

The freezer should ideally be in or near the kitchen to save time and energy, but if it is a large chest freezer it may have to be in the utility room.

Freezers with external condensers (the exposed pipes at the back) collect dust and can be awkward to clean. Fan-cooled condensers in the freezer body are more compact but are noisy. The best type are "skin condensers," in the form of pipes in the freezer walls.

All freezers should have an interior light, and be on castors for easy cleaning behind them.

A drainage outlet, pulled out of the base of the unit, will make defrosting any type of freezer an easier job. This is particularly useful in a chest freezer.

Appliances/2

A combination refrigerator/freezer with separate doors may have the freezer below or beside the refrigerator. Placing it above the refrigerator is not sensible as heat rises. The size of the freezer can vary considerably, from about one-sixth the capacity of the refrigerator to the same capacity, and the choice will depend on the cook's needs and the space available in the kitchen.

There are two types of refrigerator/freezers: One where the two parts are controlled separately with two compressors (the refrigerator and freezer are usually of equal size); and the other where the two parts are run by a single compressor (the freezer is generally smaller than the refrigerator and sits on top). The former is more expensive but the single compressor model may be somewhat more expensive to run because the freezer may have to be kept colder than necessary to maintain the refrigerator at an acceptable temperature.

In a combination, if the freezer is of a reasonable size, it should have separate temperature controls, ideally incorporating a fast-freeze switch. Like an upright freezer, pull-out drawers at the top, baskets at the bottom and shelves on the doors make the packages easy to see and get to. Be sure the pull-out drawers and baskets have stops to prevent them tipping out. They do have the disadvantage of becoming impossible to move if they get iced up.

It is a common misconception that cold air falls out every time the door of an upright freezer

is opened, thus making it less economical to run than a chest freezer. In fact, the extra running cost is due to upright freezers being less well insulated than the chest freezers.

The upright has the advantage over the chest freezer in providing more chilled surfaces with food that is more accessibly stored, and it takes up less floor space.

★ **Drawers or shelf fronts should have an open grille to reveal what is inside; transparent plastic may frost up.**

★ **A chest freezer is cheaper to buy than an upright, but it is awkward to use, as several shelves or baskets may have to be removed to reach the bottom layer.**

★ **A chest freezer must have a counter-balanced lid that will stay open.**

★ **If the top is covered with plastic laminate it can provide an extra work-surface.**

★ **A separate fast-freeze compartment in freezers is a good idea. Fresh food should not come into contact with already frozen food which could be partially defrosted and, if this were to happen several times, it could cause it to deteriorate**

The dishwasher saves time and energy and is more hygienic and generally more efficient than washing up by hand.

The dishwasher must be sited near the sink as those models without a pre-rinse program require the dishes to be rinsed before they are loaded into the machine. It is also more economical to have all water-using appliances plumbed into approximately the same place.

To be truly economical the dishwasher should be run only when full. The pre-rinse program will prevent food drying on, so the breakfast dishes can wait in the machine for the lunch or dinner dishes, and they can all be washed together.

Some machines offer different programs, including an 'economy' one set at a lower water temperature for easily-cleaned dishes. Normally the water is hotter than hands could stand—about 150°F—so grease is removed and bacteria destroyed.

Buy the largest dishwasher that space and budget permit, even if it means buying some more (and suitably dishwasher-proof) dishes. The dishwashers which are large enough to tackle 10 to 14 place settings are no more expensive to run than one that will hold a maximum of six settings. Take along some dinnerware when choosing a dishwasher, to see how much it will hold and if it fits well.

With dishwashers, always expect a few items not to be properly cleaned first time around—"rejects" that must be left in the machine for a second cycle.

Small appliances
A large table-top food-mixer with integral bowl and with attachments for different jobs—slicer/shredder, grinder and blender—will take all the drudgery out of making large quantities of cake batter, pastry and bread doughs. It is really worth buying if much baking is to be done.

A food processor, which uses blades rather than a beater, performs numerous jobs without needing any additional attachments. It is quick and convenient.

A hand mixer, the small portable version of the table mixer, is convenient to use with one hand and is cheap. It can be hung on the wall.

A blender, consisting of a goblet sitting on an electric motor which drives the cutting blades, is worth having to facilitate the making of such things as PURÉED soups or MAYONNAISE.

A food processor will not beat egg whites, but that is an easier task than the laborious chopping and grinding and grating of breadcrumbs which the processer does quickly. The ideal combination is a hand mixer, a big blender and a food processor.

Electric can-openers, which are far safer and more convenient than the manual version, can be installed in a cabinet or on the wall.

An electric slicer which has an adjustable cutting width will slice meat, cheese and bread.

A pressure cooker will quickly cook food that would normally take a long time in an ordinary saucepan. The controls should allow it to be set to low as well as to high pressures.

Buying equipment

Knives

These are essential:
1 General kitchen knife
Utility knife with a stainless steel blade 8 in long; can be used for chopping, slicing, paring and cutting up poultry.
2 Small fruit knife
Stainless steel blade with a serrated edge to cut through skins and "saw" slices without squashing delicate interiors—and a sharp tip for piercing skins prior to peeling them.
3 Scissors *Perform many functions and so come in various forms: With bone-cracking notches on one blade; or one blade serrated. Be sure that the blades meet smoothly along their full lengths. Buy a pair that can be unscrewed to facilitate cleaning and sharpening.*
4 Peeler *When used properly (held by the handle only) the blade pivots freely to adapt to the contours of the object being peeled. A double cutting edge makes it possible to peel in both directions (and accommodate the left handed). A sharp tip is useful for digging out blemishes. It is too difficult to sharpen the blade— replace the peeler regularly instead.*
5 Metal spatula *The blade should be sturdy and evenly flexible along its full length and have a blunt edge for getting under cakes and breads without scratching pans. It is also useful for smoothing iced surfaces.*
6 Bread knife *Get a long one, at least 12 in. Deep serrations give greater efficiency.*
7 Carving fork *One, as shown, 10 in long with curved tines can also be used to lift roasts. Note the guard against knife slips. Longer, straighter tines are necessary for coping with bigger roasts.*
8 Sharpening steel *The bigger, the better: Be sure the handle has a good grip and an efficient guard at the hilt.*
9 Carving knife *Get one with a broad and rigid blade at least 8 in long.*

The professional chef carries his set of kitchen knives around with him—like any skilled craftsman with the tools of his trade—and would seldom consider letting anyone else use them, nor would he be happy using borrowed knives. It is hardly surprising then that the main criterion in choosing a knife is how it feels in the hand. The handle should have a comfortable secure grip and the whole knife should feel reassuringly heavy and balanced—pivot the handle/blade junction on the edge of the open hand; the handle should fall gently back into the palm. Buy knives with handles riveted to the blade as others inevitably come loose. When buying knives any economy is false; a good set of knives will not only last a lifetime, but will pay for themselves many times over in saved labor.

Then collect the following as you need, and can afford, them:
10 Filleting knife *With a thin, flexible blade at least 7 in long, keep especially sharp, particularly at the tip.*
11 Cook's knife *The gentle curve of the blade to the tip gives a neatly pointed end for fine work. Using the tip as a pivot and rocking the blade gives an efficient chopping action. An 8-in blade is the best to start off with.*
12 Cleaver *Buy one that is as heavy as you can handle with ease. The heavier it is, the less force you need to impart the same power. For storage, hang using the hole at the top of the blade.*
13 Grapefruit knife *Stainless steel, slightly flexible, blade serrated on both sides and curved to fit the shape of the fruit.*
14 Freezer knife *Rigid blade at least 12 in long, serrated deeply on both sides and used like a saw. The hooked tip is useful for prying and lifting.*
15 Smoked salmon/ham slicers *Blades should be at least 10 in long, and only slightly flexible. The indentations on the blade cut down friction and keep thin slices intact.*
16 Fruit knife *Small cook's knife with a stainless steel 4-in blade, serrated for the same reasons as the small fruit knife 2, but able to cut larger fruit.*
17 Small vegetable knives *Similar to knife 2, but not serrated. For peeling, paring, turning and other intricate work.*
18 Poultry knife *Like a small filleting knife, with a blade about 4 in long for cutting up birds.*
19 Paring knife *Small 3-in stainless steel blade to peel fruit or vegetables which are too soft for a peeler.*
20 Boning knife *At least 4 in long, the thin, very rigid blade must be kept particularly sharp,*

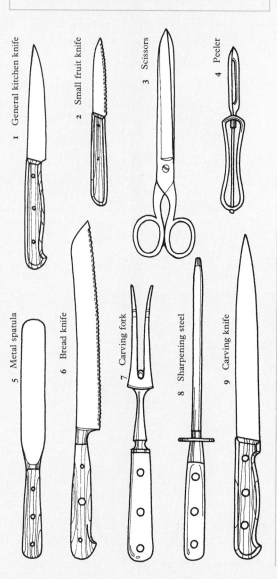

1 General kitchen knife
2 Small fruit knife
3 Scissors
4 Peeler
5 Metal spatula
6 Bread knife
7 Carving fork
8 Sharpening steel
9 Carving knife

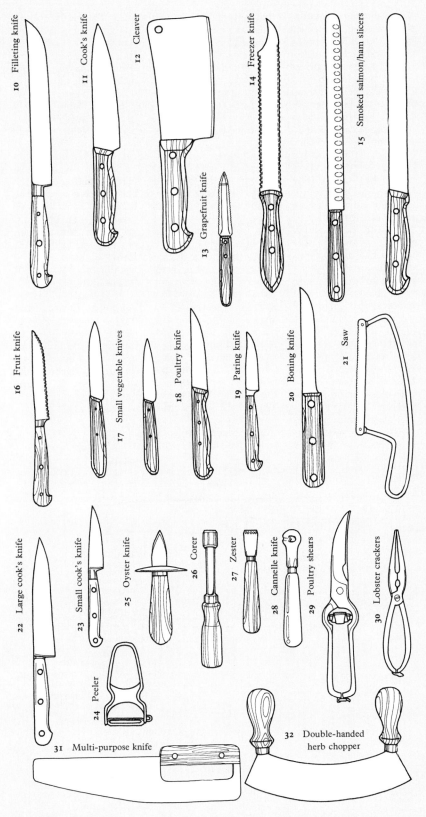

10 Filleting knife

11 Cook's knife

12 Cleaver

13 Grapefruit knife

14 Freezer knife

15 Smoked salmon/ham slicers

16 Fruit knife

17 Small vegetable knives

18 Poultry knife

19 Paring knife

20 Boning knife

21 Saw

22 Large cook's knife

23 Small cook's knife

24 Peeler

25 Oyster knife

26 Corer

27 Zester

28 Cannelle knife

29 Poultry shears

30 Lobster crackers

31 Multi-purpose knife

32 Double-handed herb chopper

especially at the tip which does most of the work.

21 Saw For use in butchery or with frozen meats. Get the type of saw which has a replaceable blade.

22 Large cook's knife The broad, heavy flat of the blade makes a useful mallet.

23 Small cook's knife 3-in blade, for fine work like dicing shallots.

24 Peeler Another version of **4**. Not as versatile, but peels large areas faster.

25 Oyster knife Short, rigid, pointed blade with good grip and a guard to save hands if the knife slips. (Clam knives are similar but have longer, more pointed blades and sharper tips.)

26 Corer Stainless steel blade which must be strong and rigid to withstand the force and torsion applied when coring.

27 Zester Stainless steel blade has a row of holes with sharpened edges to strip off the outside layer of citrus peel without removing any of the bitter pith beneath.

28 Cannelle knife Stainless steel blade with a sharpened notch for cutting decorative grooves.

29 Poultry shears At least *10* in long to cope with all varieties and sizes of bird. The notch cracks bones, the spring keeps the blades open between cuts and one blade is usually serrated for cutting cartilage. Cooks with small hands should use their poultry knife instead.

30 Lobster crackers Can also be used like pliers (e.g., to remove small bones from smoked salmon).

31 Multi-purpose knife A particularly safe design which also gives a lot of blade for a short knife and is versatile enough to cut poultry or slice mushrooms.

32 Double-handed herb chopper (*Mezzaluna*) Single-blade version best used with a rocking action for chopping herbs in a matching bowl. It can come with up to four blades in parallel for chopping herbs in bulk.

Heavy-pressure cutting
Hold the knife with the hand close to the blade.

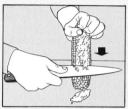

Scraping
Hold the knife with the hand low down the handle and the thumb on the blade.

Chopping and slicing
Hold at mid-handle. Use the knuckles of the other hand as a guide.

Precision cutting
Keep the hand low down the handle for delicate jobs requiring precise control.

The knife as a mallet
Use the flat of the blade for crushing or beating.

When choosing a knife, the first thing to consider is its blade. The composition and qualities of different blade steels are set out in the chart below. Good blades are forged into shape and not molded. Forged blades are stronger and take on and keep a sharper edge. The part of the blade that extends into the handle is called the "tang." The best knives have a full tang that runs the whole length of the handle and gives the best overall balance. Covering the tang is the handle material, secured to it by brass, aluminium or steel rivets. Probably the best handles are made of wood impregnated with plastic to seal it. Plain wooden handles are non-slip, tough and attractive; less expensive plastic handles are far easier to keep clean but don't provide the same good grip. The plastic-impregnated wood gives a good compromise. Always check that the junction between tang and handle has no gaps and that the heads of the rivets are flush with the handle's surface; these crevices are breeding grounds for micro-organisms.

To protect your investment, knives must be well cared for. They should be sharpened frequently with a steel (except for serrated blades) and reground by a professional at regular intervals. Always use a knife in conjunction with a chopping board.

Clean knives with care immediately after use. Never soak them or put them in a dishwasher as this may warp handles and, ultimately, the blade itself. The best way to clean a knife is to wipe it with a damp cloth wrung out in warm suds, working from the back of the blade for safety. Then dry it with a clean towel. To remove stains, rub the blade with half a lemon sprinkled with salt. To get stubborn spots off a carbon steel knife use a scouring pad (but take great care not to rub the edge) or rub with a wet cork dipped in scouring powder.

Stored loosely in a drawer knives can damage each other's blades and cut the hands. If there is no alternative form of storage, cut a cork in half lengthwise and embed the tip of the blade in it. This will protect the tip and help keep the knife from moving around. The best form of storage is a wooden block with a slot for each knife.

Always carry a knife by holding it at the side of the thigh, pointing downwards. Never try to catch a falling knife and never run a finger along the cutting edge to test its sharpness—test by rubbing a finger gingerly *across* the edge.

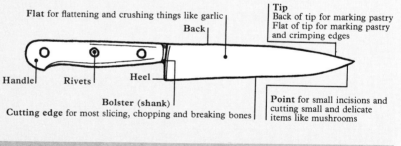

Flat for flattening and crushing things like garlic

Back

Tip
Back of tip for marking pastry
Flat of tip for marking pastry and crimping edges

Handle | Rivets | Heel

Bolster (shank)
Cutting edge for most slicing, chopping and breaking bones

Point for small incisions and cutting small and delicate items like mushrooms

Metal	Advantages	Disadvantages
Carbon steel: Iron and carbon.	Easy to sharpen, keeps its cutting edge well.	Brittle, corrodes quickly, discolors easily. Must be dried immediately after use. Less suitable for cutting onions or high-acid foods (knife and food discolor instantly and knife has to be wiped constantly).
Stainless steel: Iron with at least 4% chromium and/or nickel.	Strong, does not rust. Cuts acid foods.	Difficult to sharpen and blunts very readily.
High-carbon stainless steel: Iron with carbon plus at least 4% chromium and/or nickel.	Practical for cutting all foods. Does not rust. Easy to achieve and maintain a good edge.	Expensive. Must be sharpened with a very hard steel.

1 Hold steel on non-slip top. Hold knife low down handle, edge to steel at 45°.

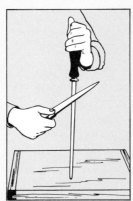

2 Bring knife down steel, keeping angle constant and drawing it towards body.

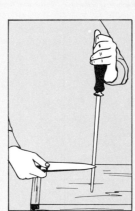

3 When the knife nears bottom of the steel, the tip should be against the steel.

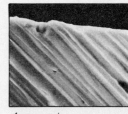

At 3,000 times magnification, the microscope shows knife edge honed on an oiled stone.

Photo © 1977 Times Mirror Magazines

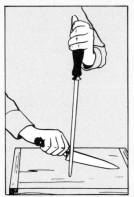

4 Reverse the procedure: Drag the other side of the knife blade up the steel.

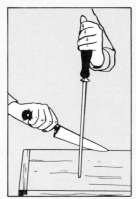

5 Draw upwards, keeping the angle at a constant 45°, but pushing the blade away from the body.

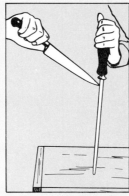

6 Finish with the tip of the blade against the top of the steel. Repeat both sequences until the blade is sharp.

The same blade again, honed on a stone, but without the lubricating oil; there is a more ragged edge.

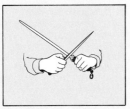

Or, Hold the steel in one hand, the knife in the other. Place the handle ends of each together at 45°.

2 Keeping the elbows against the sides, raise them and part the hands so that blade travels up steel.

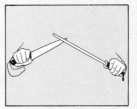

3 Finish with the knife tip near the tip of the steel.

After honing on a stone the edge is sharpened on a steel. This smooths out ridges to give a perfectly sharp edge.

4 Repeat, holding the other side of the blade against the other side of the steel.

5 Repeat the entire sequence several times until the blade is sharp.

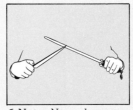

6 Note: Never sharpen one section of a blade. Go from handle to tip each time.

That edge merely run over a piece of wood several times. Any carelessness can cause as much damage.

7,000 times magnification of an edge worn by simple use and in need of regrinding.

Pots and pans

The essentials:

1 Tea kettle The bigger the better. Be sure that the handle is stout and secure. A curved spout is less liable to spurt boiling water.

2 Roasting pans Get several sizes (a small roast in a large pan allows the juices to spread too thinly and burn). The pans must be rigid with high sides.

3 Fish dish Oval, to match the shape of the fish and keep it moist by minimizing evaporation.

4 Gratin dish A roasting pan with low handles to enable it to be taken from the oven and put to broil.

5 Frying pan The heavier the better. Buy several sizes so food is never crowded; start with one 10 in diameter. The sides should be well flared out to give easy access and a large surface area for rapid boiling down.

6 Dutch oven Made from highly conductive material, deep enough for a large piece of meat or bird. The concave lid recirculates juices.

7 Saucepan Deep and straight-sided to hold the heat well and minimize evaporation. Buy three or four ranging in capacity from 1 quart to 6 quarts.

8 Omelette pan Like a small frying pan, preferably of carbon steel, with edges curving into the base, making easier the folding and serving of omelettes.

9 Lipped saucepan Light with a good grip to the handle. Pans lipped on both sides are better.

10 Sauté pan Like the frying pan, but the deep straight sides allow both vigorous shaking of the food and more control over sauce reduction. Get several—including a large one, about 12 in diameter, and one smaller, about 8 in.

11 Milk pan With a non-stick lining, for heating milk and sauces.

12 Marmite Large stewing pan with deep straight sides for long, slow cooking with little evaporation.

13 Stewing pan Smaller version of the marmite.

Get the right pan, the right size, made of the right material, for each job. Many can perform two or three functions, but it is essential to have a variety of pans. Don't necessarily buy a "matching set," buy pans of various makes, materials and types to suit various needs. Cheap, thin, light pans dent, wear out quickly and conduct heat unevenly – burning food in "hot-spots." Invest in heavy-duty pans with thick, well-ground bases, flat both inside and out (they absorb heat more efficiently, heat up evenly and oil inside them forms an even pool). Look for stout handles with a comfortable grip, preferably riveted to the pan, angled up and away from heat sources. Buy pans that are stable when empty, that are the right size for your burners and that have accompanying well-fitting lids.

Then collect the following as you need, and can afford, them:

14 Vitreous enameled cast-iron gratin dish Suitable for long, slow cooking in the oven, and more pleasant-looking to serve directly on the table.

15 Baking dish Shaped for poultry and game.

16 Large roasting pan As big as the oven can take, leaving at least a couple of inches on each side to allow air circulation.

17 Pancake pan Like an omelette pan with lower, more flared sides so that it is easier to get a spatula under the pancake.

18 Heavy-duty skillet For pan frying at high temperatures. Cast-iron, it has lips for pouring off juices and fat.

19 Round gratin dishes Get a set ranging in size from 4 in to 10 in, they are useful for vegetables and other accompaniments.

20 Sugar boiler Copper without the usual tin lining as tin melts at the high temperatures used in sugar cooking. Lipped, with a stout handle, for safe pouring.

21 Saucepan/water boiler Utility saucepan made so that it can also be used in conjunction with inserts 24 and 27 (below).

22 Pan grill/broiler Larger version of 18. Note second handle; ridged bottom gives striped effect of open-fire grilling.

23 Covered saucepan As 21.

24 Double-boiler insert which fits tightly on top of 21 to form an efficient double boiler with a large capacity.

25 Double boiler Handles angled toward one another to facilitate picking up as one unit.

26 Butter melter Small pan/ladle, usually with a copper bottom, also useful when clarifying butter.

27 Steamer insert As 24 with steaming holes in the bottom. Useful for steaming, say, greens on top while a root vegetable boils in the base.

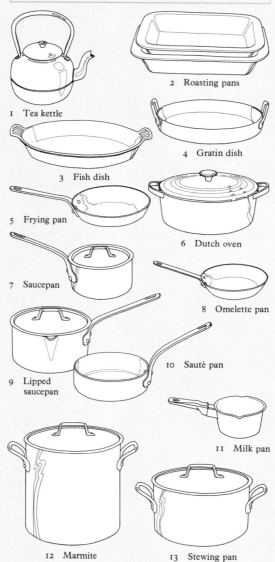

1 Tea kettle

2 Roasting pans

3 Fish dish

4 Gratin dish

5 Frying pan

6 Dutch oven

7 Saucepan

8 Omelette pan

9 Lipped saucepan

10 Sauté pan

11 Milk pan

12 Marmite

13 Stewing pan

14 Vitreous enameled cast-iron gratin dish

15 Baking dish

16 Large roasting pan

17 Pancake pan

18 Heavy-duty skillet

19 Round gratin dishes

20 Sugar boiler

21 Saucepan/water boiler

22 Pan grill/broiler

23 Covered saucepan

24 Double-boiler insert

25 Double boiler

26 Butter melter

27 Steamer insert

28 Steamer

29 Bain-marie pan

30 Blanching basket

31 Casserole

32 Self-basting covered baking pan

33 Covered frying pan

34 Large stewing pan

35 Deep-frying pan with basket

36 Stockpot

37 Terrine

38 Fish kettle and steaming platform

39 Covered baking pan

28 Steamer *Should be large to give plenty of room for the steam to circulate.*

29 Bain-marie pan *Used with a matching ceramic bowl as a double boiler, particularly for sauces.*

30 Blanching basket *Sturdy, with a long handle and sized to fit the largest pan to give greatest scope. Mesh must be small for peas and other small items, and for use in pasta cooking.*

31 Casserole *Get a large one holding about 4 to 5 quarts. Be sure that it fits in the oven and has a base that is suitable for use on burners.*

32 Self-basting covered baking pan *Unique system of indentations encourages juices to fall back evenly across contents.*

33 Covered frying pan *Useful when cooking food that produces splattering. High lid also makes it suitable for steaming, braising and stewing.*

34 Large stewing pan *As 13, about 7 to 9 quarts in capacity.*

35 Deep-frying pan with basket *Thick and deep, about 4 to 5 quarts. Be sure the basket is a good fit, has good handles, and a fine mesh to keep the fat free of particles.*

36 Stockpot *Deep and straight-sided, as the marmite, for long slow cooking with the minimum of evaporation. 7 to 9 quarts is a good size. Some pots have small taps near the bottom to draw off fat-free stock.*

37 Terrine *Rectangular in section for the manufacture of the classic PÂTÉ. Lid is convex to allow for the expansion of pâté during cooking, and has vents to let excess moisture escape.*

38 Fish kettle and steaming platform *Made to match the shape of a large fish, it should be big enough to hold one at least 20 in long. The matching platform should fit well and have handles that stand above the liquid.*

39 Covered baking pan *Larger version of 32 with a lid which circulates juices more conventionally.*

Materials

Equipment chosen for different jobs in the kitchen should be made from the appropriate material. Different materials also need to be handled and maintained in different ways. Anything made of metal will automatically be a good conductor of heat, although metals differ in the amount of heat they retain. Copper and aluminum, for example, take up heat fast but also lose it quickly, while cast iron holds heat much longer. Glass and earthenware are slow to take up heat, but retain it well, so are best suited for use in the oven or serving dishes.

Seasoning

Cast-iron, carbon steel and vitreous enamel surfaces must initially be "seasoned" to stop food from sticking to them and, in the case of cast iron, to prevent rusting and corrosion. Brush the inner surfaces of a cast-iron vessel with flavor-free oil, pour in $\frac{1}{4}$ in of oil and put the pan in a cool oven, 250°F, or, alternatively, put it on low heat on top of the stove for an hour. Leave the pan to cool, pour off the oil then wipe it out with a kitchen towel. For vitreous enamel, brush with oil and put the vessel in an oven set at 300°F for an hour and leave it at room temperature for 12 hours before wiping it clean.

Unglazed earthenware is "seasoned" before each use by allowing it to absorb water before cooking so that it does not absorb cooking juices but gives off steam to keep food moist. Fill the vessel with scalding hot water and let it soak for at least an hour.

	Advantages/uses
Cast iron	Conducts heat well, evenly and slowly. Retains heat for a long time. Used mainly for frying pans, griddles or casseroles.
Stainless steel	Conducts heat well. Durable; does not pit or rust. Easy to clean, has no effect on food flavor. Used for all types of equipment. High-carbon type makes the best knives.
Copper	Conducts heat well. Attractive. Does not rust or pit. Used mainly for pans and molds. Unlined copper bowls have catalytic effect which aids the beating of egg whites. Must be lined with tin for most uses—unlined vessels react with most foods, producing mildly toxic compounds. Lining should be at least $\frac{1}{8}$ in thick; it is easily scratched by metal utensils and must not be heated over 425°F.
Aluminum	Conducts heat well. Does not corrode. Light and easy to clean. Inexpensive. Makes good foil wrapping for storage. Used for all kinds of pans, bakeware and other equipment.
Glass	Good heat absorption and conduction. No adverse effects on food. Inexpensive. Does not deteriorate or stain (although oven glass does cloud in time). Used for bowls, baking dishes, oven-to-tableware, storage.
Earthenware	Absorbs heat well and retains it for a long time. Does not stain; if glazed it has no effect on taste of food. Good for casseroles, chicken dishes, baking dishes, bowls, storage jars and crocks.
Vitreous enameled coating	Conducts heat well and retains it for a long time. Does not rust or corrode. Makes a good covering for cast iron, which is otherwise prone to corrosion. Attractive for stove-to-table utensils. Used for pans, casseroles and gratin dishes.
Non-stick materials	Food does not stick during cooking. Can be used with very light oiling. Coating does not affect heat-conducting properties. Used for frying pans, milk pans, saucepans and bakeware. No adverse effects on taste of food.
Plastic	Cheap, durable, does not stain. Good for pitchers, measures, storage and non-scratching kitchen utensils and for handles as it does not conduct heat. Plastic film and bags make good airtight wrappings; unaffected by low temperatures.
Wood	Attractive, not easily broken. Ideal for serving bowls, chopping boards, pan and knife handles and spoons and scoops.
Rubber	Durable and flexible—a particular asset for items such as ice-cube trays, sweet molds, spatulas and bulb-basters.

Disadvantages	Maintenance
Heavy to use. Liable to rust, pit and stain. Acid foods may react with it, become discolored and have their flavor impaired. May crack if dropped. Needs careful maintenance.	Season before use. Wash with water and a stiff brush. Dry thoroughly immediately after washing. Do not scour. Oil lightly after each use and before storage. Handle carefully to prevent breakage.
If too thin, may buckle in use and tend to conduct heat unevenly, leading to development of "hot spots." Thus has to be thick and, therefore, expensive.	No seasoning required. Wash with soap and water. Scour if not concerned about preserving the surface shine. To remove burnt-on food, fill with cold water, bring to the boil, allow water to cool then wash as above. If this does not work, cover the residue with a layer of water to which dishwasher detergent has been added (one teaspoonful for each cupful of water) and simmer for 15 minutes (in well-ventilated conditions as this produces fumes). Let cool, empty the pan and chip away the crust with a wooden spatula.
Expensive, needs much maintenance. Some copper vessels, notably FLAMBÉ dishes, are lined with silver which is both attractive and durable but prohibitively expensive.	No seasoning needed. Wash inside with soap and water—never scour (which wears away the lining). Polish outside with commercial cleaner or clean with vinegar and salt. To remove burnt-on food, soak in warm water. To remove any lacquer used by the manufacturer to give a protective coating, soak for 15 minutes in boiling water with one teaspoon of baking soda for every 2 pints dissolved in it. Has to be re-tinned professionally whenever the copper shows through.
Thin metal warps easily during use. Reacts with acid and alkaline foods, discolors and may spoil the taste of these foods.	No seasoning needed. Wash with soap and water; can be scoured. If discolored, treat with 2 teaspoons of cream of tartar dissolved in each 2 pints of water, bring to the boil and simmer for 15 minutes; or boil any acid fruit (rhubard, apple or gooseberries) peel or trimmings in water in the pan.
Must be "ovenproof" for use in the oven and "flameproof" for use on the burners and in the oven. When used on burners an asbestos pad or metal ring is necessary to dissipate heat. Not good for browning food.	Needs no seasoning. Easily washed in soap and water. Soak well to remove any burnt-on food. Can be scoured with a nylon pad but burn marks may be impossible to remove. Handle carefully to prevent breakage.
May heat unevenly. Must be "ovenproof" for use in the oven and needs heat dissipater for use on burners. Not good for browning. Easily broken and will break or crack if subjected to sudden temperature changes. If unglazed, earthenware is liable to absorb and transmit flavors.	Season unglazed vessels well before each use. Wash glazed vessels with warm soapy water and a brush; do not scour. Never wash unglazed pots with soap as they will absorb it and transmit its taste. Handle carefully to prevent breakage.
Not good for quick browning. Enamel can crack if vessel is dropped or heated/cooled too quickly. Liable to stain. Enamel is easily chipped or scratched by metal utensils.	Season first before use. Wash with hot soapy water. To remove burnt-on food, soak well and scour with a nylon pad. If discolored, treat with dilute bleach: 1 tablespoon to each 2 pints of water.
Cannot be used with metal utensils which scratch it too easily. Low-quality finishes wear off quickly. Baked food will not brown unless pans are greased. Discolors at high temperatures.	Needs no seasoning. Wash in soapy water; never scour. Remove burnt-on food by soaking in warm water.
Melts at high temperatures so cannot be used on, or in, the stove. Food kept in unventilated plastic may sweat.	Wash in soap and hot water.
Burns at high temperatures so cannot be used in or on the stove except for stirring. Softwoods are porous and absorb and transmit food flavors.	Wash spoons and handles quickly in warm water. Do not soak, or wood may warp or split. Scrub with detergent or diluted bleach. Then rub or brush with linseed or salad oil to counteract drying effect.
Melts at high temperatures. Small range of uses in kitchen. Tastes nasty—never lick rubber spatulas.	Wash with soap and warm water—use of very hot water will cause rubber to perish quickly.

Utensils

The essentials:

1 Ice tray *Flexible rubber for easy unmolding.*
2 Turner/drainer *Broad enough to lift large objects.*
3 Flexible spatula *Be sure head is securely bonded to the handle.*
4 Ladle *Choose one with a large bowl and long handle.*
5 Balloon whisk *Most efficient for beating in air.*
6 Basting spoon *Heavy-duty, deep, long-handled.*
7 Corkscrew *Be sure screw is a spiral—straight metal with a spiral edge only tends to rip corks.*
8 Strainer *Must sit stably. Nylon/stainless steel.*
9 Perforated spoon *As 6, but drains.*
10 Wooden corner spoon *Reaches into the corners of pans.*
11 Colander *Should be stable with no holes near handle or rim.*
12 Wooden spoon *Plain version of 10. Get a good assortment of sizes.*
13 Can opener *May wear out quickly, but efficient and cheap.*
14 Pitcher *1 qt capacity, glass or ceramic.*
15 Bottle opener *Can opener at the other end.*
16 Measuring cup *Clear plastic, calibrated for liquids and dry-stuffs.*
17 Measuring pitcher *Clear with large capacity.*
18 Pepper mill *Wooden, with screw-type action.*
19 Salt mill *As 18— avoid side-key type.*
20 Soufflé dishes *Get two or three ranging from $1\frac{3}{4}$ cups to $3\frac{3}{4}$ cups. Straight sides, half diameter of base.*
21 Ramekin *Small 20, for individual dishes.*
22 Pudding basins/mixing bowls *Same capacities as 20, in thicker, tougher porcelain.*
23 Dish towels *Buy plenty. Good, pure linen will not shed lint on glass.*
24 Large soufflé dish *As 20, with lower sides for cooked-through soufflés.*
25 Mixing bowls *Classic thick, stable ceramic bowls.*
26 Grater *Three types of blade on one side. Easy to clean.*
27 Chopping board *As thick and big as possible.*

"Utensils" describes all the other equipment needed by the cook and not included in any of our other classifications: everything from the humble mixing bowl to complex mechanical devices for shredding and cutting. A utensil is defined as something that is useful, and usefulness must be the principal criterion in the choice of all kitchen tools, particularly those termed "gadgets." What is really useful to one cook may hinder another. It must also be determined whether or not a device will really perform the function it is supposed to perform in an efficient manner. Similar results might well be achieved using more basic implements—which are more easily washed, have fewer parts to go wrong, and have a longer and more flexible working life. In every case, look for sound, robust construction.

Then collect the following:

28 Savarin mold *Ring shape gives maximum surface for heat conduction.*
29 Copper mixing bowl *Unlined; chemical action aids beating of egg-whites.*
30 Charlotte mold *Classic shape for setting Charlotte puddings.*
31 Measuring pitcher *Durable metal measure.*
32 Fish mousse mold *Metal for setting gelatin mousses. Not for oven use.*
33 Tall jelly mold *In ceramic or lined copper.*
34 Decorated mold *Patterned version of 30.*
35 Bombe mold *For molding ice-cream. Best with a vacuum-release top.*
36 Meat thermometer *Spike, inserted into meat, measures internal temperature.*
37 Funneled mold *For cakes and jellies, in rustproof metal. Funnel speeds cooking and cooling.*
38 Flat mold *Metal mold as 34.*
39 Juice squeezer *Simple design, in toughened glass or plastic.*
40 Bottle stopper *Expanding stopper for resealing bottles.*
41 Oven thermometer *For accurate measurement of oven temperature.*
42 Small decorated molds *For individual servings.*
43 Pie/pâté mold *Metal with drop sides.*
44 Egg timer *Get one with timing which matches preferred egg softness.*
45 Egg piercer *Has steel pin for pricking eggs to prevent cracking during boiling.*
46 Sifter *Buy two, big- and small-holed, for heavy and light dredging.*
47 Drum sieve *Flat-bottomed flour sieve with metal mesh and wooden sides. Buy in several sizes.*
48 Broiling grid *Long-handled hinged grid holds food between its two halves over open fires.*
49 Pan rest *Wooden triangle keeps hot pans off easily-marked surfaces.*
50 Egg slicer *Wire cutters slice hard-boiled eggs cleanly and evenly.*

1 Ice tray
2 Turner/drainer
3 Flexible spatula
4 Ladle
7 Corkscrew
5 Balloon whisk
6 Basting spoon
8 Strainer
9 Perforated spoon
11 Colander
10 Wooden corner spoon
13 Can opener
12 Wooden spoon
15 Bottle opener
17 Measuring pitcher
14 Pitcher
16 Measure
18 Pepper mill
19 Salt mill
21 Ramekin
20 Soufflé dishes
22 Pudding basins/mixing bowls
23 Dish Towels
24 Large soufflé dish
25 Mixing bowls
26 Grater
27 Chopping board

28 Savarin mold

29 Copper mixing bowl

30 Charlotte mold

31 Measuring pitcher

36 Meat thermometer

32 Fish mousse mold

33 Tall jelly mold

34 Decorated mold

35 Bombe mold

41 Oven thermometer

37 Funneled mold

38 Flat mold

39 Juice squeezer

40 Bottle stopper

45 Egg piercer

46 Sifter

42 Small decorated molds

43 Pie/pâté mold

44 Egg timer

47 Drum sieve

48 Broiling grid

49 Pan rest

50 Egg slicer

51 Funnel

52 Preserving funnel

53 Metal heat diffuser

54 Garlic press

56 Mandoline grater

55 Splash guard

58 Rotary shredder

59 Ice-cream scoop

57 Jelly bag

61 Butter print

60 Fruit juice press

62 Food mill

63 Mincer/grinder

64 Oven gloves

65 Milk saver

69 Scales

66 Vegetable brush

67 Asbestos pad

68 Roasting rack

70 Wall-mounted can-opener

51 Funnel Get one with a widely flared top and a tube which fits narrow bottles.

52 Preserving funnel Metal with wide spout for filling wide-necked jars with jams and pickles.

53 Metal heat diffuser To reduce heat under glass and earthenware vessels on stove top, and for controlled simmering.

54 Garlic press Best with thick handles and pivoted pressing foot.

55 Splash guard Fine wire mesh with long handle. Covers pans but allows vapour to escape.

56 Mandoline grater Adjustable steel blades mounted on wooden base.

57 Jelly bag Flannel, for filtering juice for jellies. Loops for hanging it from upturned stool legs.

58 Rotary shredder With several discs for varied sizes of cut.

59 Ice-cream scoop Spring action, molds ice-cream or vegetable purées into ball shape.

60 Fruit juice press Juice rises above press foot and is poured out via the lip.

61 Butter print Carved wood for decoration.

62 Food mill Hand-operated mill for puréeing. Should have several discs of different gauges.

63 Mincer/grinder Choose one with a clamp rather than a suction base. Have blades sharpened or replaced regularly.

64 Oven gloves The thicker the better. Must be washable.

65 Milk saver Glass ring placed in pan of milk prevents it rising and spilling over as it boils.

66 Vegetable brush Buy one with tough nylon bristles.

67 Asbestos pad For simmering, as **53**.

68 Roasting rack Keeps meat clear of fat.

69 Scales For use with metal weights (which may be very expensive if certified as standard—but very accurate).

70 Wall-mounted can opener Expensive but durable and convenient.

Utensils /2

71 Wire skimmer Long-handled for lifting solids out of liquids and removing scum from stock.

72 Cheese-wire Long wire with wooden handles for cutting large cheeses.

73 Beating/blending sieve Flat wire mesh to get sauces and purées smooth.

74 Coil-rim whisk Ideal shape for shallow whisking.

75 Flat colander Perforated only on its flat base. For draining off liquids into bowls or pans.

76 Lipped ladle As 4, but with pouring lip.

77 Scraper Steel with metal handle for scraping pastry boards clean.

78 Mortar and pestle Pestle crushes herbs and spices in the bowl (mortar). Stone (because of its weight and surface texture) is more effective than glass or wood.

79 Lemon squeezer Wooden reamer is pushed into the halved fruit.

80 Butter curler The serrated metal hook is drawn across butter to make decorative curls.

81 Folding steaming platform Perforated platform stands on legs; folding side panels adjust to fit any pan.

82 Salad drying basket Folding, wide-mesh, metal basket drains well and saves storage space.

83 Olive pitter Metal prong pushes stones out of olives or cherries held in the porcelain ring.

84 Double-mesh strainer Double layer of fine mesh strains finely.

85 Sauce strainer Shallow, for straining sauce or gravy into a sauceboat.

86 Tea strainer Also strains small amounts of any liquid.

87 Rotary grinder Small amounts of cheese, herbs or nuts placed in the top are ground by rotating cylindrical metal graters.

88 Butchers' hooks For hanging meat and poultry. Should be sturdy metal.

89 Éprouvette and pèse-sirop (saccharometer) Tall glass éprouvette holds cooled syrup. Meter floats in it to measure its density.

71 Wire skimmer

73 Beating/blending sieve

72 Cheese-wire

74 Coil-rim whisk

75 Flat colander

76 Lipped ladle

77 Scraper

78 Mortar and pestle

79 Lemon squeezer

80 Butter curler

81 Folding steaming platform

82 Salad drying basket

83 Olive pitter

89 Éprouvette and pèse-sirop (saccharometer)

85 Sauce strainer

84 Double-mesh strainer

86 Tea strainer

88 Butchers' hooks

87 Rotary grinder

90 Sugar thermometer

92 Conical strainer

93 Light wire whisk

94 Collapsible sieve

91 Timer

95 Steaming platform

96 Standing colander

97 Steaming basket

98 Skimmer

99 Perforated ladle

101 Melon scoop

102 Gravy ladle

104 Wooden basting spoon

105 Bulb baster

108 Spaghetti rake

110 Wooden spatula

112 Birch whisk

113 Meat mallet

114 Corner spoon with hole

117 Long flexible spatula

119 Bottle opener

120 Pickle spoon

121 Wooden skewer

123 Butcher's skewer

125 Kebab skewer

100 Steak batt

103 Potato masher

106 Wooden scoop

107 Flour scoop

109 Lobster pick

111 Ice pick

116 Rotary beater

115 Meat pounder

118 Tongs

122 Chicken brick

124 Larding needle

126 Trussing needle

90 Sugar thermometer *Registers temperatures from 50 to 500°F and indicates degree of "crack" of boiling sugar.*

91 Timer *Timing from one minute to about an hour. Portable and loud.*

92 Conical strainer *Best shape for straining large amounts of liquid.*

93 Light wire whisk *Flexible. Best design for beating out lumps.*

94 Collapsible sieve *Wide-mesh sieve folds flat for storage.*

95 Steaming platform *Raised metal platform with handles; stands inside pan.*

96 Standing colander *Legs keep contents clear of draining liquid. Frees hands to empty heavy pans.*

97 Steaming basket *Perforated metal; for use inside a pan.*

98 Skimmer *Like a flat perforated spoon for removing fat from liquid.*

99 Perforated ladle *Lifts solids out of liquids.*

100 Steak batt *Flat metal mallet for flattening and tenderizing (breaks down meat fibers).*

101 Melon scoop *Stainless steel, it is embedded and turned in vegetable or fruit flesh to make balls.*

102 Gravy ladle *Lipped for easy serving.*

103 Potato masher *Metal plate with V-shaped holes. Good for quick coarse mashing but not professional creaming.*

104 Wooden basting spoon *Long-handled with deep bowl.*

105 Bulb baster *Syringe-type baster in plastic with rubber bulb. Also useful for skimming off fat or for extracting fat-free stock from under a layer of fat. Dismantle before washing and dry thoroughly.*

106 Wooden scoop *Best for salt as it does not corrode.*

107 Flour scoop *Ideal shape for handling dry ingredients. Buy a selection of sizes for various foods.*

108 Spaghetti rake *Spaghetti does not slip off the wooden prongs.*

109 Lobster pick *Steel prong for getting meat out of lobster legs and claws.*

110 Wooden spatula *Best material for use with pans which are easily scratched.*

111 Ice pick *Metal spike for breaking ice.*

112 Birch whisk *Flexible, good for shallow liquids and does not scratch.*

113 Meat mallet *Spiked wooden mallet, as* **100.**

114 Corner spoon with hole *Gets into pan corners and the hole allows liquid to pass through, preventing spillage during stirring.*

115 Meat pounder *As* **100,** *with good-gripping plastic handle and smooth metal base (moistened, it prevents tearing of meat).*

116 Rotary beater *For easier beating. Wash immediately after use, keeping working parts at the top out of the water.*

117 Long flexible spatula *Ideal for getting last bit of food out of jars and for scraping bowls.*

118 Tongs *Metal tongs for lifting food. Make sure that the ends meet.*

119 Bottle opener *Adjustable strap hooks around any neck size and gives firm grip. Removes difficult tops.*

120 Pickle spoon *Perforated wood for draining olives or pickles.*

121 Wooden skewer *About 8 in long for holding edges of stuffed meat or fish together. Use in oven, not under broiler.*

122 Chicken brick *Clay container seals chicken in to cook in its own juices. Never wash with detergent which will be absorbed and taint food.*

123 Butcher's skewer *Metal skewer for holding meat in shape. Buy several, 4 in to 12 in.*

124 Larding needle *Lengths of lard gripped by the teeth at the hinged end are threaded through meat.*

125 Kebab skewer *Metal, about 16 in long.*

126 Trussing needle *Metal with large eye for sewing up stuffed meat and poultry.*

Bakeware

The essentials:

1 French sponge pan (moule à manqué) Sloping sides ease unmolding and decoration.

2 Cake rack At least 1 in high, allows baked items to cool without sweating. Buy a big one.

3 Deep cake pan For large fruit cakes. Heavy-duty or double base prevents burning. Get two sizes, about 3 in deep.

4 Sandwich pan Get a pair; the standard size is 8 in by $\frac{3}{4}$ in.

5 Muffin tin The larger the better—all the moulds need not be filled.

6 Spring form pan For use where unmolding is difficult. The sides unclip.

7 Baking sheet Must fit the oven exactly (leaving 1 in around the edge for circulation), and be heavy-duty. A lip makes handling easier.

8 Flan ring About 1 in deep, in various diameters. Used on a baking sheet for molding pastry into a case. Rolled edges give rigidity.

9 Lipped baking sheet As 7, for use where there is chance of overflow. Sides higher than $\frac{1}{2}$ in inhibit the flow of air.

10 Large flan ring As 8, about 10 in wide but shallower, $\frac{1}{2}$ in, so fillings cook evenly.

11 Rolling pin Wooden pin without handles gives even pressure, maximum surface area and is easier to wash. Get one about 20 in long, 6 in round.

12 Pie dish Glazed ceramic, about 2 in deep to allow slow cooking of fillings before crust browns.

13 Pastry brush Buy a good-quality brush with thick, tightly-packed bristles which will not shed.

14 Loaf pan Sides slope out for large surface area.

15 Icing bags and nozzles Nylon bags with sewn seams wear better than plastic. Get one bag 12 in long for icing and another 16 in long and a large nozzle for bulkier mixtures. Metal nozzles give better definition than plastic.

In general, bakeware for pastries, bread and cakes is light- to medium-weight, to conduct heat quickly to its contents. Shiny surfaces give the standard, light, evenly browned crust. Duller, enameled or non-stick surfaces (which absorb more heat) give a darker, thicker crust. Buy pans with removable bases to make unmolding and cleaning easier. Pan size is critical as it must match the quantity of mixture, or vice versa. If a pan is too big, the mixture may cook too fast and may not rise or brown properly; if too small, the mixture may cook too slowly, not rise uniformly, develop an uneven texture, or even overflow and burn. Cake pans should be filled between a half and two-thirds full.

Thick ceramic dishes are used for long slow baking, as in the making of custards.

Then, in addition:

16 Jelly roll pan Heavy duty, at least 1 in high, about 14 in by 10 in.

17 Muffin tin As 5.

18 Langue de chat/sponge mold As 5 and 17. Molds should be about $3\frac{3}{4}$ in long.

19 Long loaf pan As 14, twice as long (13 in).

20 Large muffin tin As 5, deeper molds about $3\frac{3}{4}$ in in diameter.

21 Madeleine sheet As 17 but traditional shape.

22 French flan/fudge frame Rectangular version of 8 and 10. 14 in by $4\frac{1}{2}$ in is a good size.

23 Gingerbread pan 11 in by $4\frac{1}{2}$ in.

24 Square sandwich pan As 4, get a pair about 8 in square.

25 Terrine Can also be used as a pie dish.

26 Large square cake pan As 3: 14 in square by $4\frac{1}{2}$ in deep.

27 Bread baking pot Terracotta simulates baking in old brick ovens.

28 Small square cake pan As 26. Get various sizes to make tiered cakes.

29 Heart-shaped cake pan As 3.

30 Sandwich/flan pans As 4. Levers ease unmolding. Get two or three from about 8 in to 10 in in diameter.

31 Oval baking dish Ceramic for slow baking.

32 Heart-shaped cake/mousse mold Smaller, lighter 29.

33 Horseshoe cake mold As 3.

34 Fluted flan pan. As 30, conventionally for sweet flans (plain edges denote non-sweet). Get a set ranging in diameter from 8 in to 12 in, about 1 in deep.

35 Deep flan dish Ceramic, for slow cooking. Sides give a corrugated edge to strengthen QUICHE casing. Base unglazed to allow more heat into center to crisp bottom. Get several, ranging from 7 in diameter, $1\frac{1}{2}$ in deep to 11 in by $2\frac{1}{4}$ in.

1 French sponge pan

2 Cake rack

3 Deep cake pan

4 Sandwich pan

5 Bun/muffin sheet

6 Spring form pan

7 Baking sheet

8 Flan ring

9 Lipped baking sheet

10 Large flan ring

11 Rolling pin

12 Large pie dish

13 Pastry brush

14 Loaf pan

15 Icing bags and nozzles

16 Jelly roll pan

17 Muffin tin

18 Langue de chat/sponge mold

19 Long loaf pan

20 Large muffin pan

21 Madeleine sheet

22 French flan/fudge frame

23 Gingerbread pan

24 Square sandwich pan

25 Terrine

26 Large square cake pan

27 Bread baking pot

28 Small square cake pan

29 Heart-shaped cake pan

30 Sandwich/flan pans

31 Oval baking dish

32 Heart-shaped cake/mousse mold

33 Horseshoe cake mold

34 Fluted flan pan

35 Deep flan dish

36 Deep flan pan

37 Fluted French sponge pan

38 Flan dish

39 Spring form tube pan

40 Flan/cake ring

41 Raised pie pan

42 Angel cake pan

43 Raised pie mold

44 Icing set

45 Small flan dish

46 Patterning comb

47 Chocolate/cake mold

48 Decorative cutters

49 Pastry cutters

50 Ornamental cutters

51 Icing nails

52 Pastry blender

53 Muffin ring

54 Tartlet mould

55 Ceramic baking beans

56 Pastry/pasta wheel

57 Circular cake rack

58 Marble pastry slab

59 Pie funnel

60 Icing turntable

36 Deep flan pan Version of **34** with sides about $1\frac{3}{4}$ in deep, for tarts with a layered filling.
37 Fluted French sponge pan As **1**.
38 Flan dish Shallower version of **35** for tarts.
39 Spring form tube pan As **6**, funnel allows heat to reach center of cake when using a rich mixture such as for KUGELHOPF.
40 Flan/cake ring Heavy-duty fluted version of **8**.
41 Raised pie pan Sides unclip and detach from the base. Used for PÂTÉS as well as the traditional game pie.
42 Angel cake pan As **39**, with narrower funnel.
43 Raised pie mold Wooden block to shape WATERCRUST pastry.
44 Icing set More bags and nozzles to produce different decorative effects with various mixtures.
45 Small flan dish As **35**, for individual flans.
46 Patterning comb Straight sides for smoothing icing and a serrated edge for decorative markings.
47 Chocolate/cake mold Two molds clip together.
48 Decorative cookie cutters Top edge is rolled to safeguard fingers and keep shape rigid. Cutting edge must be sharp.
49 Pastry cutters As **48**, crinkled or straight edges.
50 Ornamental cutters As **48**.
51 Icing nails Bases for trellis and flower icing.
52 Pastry blender Wires ease blending.
53 Muffin ring Small version of **8**.
54 Tartlet mold Small version of **34**, normally circular; oval shape shown is a barquette.
55 Ceramic baking beans For baking BLIND.
56 Pastry/pasta wheel Cuts pastry without drag.
57 Circular cake rack As **2**.
58 Marble pastry slab Keeps pastry cool.
59 Pie funnel Ceramic tube supports pie crust and lets vapor escape.
60 Icing turntable Must be stable and turn smoothly.

Specialist equipment

1 Confectionery mold
Rubber mold with 50 or
more holes in several
different shapes for sweet
mixtures like chocolate,
marzipan and fondant.
Flexible for easy
unmolding.

2 Salamander Heavy
iron plate set at the end of
a long handle. Plate is
heated in an open flame and
used for glazing and quick
browning as in CRÈME
BRÛLÉE.

3 Easter egg mold
Stainless steel, glass or
plastic mold. Oil lightly
then brush in cool melted
chocolate, pausing
occasionally to let it set in
stages. Metal and glass
molds give the quickest,
most even set.

4 Petits fours molds
Tinned metal molds for
baking petits fours or
molding chocolates. Oil
before using.

**5 Coeur à la crème
mold** Porcelain heart-
shaped mold with a
perforated base to drain
away the liquid whey
produced in the
making of this simple
classic French dessert. Buy
small individual ones or one
large mold 6 in wide.

6 Hamburger press
Plastic with a metal spring
inside. The base unlocks to
expose two surfaces which
are then covered with wax
paper discs and the meat
placed on the lower one.
The base is closed again
and the top pressed down to
produce a perfectly shaped
hamburger.

**7 Steamed pudding
bowl** A metal pudding
bowl with a hinged, clip-
fastening leak-proof lid and
central loop handle. Buy
one large enough to allow
room for the contents to
rise.

8 Ice-cream maker
Electrical appliance for use
in the freezer of some
refrigerators. Revolving
paddles produce smooth,
uncrystallized ice cream. A
thin power supply cord
allows the refrigerator or
freezer door to be shut
during use.

Buy specialist kitchen equipment only after
careful consideration. Even if the urge to make
chutney or have a fondue party is irresistible, it
is not worth spending a lot of money on an item
that will be used perhaps only once and will then
merely take up valuable storage space. First,
decide whether or not the item really is a
necessary and good investment by testing the
possibilities of the equipment already in the
kitchen which might do instead, and also by
thinking in the long term. If cooking for a
family, then buying a mold for making Easter
eggs, for instance, may well be worthwhile. But
first try to borrow a particular item from a friend
or neighbour to test its possibilities thoroughly.
The specialist equipment chosen here is a selection of the more practical items available.

9 Tongue press A
cooked tongue, or other meat,
is pressed by a metal plate
attached to springs and
locked in place with clips
that hook over the sides of
the bowl. This keeps it in a
rolled position while it cools
and sets in jellied juices.

**10 Sandwich
toaster/waffle iron**
Aluminum or cast-iron
toaster for use on an open-
flame burner. Check that
the two halves fit smoothly
and that the handles are
long and insulated. SEASON.

11 Gridle Heavy
aluminum, iron or steel
plate for gridle scones and
crumpets. Make sure the
base is thick and quite flat.
The handle should drop
down for storage.

12 Smoke box Metal box
for smoking fish, cheeses
and other small items of
food. Smoke from wood
chips rises through holes in
the base of the upper
container. Use only
outdoors or in fireplace.

13 Waffle iron As 10,
specifically for making
waffles.

14 Barbecue grill Cast-
iron grill to fit the top of a
brick-built, charcoal-fired
barbecue. Do not wash;
simply scrape and oil.

15 Barbecue fork Long-
handled two-pronged fork
for turning and lifting
food on the grill.

**16 Copper preserving
pan** Good for jam making
but not for soaking fruit or
making preserves containing
vinegar as the acids react
with the metal. About 16 to
22 pints.

**17 Lipped preserving
pan** Aluminum pan for
making pickles, chutney and
jam. Similar capacity to
16, with useful pouring lip
and folding handle that will
fix rigidly upright.

18 Fondue set Consists of
an oil lamp heater, a metal
grid and a heavy metal pan
for cooking food at the
table. The pan illustrated is
for a melted cheese mixture
into which bread is dipped.
A meat fondue is taller,
waisted, and has a lid.

19 Fondue fork Wooden
long-handled fork for
dipping food in fondue pan.

1 Confectionery mold
2 Salamander
6 Hamburger press
3 Easter egg mold
4 Petits fours molds
5 Coeur à la crème mold
7 Steamed pudding bowl
8 Ice-cream maker
9 Tongue press
10 Sandwich toaster/waffle iron
11 Gridle
12 Smoke box
13 Waffle iron
14 Barbecue grill
16 Copper preserving pan
19 Fondue fork
15 Barbecue fork
18 Fondue set
17 Lipped preserving pan

Exotic equipment

1 Baguette (French bread) pan Metal container at least 15 in long, with compartments 3 in wide for holding bread dough. Allow enough room for the dough to expand lengthwise during cooking.

2 Snail plate Round cast-iron or oven proof earthenware plate with six indentations to hold snails in their shells. Can be used for cooking and serving. Buy one dish per person to be served.

3 Snail tongs Tongs for picking up cooked snails. They open as the handles are pressed together. The snail is extracted with a small two-pronged fork.

4 Birds' nest soup maker To make the authentic Chinese soup, swallows' nests are placed between the two sieves (they are joined by a hinge at the handle) and held in boiling soup so that the saliva holding the nest together leeches out. Can also be used for making game chip baskets. Dip the sieves in oil, then place thinly sliced potatoes between the two parts and deep fry.

5 Ravioli rolling pin Wooden rolling pin about 6 in long for rolling out ravioli or small amounts of pastry. Good for keeping children amused in the kitchen.

6 Paella pan Broad, shallow, flat-bottomed, two-handled pan that gave its name to the traditional Spanish rice dish. Best made of heavy metal—if it is iron, season it before use. The paella is cooked and served in the pan, which makes a useful extra frying and sautéeing pan. Sizes range from about 8 in to 18 in in diameter.

7 Brioche molds Fluted, tinned metal molds for cooking rich yeast BRIOCHE dough. Grease lightly before use and half fill with unrisen mixture. Allow to rise before baking. The molds can also be used for gelatins and cakes—the funnelled one makes an excellent, and decorative, angel food cake pan.

Buy the genuine article for exotic cuisine to give a really professional finish. It is certainly possible to make couscous in a conventional steamer or bake brioche dough in an ordinary cake pan, but the results may lack the authentic touch.

As with specialist equipment think carefully before investing in exotic equipment. The most practical items are those that have multiple uses—the brioche molds, for example, can be used for cake and jelly making, the pizza pan as a baking sheet, and the ravioli tray as a sweet mold.

When choosing the more expensive items such as the wok or the pasta machine, take particular care to examine materials and manufacture for good quality.

8 Pizza pan Essentially a round metal baking sheet 10 in across with a slightly raised rim to support the edges of the pizza crust. Buy at least two.

9 Wok Round-bottomed thin metal pan for true Chinese stir-frying. The sloping sides allow vigorous tossing and turning with the long-handled spoon without the food spilling. On a Western stove a metal stand or converter is necessary to rest the wok so that it doesn't have to be held all the time. Because of its shape, a wok can also double as an economical deep-fryer.

10 Ravioli cutters Round or square metal cutters for making ravioli shapes from prepared, stuffed dough (as below).

11 Ravioli tray Metal tray for quick ravioli making. The dough is rolled very thinly with **5**, then spread over the tray. (A small piece of dough is used to press it into the indentations.) Stuffing is put in the mold, the dough is brushed with egg, more dough placed on top and the whole tray rolled again.

12 Couscous steamer The deep lower pot, about 16 pints in capacity, holds meat and vegetables simmering in stock, while the crushed wheat or millet (the traditional North African couscous) steams in the upper container which has a perforated base and lid. The seal between top and bottom sections must be tight. It is also useful for steaming vegetables in bulk.

13 Pasta machine Hand-operated machine for kneading, rolling and cutting pasta dough. It should be made of rust-resistant metal and be able to be clamped securely to a work surface. Choose one with rollers that adjust to several positions to alter the thickness of the dough, and with rotary cutters that give a range of different widths of cut strips.

1 Baguette (French bread) pan

2 Snail plate

4 Birds' nest soup maker

3 Snail tongs

5 Ravioli rolling pin

6 Paella pan

7 Brioche molds

8 Pizza pan

9 Wok

10 Ravioli cutters

11 Ravioli tray

12 Couscous steamer

13 Pasta machine

Storage containers

1 Storage jar For keeping dry ingredients. Available in glass, plastic or earthenware. Must have a well-fitting stopper.

2 Salt box Wooden box with a hinged lid. Hang it near the stove.

3 Butter/jam dish Ceramic lidded dish for short-term storage.

4 Cheese dome Pottery cover with an air hole to stop cheese sweating. Buy one big enough to cover several good-sized cheeses.

5 Cheese dish As *4*, but with a matching base. Shaped to match a wedge of round cheese.

6 Open jar Useful only for short-term storage or for foods like garlic which must not be covered.

7 Cruchons Glass storage bottles for beverages only. A spring clip on the stopper snaps on to the bottle neck to give an airtight seal.

8 Preserving jars Toughened glass jars for bottling fruit and tomatoes, each with a glass or metal lid, rubber ring seal and spring clip. Sizes range from *1* pint to *3* pints.

9 Crock Glazed earthenware lidded vessel for storing and maturing pickled or salted foods.

10 Jars For keeping utensils close to their point of use or short-term storage of fats and stocks.

11 Vegetable basket Metal wire basket for short-term storage of vegetables.

12 Bread box As *9*, prevents bread drying out.

13 Aluminum foil Tough airtight wrapping for foods. For economy, keep it in three widths—*12*, *20* and *24* in.

14 Plastic wrap Transparent film sticks to itself and to most food containers. For covering bowls or wrapping food.

15 Freezer bags Heavy-gauge plastic bags in all sizes seal out the air, prevent "freezer burn" and allow freezing of liquid mixtures in any shape.

16 Freezer tape Waterproof adhesive tape for airtight sealing of bags of food for the freezer.

A kitchen storage system should provide the means to keep food fresh and ensure that utensils and ingredients in regular use are easily accessible. The aim of good food storage is to exclude the spoiling agents—light, air, moisture, insects and microorganisms. For short-term storage, in or out of the refrigerator, most things need a cover of some kind—a lidded container, dome, metal foil, plastic wrap or a plastic bag. For long-term storage choose containers made of opaque, rustproof materials with airtight lids. Always buy some containers that are larger than needs would seem to dictate, as future requirements are almost certain to be greater. Food deteriorates more rapidly if tightly packed but can go stale in over-large jars. Get a good variety of shapes and sizes. Items that can be hung near their point of use save space.

1 Storage jar

2 Salt box

3 Butter/jam dish

4 Cheese dome

5 Cheese dish

6 Open jar

7 Cruchons

8 Preserving jars

9 Crock

10 Jars

11 Vegetable basket

13 Aluminum foil

14 Plastic wrap

16 Freezer tape

12 Bread box

15 Freezer bags

Buying food

Shopping

Buying food well demands that the cook balance gastronomy, nutrition and economy with the restraints of quick shopping and speedy cooking.

No two cooks shop in the same way, although most people do shop more often for fresh food and less often for basics. There are several good rules:

1 Make a list before setting out and stick to it. Impulse buying is difficult to resist but it can be wasteful. If, on Monday, the cheap strawberries in the market look just right for making jam but there is not going to be time to make the jam before the weekend, those cheap berries will go to waste, causing unnecessary expense rather than saving money. Of course, it is not always possible to stick strictly to the shopping list. If a meal is planned around pork chops and the butcher has none, the whole menu may have to be changed; if spare ribs are substituted for the pork chops, they would be nicer with a BARBECUE SAUCE than APPLE SAUCE, and with large BAKED POTATOES rather than small SAUTÉED ones. In such circumstances it is essential to buy only replacements for original items on the list, and not to allow this to trigger off impulse buying of extras.

2 Never buy on an empty stomach. It is almost impossible to avoid impulse buying when hungry. Thus, the best time to shop is immediately after breakfast. Also the broadest range and the freshest produce is likely to be available at this time.

3 If buying expensive food, and shopping around for good prices, take a calculator to help compare prices of similar items of different size and pack quantity.

4 Keep a noteboard on the kitchen wall, and write down things that are running low *before* they run out.

5 If shopping once a week for basics, check the list *and* the shelves before leaving home.

6 Put everything away as soon as possible. Frozen and fresh foods deteriorate rapidly. Before filling the refrigerator check what is left in it, and move food to the front or, if necessary, throw it away. Put things on the correct shelves (see pages 174/5).

But having decided what, when and how to buy, how is the shopper to know what is worth buying?

Most of us can tell if vegetables are fresh, but what about beef? And what about eggs? And how can we be sure that dried beans are not three years old? The following pages give detailed guidance on individual foodstuffs, but there are a few general principles.

A shop with a large turnover is likely to have fresher food than a small one whose helpful owners try to stock everything for their few customers. If a small shop's total stock of dried apricots takes two years to shift, some unfortunate customers are going to get darkened, bullet-hard fruit. For this reason, too, buy unusual ingredients from shops where they are not regarded as quite so unusual. Spices will be fresher in a spice shop or specialty delicates-

sen where large quantities are sold all the time; STRUDEL (FILO) PASTRY will probably be better from a Greek grocer; and PARMESAN CHEESE from the Italian cheese shop, and so on.

It is, of course, worth making friends with suppliers. Butchers and bakers favor the customer who tells them how good their beef was, or that their wholemeal bread is the best in town.

They obviously prefer the shopper who pays bills on time, and does not let young children rampage through their establishment.

Being friends with the shopkeeper has other advantages, too. Friendly butchers will advise on cuts of meat, how much to buy, how salty the ham is and what special delights are hidden in the cold room. They will also, with luck, grind favored customers' kitchen knives, have their shopping delivered for them, and perhaps even cash their personal checks.

Part of a good relationship with a supplier is being forthright about anything that has gone wrong. Shopkeepers cannot put something right if no one tells them about it. If the best end of lamb was so badly CHINED that the meat saw had gone straight through the eye of the meat, or the fish steaks were so badly hacked that they varied in thickness from a sliver to a doorstep, the person responsible should be told about it. It is true that two days after the event, when the offending food has nonetheless been eaten, it cannot be examined. But the shopkeeper has no reason not

to believe the customer, and every reason to make sure that it doesn't happen again. It may not produce an instant cash refund, but only a very bad businessperson will fail to be more careful.

Good shopkeepers do not mind questions, and will certainly let the customer examine the goods carefully before purchase. Some, especially those selling fruit, may not be keen on every customer handling produce that might easily bruise, but they should be prepared to hold them out for careful scrutiny, and to test their firmness. Many shopkeepers, especially if selling loose fruit, will give a customer a plum, for example, to taste if he or she proposes to buy a quantity. This is not the case in supermarkets which normally sell wrapped fruit. If the fruit should turn out to be tasteless, bad, underripe or in any way unsatisfactory, take it back. It may have marred the previous night's meal, but a refund or exchange goes some way toward restoring confidence in the supermarket, and the management is alerted, which will, in time, improve the quality of the produce they sell.

Supermarket shopping is less personal, but the manager's brief from his employers is sure to be "the customer is always right." So, if something is wrong, complain about it promptly but politely. A good-tempered, pleasantly delivered complaint is more likely to get the offending article credited, refunded or exchanged.

Bulk buying is tempting if the price is very good. It also means fewer shopping trips. But there are snags:

1 The bargain is often not a bargain at all. "Economy size," "giant size," do not necessarily mean that the food is, measure for measure, cheaper than its smaller relatives. For example, half a lamb for the freezer may seem, by weight, very cheap. But on that carcass is a lot of fat and bone not normally sold.

2 For those who habitually eat only plain roasts and steaks, buying a quarter of a carcass is quite inappropriate. The tough cuts, the ground beef, stewing meat, braising steak and pot roasts could stay in the freezer for months, when the broiling steak had long since gone.

3 Variety is generally important to the appetite, and ten boxes of the same breakfast cereal, or a freezer full of one kind of meat or fish can only make the cook's job harder.

4 It is difficult to eat large quantities of food fast enough. For example, flour and oatmeal go stale, and even cans can become leaky and "blown" if kept too long. A cool, dry storage place helps, but any damp will rapidly accelerate deterioration.

5 The cheaper "bargain offer" bulk purchases of little-known brand-names are often of inferior quality. Buy a single pack to try it out before buying more.

6 Bulk buying locks up a lot of money. In inflationary times, the customer generally saves money by buying ahead. Prices, however, do sometimes come down.

Buying meat and poultry

Always try to buy meat and poultry from a good butcher who is reliable, helpful and whose meat tastes good and weighs what the ticket says it should weigh.

The only way to know if a butcher's shop is good is by buying their meat. The only comfort in such a risky testing method is that, if they are no good at all, their inadequacies will reveal themselves quickly. Someone who sells poor-quality re-frozen lamb is unlikely to sell good ground beef or really first-class chickens and game birds.

The general look of the shop also tells the shopper something about the butcher's standards. If the floor is clean, if the place smells pleasantly fresh, if the assistants have clean fingernails and they have smiles on their faces, the chances are that the owner is careful about even more fundamental things, like the quality and freshness of the meat.

Tender or tough?

For today's customers, tenderness in meat is often even more important than flavor. The younger the animal, the less muscular and more tender will be its flesh. It will, however, lack the flavor of an older, more mature beast. A week-old calf will be as tender as margarine and have about as much flavor. A bullock that has pulled a cart all its life will be extremely tough but its flavor will be strong and rich. For it is the muscular tissue that contains the "extractives"—substances related to the base chemicals in tea and coffee, that, when cook-ed, become tasty. To get the best of both worlds, meat producers try to limit the exercise the animals take while allowing them to grow toward, if not to, maturity.

Because they are most in demand, the tenderest cuts of the animal are the most expensive. These come from the more inactive parts of the body: The saddle, loin and rump of beef and venison are tenderer and more expensive than the neck and legs.

Maturity is one of the three factors affecting flavor of any meat. The second is diet. A wild bird feeding in woods and marshes, on insects, berries, seeds and corn will have a stronger flavor than its domesticated cousin feeding on bone-meal pellets. The third factor is aging. The longer the meat is aged, the stronger and more gamy will be its taste.

Except with game, however, aging is done more to tenderize the meat than to increase its flavor. Meat cooked immediately after slaughter would taste acidic because of the lactic acid that is created in muscle tissue by exercise; and the muscle tissue would be rigid due to rigor mortis, which can last for as much as 30 hours. But more important is the enzyme activity, causing chemical changes in the flesh, which takes place in the carcass after death. Meat aged at $35°$ F will become increasingly tender the longer it ages. If the meat is aged at higher temperatures, the enzyme activity increases and the meat tenderizes faster. Higher temperatures, however, might encourage bacterial growth and cause the meat to go bad before it becomes tender. Some enzyme activity continues even if the meat is frozen and the formation of ice crystals means that freezing meat can be said to tenderize as it solidifies and thus bruises the fibers of the meat). However, the inevitable loss of juices from the meat, and subsequent risk of dryness after cooking is a disadvantage that outweighs the minimal tenderizing effect.

Butchers tend to age meat for shorter periods than they once did for several reasons:

1 The Western public, increasingly reared on bland factory-farmed foods, is growing reluctant to eat anything with too strong or gamy a flavor.

2 The expense of storage makes prolonged aging uneconomic. Storage itself is expensive, the carcasses lose saleable weight, and capital is tied up in stock.

3 Modern breeding, rearing and feeding methods have meant that the flesh of animals is generally more naturally tender at slaughter and therefore needs less aging. (For example, pictures of pre-war chickens show a completely different bird from a modern broiler—chickens used to have less breast, be longer in the body, and have darker flesh. Good steak used to be dark and marbled with fat, but modern breeding and slaughtering policies, with animals killed at about 18 months, rather than the traditional three years, has meant paler meat without any marbling.)

Buying meat

The last and most important factor affecting the taste and tenderness of all meat is the cooking method chosen.

There is a seeming paradox in the fact that long, slow cooking tenderizes tough meat, yet the less a steak is cooked the more tender it is. Half-cooked or rare meat, such as medium-rare sirloin steak, is tender simply because it retains the softness of raw meat. The heat has not had time to have any effect on the fibers. But as the heat penetrates the whole piece of meat the fibers shrink and toughen, and the juices cease to flow, set solidly, and finally dry up. The meat is now at its toughest, which explains the chef's reluctance to serve well-done steaks. One cannot produce a steak that is both tender and juicy and well-done. But further cooking—long slow stewing rather than fierce broiling—will tenderize that tough steak by breaking down its connective tissue. On the other hand, a sirloin steak will never cook to the tenderness of, say, oxtail, which may be so tender it can be cut with a spoon. This is because oxtail, like most of the muscular active parts of the animal, contains plenty of connective tissue which, subjected to steady gentle heat, will convert to gelatin, giving the stew its characteristic soft, almost sticky, tenderness. Less-active parts of the body, like the sirloin steak, have little connective tissue and, therefore, no hope of the same degree of gelatinous softness. Cook them as rapidly as possible.

Storing meat and poultry

Most meat from the butcher is already aged on purchase, and will only be stored at home for convenience. If the proposed storage temperature is higher than 60°F, the food should be cooked within 24 hours. If the food is to be kept in an unrefrigerated place at, say, 50°F, meat will keep satisfactorily for 48 hours, and domestic poultry for 24 hours. If meat is refrigerated at 35°F it will keep safely for up to a week, but will become drier than is desirable.

Even if refrigerated, poultry should not be kept more than four days, and variety meats should be eaten as fresh as possible—preferably on the day of purchase. If food cannot be eaten within these time limits, it should be frozen or salted. If meat or poultry *has* to be stored, remove it immediately from its wrappings, especially if the wrapping material is plastic. Meat tends to "sweat" in non-porous plastic, creating a slightly steamy, damp atmosphere around it, and although the flesh will not dry out, it will become slimy and there will be a danger of bacterial growth.

To counteract hardening and drying out of meat and poultry, spread butter or margarine carefully all over the surface to form a seal, or cover loosely with foil or a butter-wrapper (butter side down).

Buying variety meats

Traditionally underrated, and therefore generally inexpensive, they are highly nutritious. They must be used, or frozen, on the day they are bought.

Liver and heart

should not have too strong a smell and liver, though it may be bloody, should not be wrinkled or discolored.

Calves' liver should be pale milky-brown with a fine even texture. It is the mildest and most delicate of the livers, moist and tender when cooked, with a fine, almost PÂTÉ-like, texture.

Lambs' liver is darker in color, more reddish-brown and smooth. It has a coarser texture and a stronger flavor than calves' liver. It is also slightly tougher and drier when cooked.

Pigs' liver is cheaper, dark-brown in color, close-textured and strong in flavor. It is seldom eaten on its own and more often used in TERRINES and PÂTÉS.

Beef liver is dark purplish-brown. The cheapest of the livers, it needs soaking or BLANCHING to reduce the strong flavor before being used with other ingredients for stews or for braising.

Lambs' hearts are good stuffed and cooked slowly in liquid to tenderize the lean tough flesh.

Beef heart is large, tough and strong-flavored so requires long slow cooking. The meat is lean, highly nutritious and often inexpensive. It may be ground for terrines, stuffed, braised or boiled.

Kidneys are sold either in their own protective layer of fat or loose. If they must be kept, they keep better in the fat. They should smell mild and pleasant, be smooth and clean-looking, feel soft and not have discolored dark patches.

Veal kidneys Pale milky brown, with creamy white fat, shaped like a bunch of grapes. They are generally in short supply and, therefore, expensive, but are good fried, roasted or in sauces.

Lambs' kidneys Medium brown, sometimes faintly bluish, firm-textured and egg-shaped. Good flavor, neither over-strong nor insipid. Broil, fry or serve in sauce.

Pork kidneys Pale brown, similar in texture to lambs' kidneys but longer. Tender, and good fried or used in casseroles.

Beef kidneys Dark purplish flesh, shaped as veal kidney but larger. They have a strong flavor and are tough-textured. They are good in stews or pies when mixed sparingly with beef.

Heads

Occasionally, whole heads of calves, pigs or sheep become available. They should be dry-skinned and, though they smell strong, the smell should not be unpleasant or over-powering. Sheep's heads, being small, involve a lot of labor for little meat. Pigs' heads and calves' heads are more rewarding. They may be salted, then boiled and the meat used for BRAWN (head cheese), or in pies and stews.

Beef cheek, though not the whole head, is sometimes sold, and is normally used for head cheese or in pies.

Pigs' heads, cooked whole and decorated, are sometimes used at banquets in place of the now unavailable boar's head.

Feet

Calves' feet are seldom sold to the public but are a good source of GELATIN for setting STOCKS.

Pigs' feet are good for enriching and setting stocks, but they may also be boned, stuffed, braised, served hot with MUSTARD SAUCE or hot or cold with VINAI-GRETTE. They are rich and gelatinous.

Tripe

Tripe can come from all cud-chewing animals, being the first and second stomachs, but in practice only beef trips is sold. The first stomach (blanket tripe) is smooth; the second honeycombed. Tripe is sold parboiled, but needs much further boiling to tenderize it. Ask the butcher exactly how much more boiling it will require. Avoid gray, slimy, flabby or strong-smelling tripe. It should be thick, firm and very white. Stew, boil or deep fry.

Marrow bones

Marrow bones are from the thigh and upper front legs of beef which the butcher saws across into short cylinders. Boil whole and serve in a napkin, allowing the diner to extract the soft rich marrow and eat it on toast. The marrow is also used as flavoring in other dishes, such as *entrecôte à la bordelaise*, in which it moistens and flavors the steak.

Tongues and Tails

Beef tongue is the most commonly available, and may be bought fresh, smoked or salted in brine. The tenderest and fattiest portion of the tongue is the thick end; the tougher, the finely-grained lean tip. Fresh tongue should feel soft, though it may have a rough, pigmented patchy skin. Smoked or salted tongue has a firmer, bouncier feel.

Lambs' tongues are generally sold by weight and fresh, not salted. They should smell pleasantly fresh, and should be light pink, though the skin may have pigmented dark areas. They are tender, full of flavor and, usually, inexpensive. Stew and serve hot with a sauce, or cold in their own stock which sets to a jelly.

Oxtail is the only generally commercially available tail. It is sold skinned and jointed. Large, fat tails with plenty of meat are best. Thin tails are probably cows' tails and will be comparatively pale in color, both raw and when cooked, and have less flavor. Oxtail meat should be dark, and the fat creamy and firm. Oxtail, containing plenty of connective tissue, cooks to a meltingly tender, almost sticky stew with a rich, hefty flavor.

Sweetbreads and Brains

Calves' brains are the most expensive, having an exceptionally creamy texture and delicate taste when cooked. They should be soft-skinned and pale pink, with a faint, fresh smell.

Sheep's brains are less delicate, but similar.

Sweetbreads are the thymus glands from the throat, or the pancreas from the body, which is more delicate and tender than the thymus glands, but both are tasty. When raw, sweetbreads should be sweet-smelling, evenly pink, smooth and soft. **Calves' sweetbreads** are the most expensive. They are soft and delicate, though not as creamy as brains when cooked.

Beef sweetbreads are rare but have a good flavor.

Lambs' sweetbreads are more common, but are not as fine as calves', lacking the great delicacy of taste and texture.

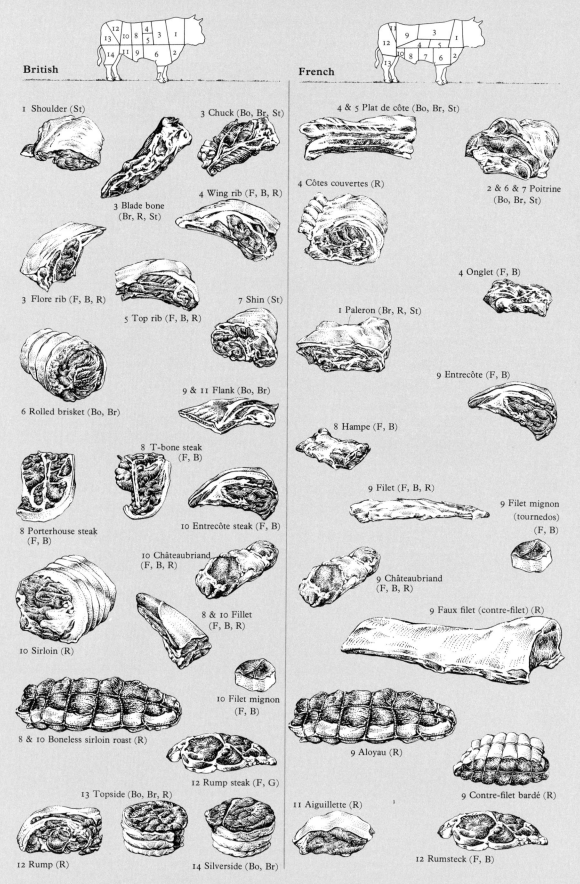

British

French

1 Shoulder (St)

3 Chuck (Bo, Br, St)

4 & 5 Plat de côte (Bo, Br, St)

3 Blade bone
(Br, R, St)

4 Wing rib (F, B, R)

4 Côtes couvertes (R)

2 & 6 & 7 Poitrine
(Bo, Br, St)

3 Flore rib (F, B, R)

5 Top rib (F, B, R)

7 Shin (St)

4 Onglet (F, B)

1 Paleron (Br, R, St)

6 Rolled brisket (Bo, Br)

9 & 11 Flank (Bo, Br)

9 Entrecôte (F, B)

8 Hampe (F, B)

8 T-bone steak
(F, B)

10 Entrecôte steak (F, B)

9 Filet (F, B, R)

9 Filet mignon
(tournedos)
(F, B)

8 Porterhouse steak
(F, B)

10 Châteaubriand
(F, B, R)

9 Châteaubriand
(F, B, R)

8 & 10 Fillet
(F, B, R)

9 Faux filet (contre-filet) (R)

10 Sirloin (R)

10 Filet mignon
(F, B)

8 & 10 Boneless sirloin roast (R)

9 Aloyau (R)

12 Rump steak (F, G)

13 Topside (Bo, Br, R)

11 Aiguillette (R)

9 Contre-filet bardé (R)

12 Rump (R)

14 Silverside (Bo, Br)

12 Rumsteck (F, B)

44

Beef cuts

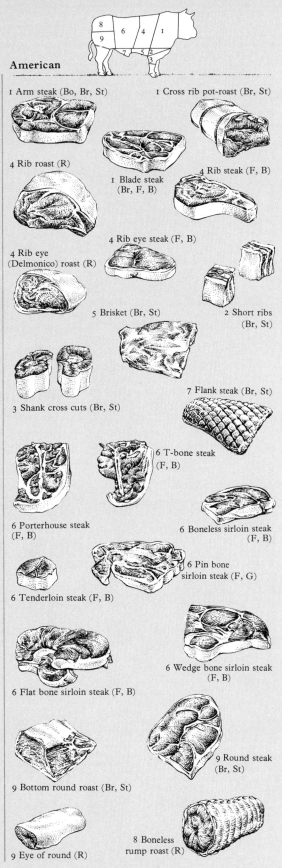

American

It used to be safe to say that deep-colored meat was well aged and would, therefore, be tender; and, conversely, that pale meat was not yet properly aged and would therefore be tough. Today it is not quite that simple. Some modern beef cattle breeds have naturally paler flesh and cattle are now killed at a much earlier age so pale flesh is more likely to be an indication of youth than of inadequate aging. Well-aged meat has a dull look. Freshly-killed meat is bright and shiny, with a taut texture and bleeds when cut. The fine veining of marbled fat is rarely seen today. The animals are killed too young to have gathered much fat (and they are bred to produce the minimum of fat). The fat does tell us something: yellowed fat indicates an older (tastier but tougher) animal; white fat a young one.

Long slow cooking will tenderize the toughest meat, but if you are buying broiling or frying steak, the only sure way to tell if it is tender is to pinch a piece of it. If it is resilient and bouncy the meat will be tough; if it can easily be squashed to a paste, the steak will be tender. Few butchers will let customers handle the meat in this manner; do it at home to find out if the cut in the freezer, which has lost its label, is tender enough to roast or is tough and will have to be braised.

It is commonly thought that any ground beef will do for hamburgers. However, if the meat has come from the tougher parts of the animal, it will make a tough hamburger. Ground stew meat is best used for meatballs or meatloaf which require long slow cooking.

Ground beef should be cooked or frozen within 24 hours of purchase. The air incorporated into the meat by the grinding process encourages the breeding of microorganisms and the meat, therefore, deteriorates rapidly.

Venison (deer meat) is lean and dark in color. It should have the dullness characteristic of well-aged meat. If it is shiny, wet-looking and taut, it has been killed recently and needs further aging. For steaks and sautés buy the tender saddle and fillet; buy haunch and shoulder to make stews, pies and casseroles.

1 Arm steak (Bo, Br, St)

1 Cross rib pot-roast (Br, St)

4 Rib roast (R)

1 Blade steak (Br, F, B)

4 Rib steak (F, B)

4 Rib eye steak (F, B)

4 Rib eye (Delmonico) roast (R)

5 Brisket (Br, St)

2 Short ribs (Br, St)

3 Shank cross cuts (Br, St)

7 Flank steak (Br, St)

6 T-bone steak (F, B)

6 Porterhouse steak (F, B)

6 Boneless sirloin steak (F, B)

6 Pin bone sirloin steak (F, G)

6 Tenderloin steak (F, B)

6 Wedge bone sirloin steak (F, B)

6 Flat bone sirloin steak (F, B)

9 Round steak (Br, St)

9 Bottom round roast (Br, St)

9 Eye of round (R)

8 Boneless rump roast (R)

Bo: Boiling
B: Broiling
Br: Braising
R: Roasting
F: Frying
St: Stewing

British

French

1 & 2 Scrag (Bo, Br, St)

2 Shoulder (Br, R)

2 Boneless épaule bardé (Br, R)

2 Collet (Bo, St)

5 Boned rolled breast (Br, R, St)

2 Middle neck (Br, St)

4 Poitrine (flanchet) (Br)

3 & 6 Carré bardé (R)

4 Best end neck (R)

4 Rib chop (F)

3 & 6 Carré (R)

3 & 6 Côte (F)

6 Loin (R)

6 Loin chop (F)

8 Longe (R)

3 & 6 Pavé (F)

6 Escalopes (F)

6 Boneless sirloin roast (R)

8 Filet (R)

8 Escalopes (F)

8 Knuckle end of leg (Bo, Br)

7 Leg (R)

11 Jarret (Br)

10 Cuisseau (noix) (R)

46

Veal cuts

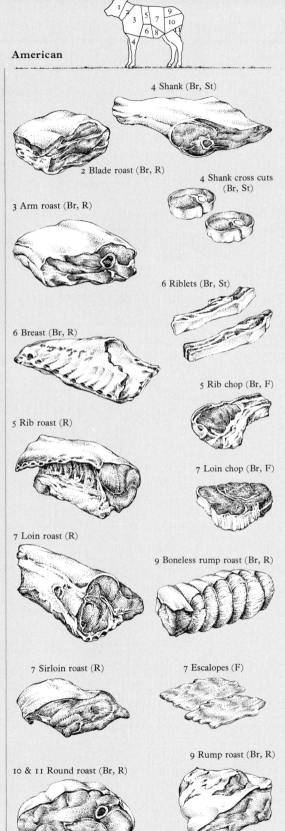

There are two kinds of veal: milk-fed and grass-fed. The flesh of calves fed on milk is naturally more expensive, very pale, and has a mild flavor. Grass-fed veal is cheaper, slightly tougher, and has a stronger flavor. Grass-fed veal is usually sold as stewing veal as the long slow cooking it will receive will break down any toughness. Roast or fry milk-fed veal. Do not broil it—being practically fat-free, it becomes very dry. Both types of veal should be pale pink, without a hint of bloodiness. They should smell milky and fresh, not at all like beef. The cuts of veal more closely resemble those of lamb or pork than beef cuts. The most prized (and expensive) are the cushion end of leg, the loin, and the best end of neck. All are used for roasting or frying as cutlets or scallops.

The morality of eating veal is a problem which disturbs many people. It is illogical and sentimental to accept the slaughter of two-year-old beef cattle while objecting to the killing of their younger brothers, but the methods used to rear veal calves can be distinctly cruel.

The inhumanity of intensive rearing of veal animals has led to a reputation which enlightened veal farmers are trying hard to lose by allowing the calves deep bedding, milk on demand, room for free movement and natural hours of light. Many modern farmers also feel that these more comfortable conditions for the animals lead to contented beasts and, thus, to better veal which yield them higher prices. Unhappily, both types of veal farming continue and the cook troubled by this thought will find it difficult to isolate and boycott veal produced by the other type of farm.

As the animal is so young and consequently needs little tenderizing, it is aged only briefly, usually about a week. Veal, in large pieces, may be stored for several days. Once sliced or beaten out into scallops, it should be cooked within 24 hours. The slices tend to lose their juices, developing a slimy coating, which is unpleasant and a potential bacteria breeding-ground.

2 Blade roast (Br, R)

4 Shank (Br, St)

4 Shank cross cuts (Br, St)

3 Arm roast (Br, R)

6 Riblets (Br, St)

6 Breast (Br, R)

5 Rib chop (Br, F)

5 Rib roast (R)

7 Loin chop (Br, F)

7 Loin roast (R)

9 Boneless rump roast (Br, R)

7 Sirloin roast (R)

7 Escalopes (F)

9 Rump roast (Br, R)

10 & 11 Round roast (Br, R)

Bo: *Boiling*	Br: *Braising*	F: *Frying*
B: *Broiling*	R: *Roasting*	St: *Stewing*

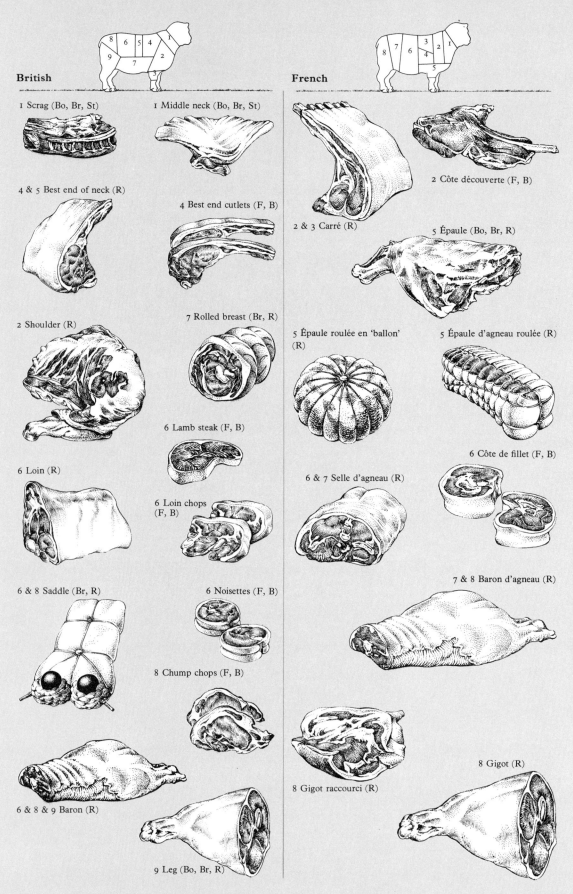

British

1 Scrag (Bo, Br, St)

1 Middle neck (Bo, Br, St)

4 & 5 Best end of neck (R)

4 Best end cutlets (F, B)

2 Shoulder (R)

7 Rolled breast (Br, R)

6 Loin (R)

6 Lamb steak (F, B)

6 Loin chops (F, B)

6 & 8 Saddle (Br, R)

6 Noisettes (F, B)

8 Chump chops (F, B)

6 & 8 & 9 Baron (R)

9 Leg (Bo, Br, R)

French

2 Côte découverte (F, B)

2 & 3 Carré (R)

5 Épaule (Bo, Br, R)

5 Épaule roulée en 'ballon' (R)

5 Épaule d'agneau roulée (R)

6 Côte de fillet (F, B)

6 & 7 Selle d'agneau (R)

7 & 8 Baron d'agneau (R)

8 Gigot raccourci (R)

8 Gigot (R)

48

Lamb cuts

American

The mutton our great-grandparents knew is rare today. Almost all sheep reared commercially are killed young enough and small enough to be graded as lamb. There is a difference between spring lamb and lamb from the larger, older animals killed later in the year. Spring lamb is pale pink, tender and mild and sweet in taste. Older lamb meat should be brownish-pink in color—neither very red nor greyish. As the animals are killed before they are old enough to have become muscular, almost all lamb cuts can be roasted or broiled. The fattier, cheaper cuts of lamb such as breast and neck are also suitable for soups, stews and casseroles. Because the whole lamb carcass is tender, prolonged hanging is rare. Most lamb is hung for about a week.

A few baby lambs are killed for the specialist trade even before they are weaned. The sweetness of their flesh is remarkable. However, they must be ordered in advance, are generally only available for a few weeks in the spring, and are prohibitively expensive. A leg from such a lamb would only feed two or three people.

Most lamb is shipped and stored frozen, and the quality varies widely. It is almost impossible to tell from the look of the meat if it has been in cold storage for three years or one week. Although the meat does freeze well, there is no question that the less time it remains frozen the better it will taste. Lamb can be butchered while still frozen, with electric saws going straight through flesh and bone regardless of correct butchery cuts. This means that the piece of meat, once thawed, may turn out to be ruined by such bad butchering. If possible, do not buy lamb while it is still frozen. It is at least possible to have a good look at thawed or fresh lamb.

3 Rib roast (R)

6 Fore shank (Bo, Br, St)

1 Neck slices (Bo, Br, St)

2 Square shoulder (R)

3 Rib chops (F, B)

2 Cushion shoulder (R)

2 Blade chop (Bo, Br, F, B, St)

6 Boneless riblets (Br, St)

5 Breast (Br, R)

6 Riblets (Br, St)

4 Loin roast (R)

5 Rolled breast (R)

4 Boneless loin roast (R)

4 Boneless double loin chops (F, B)

4 Loin chops (F, B)

7 Sirloin roast (R)

7 Sirloin chop (F, B)

7 Sirloin half of leg (R)

7 Boneless leg rolled (Br, R)

7 Leg chop (F, B)

7 Combination leg (Br, R)

7 Shank half of leg (Bo, Br, R)

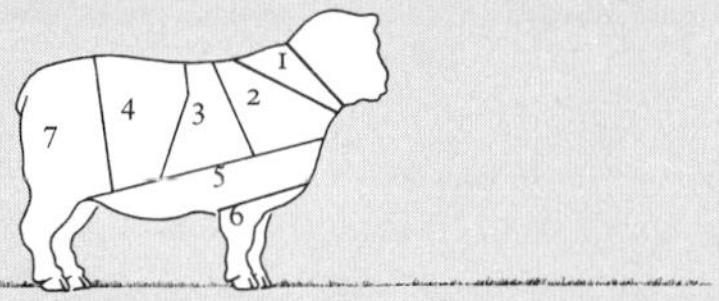

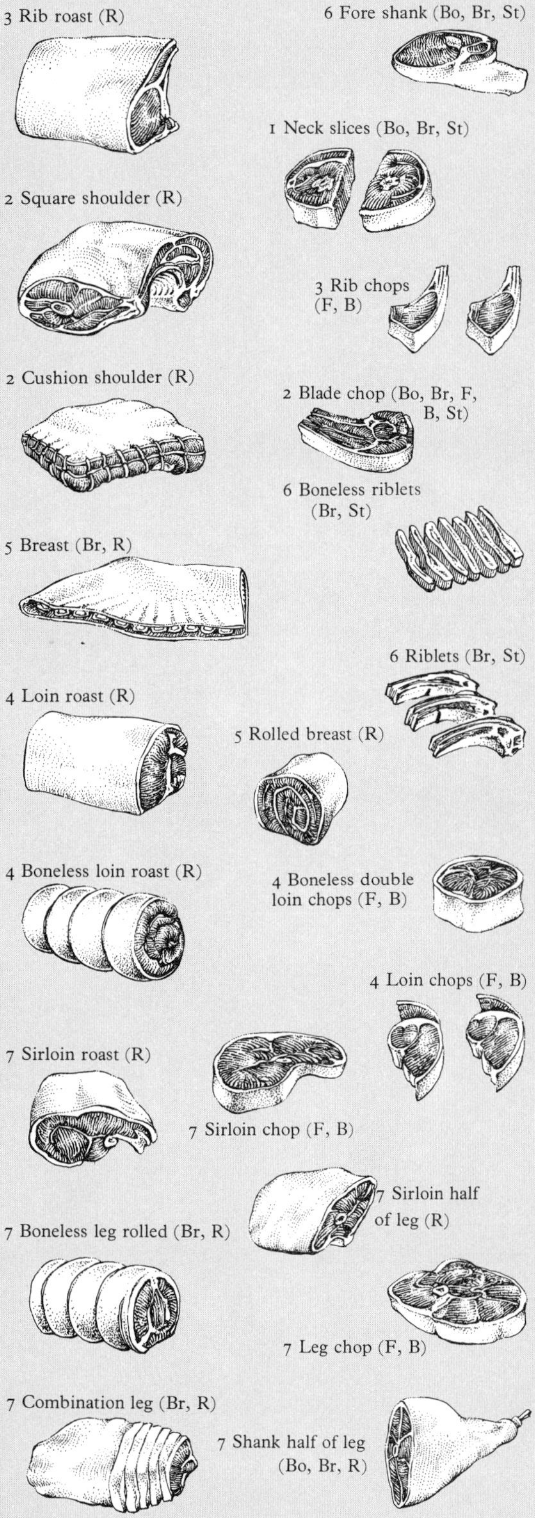

| Bo: Boiling | Br: Braising | F: Frying |
| B: Broiling | R: Roasting | St: Stewing |

British

French

2 Spare rib

2 End collar

3 Blade

2 Échine

1 Tête de porc

2 Spare rib chops

4 Fore slipper

2 Prime collar

5 Plat de côtes (petit salé)

2 Palette

4 Butt

4 Hand and spring

4 Small hock

5 & 6 Loin

2 Middle collar

5 & 6
Loin chops

3 Carré

3 Côte

5 Short back bacon slices

7 Streaky

2 Back fat
(for larding and barding)

7 Lard fumé

7 Spare ribs

7 Belly

7 Streaky bacon slices

7 Poitrine

5 Middle cut

6 Top back bacon slices

6 Fillet

7 Lard salé

6 Filet

8 Chump chop

6 Oyster cut

8 Long back bacon slices

9 Fillet half leg

9 Hock

9 Jambonneau

8 Jambon

9 Middle gammon

9 Knuckle

10 Trotter

10 Pied

Pork and bacon cuts

Modern transport and refrigeration methods have made pork generally available throughout the year. It was once only available in winter, and even today it is still regarded as a dish more suitable for cold weather as its high fat content provides extra calories to fuel the body in cold conditions. Pork flesh should not be red or bloody. It should be pale pink—practically colorless. Hogs bred for the fresh pork market are killed while young and tender and do not carry excessive fat. The fat should be firm and white, and the skin pale and dry. Bacon hogs are fattened to a greater weight and age. Almost the entire animal (usually in two half-carcasses, split down the middle) is immersed in brine for up to a week, then aged. It is then known as "green," fresh or unsmoked bacon.

Pork may be satisfactorily stored for brief periods but is best eaten soon after purchase, especially small cuts, such as chops, which quickly become slimy if covered, and dry if left open.

Gammon is a hind leg of bacon, while *ham* is, strictly, gammon that has been brined (or cured in dry salt) and possibly smoked, separately from the rest of the hog. Hams are traditionally cured and smoked to local recipes giving them their distinctive flavor. Virginia hams, for instance, owe their sweetness to the peaches and peanuts on which the hogs are fed. The meat is cured in salt mixed with sugar, and smoked over hickory and apple wood.

Making bacon was originally a method of preserving pork, allowing households to keep meat for months. Today's bacon is much milder and less salty. Home-cured bacon, however, will still be salty and, unlike most commercial bacon, needs to be soaked before cooking.

Both green and smoked bacon flesh is reddish-pink. Green bacon has a pale whitish rind, smoked bacon has a yellowish-brown rind. Smoked bacon does keep slightly longer than green bacon. Avoid bacon that is dry, hard, dark or patchy in colour. It should be sweet-smelling, moist, without being wet, and even-colored. Cut slices should be floppy rather than stiff and hard.

To test if bacon might need soaking before cooking, cut a tiny piece off the meat and eat it. (If squeamish about eating raw bacon, fry it first.)

Bacon, unlike fresh meat, does not suffer from being kept in plastic wrap in the refrigerator. Green bacon slices will keep perfectly well for five days, smoked slices for a week. Large pieces of commercially-cured bacon may be kept loosely wrapped in the refrigerator, or hanging in a muslin bag in a cool place, for a week. Home-cured keeps for months.

All pork and bacon cuts can be roasted, fried or broiled, but the fattier cuts are usually ground or stewed or braised.

American

1 Blade Boston roast

1 Neck bones

1 Boneless blade steak

2 & 3 Fresh arm picnic

1 Boneless blade Boston roast

2 Arm steak

3 Fresh hock

2 Arm roast

4 & 5 Country-style ribs

4 & 5 Center loin

4 Fat back (for larding and barding)

4 & 5 Blade loin

4 & 5 Sirloin chop

4 & 5 Blade chop

7 Spare ribs

7 Salt pork

7 Sliced bacon

7 Slab bacon

4 & 5 Sirloin

4 & 5 Sirloin cutlet

4 & 5 Rib chop

4 & 5 Canadian-style bacon

4 & 5 Butterfly chop

4 & 5 Boneless double top loin roast

5 Tenderloin

8 Boneless leg/ham

8 Smoked ham rump

8 Smoked ham shank

3 & 9 Pig's feet

51

Poultry

Fresh or frozen?
Fresh birds generally cost more than frozen because keeping a stock of freshly-killed birds, which deteriorate rapidly, is a more risky business (transport, storage and handling are all more urgent and critical).

There is, also, an undoubted loss of moisture from frozen birds; and some frozen birds, because they may not have had any aging at all, may not have developed much flavor.

The main reason for the generally slightly inferior quality of frozen birds, however, is their diet. They have usually been fed on a diet of concentrates (usually bone meal) rather than a mixed diet containing some seed or corn. This is not to say that all fresh birds are corn-fed, or that no frozen birds are. Well-flavored frozen birds are, nevertheless, an exception.

Do not confuse "fresh" with "free-range." The term "free-range" denotes birds that have had freedom of movement, but they are mostly egg-layers.

Chicken "Free-range" chickens, that have roamed farmyards pecking at the ground and have been fed on corn and scraps, are increasingly rare. Chickens reared commercially to be eaten are kept by the "deep-litter method"—confined in boxes filled with inedible "litter"—as opposed to the "battery" confinement of chickens kept for their eggs. If a young deep-litter bird is taken off its diet of bonemeal pellets three weeks before killing, and fed on corn, it will have a better flavor.

If a bird has been freshly killed it will have a faint, pleasant, fresh smell, intact feathers, clear eyes, and quill feathers that come away with a tug. If the bird is plucked and drawn, freshness is indicated by skin which is soft, smooth and dry to the touch, almost as if it has been dusted with talcum powder (wet skin indicates that the bird has probably been frozen) with an even color (not patchy) and plump flesh that feels loose with some elasticity, not tight and hard. The youth, and thus the tenderness, of a bird is indicated by a pliable beak (and feet), smooth legs with barely overlapping scales, and spurs (on male birds) no more developed than small knobs. A more general indication is a breastbone that gives slightly when pressed with the heel of the hand. On large birds only the tip of the bone will bend.

Boiling fowl Birds more than 10 months old will be inedibly tough if roasted or broiled, but their full, strong flavor is brought out in the stockpot or by stewing.

Poussin The words "poussin," "Cornish hen," "baby chicken" and "squab" (this latter used also to denote young pigeon) have different meanings in different countries, but in general they all mean a chicken small enough (1 lb to 2 lb) to be served whole to one person. A double poussin (or "spring chicken") will feed two, and weighs about 2½ lb.

Capon Emasculated cockerels eat heavily, becoming very plump. They also have pale, rich livers. Use them for parties and festive occasions as they weigh up to 10 lb.

Duck Ducklings are killed at about eight weeks old. When buying fresh dressed ducks avoid any which have slimy or patchy skin as this indicates that they have been kept too long. Also avoid ducks with badly plucked legs which are time-consuming to deal with. Buy 2 lb weight per person as the fat content of duck is high and most of it runs from the duck during roasting. It is impossible to judge the quality of a frozen duck, so buy only from reliable suppliers.

Goose A 10-lb goose will feed six people. It is less fatty than duck but is otherwise similar; larger geese can be tough.

Turkey Today's turkeys are fattened fast and killed young, giving tender, moist, delicately flavored flesh. Hens are said to be plumper and have more flavor than cocks, but the difference is minimal. Fresh turkeys, though more costly, have a better, stronger, flavor. They can weigh anything from 10 lb to 22 lb.

The breast should be plump, soft and smooth to the touch and the back covered with a layer of fat. It is normal for the entrails of drawn turkeys, and the neck, to be bloody and strong smelling.

Guinea fowl Although classed as game, today most guinea fowl are raised commercially and sold very fresh, like chicken, rather than well-aged. If buying "in the feather," look for an abundance of healthy, beautiful gray feathers, spotted with white.

Giblets
Many frozen chickens, almost all frozen duck and some frozen turkeys are sold without the giblets. (If the giblets are included they are usually to be found in a plastic package in the body cavity, and must be removed, after thawing, before cooking.) If there is no indication whether or not the bird contains giblets, ask the supplier.

Giblets are useful for gravy, soups and stocks. They are therefore worth having, whenever possible. If buying fresh birds, make sure the giblets are included. (They will have been charged for—fresh birds are weighed before being drawn.) Poultry livers are also sometimes sold separately. They make excellent pâté, and are good fried. Avoid "high"-smelling, discolored, dry or wrinkled livers, though they may vary in hue from pale brown to purple. Greenish-yellow patches lying next to the bitter gallbladder must be removed before cooking or their tainted taste will spoil the dish, but they are not an indication that they are "off."

Fat birds, like duck, geese, and capons, have the richest livers, with a creamy texture. Turkeys have firmer, stronger-flavored livers.

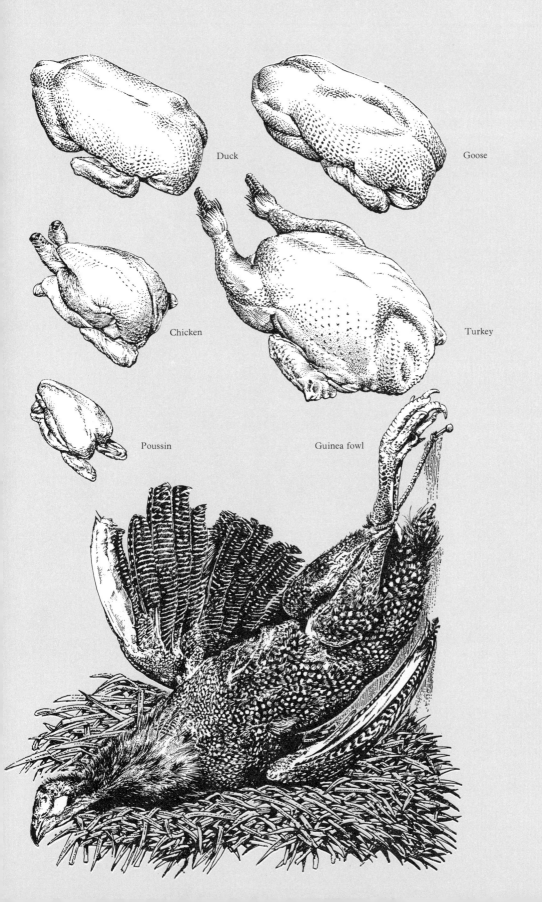

Duck

Goose

Chicken

Turkey

Poussin

Guinea fowl

53

Game

Game birds are bought aged or fresh in the feather, or ready plucked and drawn. They should not be bought cleaned if they are to be given further aging. The degree of "gaminess" is a matter of preference. Two weeks' aging in a cool place is about the maximum and will produce a very strong-tasting and rich-smelling bird, with a greeny abdomen, the skin of which tears easily. Fresh birds smell clean and pleasant and have a mild flavor. If buying plucked and drawn birds, ask for them to be barded, or buy pork back-fat and bard them at home. Casserole old birds (with rigid beaks and scaly feet). Although some game animals such as rabbits and quail are reared commercially, many are shot. Be sure they are not badly damaged, and look out for shot when preparing and when eating.

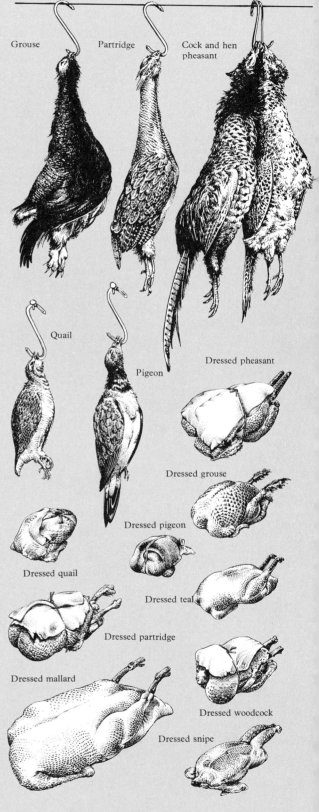

Grouse Partridge Cock and hen pheasant

Quail

Pigeon

Dressed pheasant

Dressed grouse

Dressed pigeon

Dressed quail

Dressed teal

Dressed partridge

Dressed mallard

Dressed woodcock

Dressed snipe

Quail These are small birds with plump breasts and a mild flavor.

Usually commercially raised, they may be bought dressed or completely boned and are often sold frozen.

Plumpness is all. Buy one or two per person, depending on the size of the birds.

Grouse, ptarmigan and prairie chicken These are at their best early in the season. The taste of the hen is marginally superior to that of the cock. They are delicious unaged but for the gamy flavor preferred by many, hang for 14 days in a cool, airy place (or buy ready aged).

Inspect the vent-end of well-hung birds for maggots, something even game dealers cannot always prevent. If there are any return the bird to the dealer.

Buy one bird per person. They are usually sold in brace (one hen, one cock) but may be bought singly. Roast young birds but use older birds in stews or pies.

Pheasant The hen (mottled brown all over) is plump and tender, and the cock is almost as good, with a spectacular green neck and long speckled tail feathers.

Treat as grouse, with the exception that a pheasant may serve two people.

Partridge They are small (though larger than quail), round and with browny-orange feathers.

At under six months they are *perdreux* suitable for roasting, older they become *perdrix* and are casseroled.

They may be well hung, but are generally eaten fresh, especially if plainly roasted.

Serve one or two per person.

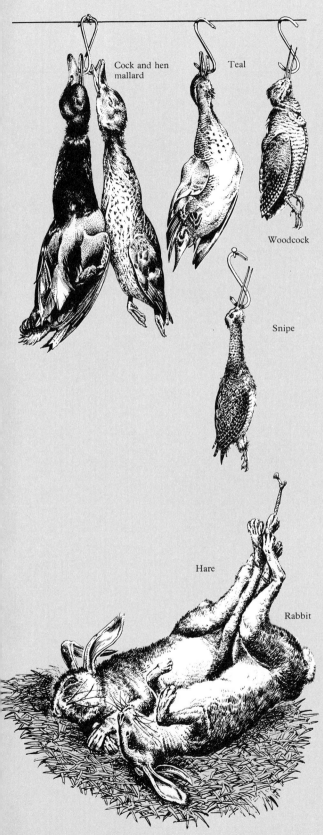

Cock and hen mallard

Teal

Woodcock

Snipe

Hare

Rabbit

Wild duck, widgeon, and teal

There are many varieties of wild duck, ranging from the large mallard to the tiny teal. Eat them all fresh for the best results. Try them slightly under-cooked in the French style. All duck are tedious to pluck so try to get the plucking done professionally, by the retailer, if possible.

Wild duck has considerably less fat than domestic duck and is therefore barded as some game birds.

Sometimes fish-eating wild duck have a slight fishy taste which can be masked, if not eliminated, by marinating, flaming in brandy or basting with orange juice.

Pigeon and squab

Wild pigeon and domestically reared *pigeonneau* or squab, which are killed when they are about four weeks old, have most of their meat on the breast. Do not bother plucking the legs as there is little meat on them. The breast is dark, lean and full of flavor. If the breasts alone are to be broiled on a skewer, casseroled or fried, allow three breasts per person (three birds for two people).

Check breastbone and feet for age as for chicken. Old birds are inedibly tough.

Snipe and woodcock

The tiny snipe and slightly larger woodcock are traditionally sold, and roasted, without drawing, the "trail" being left in the body, or removed after cooking and spread on the CROÛTON on which the bird is served.

Allow two birds per person.

Rabbit Commercially reared rabbits are sold young and plump and should have perfect fur coats, not matted, dull or patchy, and should have practically no smell. Wild rabbits may be tender and tasty or inedibly tough, depending on their age and diet. Look for the following signs of youth (and tenderness):

1 Smooth sharp claws, not roughened, rounded or hard.
2 Small, even, white teeth, not at all "bucktoothed."
3 Delicate soft ears, easy to tear, not leathery, dry and tough.

Wild rabbits are smaller and have less fat than the domesticated variety. Both must be eaten fresh. They are hung readygutted (unlike hares) for 24 hours, still with the pelt on to keep the flesh moist.

Hares Young hares (leverets) have similar characteristics to young rabbits. Young hares have a hardly noticeable harelip; old hares have a deep, pronounced one.

Hares are hung, ungutted, like game birds for five to six days, head down over a bowl to catch the blood. They are ready to eat when the back legs have ceased to be stiff.

It is occasionally possible to buy hares' blood in cartons. It makes delicious sauce.

Fish

Look for the following signs of freshness in fish:

1 Slipperiness. The skin should be shiny-bright and the fish difficult to grip.
2 Firmness, especially around the belly. If the ungutted fish is flabby and soft, press it with a finger; if the impression remains in the flesh for a few seconds, it is past its prime.
3 Tight scales. If they are coming off, the fish is stale.
4 Bulging, clear, bright eyes. Sunken, dull and opaque eyes indicate long storage.
5 Bright pink or reddish gills, not dull, brown or dry.
6 A fresh and pleasant smell.

Types of fish There are so many varieties of fish, with names varying from country to country—and even from town to town—that buying fish, especially away from home, can be a confusing business. If in doubt ask the fishmongers what they recommend and how they would cook it.

Flat fish
Brill resembles turbot though seldom grows to more than 8 lb. The flesh is grayish-white, delicate and soft. Poach or bake whole, or fry or broil fillets.

Dab Small plaice-like fish, bought and served whole. Fry or broil plainly.

Fish, unlike meat, does not toughen with age, so indications of age in a fish do not concern the cook.

Again unlike meat, fish does not improve on keeping. Even a few days' storage will leave the flesh flavorless and flabby. Frozen fish is much better than fresh fish stored too long.

If fish must be stored for a day or two, put it in a container in the coldest part of the refrigerator, scatter a couple of handfuls of ice cubes (or a scoop of crushed ice) over it, and cover the container to prevent the smell of fish tainting other food in the refrigerator. Renew the ice cubes after 12 hours or so.

If such storage is impracticable, cover the fish with a cold wet cloth. If the fish has to be stored longer than 24 hours, freeze it.

Dover sole are served whole and usually skinned on the gray-brown side only, though some chefs also remove the white side. The flesh is firm and used in a great many *haute cuisine* dishes. Serve whole small soles (about 6 oz) as a first course. Buy 1 lb sole per person for a main course.

Flounder This name is used for almost any small flat fish other than sole, but strictly denotes an inferior relation of plaice which it resembles in its color and markings. There is a distinctive row of sharp spines on its upper side.

Halibut A flat, sometimes extremely large, fish with well flavored firm white flesh, usually sold in steaks for broiling or poaching. Small "chicken" halibut weigh as little as 2 lb and are sold whole.

Lemon sole Sometimes called "poor man's sole," it has delicate, very white flesh but lacks the firmness of Dover sole. Lemon sole is flatter and rounder, with a more pointed nose than the Dover. The skin is white on one side and lightish-brown on the other. Buy sizes of about 1 lb for the best results.

Plaice Similar in shape to the lemon sole, though sometimes much larger. Plaice has one white side, the other is brownish-gray spotted with orange. Its flesh is delicious when fresh, but lacks firmness. Fry or broil.

Skate Only the "wings" are eaten. In France small skate are sometimes sold whole. The flesh between the ribs of the fins is well flavored but soft. Traditionally it is grilled and served with BEURRE NOISETTE.

Turbot Large fish (they may weigh up to 45 lb) with excellent, firm, pure white flesh, usually sold in steaks, or even in cubes for kebabs. Small turbot, large enough for two or three people, are a rare delicacy.

Round fish
Bass (freshwater) can weigh up to 8 lb they have pale, firm, delicate and delicious flesh. Cook plainly—poach, pan-fry, broil or bake. There are both black and white varieties of bass.

Bass (seabass or Mediterranean bass) called *bar* or, incorrectly, *loup de mer* in France. Bake or broil whole (they usually weigh under 3 lb) with a sprig or two of fennel. The skin is gray, the flesh white and firm.

Carp A freshwater fish, usually sold whole, weighing up to 8 lb. The fish has an ugly head and shiny colored, uneven scales. It has a good flavor. The flesh is exceptionally soft and it is rather bony. Best baked whole and stuffed.

Cod One of the most popular fish, with gray, small-scaled skin and firm white creamy flesh. It has a mild flavor and needs a crisp batter, cheese sauce or a good lemon dressing to bring it out. Cod is generally sold in large fillets, or steaks, but buy whole small cod, weighing about 4 lb, and bake them.

Eel Buy those weighing about 2 lb. If fresh, buy them already skinned, if possible. Smoked eel is generally sold in its skin to keep the flesh moist.

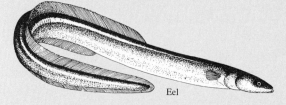

Eel

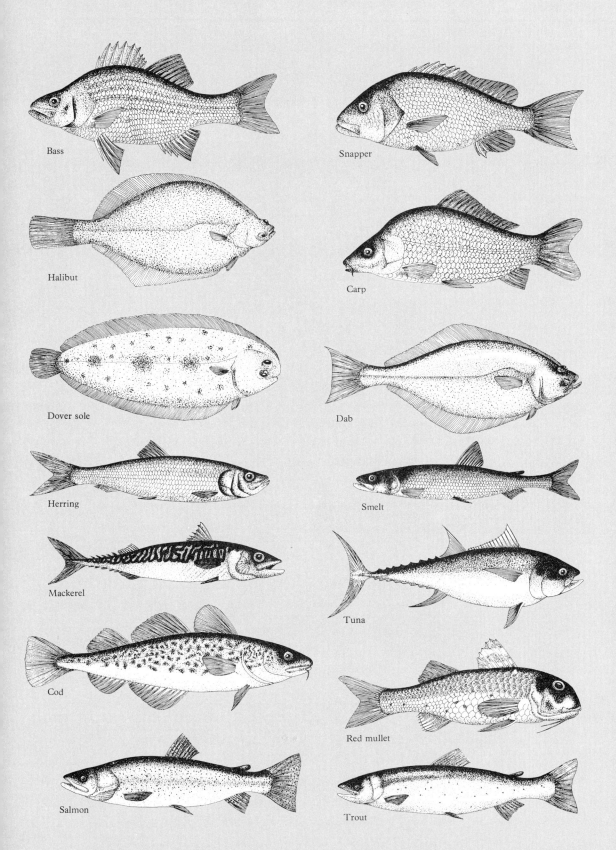

Bass

Snapper

Halibut

Carp

Dover sole

Dab

Herring

Smelt

Mackerel

Tuna

Cod

Red mullet

Salmon

Trout

Gray mullet bears no relation to red mullet as the flesh is white and soft, but of good flavor. Stuff and bake whole.

Haddock Similar in appearance to cod but infinitely superior in flavor, with large creamy flakes of firm flesh. Small whole haddocks are more readily available than whole cod. They make wonderful fish pie and are good cooked in any way.

Hake Similar in shape to cod and haddock, weighing up to 10 lb. They have a good flavor but the flesh can be dry. They are sometimes sold as "Cape haddock".

John Dory (Golden Haddock. St. Peter's fish) An Adriatic and Mediterranean fish with firm, almost lobster-like, nutty-flavored white flesh. Known as St. Peter's fish because it carries finger- and thumb-like marks on its flanks, which legend says were left by the Saint who tossed it back into the sea when it groaned.

Pike A long, ugly, bony fish, but good for stews, soups and, most importantly, *quenelles* because the sticky, gelatinous flesh binds well.

Salmon Perhaps the best of all fish, with firm pink flesh of exquisite flavor. The slight oiliness of the flesh makes it rich in taste and ideal for smoking. Early season salmon are unsurpassed in flavor and delicacy. Toward the end of the salmon season the fish may develop a muddy taste. The best fish weigh about 8 lb and are sold whole or in steaks (the best steaks coming from the middle cut, though the rich tail steaks are preferred by some). Grilse is young salmon, having spent only one season in the sea. They weigh about 6 lb and are paler and more delicate in taste. The best salmon come from Scottish and Canadian waters (either line caught in rivers or trawled in the sea).

Sea bream come in many colors and sizes but are always striking, attractive fish on the slab. The best is the Golden "*daurade*" or "*dorade*." Buy whole and bake them stuffed. Roll fillets in cornmeal, oatmeal or flour, and then fry them.

Sea trout River trout which have migrated to the sea and developed pink "*saumonée*" flesh. Called "salmon trout" by fishmongers. They are firm-fleshed and, though less rich than true salmon, are exceptionally well flavored.

Smelt are small fish which smell of cucumber when freshly caught. Gut through the gills and cook whole, either by pan-frying, deep-frying or broiling.

Snapper There are many varieties, the most well-known is the North American eastern seaboard red snapper, which is about 2 ft long and is usually served in steaks. The flesh is white with large creamy flakes of firm meat.

Gray snapper, generally larger than the red, is also good but less firm-fleshed.

Trout Lake trout or river trout, line-caught and eaten within hours, is incomparable. Shop-bought trout vary according to the fish-farming methods used, their taste and texture depending on their diet and how they were stored after killing.

Generally, the larger the trout the better will be its flavor. Look for firm, faintly pink flesh, and slipperiness of skin which is a particularly important indication of freshness in trout.

Store live trout for *truite au bleu* by putting them in a sinkful of cold water into which fresh cold water is constantly being run—this keeps it aerated. Trout quickly die if deprived of oxygen. (Regulate the flow of water carefully: too much oxygen and the trout will leap out of the sink.)

Whiting A small bony fish with little flavor but good gelatinous flesh for making pounded mixtures such as *quenelles*. Used to bind the flesh of other fish.

Oily fish
Oily fish are particularly suitable for smoking or salting, and many of the fish below are so treated, though they are also sold fresh.

Anchovies Tiny, strongly-flavored member of the herring family. Usually sold salted and canned. Used for seasoning or garnishing.

Herring Average weight 6 oz. Sold whole, they should be shiny, rather stiff to the touch, and not too strong-smelling. They may be a little bloody round the gills but should not be dry. Boniness is the chief disadvantage of herring. PICKLE or SOUSE herring fillets or broil, bake or fry them plainly.

Mackerel Small (about 12 oz), spectacularly shiny fish with green and black markings. Buy very fresh as they lose their flavor fast. Fry or bake. Good with mustard sauce.

Pilchards Strongly flavored adult sardines. They are good fresh; fry or broil them.

Red mullet Small, bony, rather stiff, red-skinned fish from the Mediterranean. Well-flavored firm flesh which is too dry to freeze well. Serve two 6 oz mullet per person; best broiled or fried.

Sardines About 4 in long, shiny gray-blue fish with an excellent flavor when fresh and broiled. Available (and good) frozen; or canned in oil, but they then have a distinctly different, though pleasant, taste.

Tuna Large fish with dense, pinky-brown flesh, resembling veal or chicken, and having little or no fishy flavor. Bake or roast (basting with plenty of butter) or casserole them. The flesh is sold in steaks or "roasts." They are available fresh from warm seas only, but are commonly available canned in oil or water.

Whitebait Baby herring or, indeed, any small fish caught in shoals. They are about 1 in long and should be fresh-smelling and slippery. Good frozen, Toss in flour and deep-fry, without gutting.

To make *taramasalata*, the Greek smoked roe pâté, wet a slice of crustless white bread and squeeze out excess water. Put the damp bread in a food processer, blender or bowl. Add two crushed cloves of garlic and about 1 cup smoked soft cod or mullet roe, skinned. Beat to a paste, then gradually add a mixture of olive oil and tasteless salad oil, beating it in slowly, drop by drop at first. As the EMULSION thickens, speed up the flow of oil to a steady stream. Continue until the required taste and texture is achieved (this usually requires about 1¼ cups of oil). Add ground white pepper and lemon juice to taste.

Smoked fish and roe

Store smoked fish for a few days in a closed container in the refrigerator, or hang in a cool dry place.

Freeze if they need to be stored for longer—but this will impair the texture.

Fish are generally cold-smoked, if they are to be cooked further before eating; or hot-smoked, if they are to be eaten as they are.

Smoked salmon is the exception to the rule, and although it is eaten without further treatment, it is cold-smoked—hung in coolish smoke which does not alter the translucency of the flesh. Good smoked salmon looks much like raw salmon flesh and should be soft and moist, with a delicate pink color. Inferior smoked salmon is tough, dry, reddish in hue and opaque.

Smoked trout is hot-smoked, with resulting opaque "cooked" flesh and a moist, tender-but-firm texture. The toughish skin of the fish should be pliable, not rigid. The flesh should not be shreddy and dry, nor mushy and wet, both of which conditions indicate that the fish may have been frozen. Frozen smoked trout has a distinctly inferior taste and texture.

Smoked mackerel

Broil cold-smoked mackerel (which has soft glassy flesh and a fairly tender skin) and serve with a piquant sauce or HORSERADISH.

Eat hot-smoked mackerel (with opaque, firmer flesh and leathery dark skin) plain as it is—with the skin removed.

Kippers are smoked herring. They are soaked in brine, then cold-smoked. Broil or poach or marinate and eat raw. The flesh should be translucent, moist and pleasant smelling. The best kippers are pale yellow. Cheaper kippers are commercially dyed to give them a dark amber color. Packaged frozen, boned kipper fillets are useful for making PÂTÉS and MOUSSES.

Smoked haddock As with kippers, the best fish are cold-smoked to a pale translucent yellow, not artificially colored to a bright orange or yellow. The best are the small whole one-portion haddock "finnan haddies" or the famous "Arbroath smokies" from Scotland. Broil or cook in milk.

Smoked eel should have oily, firm, opaque flesh. Buy them in their skins to prevent drying out.

Smoked cod and ling are often confused with the excellent smoked haddock as they are treated similarly; but they lack flavor. If haddock is not available, choose large, pale and moist fillets of cod and cook as for haddock.

Bloaters are unsalted smoked herring with a mild flavor. They do not keep well, but are delicious eaten fresh.

Fish roes

Caviar The lightly salted roes of the sturgeon. The most famous varieties are Sevruga, with small dark-grey grains, and Beluga, with large paler grains. Both should be moist, oily, translucent and fresh-smelling.

Once the container is opened, consume the caviar promptly.

Red caviar Salmon roe, salted and sold in jars. It has a good flavor but lacks the subtlety of the real thing.

Mock caviar or lumpfish roe Salty, black small grains sold in jars. Good in cocktail canapés and for dressing egg dishes.

Smoked soft cod roe or mullet roe, may be bought in jars, or fresh. It should be soft and moist, with a toughish red skin, and should smell clean and fresh. It will keep, refrigerated, for a few days but is best eaten on toast while fresh or used in smooth PÂTÉS.

Fresh fish roe (cod, trout, salmon, shad or herring) Broil, fry or deep-fry coated in BATTER female fish eggs (hard roe) and milt, or male sperm (soft roe). The roes, if bought separately from the fish, should be moist and clean-smelling. Milt is creamy, with tiny, almost invisible grains. Hard roes are less delicate, drier and more inclined to break up into grains. Buy soft roes if possible. Use roes found in fish in sauces or in stuffings for the fish, or serve them on toast (collect in the freezer until there is a usable quantity).

Seafood

If lobsters or crabs are large and strong, make sure that their pincers are bound with tape or strong rubber bands and that they cannot climb out of the storage container (a cooling rack tied across the top of a box will suffice). Fresh oysters and mussels will keep as described for up to two weeks, especially if packed in seaweed. Lobsters and crabs live for several days, but it is cruel and inadvisable to keep live creatures too long—they lose weight and they just might die anyway.

Only buy cooked shellfish from a reputable supplier. Make sure they look good and smell delicious.

To store frozen seafood
Keep frozen at the coldest possible temperatures. Enzyme and bacterial activity will continue as soon as the food thaws, so use promptly after defrosting.

Crayfish (*écrevisses*) The most delicious and delicate of freshwater creatures, pale greenish-brown in color, can weigh anything from a few ounces to 1 lb.

They will not stay alive for more than 12 hours unless kept in well-oxygenated fresh water. Arrange a continuous flow of fresh cold water to keep them aerated. They are usually sold—and are good—frozen. In this state they are pinkish, becoming brighter red when cooked. In France they are sold live, packed like tomatoes in trays. Use any bought this way promptly.

Crustaceans like lobster and crab, and molluscs like oysters or squid, have one characteristic of great importance to the purchaser: Once dead, they perish fast. For this reason, seafood is generally sold either live, frozen or already cooked. Cook killed (or thawed) shellfish immediately. After cooking its "shelf life" is much like fish: It will keep refrigerated for about four days but the quality of the taste deteriorates significantly after a day or so.

To store live shellfish: Put oysters (curved side down to prevent them losing their juices), mussels, lobsters or crabs in a container that is *not* airtight (a basket, open box or bucket) and cover with a damp cloth. Keep them in the bottom of the refrigerator (at about 41°F).

Crabs Live crabs should be quite definitely lively and feel heavy for their size.

When buying cooked crabs, hold them by the claws and shake them—they should feel solid and heavy. If they rattle as though full of water, or feel light for their size, they are of inferior quality. They must also look and smell fresh.

Lobsters Buy them between 1 lb and 2 lb in weight. Very small lobsters have too little flesh inside a lot of shell, and very large ones may have coarse dry flesh. The lobster should be blue-black, shiny and quite lively. Scratch its back with a pencil tip—a recently-caught lobster will flap its tail under it, wave its claws and arch its back. Don't buy it if the reaction is lethargic. "Cripples," or lobsters with a claw missing, are sometimes sold cheaply, but will not live for long.

Crawfish (spiny lobster, rock lobster, *langouste*) Rough-backed creature resembling a lobster without claws. Best bought live; choose as for lobster.

Shrimp and prawns (*crevettes*) There are many varieties ranging from the small brown shrimp (*crevette grise*) to the magnificent Dublin Bay prawn (*langoustine* or scampi) which, unlike the others, has claws. Prawns do not change colour when cooked. They are sold both cooked and frozen.

Squid (inkfish, *calamari*) Look for fresh squid with the ink sac intact. The ink adds body, color and flavor to a sauce. Frozen squid often has little or no ink. The smaller the animal, the more tender it will be. Buy slippery, shiny squid with a fresh smell.

Octopus Avoid any over 2 lb as they will be inedibly tough. Judge quality as for squid. They are closely related, although the octopus has a less elongated body and only eight tentacles (the squid has 10).

Oysters Buy tightly-closed, heavy oysters from a reliable supplier. Large ones are not necessarily better, but they should be plump for their size.

Scallops bought in the shell are generally already opened by fishmongers. Choose fat, moist, plump and shiny scallops which have a sweet smell. If the scallops are to be served in the shells, get the concave half, not the flat side (scallops are usually displayed on a flat shell) as they are equally decorative and are also useful for holding sauce. Shells may be put in the dishwasher, or scrubbed by hand, and may be used for years as long as they are thoroughly sterilized in boiling water each time. Frozen scallops are sold without shells. Shells may be bought separately.

Clams and mussels Make quite sure that they are still alive if buying them in the shell. If they remain open when tapped, they are dead, or dying. This applies to both long-neck (soft shell) and round (hard shell) clams. Only buy shucked (or shelled) clams from a reputable supplier and use them promptly.

Cockles Tiny clam-like creatures, sold ready-cooked, boiled or pickled in vinegar. Check for sand; they are often gritty. Boiled cockles should smell sweet and must be eaten promptly. Pickled cockles keep, refrigerated, for a week.

Whelks and winkles Both are usually sold cooked. The larger whelk is eaten like the snail; the little winkle needs a pin or "winkle picker" first to remove the scale-like cap from the opening to the shell, and then to extract the meat. Eat on the day of purchase.

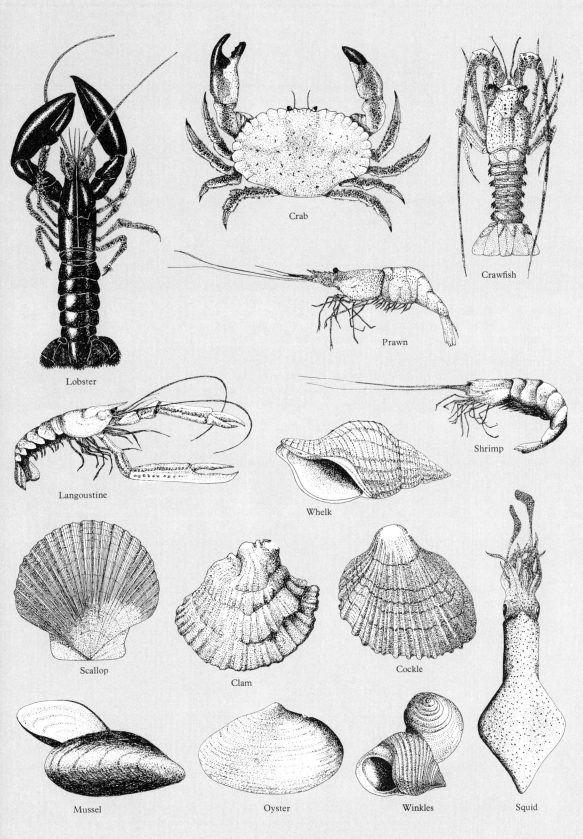

Lobster

Crab

Crawfish

Prawn

Langoustine

Whelk

Shrimp

Scallop

Clam

Cockle

Mussel

Oyster

Winkles

Squid

Vegetables

Avocado Hold the whole fruit in both palms and squeeze gently. It should give slightly. Bullet-hard ones should be wrapped in a newspaper and kept in the dark, but not refrigerated. Blackened avocadoes are sometimes a good buy if they are cheap. There is a risk they may be bad but, if not, they have a great deal of flavor.

Beans—green, snap and string Avoid any large or limp beans. They should, literally, snap when bent.

Beans—lima beans and broad beans The pods should be medium-sized but with plenty of bumps in them. Flat pods are empty; large beans have an unpleasant taste.

Broccoli (and calabrese or sprouting broccoli) These have green, white or purple immature flower-heads and are smaller relations of the cauliflower. The stalk is eaten as well as the head. Buy firm sweet-smelling ones. They soon develop an over-powerful smell, go limp, or flower.

Brussels sprouts Buy small, tight, bullet-hard ones, with very green outer leaves.

Try to buy vegetables either from a supermarket with a large and rapid turnover or from a small shop or market stall where there is simply not the opportunity to store stale produce. Stall-holders, knowing that what attracts their customers is the freshness of their wares, generally discard the day's unsold produce or sell it off cheaply.

Insist on inspecting the goods before they are put quickly into a paper bag and ask for bruised or wilting produce to be changed. This can be difficult to do the first time, but it is the only way to shop. Once merchants know their customers will not put up with inferior produce, it is then not worth their while trying to slip in some stale carrots or moldy oranges.

See pages 122/3 for suggested methods of cooking for each vegetable.

Cabbages Firmness and crispness are all. If buying hard cabbages from a market buy them with the outer leaves intact—small smooth "footballs" may have been there for weeks, with the retailer peeling a layer of old leaves off every day. (Supermarkets do peel them—only once—to make packaging easier.) They should be firm, smooth and unblemished.

Cauliflowers Open up the leaves to inspect the white head. It should be unblemished and have tightly packed florets. Leave the outer leaves on until just before cooking—they protect the flower-heads.

Celeriac Check for firmness.

Celery Check for crispness. Withered, discolored top leaves indicate age on seemingly fresh stalks.

Chicory (Belgian endive) Buy crisp white heads, avoiding slightly open buds or greenish leaves, which will be too bitter.

Eggplant Buy smooth, firm, glossy fruit which is neither wrinkled nor patchy and feels heavy and solid.

Fennel Choose white heads without dried outer leaves. If they still have their feathery tops, avoid any with yellowed or dried tops.

Snow peas are eaten pod and all; so choose small ones that are not stringy, yellowed, dry or limp. The pods must contain only barely formed peas. Once the peas are round, the pod is too stringy and tough.

Peas For ordinary peas: Buy fresh, green, crisp pods with small peas—not so small that the pod is half empty, and not so large that the peas are floury or sprouting.

Pumpkin Avoid over-large pumpkins, which can have a stringy, dry texture. It is also difficult to use all a large one before it deteriorates. Buy small firm ones, or a section of a cut large one (it is then possible to check the quality of the flesh).

Spinach Avoid yellowed, limp leaves. Carefully wash off any grit and mud. Spinach beet (leaf beet or "perpetual" spinach) has smaller leaves, but is milder in taste and more tender than all but the youngest true spinach, making it suitable for salads.

Squash Small ones are less watery. Avoid bruised or blemished ones.

Zucchini Choose those that are even-sized, firm and unblemished. Check the ends: Rot usually starts there.

Pumpkin

Avocado

Eggplant

Plum tomato

Yellow tomato

Zucchini

Mediterranean tomato

Red tomato

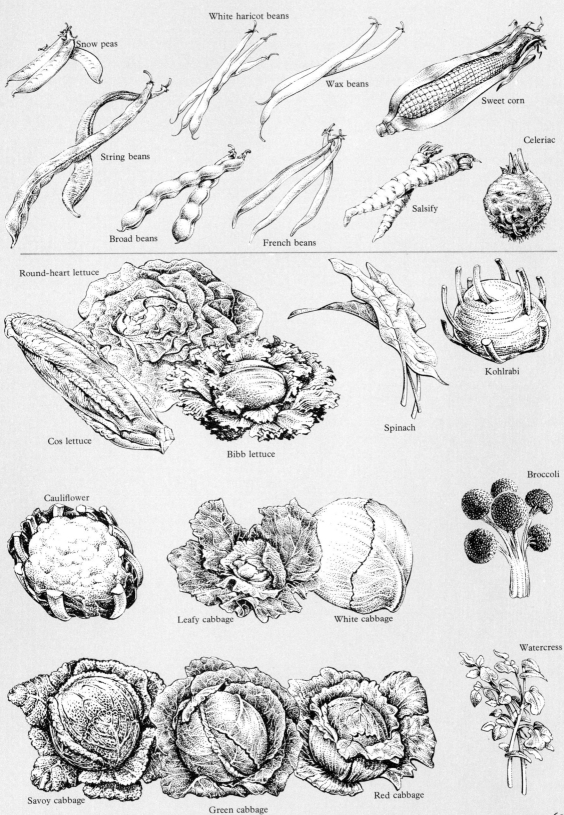

Snow peas

White haricot beans

String beans

Wax beans

Sweet corn

Celeriac

Broad beans

French beans

Salsify

Round-heart lettuce

Kohlrabi

Cos lettuce

Bibb lettuce

Spinach

Broccoli

Cauliflower

Leafy cabbage

White cabbage

Watercress

Savoy cabbage

Green cabbage

Red cabbage

Vegetables /2

Artichokes, globe The leaves should be stiff, tightly packed and evenly green, with no brown at the tips. The smaller the globe in relation to the stem, the younger the artichoke. Really young artichokes have little edible flesh on their leaves, although they are easily peeled down to their hearts.

Artichokes, Jerusalem Buy the oval-shaped type, as the more irregular kind are difficult to peel. They should feel bullet-hard.

Asparagus Choose firm, crisp stalks of an even thickness (so they will all take the same time to cook). "Spruce," or first-year asparagus, is thin and scraggy, but is a good buy. It may not look good but has good flavor.

Beets Buy bullet-hard raw small beets of even shape and size. Buy cooked beet from a market with a rapid turnover. Boiled beets quickly go moldy and it is impossible to tell if they are about to do so. Check the date-stamp on pre-packed beets.

Carrots If they still have their green leafy tops they are fresh—even if the tops are a little limp. Those bought loose without their tops, or in packets, may have been stored for months, but if the carrots are firm this does not matter too much.

Kohlrabi Medium-sized, firm ones are best. Use as turnip.

Leeks Avoid yellowed or dried-looking leeks. Small ones are crisper and have more taste.

Mushrooms Cultivated mushrooms are sold either as young "buttons", or a little older when they are half-open with brown gills, or as open "flat" mushrooms with near-black gills. The buttons are best for sauces that must stay white and for garnishing, but their flavor is mild. The middle-aged mushroom is the one most frequently sold and is good for most purposes: The cup shape lends itself to stuffing. Older, flat dark mushrooms have the most pronounced flavor—almost too rich for some. These do color sauces very dark, however, and soup made from them will be gray rather than biege. Mushrooms are sometimes worth buying in less than prime condition. If being sold cheaply because they have dried out somewhat, all they will have lost is weight (which gives the buyer more value for the money) and good looks (which don't matter if they are to be chopped). The mushrooms will swell during cooking, and will have lost nothing in flavor.

Mushrooms, wild (cep, morel, chanterelle, truffle) Mostly bought in tins in America and Britain, but widely available fresh in the rest of Europe. The same criteria apply as for cultivated mushrooms—slightly dried ones are also sometimes a bargain.

Onions Buy the big Spanish onions for salads and for a mild flavor in cooked dishes; and the smaller red type for sauces and stews. Onions should be bullet-hard. Avoid squashy or even mildly soft ones and any that are sprouting.

Onions, Welsh (*ciboules*) Judge as leeks, using the appearance of the visible top green leaves as a guide.

Potatoes The small waxy-fleshed type of potato is best for most dishes; the large, floury type is ideal for baking whole and creaming. Choose even-sized potatoes which are firm and smooth with barely developed "eyes."

Scallions Avoid limp or slimy ones. Larger ones tend to be too strong to eat uncooked in salads.

Spring onions Avoid limp or slimy ones. Larger ones tend to be too strong to eat uncooked in salads.

Rutabagas Choose medium-sized (about ½ lb) smooth, firm, unblemished ones.

Sweet corn (maize) Check the kernels inside the husk. They should be juicy and young-looking, not dry and hard. The husk should be green and the "silk," or top threads, soft and moist.

Turnips Should be firm, unblemished and as small as possible. Use the smallest raw as a 'CRUDITÉ' with mayonnaise, or cook whole.

Storing vegetables
Packing and refrigeration technology bring vegetables to the supermarket looking as if they had just been picked that morning. Obviously this is not the case; imported vegetables may be weeks, even months, old. At home, the spoilage process will be rapid unless domestic versions of the professionals' techniques are employed. Almost all vegetables store well in plastic bags in the refrigerator. Plastic bags or containers prevent limpness by dehydration. This is true of root vegetables like carrots, leafy ones like spinach and "vegetable fruits" like eggplant and tomatoes. If it is impracticable to store everything in the refrigerator, find a cool place for the rest. Store vegetables in the dark (light hastens spoilage): Wrap them in

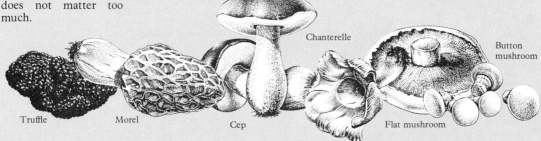

Truffle   Morel   Cep   Chanterelle   Flat mushroom   Button mushroom

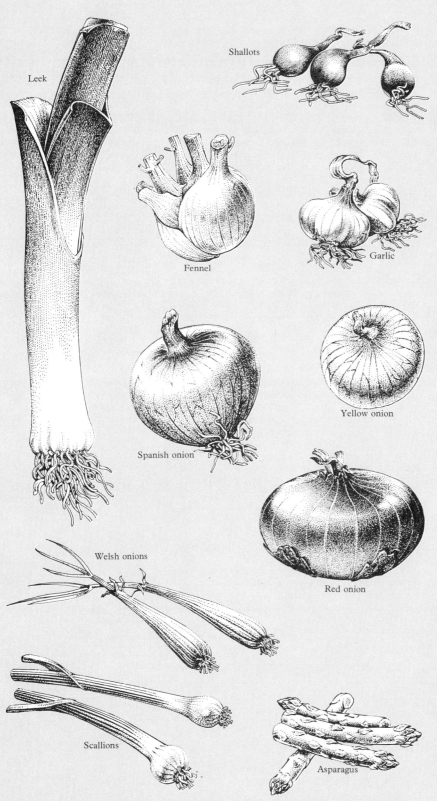

Leek

Shallots

Fennel

Garlic

Spanish onion

Yellow onion

Welsh onions

Red onion

Scallions

Asparagus

newspaper or put them in a cardboard carton with a lid. Do not use airtight containers like plastic bags or plastic containers for this form of storage as the warmer temperatures will allow "sweating" and in an enclosed space this will cause decomposition. Do not let vegetable fruits, like tomatoes, touch each other or the points of contact will go bad quickly.

Watercress, tender lettuces and leafy herbs go limp if they cannot retain water or replace lost water. Store them in plastic bags in the warmest part of the refrigerator. Herbs may also be kept in a jar of water, like flowers. Watercress needs to be almost totally submerged in water, or put to stand in a jar of water leaves down, stalks up.

Green vegetables stored in a rack in the kitchen of a centrally-heated house will wilt in a day; and even potatoes would need to be used within a week.

Dried peas and beans
Dried peas and beans, such as lima beans, red kidney beans, black-eyed peas, split peas, haricot beans and lentils, should be bought from a shop with a sufficiently rapid turnover to guarantee fresh stocks. There is a great difference between beans dried last season and those dried three years ago. As a rule, the smaller the better. Small butter beans are less inclined to break up on cooking, and have a less floury texture and a sweeter taste than larger ones.

Store dried beans in airtight containers. They will go stale quicker in an open container.

65

Fruit

Apples "Cooking apples" or very tart apples to be used in sauce, pies or baked may be bought a little unripe. Apples for eating in the hand should be perfectly smooth with an un-blemished skin. Smell apples before purchase; full-flavored and ripe apples are fragrant.

Apricots vary in quality so much that they can only be judged by their taste. If it is not possible to taste one before pur-chase, buy the smallest possible amount and eat one in the shop before buying any more.

Black currants Ripe ones are almost black, so buy containers with as few as possible that are red or the even less ripe green berries.

Cherries Sour cherries, of which the Morello is most famous, are best cooked. The sweet sort, designated tender (the heart cherry) or hard (the whiteheart cherry) ac-cording to their flesh, are best eaten fresh. Cherries should be bought firm and glossy.

Clementines are a hy-brid of tangerines and oranges, more akin to the orange in flavor and appearance. The skin is smooth, stiff and tight. They are almost seedless and somewhat tart. Like all good citrus fruits, they should be glossy and fragrant.

Plumpness, firmness and fragrance are the best indications of good quality in fruit. If fruit is shrink-wrapped under plastic, however, it is impossible to smell or taste it. Some merchants will not even permit the handling of their produce and a peach may look perfect but taste like cotton wool. The only way to be certain is to buy the smallest quantity of fruit possible, taste it, and buy more if satisfied. If buying large amounts, try asking for a sample first; with the prospects of a good sale, most retailers are prepared to give away a plum or an apple. Resist the temptation to overbuy. Fruit deteriorates rapidly and, as it is so expensive, this can result in costly waste. Buy fruit at the end of the shopping round, so that it is unlikely to be squashed or bruised by heavier purchases. Generally, the heavier fruit is for its size, the juicier and tastier it will be.

Cranberries are too tart to eat fresh, but they make excellent sauces and jellies. They range in color from a clear pink to a deep red. Look for brightly-colored, firm fruit.

Grapefruit are the larg-est members of the citrus family, so named because they grow hanging in clusters. Their color can be anything from a greenish pale yellow to a bright yellow or even a yellow-flushed pink. The flesh is norm-ally pale yellow and dis-tinctively acid, though the pink-fleshed kind is comparatively sweet. Avoid thick-skinned fruit which may be dry and tasteless.

Gooseberries Smooth yellow ones, which are almost transparent when ripe, are best for eating raw; the smaller, furry green ones are best for cooking. Buy the former perfectly ripe but the latter may be bought while still slightly firm and underripe.

Kumquats are tiny re-latives of the orange, about an inch in dia-meter and shaped like long olives. They are eaten whole without the skin, either fresh, cooked or preserved in sugar syrup (which balances the slightly bitter taste). Buy smooth and evenly-colored ones.

Lemons vary in size but biggest is not always best. The plump, smooth and thinner-skinned ones contain more juicy flesh than those with coarse, thick skins. Lemons sun-ripened on the tree have a superior flavor, but most lemons have been picked green so as to ripen en route.

Limes are much like lemons but green in color and rounder, and sharper in taste, contain-ing about one-third more citric acid than lemons of the same size. Choose firm, thin-skinned fruit.

Nectarines are related to the peach family, but are not, as some believe, a hybrid of peaches and plums. They are smaller, firmer and less juicy than peaches, and they have smooth skins. They are sold fully ripe, so buy flawless ones and eat the same day.

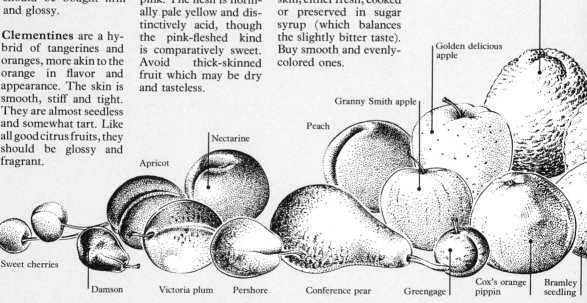

Orange

Golden delicious apple

Granny Smith apple

Peach

Nectarine

Apricot

Sweet cherries

Damson

Victoria plum

Pershore

Conference pear

Greengage

Cox's orange pippin

Bramley seedling

Oranges are selected according to their use— for eating, for juice, or for marmalade. Jaffas, navels and Valencias are all excellent for eating fresh. For squeezing, any juicy, reasonably-priced oranges are suitable. The Seville orange has a bitter tang which is good in marmalade. Always select plump oranges which show no signs of withering or mildew. Blood oranges have streaky-red flesh.

Peaches There are more than 2,000 varieties of peach, but they are generally classed either as clingstone or freestone (depending on how the flesh adheres) or as yellow-fleshed or white-fleshed. Peaches spoil easily, particularly the softer sorts, so choose those with completely unblemished skins, and about the size of small oranges.

Pears Slightly under-ripe pears are suitable for cooking, but they should not be bullet-hard. Pears are at their best when the stalk wobbles slightly. Indications that the hard-fleshed varieties are at their best are that the skin will be slightly wrinkled and the flesh softer around the stalk.

Plums The fruit should be tender (without being squashy), smooth and glossy, or with the "bloom" (a delicate patina found on freshly-picked plums and grapes) still on it. Plums for cooking may be slightly underripe.

Quinces are excellent for cooking, especially mixed with apples for jams and pies or for ice cream. Although they are not eaten raw, buy them when ripe.

Raspberries are what the Greek gods are rumored to have picked on Mount Ida when they tired of nectar and ambrosia. They are past their best if they are pitted near the top or at all mushy or moldy. Eat as soon as possible after purchase.

Rhubarb, though not a fruit, is treated as one. The best-looking rhubarb having the most delicate taste is the pale, pink, long-stemmed variety of "forced" rhubarb. Rhubarb goes limp within a few hours of being picked, but this does not affect its quality.

Satsumas are small, round, somewhat flattened members of the orange family, similar to tangerines and with something of their characteristic smell. They are seedless and loose-skinned. Their age is hard to assess from appearance, so buy and eat one first to test that they are not too tart or too dry.

Strawberries are so popular that an unfortunate amount of second-rate fruit often finds its way to the market. Be patient and resist the expensive and tasteless berries that anticipate the season. When they are properly in season, avoid mushy ones that have leaked an excess of juice into the container bottom, and beware of moldy ones as they quickly affect any wholesome berries they touch. Underripe fruit is pale and patchy and lacks flavor. Ideally, strawberries should be eaten the day they are bought.

Black currants

Cranberries

Raspberries

Gooseberries

Strawberries

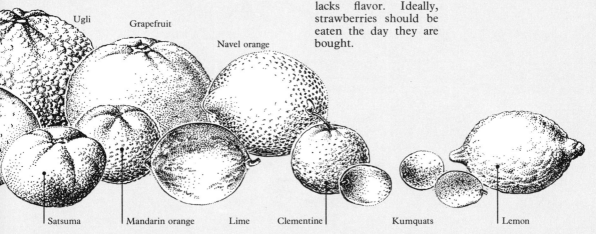

Ugli   Grapefruit

Navel orange

Satsuma   Mandarin orange   Lime   Clementine   Kumquats   Lemon

Fruit /2

Storing fruit

Some fruit, such as berries, cannot be stored satisfactorily for more than one or two days. If they cannot be used in time, freeze and use for purées, pies or ice creams.

Store citrus and hard fruit either in plastic bags (which prevents drying out) in the refrigerator or in paper bags or a cardboard box in a cool place. As with vegetables, they should not be kept in plastic in temperatures warmer than that of a refrigerator as the lack of ventilation will cause "sweating" and spoilage.

Hard fruit stored by either method will keep for up to ten days. Bananas are an exception and should not be wrapped or refrigerated, but hung in a cool place.

Wrap individual bunches of grapes separately in newspaper and keep them in the dark. If hard fruit or citrus fruit is to be stored for more than a week, wrap each piece separately in newspaper before putting them in a plastic bag in the refrigerator or in a box in a cool place. Slightly underripe apples, pears and quinces will keep like this for some months depending on the variety. Oranges will keep for three weeks, tangerines about two weeks, lemons and grapefruit about a month, but bitter oranges (Sevilles) may not keep more than a week.

Do not store strong-smelling fruit, such as cut pineapple or melon, or soft fruit such as strawberries, unwrapped in the refrigerator. Their heavy fragrance affects the smell and taste of butter, cheese and milk. Cover with plastic wrap.

Bananas Biggest is not necessarily best; small fat bananas often have more flavor than bigger ones. Bananas are at their best when there is no green tinge to the yellow skin but only a few black markings have developed. Any such marks should be in numerous spots; do not buy bananas with larges patches of black, as they are probably overripe.

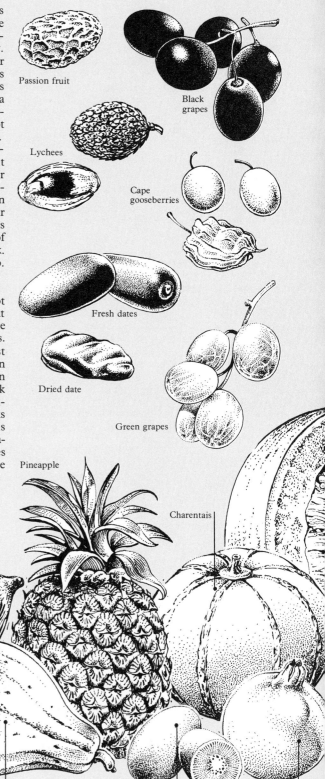

Passion fruit

Black grapes

Lychees

Cape gooseberries

Fresh dates

Dried date

Green grapes

Pineapple

Charentais

Coconut

Persimmon

Dried fig

Fresh fig

Pawpaw

Chinese gooseberries (Kiwi fruit)

Pomegranate

Cape gooseberries have crinkly, dry, pale brown husks which protect the round, orange or golden berries inside so that they may be kept up to three weeks if bought not yet ripe. (Unripe fruit is yellow-green.)

Dates are sold fresh or dried. The fresh ones are plump and glossy, approximately thumb-sized, with yellow-red to brown skins. Dried ones are a bit smaller, with the skin sunken, although it should not be shrivelled, nor should sugary crystals have formed on it.

Grapes It is impossible to tell from the look of a bunch of grapes whether or not they are sweet. Buy from a supplier who sells bunches loose so that it is possible to taste one before buying. As with plums, try to buy grapes that still have their "bloom." Avoid bunches with even a few grapes that have mold, as the rest will soon develop it.

Lychees are oval-shaped, white-fleshed, stone fruit, somewhat larger than cherries. They have crisp, scaly skins which should be brown or browny-red. The flesh should be opalescent and juicy, not gray or shrivelled.

Melons It is difficult to tell if hard green melons are ripe, so buy them only from a trusted supplier. Feel the melon, press it gently with the thumb at the end opposite the stalk. If it is bullet-hard, it is not ripe. *Ogen*, *charentais* and *cantaloup* melons have a rich smell when ripe. If the whole melon feels squashy it is probably overripe and "winey." Use such melons, which can usually be bought cheaply, to make sorbet and ice cream. Their over-strong flavor survives the taste-masking effect of freezing.

Passion fruit The fruits are plum-sized with a tough skin which is gray-purple and wrinkled when ripe. The slippery, aromatic, orange-yellow pulp is eaten fresh (with the seeds) and makes an interesting addition to fruit salads.

Pineapples Avoid any with more than 20% of the skin predominantly green—they are not nearly ripe. The skin should be deep (not pale) yellow and the leaves should be withering slightly. Smell the fruit; a good rich fragrance is a sign of ripeness.

Dried fruit The best dried fruits are moist and handsome. These need little or no soaking before cooking and are easier to chop or cut up. The flavor of the smaller, cheaper, drier fruits is often just as good, and they generally contain less preservative—but need long soaking. Store all dried fruit in an airtight container (to prevent further drying) in a cool place. In a warm kitchen moist fruit can develop mold.

Nuts Buy nuts from a shop with a rapid turnover and do not buy in over-large quantities. Nuts, especially peanuts and walnuts, go stale fast. Keep them in a cool place in an absolutely airtight container. If nuts do go stale, bake them until crisp in the oven, then chop or crush them up for use in cooking.

Honeydew melon

Water melon

Ogen melon

Bananas

Loquats

Mango

Cheeses

The list of cheeses below gives a brief international cross section of the varieties most commonly available.

1 Valençay Soft goat's milk cheese, from the Berry region of France. Look for a soft, downy rind which is either white or a faint blue. The aroma should be light, the taste mild.

2 Camembert A soft cow's milk cheese from Normandy which must be eaten at its peak of ripeness. Look for a bright-white crust and an interior that is creamy yellow-white and of even and creamy consistency throughout. The center should be neither hard nor runny. Check, too, that there is no ammonia smell. If buying a wrapped Camembert by "feel" do not press it from the top but from the sides and make sure that it is springy. Camembert is packed in wooden boxes on which its place of origin must be recorded.

3 Roquefort A soft blue ewe's milk cheese from France. Ideally, buy it by its taste, which should be strong and salty with a lingering tangy aftertaste. Look for a creamy rind (never patchy or slimy) with an even marbling of blue veins on a creamy-yellow background, and a distinctive "mold" smell.

4 Port-Salut A semi-soft French cow's milk cheese. It should have a thin, orange-yellow rind around a creamy-yellow interior that is firm to the touch and has a buttery taste and texture with a mild aftertaste.

5 Boursin A very soft triple-cream French cow's milk cheese, sold plain or with garlic, herbs or black pepper added. It is sold wrapped in foil. It should have a soft texture, very slightly crumbly. The flavor of plain boursin (or *boursault*) is mild with a distinct tang.

6 Tomme au raisin A semi-soft goat's milk cheese from Savoy. The rind is covered with a mixture of black grape pips, skins and pulp. It should be springy and yellow-white with a tangy taste. A good tomme au raisin will have a distinct, but not overpowering, alcohol smell.

Judge a cheese by its color and texture. Look for a surface that shows no sign of "sweating" and check for a smell that is never rancid or yeasty even though it might be quite strong. Always ask the advice of the retailer and, if possible, taste a sample. Cheese should always be kept covered. Wrap it in aluminum foil which, unlike plastic wrap, will not make it sweat. Wrap cheeses individually so that tastes are not transferred. For short-term storage, keep cheese in a cool place (below 50°F) where soft cheese will last 4 or 5 days, hard cheese 10 days. In the refrigerator (store on the warmest shelf) soft cheese will keep for 10 days, hard cheese for up to three or four weeks. After refrigeration, unwrap cheese about an hour before eating to let it warm up and "breathe."

7 Pont-l'Évêque A small square cow's milk cheese from Normandy. A true Pont-l'Évêque has a gold rind with distinctive crisscross markings from the straw in which it is matured. Beneath the rind it should be a soft yellow with a few small holes and it should cling to the knife when cut. At its best, it tastes strong and rich with a tangy aftertaste.

8 Brie A soft French cow's milk cheese. Like Camembert, it should be eaten as soon as it is bought or is ripe. It is better to buy it ripe and eat it immediately as it is difficult to mature at home. Look for a downy white crust and a soft, creamy texture. It should be the same glossy color almost all the way through but may have a fine, chalky, solid layer next to the skin. The body of the cheese should bulge away from the crust slightly when cut. It should be almost, but not quite, runny. An overripe Brie is runny and smells of ammonia.

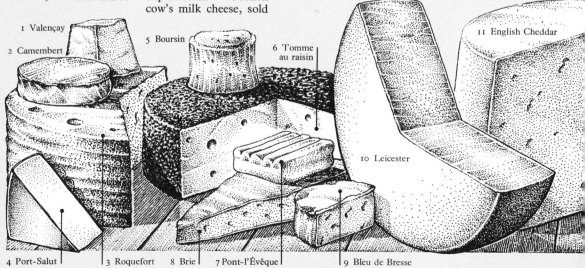

1 Valençay
2 Camembert
5 Boursin
6 Tomme au raisin
11 English Cheddar
10 Leicester
4 Port-Salut
3 Roquefort
8 Brie
7 Pont-l'Évêque
9 Bleu de Bresse

9 Bleu de Bresse A soft blue cow's milk French cheese. The veins in the cheese should be dark and even, the texture soft and creamy, the taste sharp. The skin is dry and downy to begin with on mild cheeses, becoming yellowed and slimy when overripe.

10 Leicester A hard cow's milk cheese from England which is a striking orange-red in color. It should have a loose, slightly flaky texture, a rich tangy flavor and lingering aftertaste. A good cheese for cooking, as it melts well.

11 English Cheddar A hard English cow's milk cheese. The best Cheddars are farmhouse-made and marked as such. Mild, young Cheddar is pale yellow and should have a mellow taste. The best mature Cheddar has a tangy taste and aftertaste. A good Cheddar is slightly flaky, never waxy or spongy. Inferior Cheddars have a soapy taste and a rubbery texture.

12 Feta A soft, pure-white Greek cheese made from goat's or ewe's milk. It should have a salty taste and tangy after-taste. Always buy moist or even straight from the brine in which it is traditionally stored.

13 Mozzarella A soft Italian cheese originally produced from buffalo's milk but now usually from cow's milk. It is traditionally made in small balls or bundles, tied with string at the neck, and kept in weak brine. But today it is frequently made in small blocks wrapped in plastic or waxed paper. A fresh cheese is very white and springy, never at all yellow, and has a dense, rather tough texture. It should taste creamy and slightly sweet since it is almost entirely salt-free. It does not keep more than a few days.

14 Stilton A semi-hard blue-veined English cow's milk cheese. The rind of perfect Stilton is gray-brown and rather wrinkled, the interior evenly and densely blue-veined on a very pale yellow-white background. Check for a firm, not over-crumbly texture and a strong, clean, slightly salty taste. White Stilton has the same qualities but no veining. To stop it drying out, wrap Stilton in a cloth wrung out in weak brine. Do not scoop Stilton with a spoon as this leads to drying out and waste. Instead, cut in shallow wedges from the top.

15 Edam Semi-hard Dutch cow's milk cheese with an inedible, bright red paraffin wax covering. A good Edam has a thin rind, a firm but supple texture and a pale yellow color, darkening with maturity. It should have a mild, slightly acid taste.

16 Gorgonzola A soft blue Italian cow's milk cheese. An extremely pungent cheese, its smell should be powerful but not unpleasant or rancid. It has a strong taste and a soft, creamy texture. Look for blue-green mottling between the blue "injection lines."

17 Dolcelatte Soft Italian blue-veined cow's milk cheese, similar to Gorgonzola but milder.

18 Gruyère A hard Swiss cow's milk cheese with a few holes about the size of a pea (smaller than in similar Emmenthaler). A hard rind should surround an interior of an even pale-to mid-yellow. Check its taste for a slight acidity, saltiness and a faintly sweet aftertaste.

19 Ricotta A very soft, mild white Italian cheese made from cow's milk. It should always be moist and eaten on the day of purchase. It is smooth and almost salt-free, thus ideal for cheesecake.

20 Danish blue (Danablu) A semi-soft blue cow's milk cheese. It should be very pale in color, evenly veined and never smell strong. A good one will have a sharp, tangy taste that is not too salty.

21 Parmesan Italian cow's milk cheese. It should have a brown rind (which may be blackened with a mixture of oil and umber) and a very hard crumbly texture. It should have a pale straw color and a distinct acidity, but not an over-strong taste.

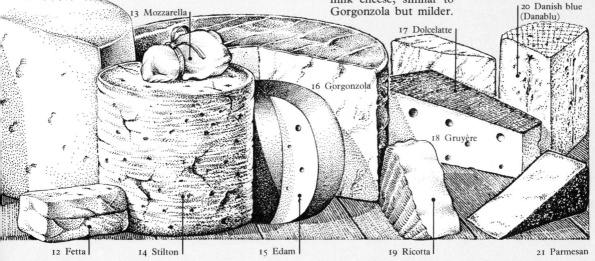

13 Mozzarella

20 Danish blue (Danablu)

17 Dolcelatte

16 Gorgonzola

18 Gruyère

12 Fetta   14 Stilton   15 Edam   19 Ricotta   21 Parmesan

Dairy products and eggs

Whole milk is sold just as produced by the cow, with the cream content left unaltered. The milk may or may not be pasteurized or homogenized as explained below.

Raw or untreated milk, rarely available commercially, is not processed or treated in any way.

Pasteurized milk is heated, but not boiled, to kill harmful bacteria without destroying the fresh flavor of the milk. Not all the microorganisms in the milk are destroyed, and the protein structure remains unaltered. This is important in making, say, junket because the protein reacts with the rennet to "set."

Sterilized milk is boiled to kill all microorganisms. It has the unmistakable flavor of boiled milk, produced by the cooking of the solids in milk, especially the milk sugar. It will keep indefinitely.

Ultra-heat treated (UHT) milk will keep for about six months. It is sterilized by heating to an even higher temperature than that used to sterilize milk—but for only one second. The advantage is that the sugar in the milk does not have time to caramelize, giving a less "cooked" flavor, though it is easily distinguishable from fresh milk.

Homogenized milk is treated so the cream is evenly distributed throughout, instead of floating on the top.

Skim milk has had the cream removed to lower the fat content, and is usually sold sterilized. It is commonly used by those on low-fat diets.

Buttermilk is the liquid whey left after milk has been used to manufacture butter. It is useful for invalids as it is more easily digested than ordinary milk, but contains much of the mineral and some of the protein content of milk.

Cultured buttermilk is skim milk with a bacterial culture added to give a tangy taste akin to that of natural buttermilk.

Canned milk or evaporated milk is sterilized milk but has a more pronounced caramel flavor due to reduction and concentration. It usually has about double the solid content of fresh milk. It keeps well and is useful in cooking.

Condensed or sweetened canned milk is a highly concentrated, thick, sweetened milk product, with a strong caramel flavor. Again it is often used in cooking, particularly in sweet desserts and in the making of confectionery.

Dried milk or powdered milk consists of dried milk solids, which must be reconstituted with water. The flavor of the mixture is similar to that of boiled milk.

Heavy cream has a high fat content. It will whip to double its volume and stay whipped. Use for floating on coffee, and for decorating desserts.

Light cream contains too little fat (about 18%) to whip. Use with coffee and for pouring over fresh fruit.

Whipping cream (or heavy cream) comes somewhere in between heavy and light cream, having a fat content of about 38%. It whips to more than double its volume, but does not hold a shape well.

Half-and-half is a thin milk and cream mixture containing only about 12% fat. Use only in beverages.

Ready-whipped cream is whipped by forcing carbon dioxide into it. The volume achieved is greater than can be created by beating in air, but it does not hold its shape.

Sour cream is light cream artificially soured and thickened by the introduction of acid. Make it by adding lemon juice to light cream.

Clotted cream is cream heated to evaporate some of the milk liquids still present in cream, so concentrating the solids. It is thick, contains about 55% fat, and has a characteristic, pleasant cooked taste. It is sometimes sold with added preservative.

Canned/bottled cream has a boiled taste, but is useful as a standby for use in cooking.

Butter is available salted, mildly salted and unsalted. The creaminess and flavor vary slightly, but perceptibly, from region to region. Yellow butter may have been colored artificially—the natural color of butter being only slightly more yellow than that of the cream from which it is made. A not-too-expensive, all-purpose salted butter is generally used for cooking, except where the recipe specifically calls for unsalted butter.

All butter contains butter fat, water and some milk particles. If butter is used for fast frying, the water causes splattering and the solids burn. The solids also make melted butter cloudy which is undesirable if it is to be used in a clear sauce.

To clarify butter, put it in a pan with a cupful of water and heat quickly until it is melted and frothy. Allow it to cool until it is solid again; lift the butter, now clarified, off the top of the liquid which has separated out and contains the other impurities.

Alternatively, heat the butter until foaming, without allowing it to burn, to drive off the water. Strain it through fine muslin or a double layer of cheesecloth to remove the impurities.

A quick way is to melt butter in a heavy pan until foaming and skim off the froth with a perforated spoon.

Yogurt is milk set to a solid by the action of a bacterial culture which, in gentle, even warmth, grows in the milk. It may be bought, flavored or unflavored, or made at home.

To make yogurt:

The ordinary bacteria present in fresh milk can interfere with the action of the yogurt culture, so fresh milk must first be boiled (to kill these bacteria) and then allowed to cool to lukewarm before adding the culture. For this reason sterilized milk (either bottled with a crown cork, or evaporated canned milk, reconstituted) is more reliable for yogurt-making.

$2\frac{1}{2}$ **cups milk**
2 tbs plain fresh yogurt

Warm the milk until lukewarm (if it has not been treated as above). Stir in the yogurt. Pour the mixture into a bowl or dish and put into a warm draught-free place until it sets (usually about 14 hours). The cooler the temperature, the slower the action of the yogurt. Too high a temperature kills the bacilli and the yogurt will not form.

Yogurt can be set in a warm closet or boiler room, a cool electric oven (set as low as possible), a vacuum flask with a wide neck or an insulated ice bucket.

Do not bother to keep back a little of the manufactured yogurt as the "starter" for the next batch—it will almost certainly have become contaminated with microorganisms which will interfere with the setting action. Get a fresh yogurt culture for each batch.

Crème fraîche is not, as a literal translation would lead one to expect, fresh cream. It is cream that has been matured for up to 24 hours and has a pleasant, slightly sour flavor. It is used on fruit and desserts and in cooking, (it can be boiled without curdling). In France it is widely available commercially, but for the less fortunate this is how it is made.

Stir together slowly a 1 pint of very fresh heavy or whipping cream and two tablespoons of buttermilk over a gentle heat until the temperature is 80°F (just *below* blood heat—it should feel cool, not tepid). Pour into a bowl and keep warm, as for yogurt, until thick.

Storing dairy products

To keep dairy produce more than a day, a cool place, preferably a refrigerator, is essential.

Keep the lids on milk bottles, the wrappers on butter and cover pitchers of cream or milk well to prevent the contents becoming tainted with the odor of other food stored nearby. Pineapple or melon, for example, can taint the taste of all dairy products stored in a refrigerator with them.

Milk and cream can be kept, refrigerated, safely for four days. Homemade yogurt, *crème fraîche* and cream cheese will keep three days, but commercially produced products will keep longer—a week or more.

Butter, wrapped and refrigerated, remains fresh up to three weeks.

If storing milk out of the refrigerator keep it in the dark. Light destroys its high vitamin B content.

Eggs The less fresh eggs are, the less flavor they retain.

Buy eggs before they are two weeks old (check date-stamp codes). Buy loose eggs only from a trustworthy supplier. To check if an egg is fresh, put it in a glass of water: If it lies horizontally on the floor of the glass it is fresh; if it stands upright it is old. If it actually rises in the glass it is stale. (As an egg ages the pocket of air at the rounded end gets bigger—the staler the egg the greater the air pocket and the more likely it is to float.) Alternatively, break an egg on to a plate. A day-old egg will have a viscous white close around a plump, round yolk. A month-old egg will have a runnier white and flatter yolk. A stale or bad egg will have a completely liquid white which runs like water from the shell the instant it is broken.

For this reason it is impossible to poach stale eggs satisfactorily because the liquid white runs all over the pan.

Brown eggs (although they may look more attractive and more natural) have no more, or less, nutritional value than white ones. The color of commercially-produced eggs is governed by chemical dyes in the chickens' feed.

Sizes of egg

Recipes generally require medium-sized eggs weighing about 2 oz. The yolk and shell together account for half the total weight, meaning that the white weighs one ounce. Conveniently, this is also about one fluid ounce if measured in volume.

Storing eggs

Eggs, provided they are not cracked, will store well at room temperature but will keep longer refrigerated. If stored in the refrigerator, remember to remove them an hour or so before use in cooking. Cold eggs don't beat easily and the yolks tend to rupture. Stand the eggs pointed end down to slow deterioration (as this keeps the air pocket up at the round end). Cracked eggs should be stored in the refrigerator, as should separated eggs, yolks or whites. Cover liquid egg tightly to prevent whites drying out, or yolk (or beaten whole egg) developing a skin. Store egg yolks with a layer of water on top to seal them off from the air.

Fromage blanc is a light, low-calorie, non-fat cheese made from skim milk. In France it is frequently eaten on its own with sugar, or used with fresh fruit in place of cream, or in tartlets or sauces. For cooks unable to obtain it, a good imitation can be made by sieving cottage cheese and mixing it with an equal amount of yogurt.

Junket Warm fresh (not sterilized) milk to blood heat. Add one teaspoon of rennet (an enzyme extract from calves' stomachs) and stir. Leave to set in a refrigerator.

Herbs

Buy or grow fresh herbs if possible. They have a better appearance and flavor than dried ones.

Freeze herbs as described on page 177.

When using dried herbs, use only one-third of the amount specified for fresh herbs. Dried herbs, having lost their moisture content, shrink in size and weight, and the flavors become more concentrated.

Basil Classically used in tomato salads, in Mediterranean vegetable soup (*au* PISTOU) and with pine nuts, pecorino cheese, garlic and olive oil to make PESTO sauce.

Bay The leaves are widely used to season soups, stews and stocks. Use with care as the flavor is strong and distinctive (one small leaf generally suffices).

Borage The leaves and flowers are used mainly to flavor summer alcoholic drinks, particularly "Pimm's." The flowers, which are bright blue, turn pink in the alcohol. The flowers are good crystallized or used to decorate salads, though they have little flavor.

Chervil or sweet cicely Use in salads, soups, and chicken dishes. Particularly good with eggs. One of the four *"fines herbes."*

Chives Use in salads, soups, cream cheeses, and with eggs. Another of the four *"fines herbes."*

Coriander Used in Middle Eastern dishes, particularly meat and chicken dishes and curries. Good, in small quantities, in salads.

Most herbs are used in very small quantities to enhance the flavor of other foods. There are some classic combinations such as basil with tomatoes, dill with pickled cucumber, fennel with fish, tarragon with chicken, rosemary with lamb. Avoid adding too many herbs. As a general rule, one herb is better than two, which provide too confused a flavor, and a little is better than a lot. The exceptions to this rule are: *bouquets garnis*, bunches of mixed flavoring herbs added to stocks, stews or soups to give a mild, diffused background flavor; the salad herbs added to lettuce which can be made more interesting with the addition of a variety of herbs (say, mint, chives and chervil) and the classic *fines herbes* in an omelette—a perfectly balanced quartet of chives, chervil, parsley and tarragon.

Cress Used to "spike" salads or sandwiches (particularly egg or cheese) or as garnish for cold food. Good also as the main flavor in a chicken - stock - based soup. Often used with mustard.

Dandelion The young leaves are good as a salad, cooked like spinach, or puréed with spinach for soup. The flowers are made into wine.

Dill Excellent in fish dishes and pickled with cucumber, or with casseroled lamb, or mashed potato.

Fennel Mostly used in fish dishes.

Land cress Good, in small quantities, in most salads or sandwiches.

Lovage Use sparingly in soups, stews and pies. It is particularly good in tomato sauces to be served with hamburgers, meat balls or other ground beef dishes. The hollow stalks may be candied.

Marjoram Good in soups, stews and sauces (especially tomato).

Mint Good in iced drinks, with new potatoes, in soups (especially cold ones), lamb dishes, tomato and green salads, and used to make mint sauces or jellies to be served with lamb.

Mustard Used in conjunction with cress and often sewn in the same tray (see overleaf).

Oregano See marjoram. Oregano is the wild form of marjoram.

Parsley The long-leaved Italian parsley or flat-leaved fern parsley are more tender and tasty for eating raw in salads, but the curled, dark-green parsley, which keeps well and is easier to chop, is preferred by many chefs for flavor and garnish.

None are good dried. Parsley is the most universally used herb in all savory cooking. It is also one of the ingredients of a classic *bouquet garni*, and another of the four *"fines herbes."*

Rocket Good in small quantities in salads, or chopped in cream cheese or sandwiches.

Rosemary Excellent with roast or broiled lamb or pork, or chicken. Use bruised sprigs to season the meat, then discard after cooking. Generally too prickly to be pleasant to eat.

Sage Excellent with pork, especially when used to season pork sausages or stuffings.

Salad burnet Good in sandwiches, iced drinks and green salads.

Savory Winter and summer savory are both excellent with beans, dried or fresh, of any kind. Best chopped and heated in butter, then tossed with the cooked beans, rather than cooked with them. Good with chestnuts in stuffing for roast poultry dishes.

Sorrel Use the leaves in salads mixed with lettuce or spinach, or in sauces or to season fish dishes. The leaves cook in seconds and lose their color quickly so add to white or VELOUTÉ sauce at the last minute and liquefy for a brightly-colored sorrel sauce.

Tarragon "French" tarragon has much more flavor than the coarser, tasteless "Russian" tarragon. Use in dishes with chicken, fish and eggs. The fourth of the *"fines herbes."*

Thyme Used widely in soups, stews, stock and meat dishes. Not good in salads unless greenhouse-grown as that variety generally has more tender leaves.

Chervil

Lemon thyme

Fennel

Common thyme

Dill

Tarragon

Sweet marjoram

Summer savory

Chives

Parsley

Lovage

Rosemary

Basil

Oregano

Spearmint

Bay

Sage

Watercress Less hot than mustard or cress, good for salads, soups (especially cold) and for garnishing cold dishes and grills.

Flowers are used in cooking for their surprising and colorful look in a green salad (nasturtium, borage, violet, clary, and rose petals) or to flavor sweet dishes. Rose petals and violet flowers may be made into a flavoring SYRUP, or into jam, or may be CRYSTALLIZED for decorating cakes. Finely ground lavender flowers may flavor cake icings, and gooseberries are given an attractive fragrance by cooking them with an elderflower before PURÉEING.

Tisanes, or herb teas, may be made with almost any herb, and have long been used as tonics and sedatives. The best tasting are those made by steeping camomile flowers or the leaves of mint or lemon verbena or bergamot (leaves or flowers) in boiling water. They are then served with a slice of lemon or lime and a little sugar.

Garlic The cloves of the bulbous head are peeled and crushed and used raw in salad dressings or fried or simmered in soups, stews or pies. Once garlic begins to sprout, the flavor deteriorates rapidly.

Horseradish root is grated fresh to serve with roast beef or used to flavor cream sauces, and is excellent with both smoked trout and mackerel.

Spices

Spices are generally the dried seeds, roots, bark or stems of certain plants, most of them grown in tropical climates. A few, such as caraway, fennel, dill and coriander, may be grown in temperate climates. Pick the seed heads before the seeds are quite dry. (They fall off the flower-head too readily if left until completely brown.) Dry the whole seed heads in an open tray or cardboard box in a warm kitchen or on a sunlit window sill. When brittle, shake out the seeds (a coarse sieve extracts stalks) and store in an airtight jar.

Most spices, however, must be bought from the supermarket or grocer. Choose a shop with a rapid turnover so that the spices will be as fresh as possible (ready-ground spices lose flavor if kept more than a few months). Use a coffee-grinder to grind whole spices, just before using them, for the best results.

Buy spices with the minimum of packaging. There is no point in paying for elaborate spice jars or ornamental shakers. Transfer the contents of a packet to an airtight screw-top jar.

Keep spices (and dried herbs) within easy reach in the kitchen, not at the back of a deep cabinet. Be sure, however, that they are in airtight containers, away from the warmth of the stove and out of any moist draughts.

Allspice (Jamaica pepper) Use in cakes, lamb dishes and CHUTNEYS.

Aniseed Use whole, scattered on bread dough before baking. Use extract in sauces to accompany fish dishes.

Capsicum See chillis, paprika and cayenne.

Caraway Use seeds whole in and on bread doughs, and ground or whole with vegetables and pickles, particularly cabbage or SAUERKRAUT.

Cardamom Mostly used ground in Eastern dishes, particularly curries. Use ground in fillings for Danish pastries. Use whole in pickles or in RICE PILAU.

Cayenne Use pods whole for pickles, and to season liquids; or ground, in cheese dishes or savory SOUFFLÉS.

Chilli Very hot ground chilli peppers.
Use sparingly for meat dishes and chutneys and pickles. Use in small quantities with shellfish, or in shellfish sauces. Or use as cayenne.

Cinnamon Use whole to flavor syrups, desserts, stewed fruit, CUSTARDS; ground in cakes, breads, meat dishes, or with sugar to make cinnamon toast (mix butter, sugar and cinnamon together in equal parts). Spread on toast. Broil until bubbling.

Cloves Use whole to flavour apple pies, stewed fruit, and to stud BAKED HAM or bacon. Use ground in cakes and meat dishes. Good in BREAD SAUCE and with sweet potatoes.

Coriander Good whole with stewed mushrooms, meat sauces, chicken dishes, pickled fish, PÂTÉS, and ground in curries and sweet custards.

Cumin Good in soups (particularly beet), in chicken dishes, curries, pork sausages and MEAT LOAVES.

Curry powder or paste A blend of powdered spices generally containing turmeric (this gives the strong orange-brown color), fenugreek, coriander, cumin, cardamom and chili.

Fenugreek Use sparingly in curries and other meat dishes.

Ginger Use fresh or canned ginger in Chinese dishes, or in chicken casseroles, curries or stews. Use dried pieces in pickles, use ground in cakes, puddings and cookies, with stewed fruit or to "spike" boiled carrots.

Juniper Good used in sausages, or any pork dishes, venison or other game, and with cabbage.

Mace Use as nutmeg.

Mustard Use the whole seeds in pickles, ground (mixed with water, wine or vinegar) to flavor sauces (particularly for pork, chicken, rabbit or kidneys) and to serve with roast pork or beef.

Nutmeg Use in meat dishes and meat sauces, also in tomato sauces and with vegetables, particularly spinach and potatoes. Use in baked milk puddings, custards and spiced wine cups.

Paprika Use generously in meat stews (like HUNGARIAN GOULASH), cream cheeses and egg dishes.

Pepper Used in almost all savory dishes.
Green peppercorns are good made into a pepper sauce, with the corns left whole.
Black peppercorns are suitable for most savory dishes either coarsely or finely ground.
White pepper is best used for white or pale dishes like VELOUTÉ sauces and mashed potatoes where the elegant smoothness and color would be impaired by the spotty appearance of black pepper.

Poppy seeds Use for topping bread dough, cakes, cookies, and in salads, particularly when fruit, such as pears, or cheese are included. Good used to flavor Danish pastry fillings.

Saffron Use, soaked or pounded in a mortar, to flavor rice dishes, chicken dishes, fish soups or cakes.

Sesame Use the seeds untoasted on bread doughs or cakes, and toasted to a pale brown in vegetable dishes, salads and cream cheese dishes.

Turmeric Use in curries, or to give curry flavor to almost any savory dish. Use to provide the color (though not the taste) of saffron to savory dishes.

Vanilla Use whole to flavor milk puddings and custards. Extract after use, dry thoroughly, then store until next time. Keep a vanilla bean in the sugar jar to make vanilla sugar for cakes and desserts.
If using extract, try to avoid the artificial or imitation variety.

Preparing food

Beef

Trimming a fillet
Remove the fatty piece of meat running along one side of the fillet. Use for stew.

2 Trim off all pieces of sinew and membrane from the surface.

3 Fold the thin end under for roasting. If cutting into steaks, remove it and use it for stew.

The first essential in butchery is a sharp knife. A blunt one is both frustrating and dangerous. The best all-purpose butchery knife is the non-flexible boning one. Remember always to hold it in such a way that, should it slip, it will slip away. Hold the meat at an angle so that the knife can be pulled to the side, not toward the body, and always cut down toward the board or chopping block, not up toward the head and arms.

Do not put prepared cuts of meat directly on top of each other, but lay them side by side on a tray, and cover them *loosely* with foil or plastic wrap (some air circulation is necessary—too tight a wrap leads to "sweating" and consequent rapid deterioration). Ideally, cuts should not be prepared too long in advance as they will inevitably bleed their moisture. The sharper the knife or grinder, the less the meat will bleed. Meat must be dry if it is to be browned successfully. When cutting meat into small steaks or strips, cut across the grain of the meat, thus avoiding pieces with long fibers. Meat cut across the grain also looks better, keeps its shape better and feels more tender than meat cut with the grain.

When tying meat for cooking, use strong, thin, non-synthetic string. There are some strings made from man-made fibers which withstand the heat of cooking, but many will melt. Elasticized netting can be bought to hold cuts in neat shapes, but it may stick to the cooked food and become difficult to remove before serving. Use metal skewers for broiling. Wooden ones char and are more suitable for use in the oven.

Cutting a fillet
Slice the thinner end of the middle into tournedos *about 1½ thick.*

2 The thicker part of the middle can be cut as one or two fillet steaks about 2 in thick.

3 The thick end produces a two-portion châteaubriand. *Cube trimmings from either end for kebabs or sautés.*

Trimming a steak
Cut off the fat as shown— all, or almost all, according to personal preference.

Steak Diane
Slice a trimmed steak horizontally without quite severing the two halves.

2 "Butterfly" it by opening it up and pressing the join flat

3 Beat gently between sheets of plastic wrap to flatten and enlarge. (Or see VEAL PREP, **Scallops 3**.*)*

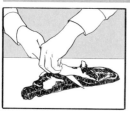

Cutting for stew
Trim off all sinew, membrane, gristle and fat.

2 Cut into 1-in cubes—no smaller or the pieces will break up.

Cutting for Stroganoff
Cut the fillet steak into slices about 1 in thick.

2 Stack the slices and cut again into thin strips.

Stuffing flank steak
Pull off thin membrane on one side. Cut and pull off fatty skin on the other.

If broiling or frying a steak with a lot of fat still on it, cut through the fat at regular intervals around the steak to keep it from curling up during cooking · For those who like rare steak and the taste of well-browned steak fat, trim off the fat and cook it separately first so that it can be well done · If tough steak must be fried or broiled, tenderize it just before cooking by beating it all over with the blunt edge of a heavy knife or with a ridged meat pounder to break down the connective tissue.

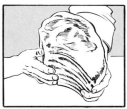

Roast rib
Roast whole as shown, only removing backbone before carving, or:

2 Cut horizontally to open up a pocket. Lift top half to cut deeper. Take care not to cut right through.

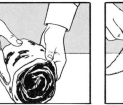

Tying a roast
Roll the meat into a neat shape, with the fat uppermost.

2 Tie and knot a loop around one end, leaving one long end of string.

2 Remove it before cooking by cutting and scraping as close to the bone as possible, leaving the thin rib bones.

3 Put the stuffing in the pocket, distributing it evenly.

3 Take the string around the meat again, looping and pulling tight (without knotting) at 1-in intervals.

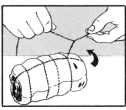

4 Then take the string under the roast lengthwise and tie it securely to the first knot.

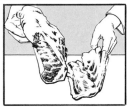

Boning a sirloin
Cut and scrape as closely as possible against both sets of bones and lift meat away.

4 Fold one side of the flank steak over the other along its full length.

If meat is to be kept for several days, rub the surface with dry mustard. This both retards deterioration and adds flavor · Render down fat trimmings for dripping. Put them in a moderate oven until they are shrivelled dry. Pour the surrounding fat into a jar for later use in frying, broiling or roasting · Freeze beef bones if they are not to be used immediately—they make excellent stock. Even bones from a rare roast contain plenty of flavor · Always remove all gristle, sinews and membranes from meat that is to be ground otherwise they clog the machine · If meat smells unpleasantly strong after a few days in the refrigerator, wash it well in cold water. If still "high," trim off the outer layers—the inside will almost certainly still be fresh · If the knife makes a hole in the meat when cutting a pocket for stuffing or boning a roast, patch it on the inside with a small piece of meat cut from a thicker part of the roast.

2 Trim off any excess fat. Tie for roasting as shown above, or:

5 Tie to secure, as for the roast shown above. There is no need to sew.

3 Cut into steaks about 1-in thick.

Veal

Barding a roast
Press the meat into a compact shape, tucking the ends under.

When best veal is prohibitively expensive, pork makes a good substitute—get slices from the leg or loin and beat out thinly as for veal scallops · Grass-fed veal is redder in color than the expensive milk-fed veal, but has good flavor. BLANCH it in lemon juice or milk, before cooking, to improve the color. Blanch veal for stews and BLANQUETTE by covering it with cold water, bringing it slowly to the boil and then draining it immediately. Keep the liquid (skimmed) for stock, but start again with fresh water or stock for the stew.

Larding a roast
Fix thin strips of pork back fat (lardons) into hinged end of a larding needle.

2 Cover with lard leaves (layers of pork back fat) or fatty bacon slices.

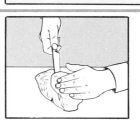

Scallops
Cutting against the grain of the meat, slice a piece of sirloin or rump thickly.

2 "Butterfly" each slice by cutting it in half horizontally without severing it. Open it out flat.

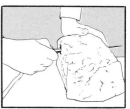

2 Push the needle through the meat, going with the grain.

3 Loop string around roast, and knot—leaving one long end of string.

3 Flatten and enlarge with a meat pounder (kept moist to avoid any tearing) or as BEEF PREP, **Steak Diane 3**.

Paupiettes
Place a spoonful of stuffing on a flattened scallop and wrap like a parcel.

3 Twist the needle as it is pushed; this makes it go through with less effort.

4 Continue looping and pulling to tighten, without knotting, at 1-in intervals.

Use best end of veal to make "crown roasts" and "guards of honor" as for lamb. When almost cooked, stuff them with a pre-cooked rice-and-watercress stuffing (mix chopped blanched watercress, cooked rice, sweated onion or garlic and fried almonds) · Stuff veal paupiettes with: Cooked rice with fried chopped chicken livers and almonds; ground veal and bacon, breadcrumbs, sweated onions and a little sage; blanched spinach, grated Swiss cheese and shreds of ham; fried button mushrooms in a thick gruyère sauce.

2 Tie each paupiette, again like a parcel, with strong cotton thread. Remove thread after cooking.

4 Grip needle with a cloth (it becomes greasy). Pull through, twisting to prevent lardon breaking off.

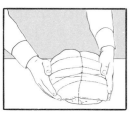

5 Turn it over. Loop string tightly around each cross tie. Secure to first knot.

Cutting for blanquette
First slice with the grain, then cut across into strips.

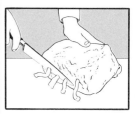

5 Repeat all over the meat at 1-in intervals, Cut off protruding ends.

Stuffing veal breast
Cut a large opening at the thick end of the meat—just above the ribs.

2 Push a hand into the cavity to enlarge the pocket and fill with stuffing.

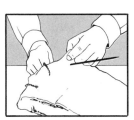

3 Sew up the end as shown, using soft, non-synthetic string.

Roast a whole veal kidney in its fat (about 50 minutes in a hot oven). The fat bastes the kidney, which should be barely pink and quite tender. Remove the fat before serving ·
If there is no time to pre-soak sweetbreads, remove the blood by pressing them under a weight for two hours instead.

If kidneys or liver smell "high", do not discard them immediately. Wash them well under cold running water. The smell should go. If it does, use the kidneys or liver promptly; if the smell is still offensive, discard.

Remove as much as possible of the tubes in the liver before cooking · If flouring liver for frying, do not overlap floured slices on a plate. Keep them separate or they will stick together and will have to be refloured.

Sweetbreads
Soak in cold water for 2 to 6 hours to whiten. Bring to the boil in court bouillon.

Liver
Use fingers to loosen the fine membrane that covers the liver.

Brains
Soak for 2 hours in cold water. Remove membranes. Blanch in court bouillon.

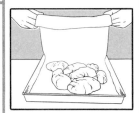

2 Cool rapidly and remove all membranes. Drain on absorbent paper.

Kidneys
Split the complete kidney cluster evenly in half.

2 Grip membrane with a cloth and pull off gently, holding liver with the other hand. Pull back, not up.

2 Poach gently for only 5 to 10 minutes. Drain, then plunge into cold water to cool. Dry and then halve.

When available (and they are usually inexpensive when they are) sheep's and calves' testicles make excellent "sweetbreads". Soak them for two to six hours to whiten them. Then cut them in half and remove and discard the tough outer skin. Bring them to simmering point in stock, then use as sweetbreads, or serve on toast with a thick VELOUTÉ sauce.

2 Cut out as much of the white core as possible.

3 Cut liver diagonally into even slices.

3 If brain is large, cut each half in half again. Pat dry with absorbent paper.

3 Slice across or dice.

Lamb

Saddle of lamb
Lay saddle skin-side down. Ease out kidneys with fatty casing.

2 Open up the fat and remove the kidneys. Discard the fat.

3 Trim off the meatless side of each flank.

4 Remove the excess fat from the meat and the strip of sinew from the backbone.

5 Turn the saddle over and shave off skin and excess fat from the back.

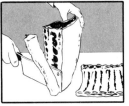

6 Turn flanks under. Prick sinew along backbone to prevent shrinking. Score fat crisscross.

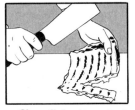

7 Tie the saddle at regular intervals to keep the shape. Remove the string after roasting.

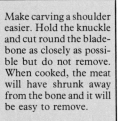

Make carving a shoulder easier. Hold the knuckle and cut round the blade-bone as closely as possible but do not remove. When cooked, the meat will have shrunk away from the bone and it will be easy to remove.

Chining and trimming a rack
Cut through meat on either side of backbone.

2 Using the knife cuts in the meat as a guide, sever the bones with gentle chops of a cleaver.

3 Chop off the thin ends of the ribs of each rack leaving bones not longer than 5 in.

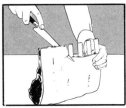

4 Trim off the fat between the rib ends to expose about 1 in of each bone. Scrape them clean.

Guard of honor
Score fat of two racks in crisscross pattern, just cutting through the surface.

Crown roast
Trim off as much fat as possible from the skin side of two racks.

2 Bring the ends of the two racks together and sew at the base and halfway up near the trimmed bones.

3 Shape the two racks into an arc with the bones on the outer side and the flesh on the inner side.

2 Push the two racks together to interlock firmly. Use the gap for stuffing.

4 Sew the other ends together as in *2*.

5 Press firmly into a crown shape. The center may be used for stuffing.

Wrap the exposed bone ends of racks, crown roasts and guards of honor in aluminum foil. This prevents them from burning during cooking. Remove after cooking and replace with decorative frills.

Trimming cutlets
Split a chined rack between each bone to cut it into small chops.

Gigot
At the thick end of the leg the hip bone is visible. Scrape and cut along it.

Noisettes
At the fatty end of each rack there is a piece of cartilage between the layers.

2 This is called the "half moon." Cut around it, work it out and discard.

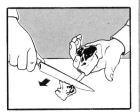

2 Scrape away fat and flesh from the tip of each rib bone.

2 Work it off, leaving the ball joint of the leg bone exposed.

3 Chine rack. (Cut meat away from backbone with a knife, saw through ribs and remove backbone.)

4 Holding a boning knife dagger-fashion, cut at either side of each bone to release it. Remove all the ribs thus.

3 Trim off almost all fat. Shorten exposed bones to a length of no more than *1* in.

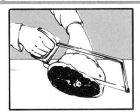

3 Roast whole, or cut off the meaty end to shorten the gigot. Use this off-cut for kebabs or sautés.

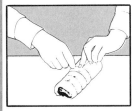

5 Cut off meatless flap at the thin end and trim away excess fat at this cut end.

6 Grip the fleshy end firmly and roll the meat up tightly toward the thin end.

Cutting a steak
Hold leg firmly by thin end and cut a slice through the larger end—to the bone.

2 Saw through the bone.

7 Tie the roll at *1*-in intervals to keep it in shape. Knot each loop separately.

8 Slice at the mid-point between each loop. A small rack gives about four noisettes; a large about six.

3 Finish cutting off the steak with the knife.

Kidneys
Slice each kidney in half lengthwise through the core.

2 Snip out the core with scissors and peel off the outer membrane.

3 For broiling, skewer open and flat to prevent curling.

Pork

To remove hairs from pork skin, use a disposable shaver or singe over a flame · Always give the butcher advance notice for ground pork. No butcher wants to put pork through a grinder used for beef. If forewarned, it can be done at the end of the day, just before the machine has to be washed anyway · Always order loin of pork with the belly flap attached. Most butchers cut it off, to sell as spare ribs, and sell the loin on its own.

Rolled, stuffed loin
Buy still with belly flap. Cut and scrape to bone. Score fat for crackling.

2 Trim off excess fat on the meaty side.

Spare ribs
Pry free a corner of skin with a knife, lift and peel the skin back.

Snipping pork chops
Cut through fat at regular intervals—to prevent curling during cooking.

3 Spread on the stuffing.

4 Bring up the belly flap to enclose the stuffing.

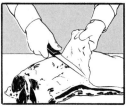

2 Use the knife to remove both skin and excess fat together.

Score crackling so that the cuts go all around the skin, deep enough to cut through to the fat but not through to the flesh · Check that crackling scored by the butcher has been properly done. If not done correctly, it does not cook crisply and is difficult to carve · Chops with the tenderloin on one side of the backbone, and those with the kidney, are the juiciest and most tender; neater "best end" chops are slightly drier · Marinade spare ribs in honey, soy sauce and lemon juice, seasoned with garlic and basil.

5 Sew up with continuous stitches at regular intervals. Use soft, non-synthetic string.

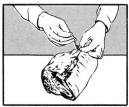

6 Knot the string securely at the end to prevent unraveling.

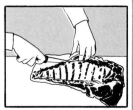

3 Trim off the fatty part beyond the tips of the rib ends.

Crackling
Score parallel cuts through the skin using a rigid knife. Rub with oil and salt.

Use best end of neck racks to make "crown roasts" as for lamb. Make sure all the fat is removed. Stuff with a sweetish mix (say, breadcrumbs, sage, sweated onions and chopped dried apricots, all bound with egg).

4 Split between each bone to cut into neat ribs.

Back fat (larding fat)
Remove rind from back fat using a long ham slicer.

2 Cut fat into even slices (or continue to cut in layers for barding).

3 Cut the slices into thin strips (lardons) for larding.

Rabbit and hare

 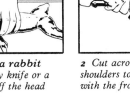

Cutting up a rabbit
Using a heavy knife or a cleaver, cut off the head and discard.

2 Cut across behind the shoulders to remove them with the front legs.

3 Cut through the base of the back to remove the hindquarters.

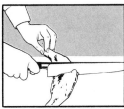

4 Split the hindquarters into two back legs.

To paunch a rabbit: split abdomen skin along length of body. Stomach and entrails come out easily. Clean inside of body cavity with a damp cloth (especially near head and tail). Skin by cutting off head and feet and working pelt off like a vest.

5 Cut the back across into two pieces.

6 Split the shoulder portion along the backbone into two front legs.

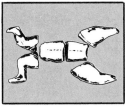

7 This produces six pieces of rabbit. Each may be split in half again to produce smaller pieces for pies.

Cutting up a hare
Cut off and discard head, trim away meatless belly flaps and remove kidneys.

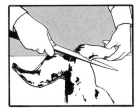

2 Cut through the flesh around each back leg.

3 Turn hare over and sever legs through the pelvis joint.

4 Twist off the remaining pelvis bones from the body, cut off the tail and discard them all.

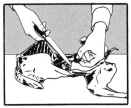

5 Cut around shoulders and through socket joints to remove each front leg.

6 Cut across lower end of carcass to divide it into two or three evenly-sized pieces.

7 At the shoulder end, heavy pressure with both hands on knife (or use of cleaver) may be required.

Paunch hares in the same way as for rabbits, but allow hares to hang first · When paunching both rabbits and hares, examine the liver. If it is blotchy and obviously diseased, throw the animal away.

8 Split remaining shoulders by cutting through ribs on either side of the backbone.

9 Remove the backbone and discard.

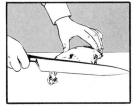

10 Chop off the knuckle ends from the hind legs.

11 The average hare cuts into 8 or 9 pieces (half are shown here skin side up).

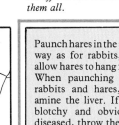 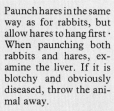 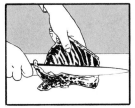

Poultry and game birds

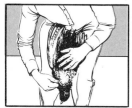

Plucking
Hold bird head down between the knees. Start with the small neck feathers.

2 Grip only a few feathers at a time. Tug them sharply downward, without jerking, to avoid breaking the skin.

No young bird need hang any longer than the time needed for the tissues to relax out of *rigor mortis*. Hanging, however, does allow enzyme activity to break down tissue and thus tenderize the meat. Older birds should, therefore, be hung slightly longer. The flesh also develops flavor—from mildly gamy to "high."

Traditionally chickens are eaten relatively fresh, ducks and geese are hung for two to three days, turkeys for a week and guinea fowl and game birds anything from four days to two weeks (although the trend is toward fresher, less powerfully high, game).

A short boning knife and a heavy cook's knife, cleaver or a pair of poultry shears for cutting up and breaking bones are essential for the preparation of poultry. It may be done as much as 24 hours in advance of cooking.

Wrap and cover to prevent drying out, but do not wrap too tightly, especially if the food was warm when covered, as the food will "sweat," encouraging the growth of microorganisms.

Singeing
Remove down and feather stubs by holding the bird over a flame.

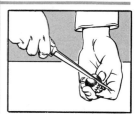

Cleaning giblets
To clean the gizzard, cut open the outer wall down the "seam."

3 Continue all over the body, leaving the quill feathers until last.

Drawing *(gutting)*
Sever the bird's neck close to the head.

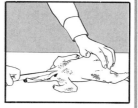

2 Lay the bird breast side down and split the neck skin by cutting along the bone.

2 Discard the inner, food-filled bag. Use gizzard, neck and the cleaned feet for stock. Use the liver for pâté.

4 Remove the quill feathers one by one with sharp, hard tugs.

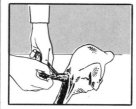

3 Peel the neck skin back and leave it attached to the body. Sever the neck close to the body.

4 Cut a slit in the belly from the vent towards the breast. Make it just large enough to insert the hand.

When drawing the guts out of a bird, take great care not to squeeze hard. If the gall sac (near the liver) is ruptured, any flesh on which its dark liquid contents spill will be so badly tainted it will have to be cut out and discarded.

5 With a heavy knife chop off the final obstinate quills with the wing tips.

5 Cover hand with a cloth and insert. Keep knuckles up against the backbone.

6 Grip the guts and draw them out gently. The cloth keeps them from rupturing.

7 Check cavity is cleared. Wipe it out with a damp cloth. Chop off feet at the knuckles.

Trussing
Chop off the wing tips (optional).

2 Put the bird on its back. Tuck the wing ends under the body.

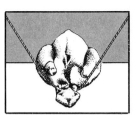

3 Take a long piece of string under the body.

Spatchcock
Cut through flesh and ribs just to one side of the backbone with a heavy knife.

4 Cross the string ends over the body. Draw them tight, enclosing the drumsticks and the body.

5 Bring the crossed-over string ends under the ends of the drumsticks. Take string ends down sides of bird.

6 Take them along the bird to the neck end. Push the neckbone with the fingers to plump up the breast.

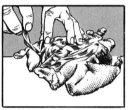

2 Open up the bird and remove the small protruding bones at the neck end.

Small game birds are usually hung by their necks. The blood cannot then run out of the body into the neck and this gives the flesh a more gamy taste. Larger birds, such as turkeys and geese are hung by their feet. The blood runs into their necks, leaving the body flesh less dark and gamy.

If hanging at home with no suitable chilly place, hang the bird out of a window, high enough to be out of the reach of pets. Do not do this in really cold weather as the bird may freeze and this will completely arrest the hanging process.

7 Tie the two string ends tightly together.

3 Chop off the backbone which is still attached to one side of the opened-up bird.

Boning
Cut open the skin at the neck to expose the breastbone (wishbone).

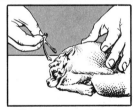

2 Cut and scrape with a short sharp knife to extract this bone.

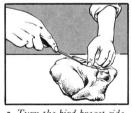

3 Turn the bird breast side down and cut along the backbone, working the flesh off the rib cage from both sides.

4 Flatten the bird by beating carefully with a rolling-pin, mallet or the flat of a cleaver.

4 Cut through the joints at each limb. Continue around carcass. Lift out rib cage.

5 If boning legs and wings, work from the inside, scraping the bones clean to free them.

6 To stuff: Open bird out, spread on the stuffing, roll up and sew.

5 Lay skin up. Push skewer through it and/or tuck drumsticks through slits in skin.

Poultry and game birds/2

Cutting up a chicken
Lay bird breast side up. Pull a leg away from the body and cut only through skin at joint.

2 Pull the leg further away, cutting the skin to free it from the body.

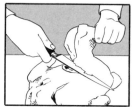

3 Turn the bird over. Feel along backbone for the soft "oyster." Cut under it and remove it with leg.

4 Turn bird over again and bend leg back to break joint close to body. Cut through exposed socket to sever leg.

5 Lay the leg skin side down and use the fingertips to feel for the knee joint.

6 Cut at the knee joint between the bones to sever the drumstick from the thigh.

Trussing with a needle
Thread trussing needle with end of ball of fine strong cotton (not nylon) string. Smooth neck flap over shoulders and back of bird to cover neck opening. Lay bird breast side up. Tuck wing tips under the back, bending them to lock over neck flap. Push needle through one wing near knee, pass it just over backbone and out at the same spot on the second wing. Go back through that wing, further down toward the tail, to make a I-in stitch. Push needle back through body to come out same distance down wing from original insertion. (*Contd below.*)

7 Use a cleaver or the base of a heavy knife to chop off the drumstick knuckles.

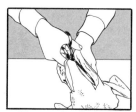

8 Cut through the breast flesh just to one side of the breastbone.

9 Use a pair of scissors or poultry shears to split the bird into halves.

10 Open up the bird. Cut each breast from the carcass along the lines where the back ribs meet the breast ribs.

Singeing fine feathers over a flame can be difficult. Instead shave off with a disposable razor · Do not truss birds if they are to be carved in the kitchen. Trussing does give a neater look at the table, but inhibits even cooking · If roasting a trussed bird, cook breast side down most of the time; lying first on one breast, then the other. This way the legs, needing most heat to cook, are uppermost, and juices run down into the breast · If poaching a trussed bird, cook breast side up in a covered pan; legs in liquid, breast cooking more slowly in steam.

11 When cutting at the wing end, extra pressure is required to cut through the collar-bone.

12 Lay breast sections skin-side up and cut them each in two diagonally, so that each wing has some breast meat.

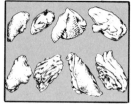

13 Chop off the wing tips.

14 Trim pieces of untidy loose skin from the finished pieces.

Trussing with a needle (contd)
Cut string, leaving enough to tie ends in a tight bow (easier to undo than a knot). Push legs close to body, slightly toward neck to plump up the breast. Thread needle as before, and truss legs to body in this position. Pass needle through legs near knee joint, and back again nearer the drumstick. Tie with bow. Use third length to tie drumsticks and "parson's nose" (tail end) together; or split flesh above vent and force parson's nose through it, close to vent, before trussing legs.

Turkey sinew removal
Break leg joints over the edge of a table by bending them backward until they crack.

2 Cut through the skin only (not the sinews) around the legs. Fix one foot firmly in a clamp, vice or door jamb.

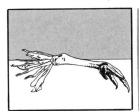

3 Pull hard on the leg while twisting the body. The leg parts at the cut, sinews intact. Repeat for the other foot.

Modern chickens are easy to cut up, their inactive life not having been conducive to their developing tough muscles and tendons. More skill and strength is required to prepare a free-range farmyard boiling fowl · Freeze chicken livers until there are enough to make a pâté: fry the livers, mash them with an equal amount of softened butter and season to taste · Capon livers are particularly rich and delicious in pâtés, but are also good broiled.

Always remove the fat around the vent. It is generally left on by retailers, but makes a dish greasy, and, in the case of factory-farmed birds, can impart a fishy flavor ·

When preparing birds for the freezer, make sure legs are severed at the rounded drumstick to pre-vent sharp bones bursting through freezer bags · Use the raw carcass and neck, feet and giblets (except the liver) of a boned bird to make stock.

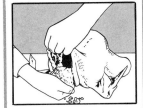

Stuffing turkey at neck end
Fill the neck cavity loosely with the stuffing.

Preparing small game
Slip a piece of string under the tail and cross the string ends.

2 Take the string ends around the legs.

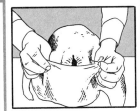

2 Put the turkey on its breast and draw the flap of neck skin up over the stuffing and cavity mouth.

Pigeon breast
Keeping the knife close to the bone, cut down the side of the bone to remove breast.

3 Draw the string tightly and knot firmly.

4 Tuck long strips of thinly cut pork back fat under the neck end and fold over to cover the breast.

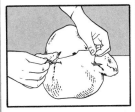

3 Sew or skewer the flap in place. (Stuff the body cavity from the vent end.)

2 Repeat on the other side. Use the carcass (with the wings and legs) for stock.

Bard a bird, or spread with butter when trussing, rather than just before roasting. This prevents drying out · For flavor, wrap quail in vine leaves, then in fatty bacon, before cooking.

5 Secure the fat by tying in two places with strong cotton thread.

Do not fill a bird with warm stuffing. The warmth can encourage the growth of microorganisms. Chill the stuffing and keep the bird refrigerated until ready to cook · To speed the cooking of roast or broiled chicken, cut deep parallel slashes into the flesh, diagonally through the breast and legs, or through the fleshiest side of pieces of poultry. Brush with butter or with a marinade.

Fish

Removing scales
Using a heavy knife, pastry scraper or scallop shell, scrape the fish from tail to head.

Skinning flat fish (sole)
Lay the fish dark side up and cut the skin across at the tail.

A sharp, flexible, not-too-large knife is the first essential. Other necessary tools are a pair of small pliers, or large tweezers, for the extraction of small bones, a scallop shell, pastry scraper or non-flexible knife for the removal of scales, a large board to work on, and a clean cloth (and perhaps a small pile of salt) to help get a good grip on the fish. Because fresh fish are slithery and slimy, the board will need frequent washing and wiping. For this reason, professionals work right by a source of running water, constantly rinsing fish, tools and board. Alternatively, put a sheet of wax paper over the board and tuck the ends firmly underneath it. The paper can be replaced when it becomes slimy, and the board stays clean. Fish skins are deceptively touch, and they blunt knives rapidly. Fish fillets and steaks may be prepared up to 12 hours in advance and kept, loosely wrapped in foil or plastic wrap, in the refrigerator. Preparation more than 12 hours ahead of cooking is not advisable as the flesh will inevitably lose moisture and taste.

Filleting round fish
Cut the head off between the gills.

2 Cut down the length of the back, keeping the knife just above the central bones and the blade flat against them.

2 Work a finger under the skin and loosen it down both sides of the fish.

Trimming fins
Trim off the fins of small round fish using scissors.

Mitering tail fins
To enhance the appearance of fish with large tails, cut a "V" out of the tail fin.

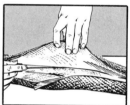

3 Lift the top fillet and work it away from the ribs and backbone using a stroking action with the knife blade.

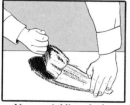

3 Use a sprinkling of salt or a cloth to get a firm grip on the tail end of skin. Pull back, not up, to peel off.

Flattening fish fillets
Use gentle downward and inward strokes with a meat pounder or rolling-pin.

Ciselé fillets
Stop curling up during cooking by cutting shallow diagonal slashes on skinned side.

4 Cut along the back again, this time just below the central bones. Then lift away the backbone and ribs.

4 Repeat for the pale side of skin, if required. Trim off the fins with scissors.

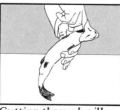

Gutting through gills
Hook the forefinger through one gill.

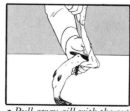

2 Pull away gill with the gut attached. Remove the other gill if necessary.

5 Run fingertips along flesh to locate remaining bones. Remove with pliers/tweezers.

Skinning/preparing eel
*(*Not a job for the squeamish.*)* *Hold firmly with a cloth. Bang its head sharply.*

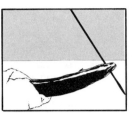

2 It may writhe even when dead so keep gripped in cloth. Push needle threaded with strong string through the eyes.

3 Cut through the skin all around the neck.

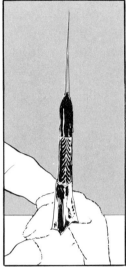

To clean fish: Slit belly from vent end toward head (belly of round fish is near the tail, flat fish nearer head). Pull out entrails. Rinse, taking care to clean blood channel close to backbone of round fish. Remove gills. Ill-cleaned fish tastes bitter.

4 Loosen the skin of the neck with a small knife or by snipping around with a pair of scissors.

5 Cut through the skin down half the length of the body.

6 Suspend the eel by the thread. Use the cloth to get a firm grip and pull the skin off slowly and steadily.

Skinning a fish fillet
Use salt or a cloth to grip skin. Push a heavy knife against the flesh to remove the fillet.

7 Cut off head and discard. Cut a slit in the body from the vent toward the head end, extract gut and discard.

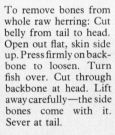

8 Cut eel into 2-in chunks. Be warned—even at this stage the body may still be writhing.

To remove bones from whole raw herring: Cut belly from tail to head. Open out flat, skin side up. Press firmly on backbone to loosen. Turn fish over. Cut through backbone at head. Lift away carefully—the side bones come with it. Sever at tail.

Filleting flat fish
Use stroking action with flexible blade held against backbone to cut off first fillet.

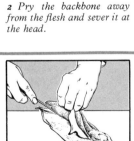

Removing the backbone through the belly
Open and slide blade between bones and flesh on both sides.

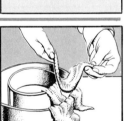

2 Pry the backbone away from the flesh and sever it at the head.

Lining a mold
Use flattened fillets, skinned side up, to line mold before adding QUENELLE *mixture.*

2 Remove second fillet similarly. Turn the fish over and repeat on the other side.

Removing the backbone through the back *Cut down back just above bones.*

2 Repeat, cutting just under central bones, keeping blade flat against them.

3 Open out fish and pry out backbone, attached bones and gut. Snip off at head.

Seafood

Killing lobster
Grip back firmly. Pierce sharply at central point where head meets body. Halve head.

2 Then split in half along the body. The creature dies painlessly at the first pierce but will continue to move.

Shellfish, more than any other foodstuff, needs to be eaten fresh. It deteriorates quickly and loses both taste and texture. It is also dangerous if at all "high." Given that shellfish is to be cooked (or eaten raw) within hours of purchase or thawing, preparation must not be done much in advance.

Oysters should be opened just before serving, having been chilled, while still live, in a bucket or tray of crushed ice. Live lobsters should be killed immediately before cooking, or by the cooking process itself, as when they are boiled.

Mussels, if they are dead on examination (if they are open and do not close when tapped) should be discarded before cooking.

Remove the digestive tract of large live Dublin Bay prawns (*langoustines*) or crayfish (*écrevisses*) by holding them down with one hand, gripping the middle tail fin with the other and twisting and pulling steadily. The threads of intestine come out with the tail fin.

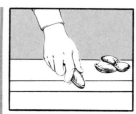

Mussels
Tap any open shells and discard those that do not close up, as they are dead.

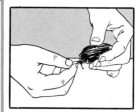

2 Scrub shells with a hard brush, knife or pot scraper to remove encrustations.

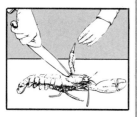

3 Extract stomach (tough transparent bag near head) and intestinal tract (thin gray thread) running down tail.

Preparing cooked lobster
Lay it on its back. Split along the belly with a heavy knife.

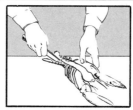

2 Cut it in half through the head and body and open it right up.

3 Tug sharply at the seaweed-like "beard" to pull it away and discard it.

Oysters
Grip firmly using coarse cloth. Push knife tip hard into hinge. Once in, twist to open.

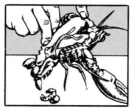

3 Discard stomach sac and intestinal trail. Take out the creamy greenish liver (tomalley) and use for sauce.

4 Remove tail meat in one piece from each half. Turn each piece over and place, pink side up, on opposite shell.

Clams
Push sharp edge of knife blade hard between the shells at the side opposite the hinge.

2 Loosen oyster from the bottom shell. (Open deeper shell down to save juices.)

Kill soft-shell crabs by piercing them through the body between the eyes. Lift the pointed ends of the shell and remove the spongy fibers between the two halves of the body. Turn on its back and remove the "apron" undershell. Wash in cold water.

Miniature crabs, less than $\frac{1}{2}$ in across, need no preparation. Toss in flour before frying, or steam or poach live. · Live mussels can be scrubbed clean quickly by tumbling them in an automatic potato peeler.

2 Once knife is in between shells twist to separate. Cut clam close to shell to free it.

Squid
Cut through the body flesh lengthwise from head to tail on one side only.

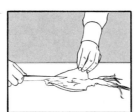

2 Open up the body.

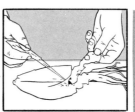

3 Pry out the clear piece of cartilage and pull the entrails up and away toward the head.

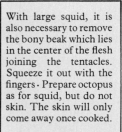

With large squid, it is also necessary to remove the bony beak which lies in the center of the flesh joining the tentacles. Squeeze it out with the fingers · Prepare octopus as for squid, but do not skin. The skin will only come away once cooked.

4 Sever the head and entrails from the body. Turn the body over and lift a corner of the skin with the knife tip.

5 Peel the skin back to remove it from the flesh and discard.

6 Cut the entrails from the head and tentacles. Discard entrails, but save ink (if any) for sauce.

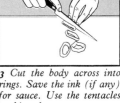

7 Scrape and peel as much as possible of the outer membranes from the tentacles.

8 Slice the body across into thin strips.

Small squid (calamares)
Cut off the head and use a finger to pull out the entrails and the cartilage.

2 Peel the skin from the body flesh and discard it.

3 Cut the body across into rings. Save the ink (if any) for sauce. Use the tentacles unskinned.

Very fresh clams are liable still to have sand in their digestive tracts. Place them in a bucket of water with a handful of barley or pet-fish food. They will ingest the food and excrete the sand · Do not confuse the intestinal tract of a lobster with its roe. The roe (if there is any) is a deep-black trail running down the body. The tract is thin, pale-to-dark gray and translucent. It *must* be removed. The roe turns a bright red when the lobster is cooked. Remove it then and liquefy in a sauce for flavor and color.

Shelling cooked prawns
Pinch off the legs and any roe from under the body. Use the roe for sauce.

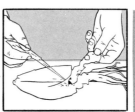

2 Loosen the crackly skin from the underside.

3 Peel off this skin and discard.

4 Break off the head and discard it.

Butterfly prawns
Split the raw prawns through undersides. Leave head intact.

2 Wipe away intestinal tract. When broiled, prawns bend up into butterfly shape.

93

Vegetables

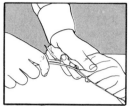

Preparing spinach
Fold the leaf in half and hold firmly in one hand. Grip the stalk in the other.

2 Pull away the stalk sharply, and discard. Tear the leaves into smaller pieces.

All the vegetable preparation techniques shown may be executed up to 12 hours before eating, cooking or freezing, except where otherwise stated. The prepared vegetables should be covered in plastic wrap and kept in a cold place. Many vegetables may be prepared as much as 24 hours in advance, but the flavor and texture will be slightly impaired. Prepared cauliflower and root vegetables may be kept for up to 12 hours in cold water, but some loss of flavor, vitamins and other nutritional content will result. Peeled potatoes must be immersed in water to prevent discoloration caused by oxidization on exposure to air. Some root vegetables, like celeriac and salsify, discolor so readily once peeled that it is necessary to soak them in water made slightly acid by adding either lemon juice or vinegar. Lettuce should be dried off well and stored in plastic bags in the refrigerator. Lettuce leaves will brown at the edges if stored longer than 12 hours. Spinach may be prepared up to 24 hours in advance, and kept in the same way.

Chopping herbs
Wash and dry thoroughly. Compress leaves into a ball in the palm of the hand.

2 Using the knuckles as a guide, slice the ball to chop the leaves coarsely.

Slicing onions
Split the onion into halves, cutting through the root.

2 Peel both halves, leaving the root intact.

3 Using the knuckles as a guide, slice with a downward and forward cutting action.

3 Scrape the coarsely chopped leaves into a pile with the knife blade.

Chopping onions
Halve and peel as above. Make horizontal cuts toward root – kept intact.

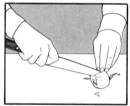

2 Make vertical cuts across these cuts, keeping the knife tip pointed toward the intact root.

3 Slice across, into dice. Discard the root, or use for stock.

4 Holding the knife tip as a pivot, chop up and down in an arc. Repeat **3** and **4** until finely chopped.

Crushing garlic
Break clove open by hitting sharply with flat of a knife.

2 Peel off all the paper-like skin.

3 Add salt to the garlic flesh to draw out moisture.

4 Chop roughly and mash to a paste with the flat of the knife.

Peeling root vegetables
Hold the peeler flat and push down and away, allowing the blade to swivel freely.

Dicing cucumber
Cut cucumber into 3-in lengths. Peel squarely to rectangular blocks of flesh.

2 Slice the blocks vertically.

Decorative cucumber slices With a fork, score deep lines in the skin along the length of the cucumber.

2 Use repeated strokes of the peeler to strip carrots into ribbons for garnish or salad.

3 Stack the slices, and cut again to produce sticks.

4 Cut across the sticks to produce dice.

2 Slice across. The fork marks give the slices a crenellated edge.

3 Make julienne strips by stacking the ribbons and slicing through the pile.

Cleaning whole leeks
Trim root fibers but leave the base intact to hold leek together. Remove outer leaves.

2 Split lengthwise from just short of the root. Turn and split again. Riffle the leaves under running water.

Degorging cucumber
(extracting juices) Sprinkle with salt, leave for 30 minutes, rinse well and dry.

Decorative carrot slices
Use a cannelle knife to pare deep grooves along a carrot.

Herbs are more easily chopped when dry. After washing, shake them in a salad basket or pat them with paper towels · Chop and dice shallots in the same way as onions, using a small paring knife · Don't peel mushrooms; wipe them with a damp cloth and trim stalk ends.

Crush garlic on a sheet of paper to avoid tainting the cutting board—flop the board over instead if you are in a hurry · Chop chives or scallion tops by holding a bunch in one hand and snipping them with a pair of scissors.

Striped effect
Peel off strips of skin, producing the pattern shown.

2 Using the knuckles as a guide, slice with a downward and forward action.

Slicing leeks
Slice, using the knuckles as a guide, before washing.

2 Separate the rings and wash well under running water.

2 Cut into blocks, or slice. Use also for zucchini.

Vegetables /2

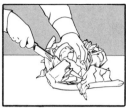

Cutting cauliflower
Hold firmly, cut off the stalk end and discard.

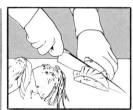

Slicing cabbage
Split in half through root, then cut in thick slices or:

2 With two angled cuts, remove the wedge of central stalk core from each half.

Preparing watercress
Wash well and shake dry. Grip the bunch round the neck at the top of the stalks.

2 Break away the outer leaves.

3 Slice roughly, using the knuckles as a guide with a downward and forward action.

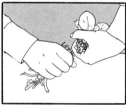

4 Or slice very thinly in the same way for salads or coleslaw.

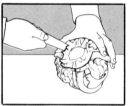

2 Grip the stalks firmly with the other hand and twist sharply. Discard the stalks or use for soup.

3 Keeping the knife tip pointed to the center, cut carefully around to form a cone shape to remove the core.

To kill any parasites in the greens, break up and soak leaves in heavily salted water for up to 10 minutes · Crisp up limp cabbage, lettuce and celery by trimming the stalks and standing them in water.

Washing soft lettuce
Agitate gently, totally submerged. Dry with abrupt, downward shakes.

Preparing asparagus
Peel any tough outer skin at base.

4 Pull the florets apart gently—do not cut. They won't then crumble and will keep their shape.

Cleaning crisp lettuce
Cut out the stalk as with **Cutting cauliflower 3.**

2 Gently separate the leaves and wash under running water.

2 Holding the bunch loosely, tips downward, tap gently to level up.

5 Break up larger florets as for whole heads, repeating *3* and *4*.

Squaring artichokes
One clean slice removes the tips of outer leaves.

2 Cut off the stalk at the base of the globe.

3 Slice off stalk ends evenly, then tie loosely in a bundle with string.

Peeling tomatoes
Immerse in boiling water for about 5 seconds.

2 The peel should then come away with ease. If it does not, re-immerse briefly.

Quartering tomatoes
Slice into quarters through core. Trim out core and push out seeds with the fingers.

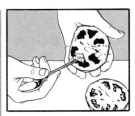

De-seeding tomatoes
Remove from halved tomatoes using a teaspoon handle.

Peeling shallots
Boil for 2 minutes. Trim off stalk and roots, leaving root base to keep the shallot intact.

If peeling only one or two tomatoes, turn briefly over a flame on a fork · The faster or harder vegetables are pushed through a food processer, the thicker the slices · The thinner the knife, the thinner the slices can be cut.

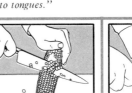

Tomato julienne
First quarter as above. Then half each quarter to make "tomato tongues."

2 Stack the tongues and slice to produce julienne strips.

2 Take care to grip only the outer skin.

Cutting off corn kernels
Peel away the outer leaves.

2 Hold cob firmly upright and cut off kernels with downward slices of a knife held firmly against the core.

Extracting juice
Hold cob firmly as shown. Slice through center of each row of kernels to split skins.

3 Peel carefully.

Château potatoes
Cut large peeled potatoes in half, or into quarters if they form a more suitable shape.

2 Use a peeler to trim them down to a barrel shape.

2 Hold the stalk firmly upright. Push out the pulp with a downward scraping of the knife blade.

Parisienne potatoes
Work melon scoop well in before turning, to produce balls.

French fries
Peel large potatoes and cut into slices.

2 Stack the slices, then cut into sticks.

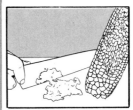

3 Remove any traces of skin and use the pulp for flavoring.

Fruit

Avocado
First cut the flesh in half lengthwise, around the stone, using a serrated fruit knife.

2 Twist the two halves gently in opposite directions to separate. Pry the stone out with the tip of the knife.

Many fruits discolor rapidly if prepared in advance. This is caused by oxidization on exposure to the air. Keeping the cut fruit at a low temperature slows down this process, and anti-oxidants such as ascorbic acid (vitamin C) inhibit the chemical reaction. Lemon juice, with its high vitamin C content, is a moderately effective anti-oxidant when painted on to the cut surface of fruit. Vitamin C, in tablet or powder form, dissolved in water, is used to make an anti-browning bath for temporary storage of fruit for bottling. However, long soaking impairs the texture and draws out the flavoring, vitamin and other nutritional content of the fruit. Carbon steel knives react with fruit in a similar way as the oxygen in the air, causing heavy discoloration, so use stainless steel knives to cut and prepare fruit.

Carefully wash and pat dry fruit that is not to be peeled to guarantee the complete removal of any traces of insecticides or other chemical sprays. Washing is likely to accelerate spoilage, so do it just before serving.

Orange segmenting
Peel both rind and pith in a spiral from the top, using a sawing action with the knife.

2 Slice down either side of each of the separating membranes to remove segments.

3 To peel for salads, first cut again into quarters then pull away the skin from the tip as shown.

Orange rind julienne
Using a swivel-headed peeler, pare the orange finely, without removing any pith.

2 Stack the lengths of peel and cut into needle shreds using a downward and forward action.

3 Do not discard the membrane core. Hold it over a bowl.

Grating rind
Use the finest openings of a grater. Remove only rind and none of the bitter white pith.

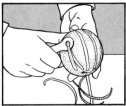

Decorated orange slices
Use a cannelle knife to score grooves in the rind from top to bottom.

2 Cut across into thin slices.

4 Squeeze it hard to extract all the remaining juice.

Slicing bananas
Hold banana gondola-style. Angled slices are uniform.

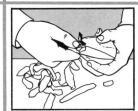

Whole pears
Peel, leaving the stalk intact.

2 Working from the rounded bottom end, remove the core using a melon baller.

3 Or, for pear halves, split lengthwise and remove the core with a teaspoon.

Pineapple boat
Split in half lengthwise through both fruit and leaves.

Pineapple cylinder
Slice off top and bottom of pineapple as shown. Discard the bottom but keep the top.

2 Cut deeply around the edge at both ends to release the flesh.

Pineapple slices
For fritters, or when core is woody, punch it out of each slice with an apple corer.

2 Using a grapefruit knife, cut around the edge to release the flesh from the skin.

3 Use the thumbs to push the flesh out of the fruit in one cylindrical piece.

4 Cut the cylinder into slices (remove the central core, as shown above, if it is woody).

Peeling grapes
Immerse for 1 minute in boiling water. The peel then comes away with ease.

3 Place the flesh flat side down and cut across into slices. Replace in the shell rounded side upwards.

5 Set the shell upright on a plate and put the slices back inside it in their original order.

6 Replace the leafy top as a "lid" to complete the effect.

Seeding grapes
Use the folded end of a bobby pin to extract seeds via the stalk end of the grape.

Melon zig-zag
Remove a small slice from both top and bottom to give a stable base to each half.

2 Cut deeply into the center with zig-zag cuts as shown. Break the two sections apart.

3 Scoop out the seeds from the center.

Skinning hazel-nuts
Bake on a tray in a hot oven until the skins split. Rub in a cloth to remove the skins.

Skinning chestnuts
Cut through skins, from top to base, down one side.

2 Place the chestnuts in water and bring slowly to the boil.

3 Drain and peel the nuts while still hot. Scrape away the pith as well.

Blanching almonds
Boil almonds for 30 seconds and then pinch off the skins.

To strip fruit like red currants or black currants from their stalks quickly, hold the stalks in one hand over a bowl and use the prongs of a fork to pull the currants off into the bowl · If currants have been frozen still on their stalks, de-stalk them by shaking the frozen fruit in a plastic container. The stalks will break off; remove them before the fruit thaws.

To separate eggs
1 Crack the egg sharply across its "equator" by hitting it against the hard sharp edge of a solid object, say the edge of a large bowl.
2 Hold the cracked egg upright over a bowl. Pull the top half-shell away from the bottom. The white will run over the sides of the bottom shell into the bowl. The yolk will lie in the bottom shell.
3 Tip the yolk carefully into the other half-shell allowing any remaining white to drip into the bowl. If the white will not fall, use the edge of one egg shell to sever the white by cutting against the other shell.
4 If the yolk membrane should rupture and some yolk drops into the white, use a yolk-free egg shell to scoop out the specks.

To squeeze oranges and lemons easily and to get the most juice from them put them in the microwave oven (for about 30 seconds) or warm them in an ordinary oven before squeezing · To soak and cook dried fruit in one operation half fill a wide-necked vacuum flask with the fruit and top up with boiling water. Put the lid on it and leave overnight. They will be soaked and cooked by the morning.

Preparation of rice To be sure that the grains of ordinary long-grain rice will not stick together in the pan during cooking, the rice must be washed thoroughly beforehand to remove all the "mill flour." Either leave the rice immersed in several changes of fresh cold water, or put the grains in a sieve and place it under fast running water for a few minutes, moving the grains around with a spoon.

Cooking food

Summary of methods

Food is cooked for several reasons: to make it more appealing, render it more digestible and, in some cases, to remove unpleasant tastes or textures. The particular method of cooking to be employed is, therefore, dictated by the ingredients at hand. One cooking method may do justice to certain ingredients but totally spoil the taste and texture of others.

The most general and important classification of cooking methods is that of fast and slow. Tough cuts of meat, such as oxtail, are only made palatable by slow processes, such as braising or stewing. Prolonged gentle heat converts the abundant connective tissue (which makes meat tough) into gelatin which gives a tender and well-flavored stew or casserole. A sirloin steak cooked in this manner would be a disaster. Lacking connective tissue, the meat would quickly dry up and become fibrous and unappetizing. Such steak retains the natural softness of raw meat if cooked very rapidly with intense heat.

Similarly, rapid boiling keeps the bright color and crisp texture of green vegetables, but some vegetables are the better for a soft casseroled texture with a mellowed and blended flavor. Stew red cabbage gently with apples and golden raisins to a soft combination of tastes and colors, or bake peas with lettuce leaves, mint, garlic, butter, sugar and onions for the dully-colored but delicious *petits pois à la française.*

The dozen or so principal cooking methods can be used on their own, or, like sweating, are generally used in conjunction with at least one other method. Some methods are, in fact, a combination of two or more other methods; a sauté is commonly a dish that has first been fried, then stewed. Many dishes require the use of more than one process: Deep-fried fritters are often made with vegetables that have already been boiled and baked; pies may contain fruit that has already been stewed.

Broiling

When meat and fish are fresh and tender, broil them to make the most of their natural texture and flavor. The drying effect of the intense heat of broiling is best counteracted by brushing the food with butter, which may also be seasoned to enhance the flavor.

Speed is the essential factor in keeping broiled food moist. A sealed outside surface should be formed quickly to prevent the juices inside the meat from running out. If the broiler is not hot enough, the seal will not be formed and the juices will escape. The broiler should, therefore, be pre-heated to the highest possible temperature before the meat or fish is placed on or under it, and the broiler tray fixed as close as possible to the heat, at least until both sides have been browned.

It is true to say that expert open-fire, or barbecue, cooking over charcoal is the best way to broil. It can also be a lot of fun to do, even if it is expensive and time-consuming, and not at all easy without a good deal of practice.

Roasting, another fast method of cooking, is best used for larger portions of tender cuts of meat, fish and poultry. Until the advent of the oven as we know it, roasting and broiling were the same process—cooking in front of an open fire, perhaps on a turning spit, to be sure of even cooking. Today roasting means cooking in an oven without any liquid other than fat. Some modern ovens or broilers have spits (rotisseries) built into them. The advantage of this is that the fat and juices run over the surface of the meat as it turns, basting the meat so that no part dries out. Meat roasted without the benefit of a spit is usually basted with fat once or twice during the process to prevent the top part of the meat from drying out and to enhance the flavor. Basting is unnecessary with fatty meats like pork or shoulder of lamb and is not strictly necessary with others—BARD them by tying pieces of back fat over them. The fat, as it melts, does the basting. Barding is essential for small birds that tend to be dry. Alternatively, roast them breast side down for half the cooking time, then finish them off other side up. This retains fat and juices in the breast.

As a general rule, cuts of meat that might otherwise tend to "bleed", such as beef, are first browned all over in a hot pan before being put to roast in the oven. Alternatively, start with an oven preheated to its highest temperature to "seal" the surface of the meat into a semi-impermeable layer (similar to that described for broiling) to reduce the loss of juices. After 20 minutes or so, lower the temperature to normal roasting level.

Shallow frying In frying, as in broiling, tender cuts of meat are treated with fierce heat for a brief time. In broiling, the fat drips off the food during cooking (and may, or may not, be served with it) whereas in frying the meat stays in the fat, at least some of which is eaten along with the food.

Food is "shallow fried" in up to $\frac{1}{4}$ in fat. Obviously, the type of fat used will affect the results. Bacon drippings, olive oil and butter all have distinctive flavors, while most other vegetable and cereal oils have little or no flavor. So choose a fat for its flavor (or lack of it), but remember that all fats cannot be heated to the same high temperatures.

Sautéing, from the French word for jumping or tossing, is essentially the same as shallow frying. Indeed the French use the same term to describe both processes. Sauté in an almost dry pan, using no more than a tablespoon of fat.

The process may be used on its own (sautéed mushrooms) or after boiling (sautéed potatoes) or before stewing (beef stew). Although a sauté is cooked by rapid frying in very little fat, there may well be subsequent stewing to be sure that the interior of the food is cooked through and to blend in sauce ingredients; but the essential flavor of the dish is derived from the initial frying. Thus, a chicken sauté consists of browned pieces of chicken with comparatively little sauce well reduced.

A chicken cooked similarly but without the browning will be more of a FRICASSÉE than a sauté. A chicken stew, on the other hand, although the bird might well have been given a preliminary frying for the same reasons as for a sauté, will be immersed in a good deal of sauce and cooked for longer than a sauté — for this reason it may be made using an older, tougher bird.

Deep-frying is a fast process in which food is totally immersed in hot fat, so all sides cook at once.

As with broiling and shallow frying, deep frying is suitable for tender cuts of meat and fish. A sealing coating of batter or egg and crumbs prevents the outside overcooking, seals in juices and reduces spluttering of the fat. Deep-frying is also the most suitable method of cooking fritters, croquettes and fish cakes which require a crisp crust and a soft, hot center. All excess fat is drained off to leave the crisp browned coating as dry as possible.

Deep-frying is a dirty process, so do not attempt it unless equipped with good ventilation and easily cleaned surfaces surrounding the deep-fryer (or a sealed deep-fryer).

After each use, filter the fat clean of any small food particles and replace it when it shows signs of breaking down (it gets dark and cloudy). Degenerated fat smokes and burns at a lower temperature, smells rancid and imparts an unpleasant flavor to anything cooked in it.

Baking is the cooking of anything in the oven. Modern roasting is a form of baking where high temperatures and basting are used to imitate old spit-roasting, open-fire techniques.

Baked foods are more usually cooked in containers at moderate-to-cool temperatures. The easily controlled overall even heat of the oven provides an efficient method for the slow cooking of tough cuts of meat. This kind of baking is commonly referred to as "pot-roasting" or "braising."

Delicate foods such as egg custards or mixtures requiring long slow cooking may even be baked AU BAIN MARIE — standing in a pan of hot water. This gentle form of heat transfer and steamy atmosphere prevents over-cooking; the center cooks through before the outside dries out or burns.

Pot-roasting is a combination of frying and baking. The meat is first browned all over in fat both to flavor and to give the look of a roast. It is then baked slowly in a covered pot in the oven, or over low direct heat, with or without the addition of a little liquid and/or some vegetables, until tender.

Braising is slow cooking in a covered pan on a bed of chopped vegetables with little or no added liquid. The braising meat cooks in its own juices and in the steam from the bed of vegetables cooking under it.

As with the pot roast, the meat is sometimes fried before braising to give a better flavor and color. The braising veg-

etables can be discarded, or used for soup, or strained or sieved to provide a sauce for the dish. Occasionally the term "braising" is used to mean baking in a covered pan without the bed of vegetables and perhaps only a little liquid; "braised celery" is celery baked in a few tablespoons of stock.

Boiling Apart from rice, pasta, green vegetables, sugar syrups and jams, few foods benefit from true boiling. The rapid agitation of a properly boiling liquid tends to toughen meat and leave it with a dry and fibrous texture. Delicate foods, like fish, would simply be broken up by the process. Boiling is thus reserved for occasions when cooking must be fast (to preserve the green color of vegetables), when the rapid agitation is needed (to keep grains of rice separate), where higher temperatures are to be achieved (sugar syrups), or where moisture has to be driven off to reduce a liquid to a thicker consistency.

The term "boiling" is often misused to describe the "simmering" or "poaching" processes.

Steaming, the cooking of food in a hot vapor rather than in a liquid, significantly reduces the loss of nutrients. It is particularly suitable when cooking for invalids, as food can be prepared without fat and thus, be made more easily digestible. The food in the upper section of a STEAMER cooks in the steam produced by the water boiling in the lower section. A well-fitting lid, to keep the steam in, is important. Care-

ful timing is essential as steamed food is tasteless if even slightly over-cooked.

Steaming is ideal for the cooking of foods that tend to break up if cooked in water, such as floury potatoes.

There is another, quite different, method of steaming as used for traditional English puddings, which require the long, slow, gentle cooking that steaming provides, but the food does not come into direct contact with the steam.

Poaching and stewing The terms "poaching" and "stewing" are often used to mean the same thing—a slow, gentle cooking in liquid. Strictly speaking, liquid at poaching temperature is barely moving. (*Simmering* water bubbles in only one part of the container; *boiling* water bubbles all over the surface; and water at a *rolling, galloping* or *fast boil* bubbles agitatedly.) Food that is poached is generally completely submerged in liquid. Food that is stewed may be cooked in a covered pan in liquid which only partially covers it.

Foods that are likely to break up, like sliced apples, are best poached in the oven where the temperature can be controlled carefully to prevent the liquid boiling.

The slower tough meat is cooked, the more tender and juicy it becomes. A cut of stewing beef, such as oxtail, will take at least 2 hours to stew at simmering temperature on the top of the stove until it is acceptably tender; poached in the oven for about 4 hours, it would be markedly more tender and succulent.

Broiling

The first essential in broiling is a broiler preheated to as high a temperature as possible. This is to seal and brown the surfaces of the food quickly, to form a crust which will trap the food juices inside. If meat is put under only a medium-hot broiler this crust will not form and the juices will leak out of the food, leaving it dry, fibrous, tasteless and unattractive.

With skilled cooking, open-fire grilling produces pleasantly smoky, well-browned meat. But a charcoal or wood fire must be lit about two hours before cooking. Such a fire, with a good bed of flameless embers (which will glow brilliantly at night, but only look dull gray in bright daylight) will cook a small lamb cutlet to perfection in 2 minutes. The outside will be dark, crisp and brown, the inside juicy and pink. A good modern stove-broiler, properly preheated, will do almost as well. The same cutlet cooked on a poor stove-broiler, where the tray cannot be positioned closely enough to the heat will take 15 minutes to be cooked through, by which time the outside will be barely brown, the juices will have leaked out and it will be uniformly dry and rather tough and tasteless. If the broiler cannot be got hot enough, do not bother with it and use the frying pan.

If, when the food is browned on both sides, it is still raw inside (as will be the case if the cut is thick) it must then be moved further away from the heat so that the inside may cook before the outside burns. It should then be turned over at regular intervals and basted with the juices from the drip tray. Obviously this method of cooking is not suitable for cuts much thicker than 2 in.

When broiling, note the following points:
1 Do not salt food prior to broiling. The salt draws moisture from the food. Salt after cooking.
2 Brush the food with butter, oil or a mixture of the two, to keep it moist, speed the browning and sealing process and enhance the flavor. This also keeps delicate foods from sticking to the rack.
3 Take food to be broiled out of the refrigerator or freezer in time to have it at room temperature before broiling. (An almost-frozen steak will still be cold inside when the outside is brown and sizzling.) This is particularly important if the steak is to be served very rare (blue).
4 Turn broiling food with spoons or tongs. Avoid piercing the meat and allowing the juices to escape.
5 The more well-done meat is, the tougher it gets.
6 Serve immediately. Broiled food, especially meat, toughens and, even if well-sealed, inevitably loses moisture and dries up if kept hot for long periods.

Broiling steaks All broiled meats should be well browned on the outside but the varying degrees of doneness are defined as follows:
Blue: The inside almost raw (but hot);
Rare: Red inside with plenty of red juices running freely;
Medium-rare: As rare, but with little free-flowing juices. Paler center;
Medium: Pink in the center with juices set;
Well-done: The center beige but the flesh still juicy.
With practice it is possible to tell the doneness of a steak without cutting it: Rare steak feels soft, almost squashy, to the touch; medium steak is firmer with some resilience to it; well-done steak feels extremely firm, almost hard.

For meat that is to be served very rare (blue) allow a brief "resting" period so that heat can permeate to the center; or warm the meat gently in oil or butter in a frying pan immediately before cooking.

Put some slices of stale bread in the bottom of the broiling pan. They absorb fat and this eliminates the smoking that usually occurs as the fat overheats · Use a paint or pastry brush to baste food. It is easier to mop up juices from the pan with a brush than it is to spoon it (which usually requires the tilting of the pan) · If the fire must be fed during the barbecueing, add the fuel at the edges, pushing the outer coals or embers to the middle. Adding new fuel in the middle means a delay while waiting for the flames to die down.

Cooking times for steaks vary with the heat of the broiler, the distance of the food from the heat, the thickness of the cut, its fat content and the density of the meat itself "open" steak with a loose texture, such as *entrecôte*, will cook faster than the same thickness and weight of the closer textured rump). The following table assumes a broiler capable of being heated to 500°F with a 1-in steak held 3 in from the heat source and then, if necessary, at 6 in until cooked to the required degree.

Fillet	
Blue	2 minutes on each side
Rare	2½ minutes on each side
Medium-rare	3 minutes on each side
Medium	3½ minutes on each side
Well-done	5 minutes on each side

Sirloin	
Blue	2½ minutes on each side
Rare	3 minutes on each side
Medium-rare	3½ minutes on each side
Medium	4 minutes on each side
Well-done	5½ minutes on each side

Rump As sirloin, but allow up to 30 percent longer in each case.

Broiling fish Fish has delicate flesh. Lay fish steaks and fillets on greased foil on the broiler pan. This prevents them sticking to the pan and breaking up when turned over. (This is not possible when broiling over, rather than under, heat. Use a fine rack, or wire mesh grill, to support delicate cuts. Grease the rack well. Fish cuts *can* be laid on greased foil and cooked over heat, but they then bake rather than broil in the true sense.)

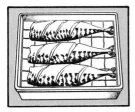

Diagonal slashes *into flesh speeds broiling.*

The gratinée top For an attractive, crunchy top to dishes as varied as SHEPHERD'S PIE or STUFFED PANCAKES, sprinkle the top of the food with dried breadcrumbs, then sprinkle melted butter all over the crumbs. The crumbs absorb the butter, giving a crisp, attractive *gratinée* top when broiled.

Substitute finely grated cheese for the melted butter to get a cheese *gratinée* top.

Dishes coated with a plain white or cheese sauce can also be browned under the broiler. Do this carefully as the top can bubble up and burn in small patches. Again, butter and crumbs or cheese and crumbs will give the best top coating.

The brûlée top Broil a sugar top coating to a golden caramel, as in CRÈME BRÛLÉE.

A crunchy sweet top is obtained by mixing sugar with the breadcrumbs-and-butter *gratinée* formula.

Unusual grills Most grills are plain, tender cuts of meat, fish or poultry. More adventurous and highly flavored dishes are possible:

Spare ribs Marinate in honey and SOY SAUCE before broiling.

Chicken breasts Open up as for CHICKEN KIEV, fill with soft stoned prunes, wrap in fatty bacon, then broil.

Duck breasts Bone and slash diagonally through the skin, sprinkle with salt, brush with honey, and broil until dark and crisp.

Pork chops Broil partially, then spread with a paste of butter, breadcrumbs and mustard, and broil again.

Lamb noisettes Prepare as shown on page 83, but roll around raw prepared kidneys, wrap in fatty bacon, secure with skewers and broil.

Horseback appetizers *Devils on horseback*: Broil stoned, soaked (but not cooked) prunes, stuffed with mango chutney, and wrapped in bacon. Serve on toast. *Angels on horseback* are oysters wrapped in bacon and broiled and served similarly. Other variations on this theme are broiled bacon rolls stuffed with raw herring roe, raw banana, or raw chicken livers.

To make sure the bacon rolls do not come undone during cooking first remove any rind, then "stretch" the bacon on a board with the flat of a knife to break down connective tissue. Roll around the filling and pack the rolls tightly side by side in the broiler tray. If serving as a cocktail snack, insert toothpicks *after* cooking.

Cake icing Make quick icing by covering the cake with thin squares of chocolate (or chocolate mint wafers), marshmallows or thin slices of marzipan, and broiling.

	Ingredients	Serve with
Fish and seafood kebab	Cubes of turbot or other white fish wrapped in thin slices of bacon	Mixed melted butter and lemon juice, fried rice
	Fresh scallops (coquilles St Jacques or fresh shrimps or crayfish tails	
	Mushrooms	
Kofta kebab	Finely ground raw lamb rolled into spicy meatballs with chopped onion, chopped mint, crushed garlic and a touch of allspice, bound with egg yolk	Spicy rice flavored with saffron or turmeric, fresh yogurt
	Blanched, peeled shallots	
	Squares of green or red pepper	
Tandoori kebab	Cubes of raw chicken which have been tandoori marinated (p139)	Some of the marinade served hot, plain boiled rice

Kebabs consist of small pieces of food, threaded on to skewers and broiled. Kebabs are a good way of "stretching" meat to make it go further. A small amount of steak can be made into an impressive dish by cutting it into 6 small pieces, threading them, interspersed with green pepper pieces, pieces of onion and whole mushrooms, on to a skewer; then broiling and serving on a bed of rice.

Meat or fish may be threaded on skewers and left in a MARINADE to absorb the taste of garlic, herbs or spices, and then broiled.

Roasting

Generally roasts are served whole and carved at the table. Part of their glory is their sheer size. A six-bone pork loin roast is so much more impressive than the same cut split into six loin chops and fried.

Another advantage of roasting is that, apart from the occasional basting (see below), the meat or poultry can be left to cook itself. Potatoes, parsnips or pumpkin may be cooked in the drippings in the meat pan, and will be all the tastier for roasting alongside the meat. A simple, but delicious, sauce or gravy can be made from the pan juices in a few minutes before serving the meat.

Because the whole oven must be kept hot for an hour or two, it is worth trying to economize on heat and fuel by using all available oven space. One reason for the traditional English Sunday meal of roast beef, Yorkshire pudding and apple pie was that thrifty cooks could not bear to have any part of the oven hot but empty.

1 First weigh the roast to calculate the time and temperatures needed to cook it.
2 Preheat the oven.
3 "Seal" or "seize" meats such as beef, veal and lamb (see overleaf) by putting them into a very hot oven for the first 20 minutes or so, before reducing to normal roasting temperature, or by quickly browning them all over in a frying pan. This will create a cooked coating that seals in the juices. If you seal by the frying method, get the fat really hot, put the meat into it and leave it there, untouched, until the surface frying is completely browned. Repeat this process until each surface has been browned. (It is impossible to brown properly without some splashing of frying fat.) This method forms a seal much more effectively than continual turning to brown evenly.
4 Place the roast on a ROASTING RACK or TRIVET to keep it up off the bottom of the roasting pan, otherwise the bottom part will simply fry in its own fat. Place in a roasting pan and put it in the peaheated oven.
5 Halfway through the cooking time, check on its progress; turn it over if well browned on top, and baste if necessary.
6 When the cooking time is up, put the roast to stand on a warm serving platter, or keep in the oven, switched off with the door wide open. Carving is easier if the roast is allowed to "rest" for some time, as the fibers relax from the taut state induced by intense heat. In particularly large roasts the heat also drives the juices into the center and resting is necessary to allow these juices to seep back into the outer layers. With ordinary, smaller, domestic roasts resting is not really necessary and the time taken to make the gravy is usually sufficient if the meat is still to be hot when served.
7 Make the gravy in the roasting pan.

Basting Dry meats such as veal and game birds cannot be placed unprotected in the oven to roast or they will become unpalatably dry. Constant basting is time, consuming and the continual opening of the oven door lowers the temperature and wastes fuel. The basting process itself is often messy and difficult. The answer is to make a roast self-basting, and there are several ways to do this:
1 BARD the roast by wrapping it in pork back fat. As the fat melts it bastes the meat beneath it. In addition the layer of fat protects the meat from the drying effects of direct heat.
2 LARD the roast by threading long thin strips (LARDONS) of back fat through it.
(See page 80 for both these techniques.)

3 Large birds and whole fish can be covered with a double layer of muslin which has been thoroughly soaked in melted butter or oil before roasting. This method is particularly good for turkeys or very large fish as, unlike foil wrapping, the muslin does allow the skin to become crisp and brown while giving continuous basting.

Very lean meats benefit from barding and/or larding. Very slow cooking is also wise, as with roast veal. Less lean meats and poultry, like beef and chicken, benefit from being coated in butter and/or oil before going into the oven.

If the roast has a fat layer, always start the roasting with that side uppermost.

Lamb shoulders and legs and well-marbled beef, although they do not have an obvious coating of fat, are fatty meats and need only an initial coating of butter and/or oil.

Although roasting is a very simple method of cooking, requiring no more than careful timing to get good results, there are some interesting variations on the plain roast. They may be filled with any number of herbed STUFFINGS; they may be BONED, ROLLED and tied to be sure of a neat shape and easy carving; they may be spread with a mixture such as mustard and breadcrumbs to give a tasty crisp crust; they may be steeped in a flavoring MARINADE, then basted with it.

Sometimes, in order to prevent the juices in the bottom of the roasting pan from burning, a cup of liquid is added to the pan. Strictly speaking this turns the roasting into baking or braising (see, for instance, FRENCH-ROAST CHICKEN).

Obviously, a long thin piece of meat weighing 5 lbs will take less time to cook than a fat round piece of the same weight, so that all times are meant only as a general guide. The essential point is that meat must reach an internal temperature of 140°F to be rare, 150°F to be medium-pink and 170°F to be well-done. A meat thermometer stuck into the center of the meat eliminates guesswork. Put it in place when the roasting is almost complete, otherwise it gets coated with grease and becomes difficult to read. Make sure that it is not touching a bone or has not gone right through the meat to touch the roasting pan.

Making gravy Gravy is made from the juices that run from the meat.
1 Pour off all, or most, of the fat from the top of the other liquids in the pan.
2 Add just sufficient flour to absorb any remaining fat and thicken the gravy slightly. Use a wooden spoon to incorporate the flour *before* setting the pan over gentle heat.
3 Scrape the bottom of the pan well to release any sediment and cooked meat "glaze."
4 Add a cup or two of water or stock, whisking or stirring all the time, until the sauce thickens.
5 Season to taste.
The pan juices will probably have enough flavor for water to be used, but stock gives more flavor and body. Use a small

piece of bouillon cube if the gravy lacks any flavor of its own.
Add a teaspoon of plum or red currant jam, or other such preserves, to gravy that is to be served with game or goose, which benefit from a little sweetness.
If meat has been roasted to a good brown color, there will probably be enough color in the juices and pieces of meat stuck to the pan bottom to give the gravy itself a good final color. If not, use commercial gravy coloring, or cook about half a teaspoon of sugar to a dark caramel in the bottom of the roasting pan, and add the flour and liquid.
If adding cider, wine, port of any alcoholic

beverage to the gravy for flavor, reduce it first by rapid boiling to moderate the harsh flavor.
Gravy should not be too thick (it should run easily off the back of a spoon). One teaspoon of flour is sufficient to thicken $1\frac{1}{4}$ cups of gravy.
Game gravies can be thickened by the addition of red currant jelly, or similar clear sharp preserves.
If there is sufficient natural juice running from the beef, gravy may not be necessary at all.
To remove all traces of fat from the top of the gravy, lay sheets of paper toweling on the surface to soak it up. Many people, particularly the French, like *slightly* fatty gravy. For households where tastes vary there are useful gravy boats with two lips, one pouring fatty gravy directly from the top, and the other bringing fat-free gravy up from the bottom via a spout.
Perfect gravy always looks shiny and never floury. Attempt to use the minimum of starchy thickening, and get the gravy to the right syrupy consistency by reducing it. This reduction will also help give a clearer, shinier look.

Thawing and cooking times for frozen turkeys and game birds

Although the thawing times in the following table can be relied on absolutely, the cooking times are dependent on an accurate oven. To be quite safe, plan your timing so that, if all goes right, the bird will be ready an hour before it is due to be served. This will give a good safety margin. When the bird is cooked, open the oven door to let it cool,

place the bird on a serving dish and put it back in the cool oven to keep warm.

Thawing in a warm room (over 18°C/65°F) or under warm water is not recommended, as this encourages the growth of microorganisms which might cause food poisoning.

Weight of turkey when ready for the oven, boned, stuffed or empty	Thawing time at room temperature 65°F in hours	Thawing time in refrigerator 40°F in hours	Cooking time at 350°F in hours	Cooking time at 325°F in hours
8–10 lbs	20	65	$2\frac{1}{4}$–$2\frac{3}{4}$	4–$4\frac{1}{2}$
11–13 lbs	24	70	3–$3\frac{1}{2}$	5–$5\frac{1}{2}$
14–16 lbs	30	75	$3\frac{3}{4}$–$4\frac{1}{4}$	$5\frac{3}{4}$–$6\frac{1}{4}$
17–20 lbs	40	80	$4\frac{3}{4}$–$5\frac{1}{4}$	$6\frac{1}{2}$–$7\frac{1}{2}$
21–24 lbs	48	96	$5\frac{1}{2}$–$6\frac{1}{2}$	8–9

for game birds:	Cooking temperature and time	
	F	Minutes
Pigeon	400	25–35
Grouse	375	25–35
Partridge	375	20–25
Pheasant	375	45–60
Snipe	375	10–12
Wild duck	400	30–35
Woodcock	375	20–30
Quail	350	20
Teal	425	20
Guinea fowl	375	60–80

Roasting /2

	Suggestions	Cooking times and temperatures
Beef	Sprinkle fat with dried mustard before roasting. Roast on an open rack with a Yorkshire pudding beneath—the drippings from the beef give the pudding flavor.	(Seal by roasting in the hottest possible oven for 20 minutes, or by frying all over. Count the cooking time from *after* sealing is complete—whichever method is chosen.) Allow 15 minutes per 1 lb for rare meat, 20 minutes for medium and 25 minutes for well-done. Roast in a preheated oven set at 375°F.
Veal	Bard, laying rosemary leaves or basil sprigs under the barding fat. Lard and dry marinate. Then bard before roasting. Stuff and sew. Bard with pork back fat.	Seal as above. Then allow 25 minutes for each 1 lb at 350°F.
Lamb	Spread with a mixture of dried breadcrumbs, chopped rosemary and mustard. Roast with a sprig or two of savory or rosemary. Press slivers of garlic into the meat as close as possible to the bone. Bone and stuff with a spicy, slightly sweet mixture. Bone and stuff with kidneys. After roasting, instead of making gravy with the pan juices, pour off most of the fat and mix the remaining juices with hot boiled pulses (flageolets, haricots blancs, butter beans).	Seal in the oven as above, then allow 20 minutes per 1 lb at 375°F. This gives slightly pink lamb. For well-done lamb allow an extra 20 minutes cooking time.
Pork	Score the rind to make CRACKLING. Then rub with oil and sprinkle with salt to give surface a crumbly texture. Bone and stuff with breadcrumb, onion and sage mixture. Bone and stuff with a fruit stuffing (apricot, prune or sour cherry). Rub with dry mustard before roasting.	Pork must be well cooked. Although incidence is increasingly rare, pork meat can carry the parasite *Trichina* which, if not killed by thorough cooking, can cause serious illness. This old fear, together with a distinct sliminess, make under-cooked pork unpalatable to most people. Sealing is not necessary. Allow 40 minutes per 1 lb at 325°F. For crackling, roast at 400°F for 25 minutes per 1 lb, plus 25 minutes over.
Bacon	Boil ham and bacon until tender, then glaze with sugar, mustard and cloves before roasting or baking.	See page 128.
Venison	Marinate and bard. Roast with a cup of the marinade. Use juices to make gravy, adding red currant jelly, port and juniper berries.	Seal in the hottest possible oven for 20 minutes, then roast at 325°F. Allow 15 minutes per 1 lb for rare meat and 20 for pink meat.

	Suggestions	Cooking times and temperatures
Chicken	Bard with fatty bacon. Stuff with sage and onion mixture. Fill cavity with a sliced lemon and fresh herbs. "French roast"—stand chicken, smeared with butter, on to the bottom of a roasting pan, add a cup of water, slices of onion, carrot, leek and herbs and use the skimmed pan juices for gravy. Coat with butter and/or oil to keep the flesh moist and give a crisp brown skin. Bone and wrap chicken around blanched fresh leeks.	Preheat the oven to 425°F. Allow 15 minutes per 1 lb. Pierce the flesh and check to see that the juices run clear—without any traces of pink—if not, cook for a further 15 minutes. White poultry should be cooked through as it may contain micro-organisms which, if not killed by cooking, can breed dangerously if the poultry is subsequently kept warm for long periods or reheated. Check for doneness with the skewer as explained above and by lifting a leg joint; it should wobble freely, not lifting the carcass with it. Always calculate cooking times on the weight of the stuffed bird.
Turkey	As chicken, or bone and stuff with a large piece of cooked ham, sausage-meat or chestnut stuffing. Sew up and roast under butter-soaked muslin as described on page 106. Use boned and flattened breasts to make BALLOTINE.	Roast large turkeys slowly, but small birds (under 12 lbs) more quickly at a higher temperature. Allow 10 minutes per 1 lb for small birds at 400°F. For larger turkeys use a cooler oven, 350°F, and allow 15 minutes per 1 lb, or an even cooler oven, 325°F, and allow 25 minutes per 1 lb. Keep the breasts covered with bacon or aluminum foil to prevent burning but remove this covering for the last 45 minutes to allow the skin to brown.
Game birds	Bard with fatty bacon. Remove bacon 15 minutes before end of cooking time to allow time for bird to brown. Serve with bread sauce or fresh breadcrumbs fried in butter until crisp and brown, red currant jelly and unthickened, but skimmed, pan juices.	See the table on page 107.
Duck and goose	Prick all over to allow the fat to escape. Roast on a trivet or rack so that the fat will run off. Stuff with a sweetish stuffing (orange and walnut, apricot and prune).	Allow 20 minutes per 1 lb at 375°F for birds under 5 lbs; 25 minutes per 1 lb at 350°F for larger birds.
Fish	Stuff with herb and breadcrumb stuffing. Roast under butter-soaked muslin. Fill cavity with fresh herbs and pieces of lemon. Roast fish, then tip pan juices into sauce boat. Put dried fennel sticks under fish. Heat a ½ cup of Pernod, light it and pour into the pan. The burning Pernod and fennel will flavor the fish.	Allow 12 minutes for very small fish (sardines, smelt); 16 minutes for "one portion" mackerel or trout and 20 minutes for a 2 lb whole fish in a moderately hot oven, 425°F. Roast larger fish for 8 minutes per 1 lb or until a skewer will glide through the flesh without resistance.

Frying

As shown in our table below some fats can be heated to much higher temperatures than others before they break down or start burning. CLARI-FIED BUTTER can be heated safely to a higher temperature than un-treated butter. Pure bacon drippings, lard, beef drippings and solid frying fat generally withstand more heat than margarine, butter or vegetable oil.

Frying steaks or chops:
1 Fry in an uncovered wide pan. (A lid traps the steam and the food stews or steams rather than frying crisply.)
2 Preheat the fat. If the fat is cool when the food is put into it the food absorbs the fat and becomes too greasy. Also, as in broiling and roasting, the food will not brown and form a crust to retain its juices. It will merely stew, losing juices, and become dry and tasteless. Even if the fat is subsequently heated to the right temperature the juices will already have run from it, preventing it from browning well and frying properly.
3 Do not add too much food at one time to the hot fat. This lowers the fat's temperature and, again, hinders the browning.
4 Fry as fast as possible until the browning is complete. Then turn down to moderate heat to cook the inside through.
5 Fried food should be served as soon as possible after cooking. (Juices gradually seep from even well-browned meat and fish, and they dry up and toughen on standing; potatoes lose their crispness and fritters deflate.)

Fats, after a period of use, begin to break down and collect tiny particles of impurities. This causes them to smoke unpleasantly at a lower temperature than brand-new fats and eventually impart an unpleasant flavor to food. Fats containing emulsifier smoke and burn at cooler temperatures than pure fats.

Glazing vegetables
Many vegetables are given a final shiny, slightly sweet, glaze by frying in a mixture of butter and sugar. The sugar melts and caramelizes to a pale toffee and the vegetables brown in the butter-and-caramel mixture. Constant shaking of the pan is necessary to prevent burning and sticking.

Small parboiled carrots cut to a uniform shape; peeled, BLANCH-ED shallots or onions; small round cooked potatoes; even-sized cubes of boiled turnip or sticks of cooked salsify, parsnip or celery, and many other similar vegetables may all be finished this way.

Raw vegetables can be cooked in the same way but because this is a lengthy process requir-

ing constant supervision to prevent sticking on the bottom of the pan, it is more usual either to PARBOIL the vegetables beforehand, or to SWEAT them in the bottom of a closed pan, adding the sprinkling of sugar and turning up the heat to fry them gently, once they are tender. Make simple fried food more tasty and interesting by adding seasonings before frying, or put simple sauces or garnishes in the pan after frying.

Fish cooked *à la meunière* is simply dusted with flour, then fried in butter until brown on both sides. The fish is put on a warm platter and chopped parsley, lemon juice, salt and pepper added to the hot butter in the pan. This is boiled up and poured, sizzling, over the fish.

Truite amandine is cooked similarly:
1 Dust the whole cleaned fish with flour.
2 Fry it in butter. Brown the skin on both sides, then turn the heat down to cook the inside.
3 Keep the fish warm on a serving dish.

4 Fry sliced blanched almonds in the butter in the pan (add more butter if necessary). Toss until evenly browned. Scatter over the fish.
5 Add lemon juice, chopped parsley and seasoning to the pan. Boil up and pour over the fish.

Eggs: Fry in clean fat (frying in a pan in which bacon or sausages have been cooked leads to sticking, and possible breaking of the yolks). If same pan is to be used (at breakfast, for instance) fry bacon, ham, sausages, potatoes, mushrooms, and bread, which all keep well in a warm oven, before tackling the delicate eggs. Pour the fat into a cup, rinse the pan, washing off any browned particles, then strain the fat back into it. Although eggs may be fried in very little fat, using enough to spoon over the eggs speeds up the cooking process. If this is not done the whites tend to burn at the edges before they are set near the yolk.

Break an egg into the hot fat. To do this, crack it smartly across its "equator" against the edge of the frying pan, separate the two sides of the eggshell over the pan and let the whole egg slip into the pan. It should sizzle at once. Eggs can be cooked slowly in warm fat but they look and taste better if the white bubbles slightly as it fries. Fry for 1 to 2 minutes, tipping the pan to one side to create a reservoir of fat to spoon over the egg until the white is set and the yolk has a milky look. Lift out with a spatula, draining

Smoke-point of fats Type of fat:	Initial	After 9 hrs use
	°F	°F
Butter	350	329
Margarine	363	338
Vegetable shortening *(without emulsifier)*	446	367
Vegetable shortening *(with emulsifier)*	365	338
Frying oils *(depending on type; peanut oil smokes less easily than corn oil)*	441-450	367-369
Lard	392	338

off most of the fat, and slide onto a warm plate. If the egg cannot be served at once, cover the plate with an upturned soup bowl and keep warm over gentle heat.

If many eggs are to be fried, they can be pre-fried, allowed to cool and rapidly reheated in clean hot fat or covered with plastic wrap and heated briefly in a microwave oven.

Sausages: Most sausages have skins which, as the stuffing expands in the hot pan, burst or split open. Avoid this by pricking carefully all over with a *thin* needle (large clumsy holes like those produced by the prongs of a fork will just provide a weak point from which the sausage skin will split) and by cooking slowly rather than briskly.

Shake the pan with rapid but careful to-and-fro and side-to-side movements; this will dislodge stuck food with less damage than prodding with a utensil.

The more bread, cereal or other filler sausage-meat contains, the more likely the sausage is to expand rapidly and burst, but even a pure pork sausage made at home will burst its skin if fried too rapidly.

Shake and turn the sausages until evenly browned all over and firm to the touch. Once they have this firm, almost bouncy, feel they are cooked. Drain on absorbent paper.

Bacon and ham: Fry slices of cooked ham to reheat and brown them, but bacon needs actual cooking.

Fry bacon in an almost dry pan, as it readily produces its own fat which can be drained off.

The perfect British breakfast The great British fry-up needs pre-planning and good timing.

Get everything else on the breakfast table, and the plates in a low oven to warm, then:

1 Fry sausages as above in a little oil. Lift out and drain. Keep warm arranged at one end of a large flat platter. Do not cover the dish, but keep warm in the oven.
2 Fry bacon in the same oil. Lift out, drain and add to the platter.
3 Add enough extra fat to cover the bottom of the pan. Fry slices of bread, holding them down with a spatula so that they brown evenly, and turn over when necessary. Drain off excess fat and add the bread to the platter.
4 Fry tomato halves rapidly (cut-side down first), lift out and drain. Add to the platter.
5 Pour the fat into a cup. Rinse the frying pan and dry it over direct heat. Pour the fat back into it, leaving behind any brown particles (use a sieve if necessary). Add more oil or fat to cover the bottom of the pan. Fry the eggs as above. Add to the platter and serve.

The perfect American breakfast Cook "hash browns" with ham and eggs using the same procedure: First fry the ham, then fry raw cubed potatoes with a little chopped onion in the same fat (adding more fat, preferably bacon drippings, if necessary). Finally, cook the eggs in the rinsed-out pan.

Waffles, bacon and maple syrup Prepare the WAFFLES first, keep hot, then fry the bacon.

Scrambled eggs are not truly fried. They are stirred over gentle heat until cooked—sometimes in a double boiler, more commonly in a saucepan or frying pan.

Beat two eggs together with a tablespoon of milk, add salt and pepper to taste. Melt a pat of butter in a heavy frying pan and pour in the mixture. Stir continually over low heat until thickened. Serve at once on hot buttered toast. For consistently good results, remember to:
1 Have the buttered toast ready on a warm plate.
2 Keep stirring *all* the time, otherwise the eggs will thicken into lumpy curds, not an overall creamy consistency.
3 Stop cooking just before the mixture has reached that desired consistency, as cooking will continue after removal from the heat.
4 Transfer *at once* onto the toast; serve promptly.

Variations:
1 **Danish egg** Stop the cooking sharply by putting the pan base in cold water. Allow to cool and mix with mayonnaise for a sandwich filling, or serve with lettuce or on buttered rye bread with anchovies and olives.

2 **Scotch woodcock** Use only the yolks of the eggs and cream instead of milk. Spread the toast with anchovy paste.

Omelettes are, classically, made with three eggs, stirred vigorously (not beaten) with 1 tsp of water and seasoning, fried in foaming butter in a heavy pan.

French omelette *Pull the edges in until the omelette is set.*

Omelette soufflé *Beat whites to soft peaks. Fold in beaten yolks. Cook slowly.*

2 *For a sweet omelette add sugar and vanilla extract to yolks and dot with jam or hot stewed fruit when set.*

3 *Fold over and slide on to a warm plate. Place under a hot broiler for about 30 seconds to rise and brown.*

Sautéing

Sautéed food is given its characteristic taste and color by initial rapid shallow frying. There may then follow some further cooking by gentle stewing in the exuded juices or, perhaps, in a flavorful sauce.

Stages in sautéing:
1 Fry the main and subsidiary ingredients in the fat. Remove them from the pan and keep them hot.
2 DEGLAZE the pan with the liquid.
3 Add the seasonings.
4 If the initial frying has cooked the main ingredients sufficiently, reduce the sauce by rapid boiling and pour it over the dish. Garnish and serve immediately.
5 If further cooking is required, simmer until the main ingredients are tender.
6 Remove them from the pan and place on a warm serving dish. Reduce the sauce by rapid boiling and, if necessary, thicken with a little BEURRE MANIÉ.
7 Pour the sauce over the dish, garnish and serve.

Vinegar chicken The chicken is first fried, then briefly stewed. This dish illustrates many interesting cooking points:
1 The alcohol/acid content of the vinegar and wine is moderated by boiling.
2 The sauce is not thickened with flour, but by reduction, and by the addition of a purée of the flavoring garlic.
3 The color and flavor come largely from the initial browning.
4 Cream, contrary to myth, may be boiled without curdling.

The sauce is a typical "saute" sauce—well reduced and not too much of it.
1 Brown eight small pieces of chicken in butter, skin side first.
2 Add five *unpeeled* garlic cloves. Cover and cook slowly until the chicken is tender, then pour off the fat.
3 Add 8 tbs of wine vinegar. Boil rapidly to reduce to 3 tbs. The fumes flavor the chicken as they are driven off. Remove the chicken and keep warm.
4 Add 1¼ C white wine and 3 tbs brandy, 2 tsp pale French mustard and 2 tsp tomato purée to the pan, then boil to a thick sauce.
5 In a heavy pan, boil 1¼ C very fresh heavy cream until it is reduced by half, stirring constantly to prevent scorching.
6 Fit a wire sieve over the cream pan and press the vinegar sauce and garlic pulp through it.
7 Mix the sauce and finish with thin raw tomato shreds, chopped chervil and salt and pepper to taste. Pour over the chicken.

Pommes sautées (a dish using pre-cooked ingredients) Melt 2 tablespoons of butter in a heavy sauté pan or frying pan. Cut boiled potatoes into unevenly shaped pieces. Toss them over *gentle* heat until they are pale brown and crumbly on all sides (about 15 to 20 minutes). Do not cook too fast—the object is to obtain pale crustiness, not the even browning of French fries or the dark tougher texture of roast potatoes. Add the leaves from a sprig of rosemary for the last 3 minutes of frying.

Grated zucchini (a dish using raw ingredients) Grate unpeeled zucchini on a coarse cheese-grater or put through the julienne blade of a food processor. Toss and shake in melted butter over moderate heat for *35 seconds only*. Season with salt and pepper and serve promptly.

Stir-frying is much used in Chinese (wok) cooking. The aim is to cook food very quickly in hot oil *without* browning it, thereby preserving a fresh taste, crisp texture and most of its nutrients. To achieve this, the pan must be hot enough to evaporate any moisture leaking from the food while the food is tossed, turned and stirred vigorously to prevent any browning. Cut into fine strips, any tender cut of meat, fish, seafood and most vegetables stir-fry well. The oil used may first be flavored by stir-frying chopped scallions, ginger root or garlic. Sauces may also be made with the de-glazed pan juices.

SAUCE BOLOGNAISE for pasta and meat for shepherd's pie are made very similarly with ground meat—the only major difference being the amount of liquid added to the mixture. The extent of initial browning largely determines the eventual flavor.
1 Brown the ground beef, a small quantity at a time, in a few tablespoons of bacon fat or oil. Get the fat very hot, put in a shallow layer of meat and press it down to a flat compact cake. Do not turn it or stir it until the underside is dark brown. (Stirring allows too much uncooked meat surface to cool down the temperature of the fat. The meat will then fail to seal quickly enough, and the meat juices will run out of the meat and into the pan giving a mixture that is gray and stewed rather than brown and crisp.) Once the underside of the meat has been well browned, turn it over with a spatula to brown the other side.
If the pan becomes too dry or brown, deglaze with a little stock, water or wine, transfer the contents of the pan into a bowl and add more oil or fat to the pan to fry the next handful of meat.
2 When all the meat is browned, fry the vegetables more gently until just turning color.
3 Pour off all the fat.
4 Put the meat back in the pan if it is deep enough to hold it all easily. Otherwise transfer everything to a casserole or larger pan, again deglazing the pan.
5 Add the seasonings and enough flour (about a tablespoon) to absorb any fat and thicken the sauce. For unthickened mixtures, skim fat with paper towelling.
6 Simmer gently until tender (30 to 40 min).

Classic name	Main ingredients	Subsidiary ingredients	Liquid for sauce	Flavour with	Garnish with
Lamb kidneys turbigo	Lamb or veal kidneys in bacon fat	Tiny sausages and shallots browned in bacon fat	30% Madeira or sherry or reduced wine 70% stock	Tomato purée, a little garlic, a BOUQUET GARNI	Chopped parsley Sautéed mushrooms
Scallopini alla Veneziana	Thinly-sliced calves' liver in butter	Sliced onions fried until golden	30% Madeira 70% stock	Garlic Black pepper	None
Foie de veau à l'Anglaise	Thick, small slices calves' liver in butter	Grilled (broiled) or fried back bacon	None	Salt and black pepper	Pan juices or BEURRE NOISETTE
Chicken Marengo	Chicken pieces in oil	Button mushrooms and tomatoes sautéed in oil	Juice from canned tomatoes, or 70% stock 30% white wine	Garlic Tomato purée	Fried eggs and crayfish tails CROUTONS and parsley
Sauté de veau aux champignons	Veal scallops, chops or cutlets in butter	SWEATED white sliced mushrooms	Equal parts reduced white wine/veal stock	Cream, salt and pepper	Chopped chervil or parsley
Poulet sauté à la Normande	Chicken pieces in butter	Pieces of fried Delicious apple	80% chicken stock or apple juice 20% Calvados	Salt & pepper	None, but add cream to sauce and boil up well
Poulet sauté Maryland	Chicken pieces, egg-and-crumbed, in butter	None	None	Salt & pepper	Fried bananas or (sweet)corn fritters
Poulet sauté à l'Indienne	Chicken joints in oil CLARIFIED chicken fat or clarified butter	Sliced onion	Chicken stock	Crushed garlic Curry powder or turmeric Ground ginger Ground cayenne	Cooked shrimps Fried almonds Lighten with yogurt/cream
Chicken paprika	Chicken pieces inb butter	Sliced onion	50% canned tomatoes 20% white wine 30% stock	Paprika Lemon juice Crushed garlic	Sour cream
Tournedos chasseur	Beef fillet steaks	SWEATED shallots Sliced mushrooms	70% BROWN SAUCE or DEMI-GLACE 30% white wine	Salt and pepper	Fried CROÛTONS Chopped chervil
Lapin aux pruneaux	MARINATED rabbit in olive oil	Chopped shallot. Puréed, sautéed prunes	Reduced red wine	Crushed garlic Lemon juice BOUQUET GARNI	None

Deep-frying

Foods are subjected to high temperatures in the deep-fryer. For this reason they are usually given a protective coating; for example, a fried fillet of fish may have an egg-and-crumb coating. This prevents a hard, unattractive skin forming on the food while allowing the inside to cook comparatively slowly. If the deep-frying is properly done, the coating forms an effective seal which prevents the flavor of the cooking food from contaminating the fat, which may be used for frying fish and then later for, say, pineapple fritters. The coating also prevents dangerous spluttering and bubbling up of the hot fat which would be produced by the rapid evaporation of excess moisture in, and on, uncoated foods.

In addition, the coating becomes a leak-proof jacket to contain foods, such as cheese or apple, that become liquid on heating. The crisp texture of the batter or crumb crust also provides a pleasing contrast with the softer inside of the fried food.

Use batter to coat wet foods such as pineapple or apple slices. Shake slightly drier foods, such as chicken or fillets of fish, in flour to give a dry surface so that the coating will stick. Then dip them in egg, which will provide the protective seal, and finally in breadcrumbs to give a crisp and crunchy texture, as:

Sole Colbert Use dried breadcrumbs. They can be rubbed or crushed to a finer texture than fresh crumbs. Fresh crumbs also shrink as they fry, many of them coming off.

Sole Colbert *Skin sole. Holding knife flat against bone, cut top fillets, but do not sever at edges.*

2 Open out. (Once fried, snip backbone at both ends and ease out. Fill with MAÎTRE D'HÔTEL BUTTER.)

3 Shake in seasoned flour, making sure both the inner and outer flaps of the loose fillets are covered.

4 Brush all over with lightly-beaten egg before pressing on fine dried breadcrumbs.

5 Deep fry, holding sole between two spatulas to keep it flat and open.

Batter is a flour and liquid mixture, of a consistency runnier than a soft dough, used to give a crisp protective coating to food that might otherwise burn or splatter when deep or shallow fried and to make pancakes, waffles or scones (see pp 154/5) and cakes.

Since the advent of the food processor, batter-making has become much less of an effort. Put any eggs and other liquid ingredients into the machine, spoon the flour on top of them and turn on the motor for a second or two—just enough to blend them without creating too many bubbles.

Otherwise, this is the classic method of mixing a batter:

1 Sift the flour into a large wide bowl, the bigger the better. There should be no lumps in the flour or the batter will not have a smooth texture.

2 Sprinkle the salt (or sugar or other dry ingredients) on top of the flour.

3 With a wooden spoon or using the hand, make a "well" in the flour to expose the bottom of the bowl. The hole should be big enough to mix liquid ingredients (say 2 eggs and a few spoonfuls of milk) without bringing in too much of the surrounding flour.

4 Using a fork, whisk or a wooden spoon or (particularly for yeasted mixtures or mixtures requiring a little warmth to soften butter or other fat) the fingertips of one hand, mix and stir the central liquid ingredients to a smooth paste.

5 Gradually incorporate the surrounding flour. With practice the stirring action of the spoon, fork, whisk or fingers flips the

liquid over the banks of flour and, as it runs back into the central reservoir, it brings with it a thin film of flour, evenly with no lumps. Pour in more liquid as the batter gets thicker. The idea is to keep it at the consistency of thick cream—this is easier to keep lump-free than a runny mixture. Once all the flour is in and the mixture is absolutely smooth, beat in the remaining liquid.

6 Leave for 30 minutes (not strictly necessary, but resting the batter allows the starch cells to swell, giving a less doughy final product). If the mixture is left for more than an hour or so it might separate but it is easily re-mixed to the correct consistency. Do not make batter more than 12 hours in advance because the mixture might ferment.

Uncoated deep-frying

Some foods, such as potato chips, are in and out of the fat so quickly that they do not need any exterior coating. Other unprotected foods, such as French fries, are given a first frying at a low, non-burning temperature to cook them, then a second frying at a browning heat.

Using the deep-fryer

1 If the deep-fryer is not thermostatically controlled, use a thermometer, or test the temperature of the fat by dropping a cube of bread into it. If it browns in 60 seconds the fat is suitable for gentle frying, at a temperature of about 360°F; if it takes 40 seconds to brown the bread it is at 375°F, moderately hot; if it takes 20 seconds the fat is very hot, about 385°F. If the bread browns in 10 seconds the fat is dangerously hot and should be cooled down. Turn off the heat and fry several slices of bread in it to speed up the cooling.

2 Cook food in small amounts. Adding too many pieces at one time lowers the temperature of the fat so that the coating will not instantly form a crisp crust. The food then absorbs fat and loses its juices into the cooking fat.

3 Once cooked, drain the food well on paper towels.

4 If the food must wait before being served, spread it out in a single layer on a hot cookie sheet or baking dish, and keep warm and uncovered in the oven, with the door open to allow the free circulation of air. Covering or enclosing the food will make the crust soggy. Try not to deep-fry too far ahead of serving.

5 Add salt, or a sprinkling of superfine granulated sugar if the food is sweet, just before serving. This accentuates the flavor and the dry, crisp texture.

6 If cooking food from the frozen state (say, frozen fish in batter or crumbs) fry in comparatively cool fat (about 350°F) to allow the inside to thaw and cook before the coating browns.

7 After use, cool the fat and strain it through muslin. This removes food particles which, if left in the fat, will become black and burnt with repeated fryings. When the fat has become at all dark it should be changed, as it is beginning to break down and will smoke readily and impart a rancid flavor.

Deep-frying is usually a quick method of cooking unsophisticated dishes, but many gastronomic marvels emerge from the deep-fryer, and experimenting with exotic combinations can produce delicious results. Several techniques that may be adapted and elaborated on are listed below:

Choux beignets
(fritters made with CHOUX PASTE)
Beignets soufflés:
Make choux paste adding about 2 to 3 tablespoons of superfine granulated sugar to the mixture. Drop spoonfuls of the paste into the hot fat. The *beignets* are done when they are puffy, floating and golden. Drain well and toss in superfine granulated sugar. Serve hot. Make a sauce by liquefying cooked apricots, or by boiling smooth apricot jam with a little water or syrup.

Beignets au fromage:
Make cheese fritters using choux paste with grated cheese beaten into it (1 oz strong cheese to each 3-egg quantity of paste). Roll the cooked beignets in grated Parmesan and serve with thin tomato sauce.

Beurrecks are made by filling thinly-rolled strudel (filo) or puff pastry, or paper-thin pancakes, with a thick BÉCHAMEL SAUCE mixed with chopped cooked chicken, tiny cubes of cheese, diced ham or tongue. Once rolled up, the parcels must be sealed well with beaten egg, coated with egg and crumbs and deep-fried. Serve with thin TOMATO SAUCE.

Villeroy fritters are foods coated in a thick sauce (usually containing finely liquefied mushrooms) chilled until solid, then coated with egg and crumbs and deep-fried. The principal ingredient may be cooked chicken, sweetbreads, brains or whole poached mushrooms. Perhaps the most exciting is:

Oeufs à la Villeroi
Poach 1 egg per person, or boil them for exactly 4 minutes. Cool in cold running water and shell carefully. Make a fine mushroom DUXELLES and mix it with an equal amount of thick WHITE SAUCE or VELOUTÉ. Liquefy the mixture if it is not quite smooth. Season it well. Put a spoonful of thick sauce for each egg on a flat plate. Carefully lay the eggs on top and coat with more sauce. Chill well. Cut around the eggs, and press the now solid sauce gently to envelop each egg completely. Coat them with flour then egg and breadcrumbs and deep-fry in medium-hot fat until brown. Serve with thin tomato sauce. When cut, the yolk is still liquid and contrasts well with the crisp crust.

Croquettes are soft, flavorful mixtures made by mixing well-reduced thick *velouté* sauce (of a consistency that will set when chilled) with other, finely chopped ingredients—diced ham, chicken, cooked flaked fish, grated cheese. The mixture is chilled, then rolled into small cylinders, chilled again until firm, then coated with egg and breadcrumbs. It is important that the crumbs be dry and fine, and it is a good idea to give the croquettes two coatings of egg and crumbs to eliminate any chance of them bursting during cooking. The fat must be very hot to harden the crust before the interior softens. Croquettes may be served with a thin, light sauce, usually tomato or SOUBISE.

Cromesquis (or krameskis) are similar mixtures, but they are dipped in batter, rather than rolled in egg and crumbs, before frying.

Attereaux are small kebabs, dipped in fritter batter and deep-fried. They are usually served with a thin tomato sauce. The best of them are made from pieces of raw white fish or seafood. They may also be made of mushrooms and chicken pieces, or of cooked ingredients such as ham, tongue and sweetbreads, alternating on a skewer.

Deep-frying /2

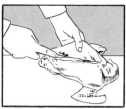

Chicken Kiev *Cut a slice down one side of the backbone.*

2 This allows the removal of the breast by cutting through the wing joint at the shoulder.

3 Cut off the pinion and scrape away the flesh, leaving a clean wing bone attached to the breast.

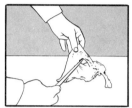

4 Skin the breast and lay it skinned side down. Remove a fleshy fillet from the middle of the breast.

5 Split the little fillet across horizontally without quite severing it. Open it out and tap to flatten it.

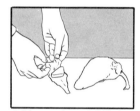

6 Place a piece of chilled MAÎTRE D'HÔTEL BUTTER *on the fillet and roll it up.*

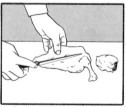

7 Split the breast across and open it out in the same way.

8 Beat it gently between two sheets of plastic wrap to flatten and enlarge it.

9 Lay the butter wrapped in the small fillet on it and roll the breast up and around that.

10 Press to close. Coat in plain egg and crumbs. Chill. Deep-fry for 8 minutes.

Chicken Kiev is a deep-fried chicken parcel which, when cut open by the diner, leaks melted butter. The butter may be seasoned with herbs and/or garlic. Chicken breasts may be prepared, as shown, in advance and refrigerated before frying. Fry them in medium-hot fat until brown and serve promptly.

Chinese sweet fritters: These exotic, crackly fritters need a cool head and some advance preparation. Coat chunks of dessert apple well in cornstarch by tossing them together in a bowl. Shake in a sieve to remove excess flour. Have ready a bowl containing ice-cubes floating in water. Set over the heat a wok or sauté pan containing a few tablespoons of sugar, an equal amount of water and a dash of lemon juice or vinegar. Dissolve the sugar and let it boil slowly to a caramel. Meanwhile deep-fry the apple chunks until brown. As soon as they are soft, drain them well on paper toweling and (using two forks) turn them carefully in the caramel. Lift each one out and drop into the water. The icy water will harden the caramel in seconds. Lift out immediately and serve. (Toasted sesame seeds may be added to the caramel to give extra flavor and texture.)

Ratatouille The ingredients of this classic vegetable dish are generally shallow fried, then stewed, but deep-frying greatly speeds up the cooking time.

Cut equal quantities of zucchini and eggplant into large chunks. Coarsely slice enough onions and green or red peppers to provide about one tenth of the volume of the first ingredients. Deep-fry everything together briefly in moderately hot, fresh, oil until barely brown and half-cooked. (Take care that the uncoated vegetables do not cause the fat to rise dangerously—lowering the basket carefully and removing it if the fat rises too quickly, repeating until the fat is sufficiently cooled to allow frying without rising.) Transfer the drained vegetables into a pan, season with crushed garlic, crushed coriander, salt and pepper, and a few tablespoons of olive oil. Add a few peeled, sliced tomatoes and stew, covered, until soft and pulpy (about 30 minutes). If still very liquid, boil the stewed mixture rapidly to reduce.

To coat foods for deep-frying with the minimum of mess put the coating (breadcrumbs, chopped nuts, beaten egg, and so on) in a deep box or plastic bag, add the pieces of food one or two at a time and shake or swivel gently so that the coating covers the food · Wear a shower cap, chef's hat or scarf around the head when deep-frying. It keeps the smell out of the hair.

Deep-fried pancakes

Use pancakes as pastry is used to make BEUR-RECKS. Put a spoonful of filling into the middle of a perfect pancake (with no holes) and fold into a small square parcel. Brush the whole parcel with egg, and roll in breadcrumbs, or dip in batter.

Deep-fry quickly until just brown. Drain and serve at once.

Make sure the filling is well chilled and, therefore, solid (but not frozen—with the exception of ice cream) before frying, that the parcel is properly sealed with egg or batter coating, and that the fat is sufficiently hot to brown a small bread cube in half a minute.

Sweet pancakes may be made similarly and dusted with superfine sugar before serving. Thin jam sauces or fruit purées are good with hot sweet fried pancakes.

Ice cream pancakes are particularly good. Wrap small blocks of ice-cream in the pancakes. Coat them well with egg or batter, then freeze them. Deep-fry briefly to brown the coating and serve at once.

Make breadcrumbs in a blender or food processor. If the bread is too moist, dry it out in the oven, then crush with a rolling pin · The easiest way to make bread-crumbs from bone-dry crusts is to grind them— they are too tough to break up easily in a blender or food processor · Crackers, cornflakes and most unsweetened breakfast cereals make good substitutes for dry breadcrumbs.

Pommes soufflées are slices of potato so fried that they inflate like little balloons.

Choose only perfect, medium-sized potatoes, peel thickly to an even cylinder. Cut into even slices, the thickness of a coin. Rinse to remove excess starch which might stick the slices together in the pan. Get two pans ready with hot deep clean frying oil. One must be at approximately 325°F and the other at 375°F.

Drop a few slices into the cooler fat and jiggle the pan gently to keep the potatoes on the move. Once the slices rise to the surface, fry, still shaking the pan, for a minute to give each slice an impermeable seal. Lift out of the pan and drain briefly, then put them straight into the hotter pan. Most will swell up as the steam trapped inside them expands. Fry to a crisp pale brown, lift out and drain on paper toweling. Sprinkle with salt and serve at once.

Ingredients	Coating	Method
Croquettes, fish cakes or cooked soft mixture. Raw chicken, and fish and seafood	Egg and breadcrumbs	Dry the food. Toss in flour, shaking off excess. Roll in beaten egg, then in crumbs.
Whole small fish such as whitebait or fresh sardines	Flour only	Dry the food. Toss in flour.
Fresh bread (for French toast)	Egg only	Dip in seasoned beaten egg and fry for snack or breakfast.
Cheese sandwiches		Make cheese sandwiches with filling in center only. Press slices together well. Dip in egg. Fry.
Pastry envelopes, stuffed pancakes		Fold soft filling (say, seafood in BÉCHAMEL sauce) in thin pastry envelopes, sealing edges with egg, and coating with egg.
Cubes of pork or chicken	Chinese batter (cornstarch mixed with egg white to a creamy consistency)	Roll first in dry cornstarch, then in batter. (Gives a puffy, light batter.)
Pineapple rings, raw apple slices, raw bananas	Sweet fritter batter Beat together: 2 egg yolks 1¼ cups flour ¼ cup sugar ⅔ cup milk ¼ tsp salt 2 tsp oil Then beat 2 egg whites and fold them in.	Dip the food in the batter.
Fish steaks or fillets, *goujons* of fish, cooked vegetables	Savory fritter batter	Mix together ingredients for sweet batter above, omitting sugar. Dip food in batter.

Sweating, braising and pot-roasting

Sweating, pot-roasting and braising are similar processes in which food is cooked slowly in a covered pan.

Sweating is the slow cooking of vegetables, frequently onions or shallots, in butter or oil over gentle heat until cooked through, softened and exuding their juices—but not colored.

It is normally used to prepare them for inclusion in stews, sauces or soups to which they are to impart a subtle flavoring but no coloring.

1 Chop or slice the vegetables finely. The finer they are cut, the quicker they will cook.

2 At the lowest of heats, melt enough butter to cover the bottom of a heavy saucepan.

3 Add the vegetables, stir once to get them well coated with the cool melted butter, and cover the pan.

4 Shake the pan occasionally to prevent sticking and burning. *Do not lift the lid to stir*, as this releases the steam, making the pan drier and the contents are then much more likely to fry than to sweat.

5 When the vegetables are soft but not browned, they are done. A finely chopped onion will sweat in 10 minutes. The cooked vegetables should be translucent.

Cover the contents of the pan with paper to trap the steam.

To make a soup on a base of sweated vegetables (like simple *Vichyssoise*)

1 Sweat the white bases of 2 chopped leeks and 2 small chopped onions in butter.

2 Add one diced, medium/large potato and continue to sweat for 30 minutes, or until the potato is half cooked and all the butter has been absorbed.

3 Add about 2 cups of chicken stock and bring to the boil.

4 Simmer gently until the potatoes are completely cooked.

5 Liquefy the soup in a blender, or push it through a sieve.

6 Add salt and pepper to taste.

7 Add about $\frac{2}{3}$ cup fresh light cream.

8 Reheat, or chill well if serving cold.

9 Serve sprinkled with chopped chives.

Note that the thickening for this soup comes from the PURÉED vegetables, and not, as is more usual, from the addition of flour to the sweated vegetables.

Some finished dishes are cooked by the sweating method only.

"Braised" red cabbage Shred enough red cabbage to feed 6 people generously (remembering the cabbage greatly reduces in volume during the cooking.) Melt 2 tbs of butter in a heavy-based saucepan and sweat a chopped onion in it.

Then add 2 tsp vinegar, 2 tsp brown sugar, 1 tbs golden raisins, 1 chopped cooking (or sharp eating) apple, salt, pepper and a pinch of ground cloves. Cover the pan tightly and sweat over a very low heat for 2 hours. Shake the pan frequently. Turn the mass with a wooden spoon every 20 minutes or so. If the cabbage is in danger of drying out at any stage, add a little water. Excess water can always be boiled off at the end. The cabbage is done when it is reduced to a dark, soft mass. Undercooked red cabbage may look appetizing but this less-glamorous well-braised cabbage has an infinitely better flavor. The final cooking of RATATOUILLE is analogous—the browner and more merged the colors and shapes of the vegetables, the less pretty they will look, but the tastier the dish will be.

Duxelles is a finely chopped mixture, always containing mushrooms, used as a base for stuffing, or as a flavoring for sauces. It is first sweated to cook the ingredients, then stirred over moderate heat to dry it off.

Put a tablespoon of oil, another of butter, and another of finely chopped shallot in a pan. Sweat for 10 minutes, then add 2 handfuls of finely chopped mushrooms or mushroom stalks, with a tablespoon of chopped parsley. Sweat for 5 minutes, or until soft and reduced. Remove the lid and stir over moderate heat until all the moisture has evaporated. This is now a dry *duxelles*, ready for use. It may be mixed with finely chopped ham, tongue, or SAUSAGE-MEAT, depending on its intended use (LAMB CUTLETS EN CROÛTE, REFORME SAUCE, VILLEROY EGGS and so on).

Braised food is sometimes simply sweated, as with the red cabbage, or stewed. ("Braised celery" consists of quarters of celery head stewed in a little stock in a covered pan in the oven; braised fennel is stewed in lemon juice, butter and a little stock.)

True braising is done on a bed of mixed diced vegetables (called a *mirepoix*) with added strong, reduced stock.

To achieve really good braising is perhaps one of the greatest challenges in cooking, and particularly so for the home cook. The essence of braised red meat is its tenderness and almost sticky juiciness obtained by constant basting with the reduced syrupy liquid.

It is a time-consuming process: The shinbones for the stock must be browned all over; the stock itself must be simmered and skimmed constantly for hours (a good restaurant chef would do it for 12 hours) and all this even before the actual braising begins.

Stages in braising meat

1 Fry the *mirepoix* of vegetables (and a few tablespoons of diced salt pork or bacon) slowly in oil and butter until browned all over.

2 Brown the meat and place it on top of the vegetable bed in a heavy casserole.

3 Add stock, made from gelatinous meats such as knuckle of veal or beef shinbones, to cover the meat. Then stew, without basting, until half cooked.

4 Lift out the meat, strain the stock, and discard the *mirepoix* (which has imparted all of its flavor).

5 Return the meat to the casserole, and reduce the stock by rapid boiling until it is thick and syrupy, and pour it over the meat.

6 There will not now be enough stock to cover the meat, and there is a danger, even in a covered pan, of the exposed top drying out, so turn the meat constantly and baste it with the liquid.

By the end of the cooking time, when the meat is tender, the stock should be so reduced as to provide a shiny coating that will not run off the meat. It will penetrate the flesh, moistening it and giving it that slightly glutinous texture of perfectly braised meat.

	Paupiettes de veau aux champignons	Jambonneaux de poulet (so called because the chicken legs look like miniature hams)
Main ingredient	Thin veal slices, battered out and stuffed with mixed veal FORCE-MEAT and *duxelles* and tied up with cotton thread (see page 80)	Boned chicken thighs, stuffed with minced chicken and sausage-meat seasoned with tarragon.
Mirepoix	Coarsely chopped carrot, onion, celery and bacon, sweated in butter	As for *paupiettes* with the addition of a few tarragon stalks
Stage 1	Brown the *paupiettes* lightly in butter. Lay on *mirepoix*. Add a few tablespoons stock.	Brown the thighs carefully in butter. Lay on the *mirepoix*. Add a few tablespoons of stock.
Stage 2	Braise slowly, turning the *paupiettes* once and making sure no steam escapes	Braise as the *paupiettes*
Stage 3	Remove the *paupiettes*. Discard the carrots. Liquefy the rest of the *mirepoix* and juices. Reduce by rapid boiling to a thick sauce. Add sweated button mushrooms and cream. Season to taste.	Remove the chicken. Press the vegetables and juices in a sieve to extract all the juice. Reduce by rapid boiling to a thick sauce. Season with more tarragon and salt and pepper.
Serve with	Sauce over the top and creamed potatoes, or noodles.	The strained vegetables beaten into mashed potato, and possibly formed into potato cakes and fried. Pour the sauce over the chicken *jambonneaux*.

Beef and veal paupiettes, or poultry cuts, are easier to braise and, for the home cook, more satisfying. They do not need the excessively rich stock, the braising vegetables are sweated rather than fried and they can be eaten, or liquefied for an accompanying sauce. Two examples are given above.

Sole paupiettes, made from flattened fillets filled with QUENELLE mixture may be cooked in the same way. Add some fish stock or white wine to an onion and mushroom *mirepoix*.

Pot-roasting is a simpler, quicker version of braising, which can be used for the more tender cuts of red meats. Sometimes no liquid is added to the pan other than the fat in which the meat is initially browned. This means, in effect, that the meat is roasted or baked in an enclosed pot. Try setting the meat on a rind of pork; it adds flavor and prevents the scorching of the meat on the bottom of the pan. Vegetables, cut larger than for the standard *mirepoix*, may also be used in this way and served to accompany the meat.

Large pieces of meat to be pot-roasted and braised benefit from MARINATING and, even more importantly, from LARDING.

Bard beef or veal paupiettes before braising by wrapping them in slices of fatty bacon · Make beef paupiettes really tasty as follows. Stop the braising process three-quarters of the way through and let the paupiettes cool in their juices. Dry them and coat with mustard mixed with a pinch of cayenne. Brush them with melted butter and roll them in breadcrumbs. Broil slowly until crisp and brown all over.

Boiling

Boiling is the perfect method of cooking ingredients such as green vegetables that must be cooked through rapidly before they change color. Boil them as rapidly as possible in an open pan. The water should be well salted (one heaped tablespoon for every 5 to 6 pints) as it then boils at a higher temperature and thus cooks the vegetables even more rapidly. Once cooked, "refresh" the vegetables by rinsing them briefly under cold water, then put them in a warm serving dish. "Refreshing" prevents further cooking by retained heat and "sets" the color. Vegetables which hold their color well, like peas or carrots, or small quantities of vegetables (say, French beans for four people) do not need refreshing, but it is vital for large quantities, especially if there is to be any delay before serving. DRIED BEANS are also cooked by boiling. As there is no color loss to worry about, and the process is a long one, they are simmered rather than fast boiled. They may even, with advantage, be stewed slowly in stock on the top of the stove or in the oven. If the proportion of liquid to beans is

right, they absorb all the liquid during cooking and there is nothing to throw away and thus little loss of taste and nutrition.

It is often recommended that dried beans be soaked in water before cooking, but this is not always necessary, especially if the beans are last season's crop. Beans known to be quite recently dried (bought from a shop with a rapid turnover) can be cooked without any prior soaking, but they will absorb more water and take longer to become tender.

Beans make excellent PURÉES. Serve them in place of the more usual accompaniments to meat, such as potatoes, noodles or rice. They are also good served whole, well-buttered, with herbs or fried onion mixed into them. Pressure-cooking works well for dried beans and eliminates the need for soaking. Pressure-cookers do vary, and it is obviously sensible to consult the manufacturer's instructions. As a general rule, 2 cups of dried peas or beans, unsoaked, will need $4\frac{1}{2}$ cups water, and cook in 30 minutes at 15 lbs pressure.

Cook rice and pasta noodles at a good rolling boil. The noodles or rice grains then won't stick to each other. Add a tablespoon of oil to the water, as this also prevents sticking. Long-grain rice, boiled in a large pan of water (salted as for vegetables) will take 10 or 11 minutes to cook. The grains, when crushed between finger and thumb, should mash to a paste, but a bit of "bite" is infinitely preferable to an over-soft texture. Similarly, noodles should always be AL DENTE. Remember that homemade pasta cooks four times as fast as dried commercial equivalents, and the cooking time depends on the thickness of the pieces of pasta. Dried VERMICELLI cooks in 2 or 3 minutes; LASAGNE takes 15 to 16 minutes.

Like dried beans, some vegetables can be boiled until all the liquid is either absorbed or has evaporated. For example, *Vichy carrots* are even-sized pieces of carrot put to boil in water that has been lightly salted and had a teaspoon of sugar and a tablespoon of butter added to it. Boil the carrots slowly so that

when all the water has evaporated they are just tender. Then glaze them in the remaining butter and sugar until brown. Shake the pan over the heat to prevent sticking. Be cautious with the salt—none will be drained off with the water in the usual way.

Boiling eggs There is considerable confusion about the correct method of boiling an egg. The easiest and most foolproof method is:
1 Holding the egg rounded end up, prick the top of the shell with a darning needle, egg pricker, or trussing needle. This allows the air trapped in the little pocket of membrane at the fat end of the egg to escape. It is this pocket of air which expands when heated and can crack the shell.
2 Bring a pan of water to the boil.
3 Lower the eggs into the water using a perforated spoon.
4 Time the cooking from that moment.
Three minutes will cook a medium-sized egg until the white is barely set—indeed the white closest to the yolk will still be runny;
Four minutes gives a runny yolk and a just-set white;
Five minutes gives well-set white and moist, but not runny, yolk (set on the rim and thick but wet inside);
Eight minutes gives a nicely hard-boiled egg;
Ten minutes will give a yolk sufficiently cooked to be dry and crumbly when mashed;
Just a few minutes more than 10 will give an egg with a yellow-green rim to the dry yolk and tough, unpalatable white.

Dried beans and cereals	Recommended pre-soaking time	Boiling time (approximate)
Lima beans	4 hours	30 minutes
Haricots blancs	2–3 hours	$1\frac{1}{2}$–2 hours
Butter beans	12 hours	2 hours
Chickpeas	Overnight	2–3 hours
Lentils	No soaking	20 minutes
Split peas	30 minutes	$1\frac{1}{2}$–2 hours
Brown beans	2–3 hours	2–3 hours
Red kidney beans	2–3 hours	2 hours
Buckwheat groats	No soaking	30 minutes
Hominy grits	12 hours	3 hours
Cracked wheat	12 hours	12 hours
Barley	No soaking	40 minutes
Coarse oats	No soaking	40 minutes
Rice	No soaking	10 minutes

Steaming

Steaming The terms "boiling" and "steaming" are often loosely used interchangeably and even to describe forms of simmering, poaching or stewing. True steaming—the cooking of food in steam—except for fat-free diets, is normally only used to cook vegetables. As the cooking medium is hot vapor and food is not immersed in liquid there is significantly less loss of nutrients.

Steamed potatoes Cut the potatoes to a uniform shape and size and place in the top half of a steamer with the water below set to boil vigorously. The advantage of this method, especially with floury potatoes, is that none of the starch is lost in the water and there is no violent agitation to break up the potatoes.

Couscous, the Arab dish of processed wheat (rather like coarse farina or semolina) may be steamed over stewing vegetables in this way. The cooked vegetables are served on a bed of couscous, and a spicy sauce made by mixing together:

3 tbs hot stock
1 tsp cumin
1 tsp ground coriander
$\frac{1}{2}$ tsp chili powder
3 tbs tomato purée

To improvise a vegetable steamer fit a sieve over a pan of boiling water so that the bottom of the sieve just clears the surface of the water.

Line the sieve with a piece of muslin, and cover with aluminum foil and a lid, to contain the steam.

Vegetables can be steamed in their own juice. Spinach, for example, may be put, wet from washing, into a covered pan and shaken over moderate heat for about 5 minutes. It will then be soft, bright green and much reduced. Press to extract excess moisture, add a tablespoon or 2 of butter and season.

Stand asparagus in a tall pan, or asparagus steamer: The stalks boil in the water until tender; the delicate tips steam.

Cook fish steaks in their own juices by putting them on a plate set on top of a pan of boiling water and covering them with another (upturned) plate or aluminum foil. Thin salmon steaks, for instance, cook in 8 to 10 minutes. Add butter and seasoning, if not cooking for a special diet. Use only the freshest of fish,

Put fish steaks between two plates over boiling water.

Steamers are more normally used to cook food in containers heated by the steam. The *English steamed pudding* comes into this category. Make the cake mixture, put it into a buttered pudding bowl, cover it —to seal the steam out— and cook in the steam. Once cooked, turn it out and eat it hot with a sweet sauce or custard. Most such mixtures can be baked in the oven in a buttered cake pan, but this will not give them the same soft open texture

which is the glory of the traditional steamed pudding. Suet puddings come in two guises— sweet and herbed.

In sweet puddings, such as Christmas pudding, the suet is mixed with everything else and the mixture is steamed for 6 to 10 hours, depending on its size. The mixture may also be boiled in a cloth to give the traditional cannonball shape. It is served with HARD SAUCE.

Herbed suet puddings are made with suet pastry, which lines the greased pudding bowl. This is filled with a meat mixture (steak, chopped onions, herbs and chopped kidney) moistened with stock and covered with more suet pastry and then steamed. The result is a soft but flaky crust, with a tender stew-like center.

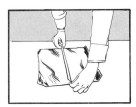

Steamed puddings
Butter aluminum foil, pleat.

2 Place foil, buttered side down, over bowl and tie around the rim.

3 Pleat allows for expansion. Strip of folded foil lifts bowl.

Basic steamed pudding
Cream $\frac{1}{2}$ C butter with equal amount of sugar. Add $4\frac{1}{2}$ tbs milk and 3 drops vanilla extract. Beat in 2 beaten eggs, little by little to prevent curdling, and fold in $1\frac{1}{2}$ C flour sifted with $1\frac{1}{2}$ level tsp baking powder.
Turn mixture into a greased pudding bowl and cover. Steam for about $1\frac{1}{2}$ hours. Top up the water in the steamer or saucepan every 20 minutes.

Variations		Serve with
Apricot sponge	Put tinned apricots and brown sugar at the bottom of the bowl	Warm golden syrup or maple syrup
Date pudding	Place halved dates around the buttered bowl before adding mixture.	Custard
Ginger pudding	Put $\frac{1}{2}$ tsp ginger into the mixture, and chopped preserved ginger, sugar and butter in the bottom of the bowl before adding the mixture.	Sauce made by heating ginger marmalade with a little water (or any clear marmalade plus 1 tsp powdered ginger)
Chocolate pudding	Replace 3 tbs flour with cocoa.	Chocolate sauce.

Cooking vegetables

	Preparation (Methods other than boiling or steaming are included)	Suggested method of cooking	Cooking time	Suggested garnish or seasoning
Artichoke, Jerusalem	Wash and peel.	Steam, sweat or boil.	30–40 min	Melted butter, black pepper and lemon juice.
Asparagus	Wash, remove hard ends and peel tough outer skin if necessary. Tie in bundles.	Steam or boil in unsalted water. Stems will cook slower than heads, so stand bundles upright with heads above water level, or lay flat and cook until middles are cooked and stalk ends are still tough.	10–15 min	Hollandaise sauce or melted butter (seasoned with salt, pepper and lemon juice) served separately.
Beans, runner	String. Wash. Cut into 2-in lengths.	Boil in salted water.	7–10 min	Melted butter, chopped fresh savory or thyme.
Beans, string	Wash, top and tail. String if necessary.	Boil in salted water.	8–12 min	Melted butter, sautéed almonds.
Beet, young	Wash but do not peel.	Boil in salted water. Then peel.	1–2 hrs	White sauce or melted butter with chopped raw onion or sour cream and chopped chives.
Black salsify	Wash, peel and cut into 2-in lengths.	Boil, steam or sweat.	15–20 min	BEURRE NOISETTE.
Broadbeans	Shell. (If very young they may be boiled whole.)	Boil in salted water. If tough, remove outer skins after cooking.	7–10 min	Melted butter and fried bacon bits, or white sauce, or sautéed chopped walnuts, or chopped fresh savory or thyme.
Broccoli	Wash. Remove tough leaves or stalks.	Boil in salted water.	8–15 min	Melted butter or hollandaise sauce.
Broccoli, sprouting	Wash. Remove hard stalks.	Boil in salted water.	6–10 min	Melted butter.
Brussels sprouts	Trim off outer tough leaves. Trim stalks. If large, make a deep cut in base.	Boil in salted water.	6–12 min	Melted butter, pinch of nutmeg or caraway seed.
Cabbage, Chinese	Wash. Slice coarsely.	Stir-fry, sweat or boil very briefly.	4–6 min	Melted butter, lemon juice. Black pepper.
Cabbage, red	Wash. Shred finely.	Stew gently in a covered heavy pan, with butter, chopped onions, chopped apples, golden raisins, salt, pepper, sugar and a little vinegar. Turn frequently.	2–3 hrs, or until very soft	
Cabbage, spring	Wash. Shred very finely.	Stir-fry or boil in salted water.	Stir-frying: 10 min Boiling: 5–7 min	Melted butter and caraway seed.
Carrots	Peel and slice or cut into sticks or peel and grate coarsely. Do not salt.	Boil in salted water with a pinch of sugar if in sticks or thick slices. Stir-fry in butter if grated or sliced paper-thin.	8–10 min 2 min	Melted butter and chopped mint. Salt, pepper, pinch of sugar or dried ginger.
Cauliflower	Wash. Break into florets. Remove large stalks.	Boil in salted water.	12 min	Browned butter (BEURRE NOISETTE) or white sauce.
Celery	Wash and cut in 2-in pieces.	Boil in salted water.	15–20 min	White sauce or chopped dill and melted butter.
Chicory	Wipe dry. Leave whole.	Steam, or bake covered in water with lemon, chopped tarragon and thyme.	Steaming: 20–30 min Baking: 1–1½ hrs	Steamed: White sauce. Baked: Melted butter, chopped parsley.
Curly kale	Wash. Remove tough stalks.	Put in covered pan with no water. Shake over moderate heat. Drain.	6–10 min	Melted butter, pinch of nutmeg and lemon juice.

	Preparation (Methods other than boiling or steaming are included)	Suggested method of cooking	Cooking time	Suggested garnish or seasoning
Leeks	Wash. Remove outer leaves and tough dark green part. Split if large.	Boil flat in salted water in roasting or frying pan. Lift out with a draining spoon.	10–15 min	Melted butter and black pepper or white sauce.
Mushrooms	Do not peel unless very tough. Wipe and trim off any ragged stalks. Quarter if large.	Sweat in butter with squeeze of lemon juice to prevent discoloration, Or broil, brushed with butter.	4–8 min	Melted butter, black pepper and lemon juice, or a little heavy cream or sour cream.
Onions	Peel.	Boil or bake. If baked, peel after cooking.	Boiling: 20–30 min Roasting: 1–2 hrs	Boiled: Toss in butter plus pinch of sugar until pale brown. Baked: Melted butter.
Parsnips	Peel, and cut up if large.	Boil in salted water. Or boil and mash. Or roast with butter.	Boiling: 20–30 min Roasting: 1–2 hrs	Melted butter, black pepper. Nothing if roasted.
Peas	Shell.	Boil in salted water with a good pinch of sugar and a sprig of mint.	5–20 mins	Melted butter. Chopped mint.
Potatoes	Peel for steamed or boiled (except new). Scrub and rub with salt for baked. Blanch 5 min then scratch with fork for roast.	Steam, boil, sweat, bake, roast or deep fry.	Roast: 1–1½ hrs Other methods: Up to 30 min	Melted butter and chopped parsley or mint or dill for boiled and steamed
Pumpkin	Wash and peel. Cut into 2-in chunks.	Roast with butter and lemon juice. Steam or sweat in butter.	Roasting: 1–2 hrs Steaming, sweating: 30 min	Nothing if roasted. Melted butter and chopped parsley.
Rutabaga and turnips	Peel thickly. Slice.	Sweat or steam. Mash. If very wet, shake over heat to dry.	20–30 min	Whole: Melted butter and/ or chopped parsley. Mashed: Plenty of butter, salt and pepper.
Salsify	Wash and cut into 2-in lengths.	Boil. Peel after cooking.	15–20 min	BEURRE NOISETTE.
Sea kale	Wash and remove any tough stem.	Boil in salted water or steam.	10–20 min	Hollandaise sauce, or melted butter (with salt, pepper and lemon juice).
Shallots	Peel.	Boil in salted water. Steam, sweat or roast with butter.	8–20 min; more for roasting	Steamed: White sauce. Boiled: BEURRE NOISETTE.
Snow peas	Wash, top and tail.	Stir-fry, sweat, or boil.	4–6 min	Melted butter only. None if stir-fried.
Spinach	Wash well. Pull away stalks.	Put into covered pan without any water. Shake over moderate heat. Drain and squeeze dry.	4 min	Melted butter, grated nutmeg or crushed fried garlic.
Squash	Wash and peel if tough-skinned. Cut into 2-in chunks.	Baked covered in moderate oven brushed with melted butter, or steam.	Baking: 30 min Steaming: 10–20 min	Browned butter (BEURRE NOISETTE) and chopped parsley or white sauce.
Sweet corn	Remove outside leaves and thread-like fibers.	Boil in salted water, or steam.	5–6 min Steam: 15 min	Melted butter and freshly ground black pepper.
Zucchini	Peel strips of the skin lengthwise, leaving half; or grate coarsely, including skin. Do not salt.	Boil in salted water, or sweat in butter. Stir-fry in butter.	Boiling: 4–6 min Sweating: 5–10 min 35 secs	Melted butter or BÉCHAMEL SAUCE. Salt and pepper.

Poaching

Poaching Is long, slow, gentle cooking in barely simmering liquid either in the oven or on the stove. There is a skill acquired only by considerable experience, in telling when a large whole item is cooked. A fish, when cooked, will feel firm to the touch and the skin will peel off easily. A ham or large piece of bacon is cooked when the meat has shrunk back from the bone, or if boneless, when the whole thing has visibly shrunk in size by about one-fifth. The rind, or skin, will peel off easily. Until sufficiently experienced, stick rigidly to times in recipes.

Hams and thick pieces of bacon If a piece of the uncooked flesh tastes excessively salty, first soak overnight in cold water to bring out some of the salt. Then put it in a deep pot and cover it with boiling water. Add a celery stick, half an onion, a couple of carrots, two bay leaves, a dozen peppercorns and a dash of vinegar. *Do not salt.* Simmer or poach gently for at least 25 minutes for each pound in weight.

Poached meat dishes "Boiled" tongue and beef are cooked in the same way as the ham described above. A piece of rolled, boned beef weighing 6 lbs, cooked overnight in the bottom oven of an old-fashioned solid fuel stove will, however, be more tender and juicy than one simmered for 4 hours.

If the meat is to be cooled rapidly, stand it in a pan of cold water in the sink. Arrange that cold water can flow steadily into the pan while some drains away.

Whole chickens First make the stock with the neck, giblets and some onions. Stock takes at least an hour to develop much flavor. If the stock ingredients were simply put into the water with the chicken, by the time the chicken was cooked the stock might be fairly tasty, but the chicken would have lost more flavor to the stock than it might otherwise have gained.

Poach the chickens, untrussed, almost completely submerged in the stock until a skewer will glide easily into the thigh, and the drumstick, when lifted, will wobble independently from the body. If the drumstick feels stiff, and lifts the whole chicken with it, the bird is not cooked.

The advantage of poaching untrussed chicken is that the legs, not being held against the body, cook almost as quickly as the breast and there is less danger of overcooking the white meat while waiting for the dark meat to cook.

Poached eggs *Boil 1½ in water in a shallow pan. Slip eggs in one by one.*

3 *Use a perforated spoon to lift the eggs out of the water when they are just milky-looking, with set whites.*

Whole fish Let a COURT BOUILLON cool. Put the cleaned fish into a suitable fish steamer with the head and tail just clear of the ends. Cover with cold *court bouillon*, then bring slowly to the summering point. If the fish is to be served cold, turn the heat off immediately and put the cover on the steamer. Once cold, lift it out, skin it and serve. This treatment works for any size fish as, the larger it is, the greater the volume of liquid around it will be; therefore, the longer it will take for that water to heat and to cool and hence the longer the cooking time, If the fish is to be seved hot, bring to the boil as above, then poach (with the liquid barely moving) for 4 minutes for each pound in weight. Remove it from the liquid, and serve. (Starting with a cold *court bouillon* does produce moister flesh, but if this is not practicable, put the fish into hot *court bouillon* and allow 6 minutes to the pound, then remove at once.)

2 *Keep just simmering. Draw spoon across surface to keep eggs apart.*

4 *Drain them on paper toweling. Trim off any untidy edges.*

Poaching seafood So-called "boiled" lobsters, crabs, and so on, should, in fact, be poached. Large crabs and lobsters are sold alive. Plunge them, head first, into fast-boiling water or *court bouillon*, then poach gently for 18 to 25 minutes, depending on their size.

If the lobsters or crabs are to be served cold, the flesh will be juicier if the liquid is cold when the animals are put into it. Boil the *court bouillon* and let it cool again before the creatures are put into it. The liquid then contains no oxygen and anaesthetizes the creatures. Leave them in the deoxygenated liquid for 30 minutes, by which time they have died painlessly, then cook them.

Put shrimp, prawns, crayfish, scallops, clams and mussels into cold *court bouillon* and bring them gently to simmering point, by which time they will be cooked.

Seafood must not be over-cooked, otherwise the flesh becomes rubbery and tough. If the seafood is not to be used at once, stand the pot in a pan of cold water to cool it rapidly, leaving the seafood in the cooking liquid to keep it moist.

Cook large squid longer; stew them gently for up to 2 hours. Poach octopus slowly for a similar period.

Clams and mussels may also be cooked in their shells in a minimum of stock, or wine or *court bouillon* (plus seasonings such as parsley, dill or onion).

Add a glass of wine to the cooking liquid and sprinkle with chopped parsley to create the classic French dish, *moules à la marinière.*

Stewing

Stewing is best explained by giving an example, as below:

Family beef stew
1 Well brown cubes of gristle-free stewing beef in fat. Lift them into a casserole or pan. DE-GLAZE the pan with stock, as necessary.
2 Brown small, peeled onions, carrots and turnips and add to the meat.
3 Half cover with good stock, add a BOUQUET GARNI, salt and pepper, and a tablespoon of pearl barley for each pint of stock, to thicken the liquid. BEURRE MANIÉ may be used instead to thicken after cooking, as may flour (1½ tbs per pint of liquid) added after frying the vegetables.
4 Stew until the meat is tender (2 to 3 hours), stirring once or twice to be sure of even cooking.
5 Sklm off the fat, or remove with paper towels.

Stewing fruit
1 Make a SYRUP flavored with orange rind, lemon rind, cinnamon sticks or cloves.
2 Put fruit in a shallow baking dish. Pour hot syrup over it and cover.
3 Stew in the oven until tender (or very gently in a pan on the stove).

Classic stews	Main ingredient	Secondary ingredients	Liquid	Seasoning	Remarks
Carbonnade	Stewing beef in thin slices or cubes	Sliced onions	Beer and stock in equal proportions	BOUQUET GARNI, brown sugar, salt and pepper	Has slightly sweet taste from pinch or two of brown sugar
Boeuf à la bourguignonne	As above	Button mushrooms, fried bacon, salt pork, pearl onions	Red wine and stock in equal proportions	BOUQUET GARNI, crushed garlic, salt and pepper	Browning is very important, and is good reduction of the sauce
Veal goulash	Stewing veal	Sliced onions. seeded, skinned tomatoes, potatoes (optional)	Water and stock cube or veal stock and 20 per cent white wine	Tomato purée, garlic, plenty of paprika, lemon, salt and pepper	Veal and onion only lightly browned in butter
Veal *blanquette*	As above	Sliced onions, mushrooms or carrots (optional)	Water and stock cube or veal stock Cream and egg-yolk LIAISON	Garlic (optional), lemon, salt, pepper, BOUQUET GARNI	Veal and onion are not browned, just simmered in stock
Lancashire hot-pot	Stewing lamb	Sliced onions, sliced potatoes	Lamb or veal stock, or stock cube and water	Thyme, salt and pepper	Onions, lamb and potatoes (not browned) packed in layers in casserole. Stock added.
Navarin de mouton	Mutton or stewing lamb	Small potatoes, pearl onions	Veal or lamb stock, or stock cube and water	Sugar, garlic, tomato purée, salt and pepper	The potatoes are not browned. A teaspoon of sugar is CARAMELIZED in the frying fat to give color and flavor.
English-style curry	Shoulder of lamb in cubes	Chopped onion	Lamb or veal stock, or stock cube and water	Plum or apricot jam to sweeten sauce, coconut milk, CURRY PASTE, golden raisins, salt and pepper	Serve with plain boiled rice, POPPADUMS, CHUTNEYS and RELISHES. Thicken sauce with BEURRE MANIÉ if necessary.

Baking

Baking is a most satisfying method of cooking. There is no messy splattering of fat, the foods need little attention once in the oven, and cheaper cuts of meat and fish may be baked to great effect.

Baked chicken Fry some chicken pieces lightly in butter. Line the bottom of a heavy casserole with a layer of sliced potatoes, add a layer of sliced onions, then put in a few of the chicken pieces. Cover these with more potatoes, more onions and so on, finishing with a top layer of potatoes. Pour in stock to come half-way up the pot and add the butter in which the chicken was fried, plus, perhaps, another tablespoon of butter. Bake in a slow oven for $2\frac{1}{2}$ hours, or until tender. From time to time check to be sure that all the stock has not evaporated, and add more if necessary. By the end of cooking there should be not more than a cup or so of stock. Serve from the pot.

Baking fish in milk or wine
1 Grease a small ovenproof dish. Lay fish fillets or steaks in it.
2 Add enough milk or wine or fish stock (or a mixture of wine and fish stock or fish stock and milk—but not wine and milk, which curdles) almost to cover the fish.
3 Scatter seasonings—such as salt, pepper, bay leaf, sliced onion, tarragon, parsley, fennel or dill—over the dish.
4 Cover with foil or a lid and bake in a moderate oven until the fish feels firm to the touch—about 25 minutes for medium-sized pieces.

5 Lift them out, and skin them if necessary.
6 Reduce and thicken the liquid to make a sauce, and finish with cream, tarragon, lemon, or even cheese, cooked sliced mushrooms, or shrimps, or scallops.

Small whole fish may be baked similarly in melted butter and lemon juice with no covering. The effect is half that of roasting, giving a crisp top skin and moist flesh. The oven must be hot. Serve the fish with lemon halves and the juices from the pan. ROASTING UNDER MUSLIN is excellent for whole salmon.

Fish pie Cook white fish in seasoned milk as described above, and make a creamy sauce (VELOUTÉ) with the cooking liquid. Flake the cooked fish and mix with chopped parsley and sliced hard-boiled eggs (and any cooked seafood or cooked mushrooms). Put into a pie dish, top with a layer of mashed potatoes, and scatter dried breadcrumbs and melted butter or grated cheese on top. Reheat, and brown the top under the broiler.

Baked potatoes Potatoes for baking are pricked all over (to prevent bursting as the inside expands when heated) and put in a moderate-to-hot oven until tender. A medium-sized potato takes an hour to cook. Cooking may be speeded up by putting a metal skewer through the potato to conduct the heat more rapidly to the middle. For a soft shiny skin, oil the potato and wrap in foil before cooking. For a crisp dry skin, wet the potato and rub it in salt. For a crisp, but not too hard, shiny skin, oil and salt the potato but cook it unwrapped.

To make a good light lunch, served with a salad, split baked potatoes in half, scoop out the flesh and mix it with other ingredients; then pile this back into the potato.

Possible potato fillings:
1 Mix the mashed flesh with cubes of cooked chicken and Gruyère cheese. Put the stuffed potatoes back in the oven to brown the tops and melt the cheese.
2 Mix the mashed flesh with chopped chives and sour cream, pile back and top with slices of cooked bacon, or sliced fried kidneys.

Carrots and other root vegetables, or a mixture, may be cut to equal-sized, small sticks or cubes, and baked in buttered foil parcels with some appropriate seasoning—a sprinkling of sugar and ginger for carrots, caraway seeds for turnips, or sugar and lemon juice for parsnips. Cook for at least an hour in a moderate oven.

Baked mashed potatoes Mashed potatoes are good baked. Make *pommes duchesse* by mixing mashed potatoes with egg yolks and very little butter, season well and pipe into whorls on a greased baking sheet, then brush with beaten egg and bake until brown. Do not make the mashed potatoes too buttery or the mix will melt into unattractive patties before it has a chance to bake. *Pommes dauphinoise* are sliced, well-seasoned potatoes in layers in an ovenproof dish with plenty of butter and hints of garlic and nutmeg. Cream, or a mixture of milk and egg (1 beaten egg to each $1\frac{1}{4}$ cups), is then added to come half-way up the dish, and a GRATINÉE top of grated Gruyère cheese and dried crumbs scattered over it. A four-portion dish takes about 50 to 60 minutes in a slow oven for the potatoes to soften fully and for the top to brown. This dish is not to be confused with *pommes dauphines*, which are a mixture of $\frac{1}{3}$ choux paste (p148) and $\frac{2}{3}$ *duchesse* potatoes, formed into balls and then deep-fried.

Baked cabbage Shred a cabbage, turn it in oil to grease it thoroughly, then mix with salt, pepper, lemon juice, crushed garlic and a few juniper berries. Bake, covered, in a slow oven until translucent and much reduced.

Stuffed baked cabbage BLANCH cabbage leaves till pliable, wrap them around a flavorful FARCE filling, pack tightly in an ovenproof dish and bake in a little stock, butter or tomato sauce.

The perfect soufflé is infinitely easier to achieve than kitchen myth would have one believe, and impressive to serve. Because hot air expands and rises, any baked mixture which contains beaten egg whites (which hold trapped air) must rise. So, providing the egg whites are properly beaten (see p168) and the base or *panade* (usually containing flour, egg yolks and flavoring) is of a consistency that can easily be folded together with the egg whites, it is hard to fail with a soufflé.

Stages in soufflé making

I Make the base—this is usually a *panade* (thick white sauce) into which the yolks and flavoring (such as grated cheese, purée of leeks or cauliflower or flaked fish) is beaten. The addition of the yolks and other ingredients should only soften the base to the consistency of gently-whipped cream or a medium-thick purée of fruit.

Sometimes sweet soufflé bases are made with *crème pâtissière*, using the yolks to make the CUSTARD and adding only the flavoring—melted chocolate, orange juice and grated rind, or fruit purée.

The base must be well seasoned as there is *no* flavor in egg whites and they are going to provide half the volume of the finished soufflé.

2 Get the oven hot and put in it a baking sheet on which the soufflé will eventually be placed. This will give an initial burst of heat to the bottom of the soufflé and help it rise evenly.

3 Coat the inside of the soufflé dish with melted butter (so that the rising mixture can glide easily up the sides). The soufflé will rise above the dish anyway, but if a paper collar is tied around the dish the soufflé will have straight sides (uncollared ones have a crown of risen mixture in the middle).

4 Reheat the soufflé base, but do not let it get *near* boiling point.

5 Beat the whites to MEDIUM PEAK—preferably in a COPPER BOWL.

6 Soften the base first by mixing in 2 or 3 spoonfuls of egg white, then fold in the rest. Fold with a gentle cutting action. Over-vigorous folding can knock out some of the air painstakingly beaten into the egg whites. There should still be visible flecks of egg white in the finished mix.

7 Pour into the dish and smooth over the top. Give dish and mix a sharp bang on a counter top to dislodge any large pockets of air trapped in the mix.

8 Bake in an oven preheated to the temperatures recommended below without opening the door for at least the first three-quarters of the cooking time.

9 Test for doneness by giving the soufflé a sharp shove. If it wobbles easily, it is liquid in the middle; if rock-steady, it is dry in the middle. A slight tremble, indicating a nearly-set center, is best.

2 *Tie waxpaper around dish to project I in above the rim. Coat all of inside with butter.*

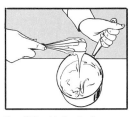
Soufflés *Make the base to a soft, just-liquid, consistency.*

3 *Beat egg whites to soft peak. Aim for a texture as near as possible to that of the base.*

4 *Fold whites into base with a lifting and turning (not stirring) action. Pour into dish.*

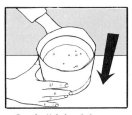
5 *Crack dish hard down on table to dispel uneven air pockets.*

Base	Egg yolks	Flavoring	Egg whites	Temperature and time
Savoury cheese soufflé				
Panade 1¼ cups milk ½ cup flour ¼ cup butter	4	Grated Gruyère cheese or strong Cheddar I tsp mustard	4	400°F 25–30 minutes
Hot chocolate soufflé				
Crème pâtissière ¼ cup cornstarch ½ cup flour 4 egg yolks 4 tbs sugar 1¼ cups milk	Already in the *crème pâtissière*	Beat ¼ cup butter and ¼ cup grated chocolate into the hot *crème*	4 beaten with 4 tsp superfine sugar	350°F 40 minutes

Baking /2

Lamb cutlets en croûte
Roll puff pastry thinly and cut into 6-in squares. Halve these into triangles.

2 *Spoon mushroom* DUXELLES *on each. Brown cutlets quickly without cooking through. Trim fat.*

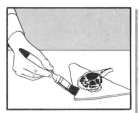

3 *Place the cutlet on top of the stuffing as shown. Brush the edge of the pastry triangle with egg.*

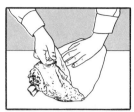

Glazed ham *Boil ham and ease off its skin while it is still warm. Leave the fat on it.*

4 *Fold the edges over to wrap up the cutlet, leaving the bone protruding. Press the edges to seal all around.*

5 *Decorate with thin pastry leaves or lattice and coat with egg.*

6 *Bake in a hot oven until brown, and serve at once.*

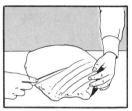

2 *Cut into the layer of fat to produce a lattice pattern.*

Pain de poisson *Make a* QUENELLE *mixture with ¾ lb fish, 3 eggs, 4 tbs bread-crumbs and seasonings.*

2 *Line a buttered loaf pan with a pig's caul, easing it into the corners.*

3 *Leave excess hanging over sides. (If unable to obtain caul, use rindless fatty bacon.)*

3 *Spread all over with mustard and stud with small whole cloves at each of the intersection points.*

4 *Put a layer of thin fillets of salmon or sole on the bottom of the pan. Coat with beaten egg white.*

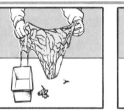

5 *Cover with a layer of the* QUENELLE *mixture. Coat with egg white. Fill with alternating layers.*

6 *Bring caul up over top. Brush with butter. Wrap dish in aluminum foil. Bake* AU BAIN MARIE *until firm.*

4 *Press brown sugar on to the mustard. Bake in a hot oven until the sugar darkens. Allow to cool.*

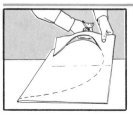

Papillotes *Fold a large piece of parchment paper in two and cut as shown.*

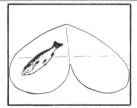

2 *Open out. Brush with oil. Lay small whole fish, or fillets, on one side.*

3 *Add lemon juice, season-ings and butter. Close. Fold edge tightly all round.*

4 *Brush with oil. Bake on an oiled baking sheet in a hot oven for 20 minutes.*

Lard leaves Thin slices of pork back fat make the best lining for pans when making PÂTÉS and TERRINES. *Cut the fat in thin slices and line a loaf pan, allowing the fat to hang generously over the side.*

Fill the pan with the pâté or terrine mixture and fold the excess fat over the top.

Cover the whole thing with aluminum foil and bake AU BAIN MARIE.

Custards are usually baked *au bain-marie* as the surrounding water bath will prevent the delicate mixture overcooking at the sides before the middle is set. The tell-tale signs of overcooked baked custards are small holes appearing in the mixture, a curdled texture and, eventually, the leaking of liquid as the mixture separates. To get the smoothest of consistencies, mix the eggs and other liquids *lightly* to avoid frothing. (First, heat the milk, with the sugar, almost to boiling point, then cool slightly.) Strain to remove any egg "threads."

Charlotte Brush CHARLOTTE MOLD *with butter. Line with slices of bread dipped in melted butter.*

2 Pour reduced thick apple PURÉE *into the center to the level of the top of the lining of bread.*

3 Cover with more buttered bread. Bake in moderate oven.

4 Bake until top is brown. Cool. Turn out carefully.

Baked custards	Basic ingredients	Secondary ingredients	Method	Temperature & time
Family baked custard	4 eggs + 2 yolks 2½ cups milk 3 to 4½ tbs sugar	Nutmeg Vanilla extract	Mix everything together and pour into a pie dish	Low oven 40–50 minutes. Bake *au bain marie*.
Bread and butter pudding	2 eggs + 1 yolk 1¼ cups half-and-half	3 small crustless slices of buttered bread 1½ tbs sugar 3 tbs currants 2 drops vanilla extract Pinch ground cinnamon	Arrange bread in shallow layers. Sprinkle sugar and fruit over each. Mix milk, eggs, currants and seasonings together. Pour over the bread and fruit.	Moderate oven for 45 minutes. Bake *au bain marie*.
Molded vanilla custard	4 eggs + 2 yolks 2½ cups milk 3 to 4½ tbs sugar	2 drops vanilla extract	Mix everything together well. Strain through fine muslin into a buttered charlotte mold. When cold, turn out.	Moderate oven for 45 minutes. Bake *au bain marie*.
Crème caramel	4 eggs 2½ cups milk 3 to 4½ tbs sugar	CARAMEL to coat mold for pie dish 2 drops vanilla extract	Coat mold or warmed dish with liquid caramel. Strain in the custard. When cold, turn out into dish with good lip (to hold the liquid caramel).	Moderate oven for 45 minutes. Bake *au bain marie*.
Crème brûlée	8 egg yolks 2½ cups heavy cream 3 tbs superfine granulated sugar	¼ tsp vanilla extract Superfine sugar for BRÛLÉE top	Make CRÈME ANGLAISE, then strain into shallow dish. Bake 8 minutes. Chill overnight without breaking skin. Give BRÛLÉE top.	Bake in moderate oven for 8 minutes only—to get a good skin on top.

Stocks and sauces

Stock

The secret of good stock is long, slow, gentle simmering, *not boiling*, and careful skimming. If stock is allowed to boil furiously, some of the fat will break down and form a stable emulsion. The liquid will then not be clear, and, even if subsequently skimmed, it will have a greasy flavor.

Fish stock is not given prolonged simmering. If fish is cooked for longer than about 30 minutes, the bones soften and impart a bitter taste to both flesh and liquid.

If keeping stock going for weeks:
a) Strain it every day, discarding the solid ingredients;
b) bring it to the boil each day to prevent fermentation;
c) skim carefully and often;
d) as new ingredients are added, keep the stock simmering to draw out their flavor. Adding fresh ingredients to luke-warm stock, left unheated, turns it sour.

The adding of potatoes clouds stock, and strongly flavored root vegetables imparts an overpowering flavor.

Trim fat or fatty skin from meat or bones before using for stock.

To store stock, simmer it down to a syrupy consistency. Keep frozen or refrigerated, to be let down with water again when needed. Brown stock so treated is called *glace de viande* ("meat glaze"); fish stock, *glace de poisson.*

Jellied stocks keep longer, so if stock is to be kept without frequent boiling, make sure that it will set by adding pigs' feet, veal bones, or any other natural source of gelatin (most poultry, veal or pork stock will set naturally if reduced sufficiently).

The best stock comes from raw bones, which retain all their flavor.

Brown stock	White stock
Coarsely chopped onion, turnip, carrot, celery Beef dripping Brown onion skins Parsley stalks Bay leaves Thyme Garlic clove Peppercorns Beef or veal knuckle Bones and perhaps pieces of raw beef Bacon, green or smoked Brown the vegetables *very slowly* in the fat, turning often to be sure of even color and no burning. Brown the meat similarly. (Bones are more easily browned in the oven.) Put everything in a large pan and simmer gently for up to 12 hours, skimming frequently and keeping the liquid level topped up over the bones. Strain, and remove fat. If required, boil down to concentrate.	Coarsely chopped onion, carrot, celery Chicken or veal bones, skin or flesh Parsley Thyme Bay leaves Green leaves of leek Peppercorns Simmer all ingredients in water, skimming frequently and topping up for 3 hours. Strain, remove fat and reduce, if necessary, by boiling.
Game stock Proceed as for brown stock, replacing beef or veal with game flesh from old birds, or carcasses. **Mutton stock and pork jelly** Mutton stock is a base for Scotch broth, and pork jelly is used to fill a raised pork pie. Proceed as for brown stock, using mutton or pork.	**Fish stock** Fish bones, heads, skins Chopped onions, mushrooms, carrots Parsley Lemon juice White wine (optional) Peppercorns Thyme Submerge solids in water. Add 20% white wine with the lemon juice. Simmer for 20 minutes if the bones are small, 30 if large. Strain, skim and reduce if necessary. **Court bouillon** Water, with carrot, onion, celery, bay leaf, peppercorns and salt, with 25% white wine or vinegar. The liquid is simmered for 20 minutes, cooled, and then used for the poaching of fish or seafood. It may then be reduced and used in place of stock.

Vegetable stock
This may be brown or white, and is used in vegetarian cookery. Follow the brown stock instructions, omitting the meat and bone ingredients and the skimming. Add water from the boiling of other vegetables.

Good-quality stock cubes and bouillon mixes, often adequate substitutes for the real thing, can be used to strengthen a weak homemade stock. Add them at the end of cooking.

Sauces
Simple combination sauces

The ingredients are mixed together, as in bread sauce; puréed (apple sauce) or strained (Cumberland sauce).

Sauces thickened with flour

Brown, white, blond and butter sauces, and related "daughter" sauces belong to this group. To make such a sauce:
1 Sweat or fry any flavoring vegetable in fat, or if using no such flavoring starter, then simply warm some fat.
2 Add the flour and cook to make a roux (see overleaf).
3 Slowly add the liquid, whisking or stirring all the time until mixture boils. (If liquid is hot it is essential to remove the pan *from* the heat and add liquid slowly to prevent roux from cooking into lumps.
4 Once the sauce boils, stop stirring, turn down to simmer and cook for at least 2 minutes to eliminate the floury taste of the roux, longer to reduce the harshness of wine or obtain a thicker consistency. This reduction will also give the sauce, particularly any brown sauce, an attractive semi-clear shine. For a really professional gloss, push the sauce through a fine-meshed conical strainer or liquefy in a blender, then strain through muslin.
5 Beat in any butter, cream or garnish. If adding butter, do this gradually, in tiny pieces, beating between addition. The melting butter will form an emulsion (see below) with the thickened sauce. Butter added all at once may just float obstinately.

The emulsion

A liquid containing tiny drops of oil or fat distributed through it in a stable suspension is an emulsion. If mixed correctly, it is possible to get a large quantity of fat (oil in mayonnaise, butter in hollandaise) held in emulsion by a comparatively small amount of thick mixture, usually egg yolks.

Even French dressing can be beaten into a temporary creamy emulsion by mixing mustard, garlic or puréed onion to a paste and adding oil as for mayonnaise, finishing with the vinegar.

Mayonnaise

2 egg yolks
1 cup olive oil (or olive oil and salad oil)
1½ tbs tarragon or wine vinegar
Squeeze of lemon
1 tsp Dijon mustard
Salt and pepper

Beat the egg yolks and mustard well with a whisk or wooden spoon. Add the oil drop by drop, beating all the time. The mixture should be very thick by the time half the oil is added. Beat in the lemon juice. Resume adding in the oil, more rapidly now, but alternating the dribbles of oil with small quantities of vinegar. (If the mixture curdles, beat another egg yolk in a separate bowl and beat the curdled mixture into that drop by drop—it will then re-emulsify.) Add salt and pepper to taste.

Mayonnaise made in a blender

Put all the ingredients except the oil in the goblet. With the machine running, add the oil in a thin, steady stream. Use whole eggs for a lighter, white mayonnaise.

Hollandaise

4½ tbs wine vinegar
6 peppercorns
½ bay leaf
2 egg yolks
½ cup butter
Lemon juice (optional)
Salt

Boil the vinegar, peppercorns and bay leaf rapidly until reduced to about a tablespoon. Strain into a small bowl or the top of a double boiler. If using a bowl, fit it over a pan of simmering water so that it does not quite touch the water. Alternatively, fill a roasting pan with water, putting one end of it over direct heat so that the water bubbles, standing the bowl in the other end which is not receiving any direct heat (as shown above). Add the yolks to the reduction. Whisk until smooth and whisk in the butter bit by bit. The butter will be smoothly incorporated, forming a thick emulsion. If it should curdle, add it drop by drop to a spoonful of warm vinegar in a fresh bowl, it will re-emulsify. Be sure that the yolks never get hot enough to scramble. When the sauce is thick, remove it from the heat and beat it well. Add lemon juice and salt as necessary.

Hollandaise made in a blender

Put in the reduction and yolks, turn on to maximum speed and pour in the melted but cool butter in a thin steady stream.

Hollandaise, chef's method

Put the vinegar reduction, egg yolks and 2 tablespoons of water in a small, thick-bottomed pan. Whisk over moderate heat until frothy and well risen. Slowly whisk in the melted butter, moving the pan to the side if it gets more than hand-hot.

Beurre blanc

Beurre blanc is much used in place of hollandaise. It is light and delicate, and typical of the NOUVELLE CUISINE.

Have ready ⅓ cup very cold, unsalted butter, cut into small dice. Simmer 4½ tablespoons white wine vinegar and 7½ of dry white wine with a finely chopped shallot until reduced to 2 tablespoons. Add a tablespoon of heavy cream and reboil. Turn the heat down. Whisk in the butter pieces, one by one. The sauce will rise and become thick and creamy. Season with salt and pepper.

Beurre monté

"Mounted" or risen butter is made and used like *beurre blanc* but can have a base of any slightly thickened liquid—either a reduction as in *beurre blanc*, or a little stock or sauce thickened with flour. Whisk in cold butter in the same way.

Clarified butter

Served with vegetables, especially asparagus, and fish, it is melted butter from which salts, water, milk and other impurities have been removed. There are three methods of clarifying:
1 Melt butter in water. Leave to set. Lift off the fat, leaving salts and other solids in the water.

2 Heat until foaming, then pour through fine muslin or a cheesecloth.
3 Melt the butter and skim off the froth with a perforated spoon.

(Cool clarified butter, poured over PÂTÉS and TERRINES, acts as an excellent seal to exclude air. It is also useful for frying as it may be heated to much higher temperatures than unclarified butter; the impurities in butter burn first.)

Reduction

Sauces may be thickened by boiling down pan juices or even stocks (providing they have been made with some solid ingredients).

Sauté pan reductions

Simple sauces are made by DEGLAZING the pan with liquid (stock, cream or wine), boiling up well, and serving over the cooked food without thickening. The following are the most common:

Bercy reduction

Deglaze with white wine. Add chopped shallot. Sweat until soft. Beat in butter, diced bone marrow (if available), chopped parsley, lemon juice, salt and pepper.

Red wine reduction

As *Bercy*, substituting red wine for white. Sweeten slightly with red currant jelly or plum jam if for game or duck.

Cream reduction

Deglaze with brandy, sherry or marsala. Add cream, salt and pepper.

Mustard and cream reduction

Deglaze the pan with stock. Add cream, salt, pepper and flavor well with Dijon mustard.

Stocks and sauces /2

Thickening agents
Sauces are thickened by one or a combination of the following:

Roux
A mixture of equal parts butter and flour: A white roux is mixed over heat without browning; a blond roux is cooked slowly until the flour is sandy in texture and pale golden-colored; brown roux is cooked over gentle heat so that the flour fries brown without the butter burning.

Buerre manié
"Kneaded butter" is a mixture of equal parts flour and butter, in this case worked to a paste. It is added in small lumps to the hot liquid at the end of the cooking process.

Cornstarch or arrowroot
These are first dissolved (or "slaked") in a little cold liquid then added to hot liquid and stirred while thickening. The result is clearer than a flour-thickened sauce, but is rather gluey.

Egg yolk liaison
Mix 2 yolks with 2 tablespoons of cream or other cold liquid. Add to the hot sauce and cook gently without boiling to thicken the yolks without scrambling them.

Blood liaison
Blood thickens on heating. Do not overheat as this causes curdling. Follow the procedure for egg yolk liaison, above.

Vegetable purées
Nouvelle cuisine uses purées of cooked vegetables (shallots, mushrooms, tomatoes or even garlic) to thicken and give body to well reduced stocks or pan juices.

Savory sauces	Mother sauces	
for red meat, poultry, variety meats and game	**BROWN**	**Espagnole** *(Mirepoix of vegetables browned in butter, flour added and browned, then brown stock and tomato and mushroom peelings; reduced by half)* **Demi-glace** *(equal parts espagnole and jellied bone stock, reduced again by half)*
for eggs, vegetables, fish, poultry, lamb, and for binding soft mixtures	**WHITE** *(seasoned milk thickened with white roux)*	
for eggs, fish, vegetables and white meat	**BLOND (Velouté)** *(White stock thickened with blond roux)*	
for grills, fish, vegetables, toast and CANAPÉS	**SAVORY or FLAVORED BUTTERS** *(soft butter, well-seasoned then chilled in a cylindrical shape so that slices can be cut off as required)*	
for eggs, vegetables, fish and meat	**BUTTER (Beurre à l'Anglaise)** *(white roux, boiling water, added butter, lemon juice and seasoning)*	
for eggs, fish, vegetables, salad, poultry and meat	**EMULSION**	**Hollandaise (warm)** *(egg yolks and butter seasoned with vinegar, peppercorns and salt)* **Mayonnaise (cold)** *(egg yolks and oil seasoned with vinegar, mustard, salt and pepper)*
for salads, hot potatoes and pigs' feet	**VINAIGRETTE (French dressing)** *(3 parts olive/vegetable oil to 1 part vinegar and/or lemon juice plus salt and pepper)*	
for lamb		
for pork		
for duck		
for poultry and game		
for white meat, vegetables and pasta		

Suitable for	Daughter sauces
broiled and roast meat, rabbit and chicken	**Chasseur** (with cooked mushrooms and tomatoes, reduced white wine and chopped parsley)
pork, kidneys, tongue and ham	**Robert** (sweated chopped onions added to vinegar, white wine and pepper and reduced by half, then added to base)
veal and tongue	**Madeira** (with Madeira)
broiled meat	**Bordelaise** (with reduced wine, sweated shallots and thyme)
game	**Poivrade** (parsley stalks, thyme, peppercorns and bay leaves cooked with a *mirepoix*, marinated in wine or vinegar, reduced by half, added to base, cooked for 30 minutes and strained)
lamb	**Réforme** (equal parts *poivrade* and base garnished with *julienne* of egg whites, gherkins, truffles and tongue)
meat and game	**Périgueux** (with cooked chopped truffles or truffle extract)
eggs, fish and chicken	**Béchamel** (seasoned with bay leaves, onion and peppercorns)
fish	**Cardinal** (*béchamel*, fish stock, truffles, lobster butter, cayenne)
fish	**Anchovy** (with anchovy paste)
fish	**English egg** (with chopped hard-boiled egg)
eggs and veal	**Crème** (with cream)
fish, eggs and cauliflower	**Mornay** (with grated cheese, little mustard and/or cayenne)
lamb, eggs, fish and cauliflower	**Soubise** (with cooked chopped onion)
eggs, fish, vegetables and meat	**Aurore** (with tomato purée)
carrots, beans, potatoes and veal	**Poulette** (with mushroom extract, lemon juice and chopped parsley)
chicken	**Suprème** (with chicken stock, cream and mushroom peelings)
chicken and sweetbreads	**Mushroom** (*suprème* with mushrooms)
all grills and vegetables	**Parsley butter** (with chopped parsley, salt and pepper)
broiled meat, toast and canapés	**Roquefort butter** (with Roquefort, lemon juice, salt, pepper)
broiled meat and fish and boiled vegetables	**Maître d'hôtel butter** (with chopped parsley, shallots and lemon juice)
broiled meat and fish and cold hors d'oeuvres	**Mustard butter** (with Dijon or English mustard)
cauliflower, veal and eggs	**Bâtarde** (with egg yolks)
turbot, cod and lamb	**Caper** (with capers)
fish	**Fennel** (with chopped, blanched fennel)
broiled steaks	**Béarnaise** (reduction of chopped shallots, tarragon and peppercorns, plus fresh chopped tarragon and chervil)
broiled meat, fish and asparagus	**Choron** (*Béarnaise* with tomato purée)
asparagus, sole and sea kale	**Mousseline** (with whipped cream)
herring, mackerel and poached fish	**Moutarde** (with mustard)
fish soups and raw vegetables	**Aïoli** (with crushed garlic)
cold meat, fish and potatoes	**Aillade** (with crushed garlic and pounded walnuts)
celery, salads and herring	**Rémoulade** (with mustard and sometimes capers, parsley, gherkins, chervil, tarragon or anchovy paste)
egg and green salads	**Thousand island dressing** (with tomato ketchup, ground chili, chopped olives, pimiento, onion, chives, hard-boiled egg, parsley)
fried fish and shellfish	**Tartare** (with chopped hard-boiled egg, capers, gherkins, onions)
salads, chicken and fish	**Andalouse** (with tomato purée, chopped sweet red peppers)
salads made with cooked vegetables	**Half-and-half cheese dressing** (equal parts vinaigrette/mayonnaise with mashed anchovies, grated Parmesan and crushed garlic)
warm pigs' feet and potato and ham salads	**Mustard vinaigrette** (with mustard)
salads containing peas, tomatoes or potatoes	**Mint vinaigrette** (with chopped mint and sugar)
tomato or pasta salads and cold veal	**Basil vinaigrette** (with chopped pine nuts and basil)
potato, green and Mediterranean vegetable salads	**Garlic vinaigrette** (with crushed garlic)
mixed salads containing fruit	**Sweetened vinaigrette** (with sugar)
any salad	**German cream vinaigrette** (with sour or heavy cream)
	Mint (boiling vinegar, poured on chopped mint, sugar and salt)
	Apple (apples, butter and sugar cooked together and puréed)
	Bigarade (duck gravy, orange juice, arrowroot and butter)
	Cranberry (cooked cranberries, sieved and sweetened)
	Bread (milk seasoned with bay leaves, onions and cloves, thickened with breadcrumbs; with pepper, salt, melted butter)
	Cumberland (red currant jelly and port simmered, orange and lemon juice, mustard, cayenne, ginger, chopped cooked shallots)
	Tomato (*mirepoix*, stock, tomato purée and fresh tomatoes, cooked and sieved; with sugar, salt and pepper)

Soups

Broths are the simplest of soups, being nothing more than the stock or the liquid in which meat, poultry, game or, sometimes, vegetables have been cooked, with perhaps added seasoning and possibly a garnish of small pasta, shredded leek or chopped parsley.

If the base stock is too strong, it can be watered down; if too weak, it is rapidly reduced by boiling, or strengthened with the addition of a stock cube.

Clear soups or *consommés* are more sophisticated. The stock, which is made with plenty of meat or poultry bones, some fresh meat, and possibly wine or sherry, is then filtered clear using blood or egg shells and egg whites as clearing agents (see ASPIC).

Consommés are often named after a classic garnish. *Consommé aux profiteroles*, for example, is served with bead-sized PROFITEROLES (CHOUX PASTE balls) floating in it. Really rich, almost sticky *consommé* is known as *consommé doublé*, because the stock (though it might have been made with beef and veal bones only) is simmered for a second time with fresh chopped lean beef (or blood) before clearing. The blood in the extra beef helps the clearing process and strengthens the flavors.

Cold *consommés* must set to a jelly; gelatinous veal bones are used in the stock-making, or gelatin is added to be sure of a set.

Iced *consommés* are served in well-chilled bowls.

Cream soups need not contain cream. But they

are "creamed" in the sense that the ingredients are rubbed through a fine sieve or liquefied.

Vegetable purées are the most common bases for cream soups. Almost all vegetables can be made into cream soups, including leftover cooked vegetables.

Chowders are soups which contain solid ingredients. They are usually made the same way as cream soups, but the solid ingredients (which are chopped to a uniform small size before being added to the pan) are left floating in the soup.

A bisque is a cream soup made from shellfish and frequently seasoned with cayenne pepper and "spiked" with brandy.

Soup-making

1 Sweat a handful of sliced onions, leeks or shallots in 1 or 2 tablespoons of butter.
2 Add 1 or 2 cups of the raw or cooked vegetables that are to form the base of the soup (chopped cauliflower, beets, potato, and so on). Cook gently, covered, until the vegetables are soft, or for 2 or 3 minutes if the vegetables are already cooked.
3 If the soup is to be thickened with flour, stir in a tablespoon or so to absorb the remaining butter and to be sure of a thick but smooth soup. Creamed soups are almost always thickened, but may not be if the ingredients include farinaceous vegetables like potatoes or parsnips. Flour is sometimes added anyway to prevent the soup from separating out later.
4 Add 4 cups of the liquid (stock, water or

milk). Stir until boiled.
5 Add flavoring and season to taste. Simmer.
6 If the soup is to be "creamed," liquefy or blend it in a food processor or push through a sieve.
7 Chill if it is to be served cold.

8 Add cream and/or garnish as desired.

To obtain a velvet-smooth texture and luxurious richness in cream soups add an EGG AND CREAM LIAISON just before serving.

	Sweated base	Other Ingredients
Chilled soups		
Vichyssoise	Onions and leeks in butter	Chopped raw potato
Creamy *borscht*	Onions or shallots and garlic in butter	Boiled beets, raw potato
Curried pea soup	Onions in butter with a little garlic	Fresh peas
Hot soups		
Tomato soup	Shallots in butter with garlic	Tomatoes (canned or very ripe fresh) Small carrot
Parsnip and thyme soup	Onions in butter	Cooked parsnips
Parsley and mushroom soup	Shallots in butter with a little garlic	1 or 2 handfuls of roughly chopped parsley Sliced mushrooms
Mussel soup or *Billi-Bi*	Shallots in butter with garlic	Mussels cooked as for MOULES À LA MARINIÈRE and any cooking liquid
Blue cheese soup	Shallots in butter	Celery
Chowders or substantial soups		
Scotch broth	Leek and onion in mutton fat or butter	Few tbs each of: Chopped carrot Turnip Split dried peas Barley; 1 or 2 cupfuls each of: Chopped raw cabbage Raw lean lamb
Corn chowder	Sliced onion Chopped bacon in butter	Equal quantities of: Potato Celery Corn off the cob Green pepper
New England clam chowder	Chopped bacon, leek and onion in butter	Clams Potatoes

Soup garnishes

Use tiny cubes of meat, ham, poultry or vegetables, fried bread CROÛTONS, chopped herbs or swirls of cream or sour cream. Serve vegetable or fish soups with a good-size spoonful of a garlic-flavored paste, stirred in at the last minute.

Rouille

Cook one green and one red pepper until soft (or use canned pimento). Drain and discard seeds and pith. Liquefy or chop, then beat to a paste with 2 cloves of garlic, 1 tablespoon of bread-crumbs, a dash of TABASCO or CHILI sauce, and gradually beat in 3 tablespoons of olive oil.

Pistou

Crush 2 cloves of garlic, Beat in 2 tablespoons of ground pine nuts, a good handful of chopped sweet basil and a little soup liquid.

Pesto

Crush 2 cloves of garlic, then beat in 2 tablespoons of ground pine nuts, a good handful of chopped sweet basil, 2 tablespoons of grated Pecorino or Sardo cheese and gradually beat in 4 tablespoons of olive oil.

Thickening	Liquid	Seasoning	Method	Garnish
None, or a little flour	Veal or chicken stock	Salt and pepper	Follow stages in soup-making. Chill	Chopped chives Cream
Flour	Milk, water from boiling beets Chicken stock	Pinch cumin Salt and pepper	Follow stages in soup-making, adding the beets and their water before liquefying	Sour cream and chopped chives
Flour	Chicken or veal stock	Salt and pepper Curry powder Lemon juice Pinch of sugar	Follow stages in soup-making	Chopped fresh mint
Flour	Water or veal stock	Pinch of sugar Salt and pepper Thyme, Bay leaf Marjoram	Follow stages in soup-making. For cream soup add 20% thick WHITE SAUCE.	Chopped parsley CROÛTONS
None	Chicken or veal stock	Salt and pepper Chopped thyme	Follow stages in soup-making	Cream and chopped fresh thyme
One slice of crustless white bread	Chicken stock	Salt and pepper	Follow stages in soup-making, adding the crumbled bread in place of flour	Add cream (about 10% of total volume). Reheat.
Flour	Fish stock	Salt and pepper	Follow stages in soup-making, adding cooked mussels and their strained liquid just before serving	Cream and a few whole mussels
Flour	90% chicken stock 10% white wine	Salt and pepper, 4 oz Blue cheese per 1 pt	Follow stages in soup-making, adding wine with stock. Beat in cheese at the end.	Cream and a few whole mussels
None	Mutton or lamb stock or Water and a mutton bone	Salt and pepper	Follow the stages in soup-making but omit the thickening (the barley will do that). Simmer everything for 1½ to 2 hours, topping up water and skimming off fat as necessary. Do not liquefy or sieve.	Shredded green leaves of leek
Flour	Milk	Salt and pepper	Follow the stages in soup-making, scraping the corn off the cob and adding any juice from the cob to the soup. Do not liquefy or sieve.	CROÛTONS, served separately
Flour	Milk	Thyme Bay leaf Salt and pepper	Scrub the clams and cook in water until shells are wide open. Reserve the cooking water. Follow the stages in soup-making, adding the cooked clams and their liquid once the potatoes are soft.	Cream Chopped parsley

Aspics and jellies

Gelatin, the most common setting agent, is present in calves' feet, veal bones, chicken bones, and commercially available in sheets or powdered form. Hot liquid mixtures containing sufficient gelatin will set solidly when cooled.

Sheet gelatin is sold in thin, transparent sheets. Four sheets (or a scant $\frac{1}{2}$ oz) are needed to set 1 pt of liquid.

Powdered gelatin is usually sold in boxes containing small envelopes, each holding $\frac{1}{2}$ oz or 2 level teaspoons (enough to set 1 pt of liquid).

However, if the liquid to be set must hold solid pieces of food (a savory jelly containing, say, hard-boiled eggs and pieces of cooked tongue) the proportion of gelatin must be slightly greater. The same is true if the jelly or mold is to sit in a warm room for any length of time.

Conversely, if the mixture is to be served well chilled, or is already fairly stiff (such as a purée of chicken mixed with thick MAYONNAISE) less gelatin is needed.

Added gelatin to a cold or a lukewarm mixture such as a mousse:
1 Put a little of the liquid from the recipe into a small, heavy pan.
2 Sprinkle powdered gelatin evenly over the surface of the liquid. (First crush any lumps of gelatin that may have formed in the package.)
3 Leave to soak for 10 minutes. The gelatin will absorb the liquid and the mixture will become spongy.
4 Warm gently until it is runny and clear, but

by no means hot. The heat must be sufficiently gentle to melt the gelatin without reducing the liquid and cooking the gelatin into strings.
5 Stir the mix into the liquid to be set. (This should be at room temperature or lukewarm.) Be sure that the gelatin is evenly incorporated.
(Put sheet gelatin into a pan or dish. Break up the sheets if it is necessary to get them to lie flat. Pour sufficient liquid, taken from the recipe, over to cover them. Soak for 10 minutes, then proceed as from step 4 above.)

Adding gelatin to a large quantity of a liquid, such as stock for aspic:
Sprinkle the gelatin over the cold or lukewarm liquid in a pan. Warm gently, then heat or boil as required.
(Soak sheet gelatin in the liquid, then heat. Or add the sheets of gelatin one at a time to the hot liquid, then heat or boil.)

When using gelatin, remember:
1 To avoid any lumps, sprinkle powdered gelatin on liquid, rather than liquid on gelatin.
2 If, when gelatin is sprinkled on liquid, one or two patches do not absorb liquid at once, swirl the pan gently but do not stir—the gelatin will stick to the spoon.
3 If the gelatin does overheat and become stringy, start all over again.
4 Most liquids and mousses will set in 4 hours if refrigeratred, but the full setting power of gelatin is only reached after about 12 hours.

Aspic
Aspic is savory jelly made from clarified stock. Fish, veal and poultry stocks form the bases of most aspics.

Clarifying stock for aspic
1 Skim off all the fat from the stock or use paper toweling laid on the surface to lift off every vestige of grease.
2 Put the cold stock in a pan so large that the liquid does no more than half fill it.
3 Add 1 or 2 cups of finely ground lean beef. This is not strictly necessary, but it adds flavor and aids the clarifying process. Simmer for 1 hour. Cool the stock.
4 For each pint of liquid, add the white and the crushed shell of 1 egg into the stock and whisk steadily with a large balloon whisk while heating the stock slowly.
5 When the liquid is frothy and milky and starts to rise, as though to boil over, stop whisking at once, allow the crust to rise briefly, then remove the pan from the heat to let the crust subside. This allows the bubbling stock beneath the egg white to swirl about so that particles of sediment get caught in the egg white. Keep the egg-white crust in one piece so that it can act later as a second filter. (If the stock is allowed to boil so vigorously that the liquid breaks up the crust, filter effectiveness will be impaired, but sometimes the stock will bubble quietly through one hole in the crust which helps the egg white in its role as a sediment trap.)
6 Simmer gently for 45 minutes, not allowing the crust to rise again.

Clearing Whisk egg whites and crushed shells in liquid over heat until rising. Let rise then take off heat.

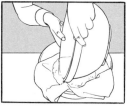
2 Repeat rising and subsiding 2 or 3 times, then simmer gently for 45 mins. Strain through muslin-lined sieve.

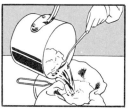
3 If still murky, slip egg-white crust into the muslin and strain again through both crust and muslin.

7 Fit a double thickness of muslin over a sieve and set it over a large bowl.
8 Pour the stock carefully through this filter into the bowl, holding back the crust.
9 If the stock is not crystal-clear, place the sieve over a second bowl and slip the egg-white crust into the muslin-lined sieve.
10 Pour aspic through the sieve once more.
11 Take a small amount of the stock and chill it to check its setting quality. If it does not set, dissolve $\frac{1}{2}$ oz gelatin powder or sheets in the stock.

Using sheet gelatin
Soak in water until soft before melting it gently in liquid.

Dicing aspic *Let aspic set in a shallow layer. Cut it across into neat even squares.*

2 Lift the aspic cubes with a moistened metal spatula. Use the aspic dice as garnish.

Savory set molds		
	Ingredients	Method
Egg mousse with anchovy	4 eggs, hard-boiled 4 anchovy fillets, mashed 3 tbs whipped cream 3 tbs mayonnaise 1 cup *consommé*	Chop up the eggs. Combine the ingredients in the order listed. Set in an oiled mold.
Chicken and tarragon mold	2 cups ground chicken flesh 2 tsp chopped tarragon Few tbs whipped cream Few tbs mayonnaise 1 level tsp gelatin in: $1\frac{1}{4}$ cups chicken stock Salt and pepper 1 egg white, stiffly beaten	Allow the stock to cool but not to set. Combine the ingredients in the order listed. Set in an oiled mold.
Cucumber and pepper yogurt mould	1 cucumber 1 cup full-fat cream cheese Few tbs whipped cream $\frac{2}{3}$ cup plain yogurt Salt and pepper Juice of 1 lemon Grated nutmeg 2 level tsp gelatin in: $\frac{2}{3}$ cup chicken stock	Allow the stock to cool but not to set. Peel and liquefy the cucumber. Combine the ingredients in the order listed. Set in an oiled mold.

Unmolding *Dip mould briefly in hot water. Pull edges loose. Jerk to dislodge.*

Sweet jellies/jello

The most common sweet jellies are bought in the form of jelly crystals or solid blocks of concentrated jelly, to which boiling water is added. For a more natural and better flavor make jellies with real fruit juice—which may or may not be clarified.

To clarify fruit juice: Proceed as for the clarification of stock (paragraphs 2 and 4 to 10).

Make the jelly by adding sugar to taste and boiling until clear and dissolved, then add gelatin to ensure a set.

Any fruit juice may be set to a jelly, and many boiled juices are clear enough not to need further clarification. Orange juice, however, loses its fresh flavor if boiled. Use a small quantity of fresh orange juice to dissolve the sugar and then allow it to cool. Use this to soak and to dissolve the gelatin, stirring the mix into juice at room temperature.

If the jelly must support pieces of fruit suspended in it, use more gelatin.

Setting molds

If the mixture is thick before setting, oil the mold lightly; if the mixture is an aspic or jelly, wet the mold. When unmolding, wet the plate so that if the mold comes out off-center it can be pushed into place.

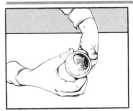

Aspic molds *Coat insides of molds with nearly-set aspic. Allow to set. Lay decoration on base.*

2 Add another thin layer of just-liquid aspic. Chill until completely set.

3 Then add savory mousse mixture (chopped chicken, eggs, mayonnaise).

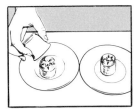

4 Chill. Add topping of aspic. Chill. Dip in hot water briefly to unmold.

Consommé

To make a good beef or chicken *consommé* proceed exactly as for clarifying stock (opposite) using strong beef or chicken stock.

Even if the stock has a good flavor, add ground lean beef or chicken flesh at the clarification stage. The ground meat is discarded but it will have added more flavor.

Good additions are a dash of sherry in beef *consommé*, white wine in chicken *consommé*, or brandy in game *consommé*. Put these in 10 minutes before the end of the simmering time to allow the alcohol harshness to mellow.

Alcohol and marinades

Wine and other alcoholic beverages are used in cooking in many ways:

1 The actual alcohol is evaporated by heating, or burnt off by flaming, leaving the residue to provide richness, body and flavor. The elimination of the alcohol is important if the dish or sauce is not to be harsh. Wines should be greatly reduced by prolonged simmering or rapid boiling to moderate the "winy" taste. A splash of unreduced wine added to a soup or sauce at the last minute can overpower other, subtler seasonings and ruin the taste.

2 Spirits or fortified wines are used as a preservative. Brandy and rum prevent food from going bad; fresh Christmas MINCEMEAT, which is uncooked, depends on alcohol and sugar to preserve it, and fruit cakes which are soaked in brandy after cooking will keep almost indefinitely.

3 Liqueurs or brandies are added undiluted and unreduced to sweet dishes. The alcohol is actually important to the taste of the dish, and must not be eliminated—sherry in trifle, Kirsch on pineapple, brandy in stewed peaches.

4 Spirits or fortified wines (with a high enough alcohol content to burn easily) are used for dramatic effect. Sweet *flambé* dishes (like *crêpes Suzette*) would taste as well without the flaming, and ordinary heating would evaporate the alcohol.

5 Occasionally, alcoholic drinks are used for marinating and macerating.

Generally, when a recipe calls for one glass of wine this means about 3 to 4 fluid oz, not a large drinking glass · Cover prunes with port and leave them to soak for several weeks. They plump up and are delicious, uncooked, with cream or custard. They are, however, quite intoxicating · Having difficulty in getting a dish with a low alcohol content to flame—add a large dash of vodka; this will raise the alcohol content without changing the taste · Turn simple pork chops into an exciting dish by rubbing them with a few crushed juniper berries and flaming them in gin · Flame BAKED ALASKA with brandy at the table for a doubly dramatic, exciting and tasty dessert.

When cooking with wine always remember the following:

1 Do not cook with wine that has turned to vinegar. Its harshness may be reduced by prolonged simmering or rapid boiling, but when it has reached this stage many other things in it may have gone bad. Better results would be achieved using good-quality bottled vinegar.

2 Wine need not be expensive to be good and the best wines for cooking are often not wonderful to drink. Slightly sweet, heavy, sunny wines are excellent once their harshness has been eliminated by boiling them down. White wines with a pronounced flowery perfume give an excellent taste to fish dishes or cream sauces. Like red wines, they need reduction to lose their "winy" (as opposed to fruity or rich) taste. If the cooking time of the sauce is less than 20 minutes, reduce the wine by itself in a small pan before adding it to the sauce at the last minute.

3 To store leftover wine for cooking, boil it down to half quantity, put it into small, dry, clean, hot screw-top bottles with as little air space as possible, or bottle it in preserving jars.

Flaming If alcohol is to burn dramatically, or indeed to burn at all, remember the following:

1 Liquids low in alcohol content, like wine, will not burn.

2 Do not add alcohol to a pan of liquid before it has been ignited or it will become so diluted it will not light. Instead, warm it in a ladle over the flame, or in a small pan, light it there and pour it, flaming, on to the dish.

3 Stand back when touching it with a match. If the alcohol is very hot the flames will flash quite high.

4 Do not panic if the flames are high. Leave the pan alone and they will die down very quickly. If there is any danger of a fire, quench the flames by covering with a lid.

Marinating

A marinade is a liquid mixture in which food is soaked prior to cooking. It has three purposes:

1 To flavor the food. For this purpose it contains spices, herbs, and sometimes vegetables.

2 To tenderize or soften the muscle fibers of meat. For this it contains an acid such as vinegar, lemon juice or wine.

3 To limit drying out and deterioration of the meat by preventing its exposure to the air. For this purpose it normally consists predominantly of oil. (Before refrigerators were widespread, marinades contained a higher proportion of vinegar as its acid content was necessary to prevent bacterial activity. Today, with marinating done in the refrigerator, drying out is more likely to be a problem than deterioration. Milder marinades, with much less of the overpowering vinegar, are now more common.)

In restaurants, the process of marinating is done for all three reasons. A lamb steak left for five days in a marinade of oil, onion, garlic, white wine and herbs will taste wonderful when broiled, will be extremely tender, and, if demand should be slow, it can stay a further three days in the marinade and remain fresh.

The home cook is unlikely to be as concerned with preservation as with flavoring, and, if the cut is cheap, tenderizing. The most useful domestic marinade for small cuts of meat, game or fish is the dry marinade.

Dry marinade

A slight misnomer, as oil and vinegar (or lemon juice or wine) are used, but the ingredients are sprinkled on the dry meat rather than forming a bath in which the meat is totally immersed. Dry marinades are more economical, as not as much oil or vinegar is required, and the resulting juices (the marinade plus any liquid which runs from the meat) are frequently used in the final dish. They may be used as a sauce, a basting liquid or, in the case of TERRINES, mixed with the FARCE before baking. The object of the dry marinade is simply to flavor the meat by prolonged contact (perhaps 24 hours). The meat should be turned occasionally to ensure even absorption. Dry marinades are often used to flavor food that is subsequently to be smoked.

Wet marinade

Food totally immersed in a marinade will be safe for at least 10 days if refrigerated. It is more economical to make only a small quantity of marinade, pour it over the pieces so that they are partially immersed, and turn them every 6 hours or so to ensure even marinating. If the refrigerator is cold enough to congeal the oil, the marinade may be spread thickly over the meat and turning will not be necessary. If the marinade is strongly flavored it should be covered to prevent it contaminating the taste of other food in the refrigerator.

Marinades should not contain salt as this draws out too much of the natural juice and color from the meat.

Dry marinade for kebabs, broiled fish and meat

Sprinkle with

Chopped shallot, thyme and parsley stalks
Crumbled bay leaf
2 parts oil to 1 part lemon juice

Variations:
Add crushed juniper for pork
Replace bay leaf with fennel seeds for fish

Garlic marinade for lamb steaks

Marinate for 3 to 5 days, then broil or fry.

About 1 cup oil
6 tbs vinegar
3 tbs red wine
3 cloves garlic, crushed
$4\frac{1}{2}$ tbs chopped thyme
2 onions, sliced
6 crushed peppercorns

Tandoori marinade

Natural YOGURT takes the place of oil in this marinade. Skin a chicken, leave whole or cube and thread on kebab skewers. Marinate for 8 to 24 hours. Roast or broil, basting with the marinade.

1 cup natural yogurt
Juice of 1 lemon
3 tbs vinegar
1 chopped onion
2 crushed cloves garlic
1 tsp chopped fresh ginger
2 tsp chopped paprika
2 tsp ground coriander
1 tsp ground cumin
2 tbs tomato purée
1 tsp mild curry powder or GARAM MASALA

Honey marinade

This is excellent for spare ribs. Marinate the ribs for 24 hours, then baste with the marinade while broiling. They should be well cooked to a shiny dark color. (Baking them in the marinade first, then broiling, will ensure that they are cooked through.)

6 tbs liquid honey
Juice of 1 lemon
3 tbs soy sauce
2 crushed cloves garlic
3 tbs chopped basil
6 crushed peppercorns

Game marinade

Use for large roasts of meat to tenderize the flesh and accentuate the gamy flavor. Use also to give meat other than game (such as lamb) a gamy taste. The vegetables used are first lightly browned in the oil to give a stronger taste, thus speeding up the permeation of the taste into the meat.

Because the marinade may have to be in use for more than 10 days, it is cooked and should be re-simmered for half an hour at least once a week. Always cool the marinade fully before replacing the meat.

1 cup vinegar
1 cup oil
1 sliced carrot
1 sliced onion
1 sliced stick celery
2 crushed cloves garlic
10 crushed juniper berries
1 crumbled bay leaf
1 sprig rosemary

Cook the vegetables and seasonings gently in the oil until the onion is just beginning to color, then add the vinegar. Allow to cool completely before pouring over the meat. Marinate large cuts for up to 14 days under refrigeration (re-boiling and cooling the marinade after one week), or for a week (re-boiling the marinade and cooling after four days) in a cool larder.

Sreviche marinade

Sreviche is fish "cooked" in marinade. Lemon juice tenderizes the raw fish, and changes its glassy look to the opaque whiteness of cooked fish. Use any filleted white fish, and cut it into thin strips. Marinate the fish for as little as 30 minutes (for small dice) or up to 12 hours for slices. Serve lightly salted and dressed with the marinade and slices of avocado and tomato.

1 onion, chopped
Juice of 2 lemons or 4 limes
Olive oil (enough to coat the fish)
Pinch of cayenne pepper
2 fresh chilies, split in half
Freshly ground black pepper
$\frac{1}{2}$ small green pepper, seeded and chopped

Minced mixtures

Any meat, if ground, produces more volume than if left in one piece. Immense variety of flavor and texture can be achieved with chopped, ground or puréed ingredients, producing dishes as diverse as country-style meatballs and the sophisticated, velvet-smooth *moussel-ines de brochet.*

Ground meat mixtures

1 If the dish is to be broiled or fried (like hamburgers), use only best-quality steak.
2 Cereal binders, such as dried cracker crumbs, breadcrumbs or some starchy addition, such as mashed potatoes or thick WHITE SAUCE are frequently added in to the mixture to "stretch" the meat, give a softer texture, absorb fat, and to bind wet or crumbly mixtures into a cohesive mass.

Do not add too much "stretcher." Pork sausages, for example, are best with little or no binder.

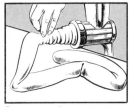

Sausages Scrape fat from inside casing. Run cold water through it. Feed on to grinder filler tube.

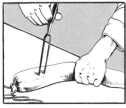

3 For salami, prick skins all over and press filling to one end. Tie other end.

3 Beaten egg added in binds crumbly mixtures well, but too much egg will produce a bouncy, too-solid texture.
4 Finely-chopped raw onions give flavor but as the onion "weeps" and shrinks during cooking, the finished dish will have an uneven, crumbly texture. Instead, sweat onions first.
5 Always cool cooked ingredients before adding them to cold raw ones (the warmth might sour the raw ingredients) especially if the raw mixture is to be kept for any length of time. If the mixture must be made more than 12 hours in advance, freeze it pre-shaped into loaves, sausages or meatballs.

Meatloaves and terrines

The main ingredient of a good terrine is the force-meat, a sausage-like mixture of raw meat, fat and seasoning, all well seasoned and perhaps "stretched" with bread-crumbs and bound together with egg.

2 Fingers control casing coming off filler to ensure tight packing for salami and loose for fresh. Tie end.

4 Use fresh at once, or freeze. Tie salami down length. Tighten weekly.

Terrine making

1 Sweat a few spoons of chopped onion, shallot and/or garlic and let them cool.
2 If the terrine contains liver, brown it in butter or grind it raw.
3 Mix 2 parts raw ground pork, liver, beef, veal, chicken, turkey or game with 1 part ground pork back fat. (If the chosen meat is pork, use a fatty cut so that there is no need for the back fat.)
4 To "stretch" the mixture, add breadcrumbs —up to 20% of the volume of the combined ground meat and fat. Dried crumbs should be pre-soaked in milk.
5 Mix well and add the seasonings, herbs and brandy, sherry or cream.
6 Bind the mixture with beaten egg to make a soft, but not sloppy, paste.
7 Grease the terrine, pie dish or loaf pan, or line it with LARD LEAVES, PIG'S CAUL or slices of rindless, streaky bacon. (Bacon has a rather dominant flavor so blanch it first.)
8 Fill the dish with the forcemeat, or spread a layer of it in the bottom, add a thin slice of cooked or raw meat, then another layer of forcemeat and so on. Finish with a topping of forcemeat.
9 Brush the top with melted butter, or fold over the lard leaves or pig's caul.
10 Cover with a square of buttered paper, then with a lid or a piece of aluminum foil. Foil directly applied could cause metallic spots on the top of the terrine.
11 Bake AU BAIN MARIE in a moderate-to-cool oven until the mixture feels firm and has shrunk slightly away from the edges (1 to 3 hours, depending on size).

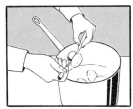

Shaping quenelles Use two wet spoons to mold egg shapes. Scoop quenelle off one spoon with the other.

12 If the dish is to be served hot as a meat loaf, cool it for 10 minutes, then turn it out on a warmed serving dish.

If the dish is to be served cold as a terrine or pâté, let it cool in the pan or dish, then turn it out, cover, and either refrigerate or press.

To press a terrine into a compact, dense block that will slice without crumbling, fit a plate or other suitable flat object on top of it so that a weight on that can press it down. Leave, weighted, overnight in the refrigerator. Run a knife around the edge and stand the pan briefly in hot water to loosen it.

Quenelle mixtures

These are soft mixtures made from white meats such as chicken, veal or fish, containing cream and usually bound with egg white. A really perfect *quenelle* should be tender enough for the weight of a heavy fork to cut it. Fish *quenelles* are the easiest to make as the gelatinous fish binds the mixture well. If the principal ingredient is not gelatinous, like chicken, the mixture must be cooked in a thin puff pastry case, or in a sausage skin. See BOUDIN BLANC.

Alternatively, bind with a CHOUX PASTE or PANADE as for *quenelles lyonnaise.*

Quenelle mixtures

Ingredients	Seasonings	Binders	Method	Serve
Quenelles lyonnaise $\frac{1}{2}$ lb salmon fillet $\frac{1}{4}$ lb pike or whiting fillet	Pinch nutmeg $\frac{1}{4}$ tsp salt	3-egg quantity CHOUX PASTE 3 egg whites $\frac{3}{4}$ cup butter	Pound the fish to a smooth paste. Beat into the cold choux paste. Add seasonings. Chill well. Beat egg whites until just frothy, then beat them into the mixture slowly. Pound the butter into the mixture (or blend in a food processor). Chill. Roll into cylinders with floured hands, or shape and poach as illustrated.	With fish VELOUTÉ
Mousselines de brochet 1 lb pike fillet $\frac{1}{4}$ lb whiting fillet	Pinch cayenne pepper White pepper Salt	4 slices crustless white bread Milk 2 egg whites $1\frac{1}{4}$ cups heavy cream	Liquefy or pound the fish to a smooth paste with bread soaked in milk. Add seasonings, and gradually beat in egg whites. Chill. Beat in cream gradually until mixture is at DROPPING CONSISTENCY. Shape and poach as shown.	On bed of rice with VELOUTÉ, or NANTUA SAUCE
Boudin blanc de volaille (chicken sausage) 3 parts white chicken meat 2 parts pork back fat	Sweated chopped onion Pinch thyme Salt White pepper Grated nutmeg	Egg whites beaten with a fork until just frothy (about one white to every $\frac{1}{2}$ lb chicken) Heavy cream, chilled	Grind or liquefy the chicken and pork fat with the seasonings to a very smooth paste. Beat in the egg whites a little at a time, and reliquefy or sieve. Chill well. Beat in as much cream as the mixture will take and still hold its shape— about $\frac{2}{3}$ cup for each 2 cups chicken flesh. Fill into sausage casings. Poach very gently for 12 minutes. Remove; cool. Brush with butter and broil.	Sprinkle with chopped parsley. Serve with mashed potatoes.

Ground meat dishes

Ingredients	Seasonings	Binders	Method	Serving	Variations
Hamburgers Best steak, no gristle	Ground pepper (salt *after* cooking to prevent loss of juice) Minced onion (optional)	Ideally, none, or up to 20% breadcrumbs	Grind meat finely. Add seasonings. Shape into thick patties. Broil or fry.	With salad or between toasted buns with chopped onion and relishes.	Eggburger: Top cooked burger with fried egg. Lamburger: Replace beef with best tender lamb. Broil with a few rosemary leaves.
Meatballs Stewing steak with about 10% fat but no gristle	Chopped sweated onion Chopped marjoram Crushed garlic Pinch of allspice Salt and pepper	20% fresh breadcrumbs Beaten egg	Grind meat. Add all other ingredients to form a stiff paste. Roll into balls. Brown all over, stew in stock.	Serve in sauce made from stewing liquid. Serve with noodles, rice or potatoes.	Add sliced, sweated onions, garlic and paprika to the meatballs while stewing. Serve with sour cream for a meatball goulash.
Pork sausages Belly of pork, boned and skinned (or any fatty cut)	Rubbed dried sage or chopped fresh sage Salt and pepper	Up to 20% fresh breadcrumbs Little (if any) egg	Grind meat. Add all other ingredients. Roll in hands. Or fill into skins. Fry or broil.	Serve with fried onions, mashed potatoes and tomato sauce	Substitute fennel or crushed juniper berries for the sage. For a spicy sausage use tender beef or lamb and add crushed garlic, nutmeg and allspice.
Salami 6 lbs pork butt or shoulder (including fat but no bones or skin)	2 cloves garlic, crushed 3 oz coarse salt 1 tsp potassium nitrate 3 tbs white wine 1 tbs black peppercorns	None	Grind meat. Add other ingredients. Pack as shown opposite. Tie ends and hang in a cool, dry place or refrigerate for one month.	Eat raw with fresh bread and butter and olives	Season with juniper, spices, or dried herbs.

Potted meats and pâtés

Potted meats and smooth pâtés

Electric mixers, blenders and processors have greatly reduced the time and effort required in the making of smooth pâtés and potted meat pastes.

Smoked fish pâtés can be made as much as three days before they are needed; potted meats and liver pâtés, if covered with CLARIFIED BUTTER, up to 10 days ahead. (All pâtés keep better if made with butter rather than cream.)

The flavored butters (see pages 132/3) are a simple form of smooth pâté and can be served in the same way. If made with clarified butter they can be used as a tasty seal.

Making smooth pâtés

1 Cook the main ingredient (poach the fish, fry the chicken livers in butter).
2 Pound, blend, liquefy, mince or grind the cooked ingredients in a food processor. If hot, allow to cool (otherwise the pâté may curdle when mixed with butter).
3 Beat in the softened butter or the whipped cream, or mayonnaise, sour cream or other main ingredient.
4 Pack tightly into a terrine dish or into individual, small ramekins, pressing down to eliminate pockets of air.
5 Cover with a thin layer of melted clarified butter or with plastic wrap and leave to set.
6 Serve chilled, with hot toast.

The addition of two stiffly beaten egg whites and 1 tsp gelatin dissolved in $\frac{2}{3}$ cup stock added to 2 cups mixture will give the pleasant, light texture of a mousse.

Confit d'oie and confit de canard (preserved goose and preserved duck)

The fat used to preserve the flesh must be either goose fat or lard mixed with an equal amount of duck fat. Duck fat alone does not solidify well. Put the cut up bird in a casserole, cover with the liquid fat (without juices or sediment) and cook very slowly in the oven until it is exceptionally tender and well cooked. Set a layer of clean fat in the bottom of a glass jar or earthenware crock. Put in the cooked duck pieces, making sure that they do not touch the sides of the pot. Add more just-liquid fat to cover. Refrigerate until set. Fill any holes with more fat and cover well. This will keep for up to three months in a cool place (refrigerated in the summer). When needed, lift out the pieces of duck, wipe off the fat and eat cold; or use in casseroles or stews.

Brandade de morue

(purée of salt cod)
Wash and soak 1 lb salt cod. Poach it for 8 minutes. Drain and remove the skin and bones. Break the flesh up into a large pan containing $\frac{2}{3}$ cup olive oil heated to smoking point. Add two or three crushed cloves of garlic and beat all the ingredients over moderate heat until they form a smooth paste. Reduce the heat and stir in alternating small amounts of oil and heavy cream until the dish has a fluffy texture. Season well and serve warm on CROÛTONS or as a dip.

	Ingredients	Method
Mushroom pâté	Mushrooms Butter Garlic, crushed Coriander seeds, crushed Sour cream Salt and pepper	Fry mushrooms in butter with crushed garlic and 1 or 2 tsp coriander seeds. Liquefy and sieve to extract seeds. Cool. Beat in sour cream (a volume about equal to purée) and season. Chill.
Duck liver pâté with brandy	Duck livers Butter Onion Salt and pepper Brandy	Sweat onions in butter, add livers. Fry until brown and just firm to the touch. FLAME with brandy. Pound everything to a paste. Season and beat in butter to taste (up to 50% volume of livers).
Chicken liver pâté with gin and juniper berries	Chicken livers Butter Onion Salt and pepper Gin Juniper berries	Sweat onions in butter. Add juniper berries. Add livers and fry until brown and firm. FLAME with gin. Pound everything to a paste. Season and beat in butter to taste (up to 50% volume of livers).
Potted turkey and ham	1 part poached turkey flesh 1 part cooked ham 1 part butter Mustard Salt and pepper	Pound the meats to a paste. Add the butter and seasonings.
Potted beef (or game of any kind)	2 parts boiled or lean beef or game 1 part butter Mustard Salt and pepper	As above
Kipper pâté	Cooked kipper fillets Butter Lemon juice Pepper	As above. (*Variation*: Use raw kipper fillets marinated for 3 days in oil, lemon juice and onion.)
Salmon pâté	2 parts cooked salmon 1 part butter 1 part whipped cream Lemon juice Salt and pepper	Beat fish to a paste. Add lemon, butter, salt and pepper, and finally whipped cream. (*Variation*: Use smoked salmon or trout with creamed horse-radish.)

Purées

Carrot purée Pass cooked carrots through a rotary sieve set over a bowl lined with a muslin cloth.

2 Close the muslin around contents. Tie around a wooden spoon handle. Twist bag round to extract juice.

Mashing potatoes Move potatoes to one side of pan. Heat milk in empty side. When boiling mix into purée.

Vegetable purées

Almost any cooked vegetable may be puréed to advantage. The resulting dishes may often be lighter, prettier and more interesting than the original ingredients.
1 Cook the vegetables, either by steaming, boiling or sweating. (Roast, baked, and fried vegetables seldom make good purées.)
2 Process or blend them or push them through a food mill or ordinary sieve.
3 Season well and add butter, cream, WHITE SAUCE, or another vegetable purée.
4 Keep warm in a covered dish, or cool and reheat as required.
5 Reheat green purées by tossing them in butter over high heat, moving the contents constantly; or heat them, covered, in a microwave oven. Reheat root vegetables, such as parsnips or potatoes, in the same way or warm through in the oven.

Virtually all puréed vegetables make good soups and many of them, notably cauliflower or spinach (especially if flavored with cheese), make good SOUFFLÉS.

Experiment with herb and spice seasonings and with purée combinations. Try a little in a small dish first to avoid ruining a whole dish with an overpowering flavor.

Suggested taste combinations

Carrot purée with added pepper, sugar and a touch of ginger.
Parsnip purée made with cream and thyme.
Broadbean purée with butter and chopped fresh savory.
Spinach purée with reduced heavy cream and nutmeg. (To reduce cream it must be very fresh and boiled rapidly in a heavy saucepan until thick.)
Celeriac purée mixed with mashed potatoes.
Puréed turnip, carrot and potato, with butter and garlic.
Mushroom and onion purée mixed with breadcrumbs and baked in scooped-out tomatoes.
Peas, puréed and seasoned with sweated onion, garlic, mint and sugar.
Sweet corn purée, beaten into mashed potato, mixed with egg and grated cheese, and fried as pancakes.
Sweet potato, mashed and mixed with egg, grated cheese and seasonings and fried as pancakes.
Puréed salsify with cream and mustard.
Purée of cauliflower and potato with cream and nutmeg, baked in a dish with a cheese GRATINÉE top.
Purée of pumpkin or acorn squash with garlic, pepper and sour cream.

Fruit purées

These are generally sweetened for use in desserts, but they may be cooked and puréed without sugar, or puréed raw and sweetened as needed.

To make cooked fruit purée

1 Cook the fruit with sugar and/or water until soft. Rhubarb, apples and most berries need no added water, but must be heated slowly at first to allow the juice to run from them. If sugar is added, the pan must be heated slowly so that the sugar dissolves without crystallizing.
2 Remove any pips from the fruit. Liquefy the fruit in a processer or blender; then, if necessary, sieve to remove shreds of skin or small seeds.
3 If a "marmalade" or very thick purée is required, boil the purée rapidly to reduce it to a thick paste. Keep the pan half-covered to allow the steam to escape and prevent spitting and splashing. As soon as the purée begins to thicken, stir frequently to keep it from sticking.

To purée raw fruit

Liquefy the fruit in a blender or food processor, or chop and push through a food mill or stainless steel or nylon sieve.

To make fresh fruit sauce (such as SAUCE MELBA with sieved raspberries) simply sift and beat in confectioner's sugar.

Raw and cooked fruit purées are used for SOUFFLÉS, for JELLIED MOLDS, JAMS and ICE CREAMS, but they may make a simple dessert on their own or with cream.

Kissel is a fruit purée, set with GELATIN or ARROWROOT to a thick, but not solid, consistency. Serve with whipped cream, or with CRÈME ANGLAISE.
Black currant kissel
Add 1½ cups fresh or frozen black currants to 1 cup sugar. Cook slowly until the juices run freely and berries are soft. Liquefy and sieve. Make up to 2½ cups with equal parts ruby port and water. Set with 2 tsp gelatin.

For a layered fool choose three fruits of attractive toning colors (such as greengage, plum, mango and rhubarb or blueberry, strawberry and red currant). Make separate purées and sweeten them to taste. Spoon the purées, with layers of whipped cream and/or custard between them, alternately into individual glasses to give a striped effect—say green purée / cream / pink purée / cream / orange purée / cream.

Hard sauce or brandy butter

Made by mixing soft, unsalted butter with confectioner's sugar and brandy, rum or any other spirit. In Britain this is traditionally served in solid spoonfuls on top of the Christmas pudding.

Bread

Breads are not much more than a mixture of flour, water and yeast. The different flours used largely account for the differences in the wide variety of breads.

Yeast doughs *Work slack dough by slapping, pinching and throwing it against sides of bowl.*

2 Knead firmer dough on a floured surface, using the fingers to draw the dough in to a ball.

3 Turn dough slightly clockwise, then use heel of hand to push it away. Repeat 2 and 3 for 10 min.

White flours (ground from wheat grains with outer bran and inner germ removed):

Strong flour (sometimes called bread flour) comes mainly from North American hard wheat, and its high GLUTEN content gives the dough a remarkable capacity to expand and rise, producing light, crisp bread.

Weak flour, household or soft flour (from soft wheat, grown mainly in Europe) has less robust and expansive gluten, and produces a less stretchy dough, which bakes to a heavier, more crumbly bread.

All-purpose flour is claimed to be suitable for cakes or breads. In practice European all-purpose flour is more suitable for cakes, containing more of the home-grown soft wheat; and in America it is more suitable for bread, as it contains more of the home-grown hard wheat.

Whole wheat flour (also sometimes called whole meal or whole grain flour) is made from the entire wheat grain including the bran casing and the wheat germ. It is nutritious (the bran is rich in fiber and the wheat germ in Vitamin B), but produces a heavier bread. Wholemeal flour is much more absorbent, so more liquid must be added in to the dough.

Stone-ground flour is produced by the ancient method of milling flour between stone rollers. It is coarser than modern processed flour and needs extra yeast to make it rise. Stone-ground whole meal flour makes the heaviest, but perhaps also the tastiest, loaf.

Brown flour is probably artificially colored rather than rich in bran and germ and will be lighter than whole meal. It may, however, also have artificial flavoring to give it a sweeter or maltier taste.

Bran gives coarseness and color, but cannot be used on its own.

Yeast is a single-celled organism which, given warmth and food multiplies amazingly, giving off carbon dioxide as it does so. In a dough the trapped gas will cause it to puff up. The more elastic the dough is, the more it will be able to rise before the strands rupture, releasing the gas.

Normally about a scant ounce of fresh yeast, or about 2 teaspoons (a little less than half an ounce) dried yeast will leaven 8 cups of flour. Other factors do affect this ratio, and recipes vary.

If yeast is to grow fast it must be given perfect conditions: Gentle warmth, moisture and food—in the form of flour, and sometimes sugar.

Fresh yeast will keep for 10 days or so, wrapped, in the refrigerator, and will keep frozen for months.

Dried yeast will remain active for some six months or so kept in a cool cabinet. Most dried yeasts are mixed with water before being added to the dough, but some are added directly.

Other bread ingredients: Water gives bread crispness. Beer gives a malty taste and milk a richer crumb and golden crust. Sugar or molasses encourage rapid yeast growth and adds a touch of sweetness.

Fat in the form of butter or lard is sometimes added to provide richness and to improve keeping quality. Butter also adds flavor.

Salt Bread needs a surprising amount of salt to taste right. Too much, however, discourages yeast growth. Three level tsp per 4 cups flour is about right.

Making bread

1 Sponging If it is fresh yeast, mix it with a teaspoon of sugar until smooth, then with a little lukewarm liquid; if dried, sprinkle it over a little lukewarm liquid and leave for 15 minutes. It should be frothy. If it is not, the yeast is dead and will have to be replaced before going to the trouble and expense of making the dough.

2 Mixing Mix the yeast into the liquid, which should be tepid or warm, not hot. Then mix this thoroughly into the flour which has been sifted with the salt.

Glazes Brush with beaten egg for a plain finish. For a crisp crust, put a roasting pan of water under the baking bread and brush frequently with salty water. For a "country" look, brush with salty water and sprinkle with cracked wheat or poppy seeds.

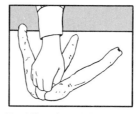

Braiding bread *Place ends together and turn them under. Push with the knuckles to fix the end.*

2 Braid the strands loosely. Tuck the other ends under as 1. Leave to rise before baking.

Brioche *To fix the heads on the bases, push the handle of a spoon through to the base of the mould.*

3 Kneading The working of the dough to ensure that the yeast cells are evenly distributed. It should start off very sticky. Do not stop kneading until it no longer sticks to the fingers and is slack, elastic and shiny. A heavy electric mixer with a dough beater kneads two pounds of flour in five minutes or so. Kneading vigorously by hand should take 10 to 12 minutes.

4 Rising Put the dough somewhere warm and leave it until it has doubled in bulk. To prevent it from sticking, the ball of dough, or its container, is usually lightly oiled. The dough must be covered, usually with an oiled piece of plastic wrap, to prevent drying out and cracking. A good rising temperature is about 90°F, at which the dough will double in volume in about an hour. Alternatively it may be left to rise more slowly overnight in a cool place or even in the refrigerator. Over-risen bread tastes too heavily of yeast and has a beery smell and coarse texture.

5 Knocking back entails punching the air out of the dough again. Because it has already been kneaded, then stretched, it will require little kneading to be smooth again. Shape into loaves or rolls.

	Ingredients	Method
Yeast quantities are given for fresh or compressed yeast. If using dried yeast, halve the weight, and sponge it with 5 tablespoons of the warm liquid before mixing.		
Plain white bread	10 cups strong white flour 3 level tsp salt 1 oz yeast 1½ tbs butter 3¾ cups water	Follow stages in bread-making, melting the butter in the water
Whole wheat bread	10 cups whole meal flour 3 level tsp salt 1 oz yeast ¼ cup lard or butter (optional) 2 tbs sugar 4½ cups warm water	Follow stages in bread-making, creaming the yeast with the sugar and adding it and the melted fat to half the water. Go slowly with the second half of the water as it may not all be needed.
Malt bread	6 cups strong white flour 1 oz yeast 1 level tsp salt 2 cups water 3 tbs molasses 3 tbs extract of malt ¼ cup butter ¼ cup raisins	Follow stages in bread-making adding the molasses, malt and raisins with the liquid. Bake in pans. Turn the pans around half way through cooking to stop uneven rising. Brush with thick SUGAR SYRUP while still hot after removal from the oven.
Kugelhopf (open-textured caky bread. The dough should be almost a pouring batter)	2 cups white flour (all-purpose, or weak) 9 tbs warm milk ¼ cup butter 4 tbs sugar 2 eggs Grated rind and juice of 1 orange ⅓ seedless raisins	Grease Kugelhopf pan and dust with fresh breadcrumbs. Follow stages in bread-making, adding sugar, eggs, butter, orange rind and juice to yeasty milk. Beat rather than knead. Put to rise for 1½ hours. Knock back. Prove in pan. Bake for 30 minutes at 375°F until shrunk at edges. Turn out. Cool. Dust with confectioner's sugar.
Brioche	2 cups white flour (all-purpose, or weak) ¼ cup butter ¼ oz yeast ¼ tsp salt 2 tbs fine sugar 2 eggs, beaten 3 tbs warm water	Follow stages in bread-making, adding eggs, melted butter and sugar with the yeast liquid. The dough should be very soft and sticky. Slap and pound the dough, throwing it down on the table-top rather than kneading it. Prove in a brioche pan or individual brioche pans.

6 Proving This second rising of the dough is not strictly necessary, but does give a lighter loaf. Once the loaves or rolls are about the size of the finished product, GLAZE them and bake.

7 Baking The bread dough will continue to rise in the oven, partly because the yeast keeps working until the heat kills it and partly because of rising steam, until the dough cooks rigid. This rising is called "oven spring" and it is likely to push away the top crust from the body of the loaf. So start in a hot oven to set the dough and kill the yeast quickly. A large loaf will take between 45 and 60 minutes. Start at 425°F, and reduce to 375°F after 30 minutes. Test for doneness by tipping it out on a cloth and tapping the underside; if it sounds hollow it is done. If not, return to the oven on its side, without the pan. When done, cool on rack.

Pastry

All non-flaky pastries may be made by the rubbing-in method used here (see below) to make plain short pastry. Sugar may be added with the flour, and eggs added with, or instead of, the water. Make the richer pastries containing a high proportion of egg and/or fat, like *pâte à pâté*, by sifting the flour onto a flat surface, making a well in the center, and gradually incorporating the surrounding flour as illustrated. If the pastry is very rich in fat and malleable (such as the three-yolk *pâte sucrée sablée*) it will probably be smooth, with the fat evenly distributed and with the texture of soft putty, needing little handling other than quick pressing into a ball. If, however, the ingredients are unevenly distributed, with streaks of fat and pockets of unincorporated flour visible, the pastry should be *fraisée* as shown in the illustration.

The ideal pastry is "short"—it is crisp and crumbly but not hard. The amount of fat added to the flour, the way the pastry is handled and the amount of water in the dough all govern the shortness. Even pastries with a little fat in them require little water. The more water is added, the harder and tougher the pastry will be. If pastry is very doughy and easy to handle it probably has too much water in it, will shrink badly in the oven, and turn out hard and tough; if it is tricky and fragile to handle, the resulting pastry will be short. The exception is the malleable, butter-laden French *pâte brisée* which has the texture of soft putty.

No two chefs can agree exactly on proportions of flour, fat and egg used in pastry doughs (in some cases they cannot even agree on their names).

There must, however, be at least one part fat to two parts flour (by weight) to make even the plainest shortcrust. The more fat the pastry has, the richer, more friable and delicate it is. If there is a high proportion of fat and egg together there is no need for any milk or water, but the dough will have to be chilled if, as is likely, it becomes too sticky to handle. This is particularly true of almond pastry and *pâte sucrée aux oeufs*. A high proportion of sugar gives the sandy, shortbread-like texture of *pâte sablée*.

Egg whites will provide a waterproof seal to a cracked flan case if re-baked briefly · Press pastry into edges of pans with a small ball of dough to avoid tearing · To get well-risen, crisp puff pastry, put a roasting pan filled with hot water in the bottom of the oven.

Short pastry *Cut cold fat into small pieces. Rub them with the flour between the fingers and thumbs.*

2 Rub until the mixture looks like crumbs. Mix in liquids with a knife then gather the dough together.

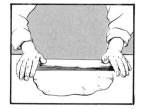

3 Press dough into a ball. Chill (wrapped if sticky). Roll out using short firm strokes of the pin.

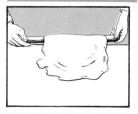

Lining a flan *Roll pastry thinly. Lift by rolling loosely on pin. Lay on flan pan by unrolling.*

2 Ease the pastry carefully into the corners to avoid any stretching.

3 Roll pin across top of pan to remove any excess pastry. Leave pastry to relax for 30 minutes.

Baking blind *Line pastry shell with paper. Fill with dried beans or rice. Bake to required degree.*

Apple flan *Fill baked case with apple purée. Fan thin slices of raw sweet apple. Glaze with jam. Bake.*

Pie tops *Put thin strips of pastry around edge of pie dish and wet them before filling and covering.*

Plate pie edge *Make parallel cuts at 1-in intervals in pastry edge. Fold corners and press.*

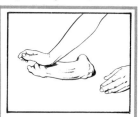

Fraiser method *Knead rich pastries smooth by smearing them with heel of the hand once or twice.*

	Flour	Salt	Butter	Chilled water	Eggs	Other ingredients
Plain shortcrust (*pâte brisée*)	2 cups plain	1 tsp	$\frac{1}{2}$ cup	5 to 8 tbs		
Rich shortcrust (*pâte brisée fine*)	2 cups	1 tsp	$\frac{3}{4}$ cup	4 to 6 tbs		
Shortcrust with egg (*pâte brisée aux oeufs*, rich flan pastry)	2 cups	1 tsp	$\frac{3}{4}$ cup	3 to 5 tbs	1 yolk or $\frac{1}{2}$ an egg	
Pâte à pâté (*croûte* doughs for pâtés)	2 cups	1 tsp	$\frac{2}{3}$ cup	4 to 6 tbs	2 yolks or 1 egg	
Sweet shortcrust (*pâte brisée sucrée*)	2 cups	$\frac{1}{2}$ tsp	$\frac{1}{2}$ cup			2 tbs sugar
Rich sweet shortcrust (*pâte sucrée aux oeufs*)	2 cups	$\frac{1}{2}$ tsp	$\frac{3}{4}$ cup		2 yolks	2 tbs sugar
Pâte sucrée sablée (rich pastry with a sugary texture)	2 cups	$\frac{1}{2}$ tsp	$\frac{1}{2}$ cup	Note: Chilled water is not used because of the high proportion of egg yolks. 2 to 3 tbs water may be substituted for 2 of the 4 egg yolks for a less rich pastry.	4 yolks	$\frac{1}{2}$ cup sugar 2 drops vanilla extract
Almond pastry (*pâte frolle*)	2 cups	$\frac{1}{2}$ tsp	$\frac{3}{4}$ cup		1 egg	$\frac{3}{4}$ cup ground almonds $\frac{1}{3}$ cup sugar 3 drops vanilla extract
Cheese pastry	2 cups	Pinch	$\frac{1}{2}$ cup			1 cup grated hard dry cheese Pinch of pepper Pinch of cayenne Pinch of dry mustard
Whole wheat pastry	1 cup plain 1 cup whole wheat	1 tsp	$\frac{2}{3}$ cup	3 to 4 tbs	1 yolk	
Suet pastry (for steamed puddings)	2 cups self-raising	1 tsp		$\frac{2}{3}$ cup (approx)		$\frac{2}{3}$ cup shredded beef suet

Pastry/2

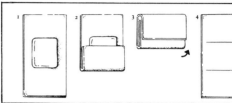

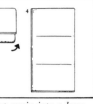

Flaky pastry *Use three-quarters weight of butter to dry flour. Proceed as for short pastry, using half the butter. Then roll dough into a rectangle. Dot half remaining butter over bottom two-thirds. Fold top third down, bottom third up and proceed as for puff pastry (see right) giving two 90° "turns" (rolls and folds). Dot remaining butter as before and give three more "turns." Chill. Use rolled thinly.*

Pâte à pâté *Sift flour on to a table-top. Make a well in the center and put in eggs, liquids, sugar and soft butter.*

2 *Use only the tips of the fingers to pinch the central ingredients together until smooth.*

Puff pastry *Mix flour with chilled water and a pinch of salt to a soft, smooth dough. Weigh. Roll with short firm strokes on a floured board into rectangles ½ in thick. Tap a block of butter (half the weight of the dough—less if inexperienced) with a floured pin to flatten it. Place the butter in the center of the dough rectangle. Fold bottom third up and top third down to enclose the butter. Press to seal the sides. Give the "parcel" a quarter turn.*

Roll out again into a long rectangle. Fold in three and chill for 15 minutes. Roll, fold, wrap and chill again. Repeat until six complete "turns" have taken place. Roll out to the thickness of a coin for EN CROÛTE dishes and pies.

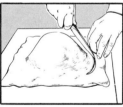

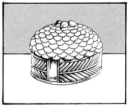

Puff pastry shell *Roll out a thin circle of pastry. Place a rolled ball of foil on top. Wet edge around ball.*

3 *Gradually work in the surrounding flour, still using only the fingertips.*

Filling a raised pie mold *Use not-too-thin pastry to line mold. Ease it into the corners.*

2 *Roll pin across the top mold to remove excess pastry. Fill with savory mixture. Cover with tin pastry.*

2 *Cover with thin sheet of pastry. Cut around edge. Brush with egg and decorate with pieces of pastry.*

4 *Flour the hands and press the dough into a ball. Chill before rolling or pressing out.*

3 *Cut out fluted circles of thin pastry. Halve. Use egg white or water to stick in overlapping circles.*

4 *Make a steam vent in the top. Decorate that with pastry leaves. Glaze with egg and bake.*

3 *Bake in hot oven until dark brown. Cut around top. Remove foil.*

Baking pastry shell on the back of a pan *Roll pastry. Lay on back of pan.*

2 *Put a second pan on top of that. Trim off the edges. Bake until crisp.*

3 *Remove top pan, allow pastry to cool slightly. Lift off cooked pastry shell.*

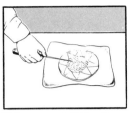

Vol-au-vent *Roll puff pastry ¼ in thick. Cut out large circle. Cut inner circle on surface only.*

2 Use back of knife tip to decorate inner section and outer rim. Use knife edge to "knock" pastry layers.

3 Bake in hot oven until risen and brown. Cut right through inner circle to release a lid.

4 Remove lid and scrape out any uncooked pastry from center. Return case to the oven briefly to dry it out.

Bouchées *Make small versions of vol-au-vent. Or, if using flaky pastry, stamp out rounds.*

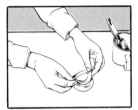

2 Stamp out smaller circles from half the rounds. Brush larger circles and rings with egg. Lay rings on rounds.

3 Prick the bases (only) with a fork.

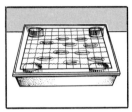

4 Bake bouchées and lids (inner circles) under a greased cake rack (to prevent uneven rising) in hot oven.

Fish in puff pastry *Bake a fish-shaped pastry base. Sprinkle evenly with semolina (to prevent sogginess)*

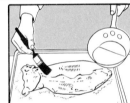

2 Lay boned and skinned fish fillets on base. Brush with butter. Add lemon juice and tarragon leaves.

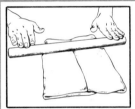

Palmiers *Roll out a thin sheet of puff pastry. Fold ends in to middle and roll again lightly.*

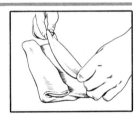

2 Fold edges into the middle once again.

3 Sprinkle with black pepper and salt.

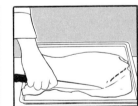

4 Cover fish with a thin sheet of pastry. Cut around the edge leaving about ½-in margin.

3 Fold in half lengthwise.

4 Cut into ¼-in slices. Press both cut sides of each slice in sugar.

5 Use metal spatula to lift base and tuck raw pastry top under it. Do this all around.

6 Make scales with teaspoon. Add pastry eye and tail. Brush with egg. Bake.

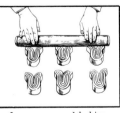

5 Lay on greased baking sheet. Roll or press out thinly and bake in hot oven.

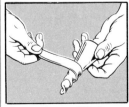

Cream horns *Wind egged strips of puff pastry round moulds. Bake upright.*

149

Pastry/3

Scalloped edge "Knock-up" pastry edge into layers with knife blade held horizontally.

2 Then use the back of the knife tip to drag edge into scallops while pinching with fingertips.

Pastry rose Flour thin strips of pastry and roll them up loosely.

2 Push fine knife blade into center of concentric pastry rings. Cut through to edge. Repeat five or six times.

3 Squeeze the pastry gently from the base to make the rose petals open out.

Plaited croûte Roll out rectangles of pastry and cut edges as shown.

2 Lay sausage-meat filling, or browned meat, down center.

3 Flap the side strips over the filling from alternate sides to give plaited effect.

4 Brush with egg. Bake brown in hot oven. Cook longer in cooler oven if it is necessary to cook the filling.

Pastry leaves Use back of knife to mark diamond shapes to resemble leaves.

The fat (shortening)

Butter gives a crisp rich crust, with an excellent flavor. Margarine gives a slightly less rich and less flavorsome pastry. Lard gives a soft, very short crust, which is lacking in flavor but gives excellent results used in conjunction with butter. Vegetable shortening gives a crust much like lard, but slightly crisper and less crumbly.

The flour

Plain flour, all-purpose flour and cake flour are all suitable for pastries. Whole meal flour may also be used, but it will need more liquid than white flour as it is more absorbent. Pastry made from whole wheat flour is somewhat heavier. Self-raising flour is sometimes used to produce a caky, rather soft, crust and is occasionally used to help lighten heavy doughs such as cheese.

To make short pastry dough in a mixing machine: Sift in the flour and salt, add diced butter and mix until the butter pieces are no bigger than coarse breadcrumbs. Add the liquids and mix to a loose ball with a pastry or dough beater. Turn out. Work for a minute or so by the *fraiser* method.

To make short pastry dough in a food processor: Put the flour, salt and diced butter in the machine and process with the knife blade for three seconds or until the mixture looks like coarse breadcrumbs. Add the liquid, process for three more seconds, until the mixture has massed together. Turn it out and work smooth by the *fraiser* method.

Choux pastry is the base for many French desserts.

½ cup butter
1 cup water
¼ tsp salt
1 cup plain flour
4 eggs

1 Put the water, butter and salt in a large pan and bring slowly to the boil.
2 Once all the butter is melted, bring the water to a full, rolling boil and immediately add all the flour at once.
3 Remove the pan from the heat and beat hard with a wooden spoon until the mixture is smooth and curls away from the sides of the pan.
4 Turn the mixture into a large cold bowl (mixer bowl if using a machine) and spread it up the sides to speed the cooling.
5 After a minute or so beat in one egg. At first the mixture will be slippery and wet, but it will soon stiffen to a solid paste. Once beaten, add the next egg, beat until smooth, then add the third egg. Beat again.
6 Mix the last egg in a cup before adding it to the mixture as it may not all be needed. The aim is to make a shiny, soft paste of dropping consistency, with the mixture just holding its shape and dropping reluctantly off the spoon in a blob, neither running off nor adhering too obstinately. Add as much of the final egg as is necessary to achieve this.
7 Keep it refrigerated until it is needed.

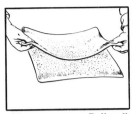

Cheese straws Roll puff pastry thinly. Sprinkle well with grated Parmesan cheese. Fold and roll again.

2 (CHEESE PASTRY can be used instead.) Fold again loosely. Cut into strips.

3 Twist each length several times. Lay on paper-covered baking sheet. Press each edge to secure. Bake until crisp.

Fleurons Use fluted pastry cutter to stamp out thin crescents of puff pastry. Glaze and bake.

Paris Brest

On a baking sheet pipe or spoon the choux paste into a fat ring shape with a hole in the middle. Bake, cool, then split and scoop out any uncooked paste. Fill the bottom half with a thin layer of good strawberry jam, whipped cream and fresh strawberries. Replace "lid;" dust with confectioner's sugar, or ICE.

Profiteroles and éclairs

Pipe choux paste on a baking sheet in little balls or long lines respectively. Bake at 400°F for 20 to 30 minutes until swollen and brown. Make a pea-sized hole in each to allow moisture to escape and dry out in the oven for five minutes. They may subsequently be filled with cream of CRÈME PÂTISSIÈRE by piping it in through the vent hole.

Gâteau St. Honoré

Bake a *pâte brisée* flan case. Fill it with *crème pâtissière*. Then pile *profiteroles* filled with sweetened whipped cream in a pyramid on top (dipping them in liquid CARAMEL first to help stick them in place). Ideally, it should be built very high, like a witch's hat, but it can be a small mound. Trickle more caramel over it or swathe in SPUN SUGAR.

Hazel-nut pastry

1½ cups flour
⅔ cup ground hazel-nuts
3 tbs confectioner's sugar
Finely grated lemon rind
¼ tsp ground cinnamon
⅓ cup butter
1 egg yolk
1½ tbs cold water

Make up as shortcrust pastry, mixing the nuts with the flour, sugar, cinnamon and rind. Rub in the butter, then mix in the yolk and water. Press to a ball. Chill.

Cookie dough Chill rich pastries wrapped in cylindrical shape. Slice off rounds for baking.

Strudel Make a pastry dough with 2¼ cups flour, pinch of salt, 1 egg, and ⅔ cup water. Beat and throw dough against a floured surface until dough is smooth and *very* elastic. Allow it to relax for 15 minutes. Cover surface with a floured cloth and roll pastry out on it—so thinly that newsprint could easily be read through it. Cut off thick edges. Spread with sweetened cooked apples or cherries spiced with cinnamon. Roll up (using cloth makes this easier). Brush with butter. Bake in moderate oven for 20 minutes.

Linzer torte

Line a flan dish with hazel-nut pastry, fill with cranberry jelly, raspberry jam or red currant jelly mixed with apple purée. LATTICE TOP it with more pastry and bake at 375°F for 30 minutes. Take out and put a small blob of clear jam jelly into each lattice square while it is still hot so that the jam will melt. Sift confectioner's sugar over the top. It will stay visible only on the lattice strips, melting into the jam.

Strudel (filo) pastry Pulling and stretching strudel dough as below, and baked strudel.

Chiffon pies

Fill chilled baked pastry shells made of *pâte sucrée* or rich flan pastry with any gelatin-set MOUSSE mixture such as raspberry, praline or lemon and orange when it is on the point of setting. Decorate once set.

Sausage rolls

Use short, flaky, rough-puff or puff pastry. Roll into long thin rectangles. Lay some well-seasoned SAUSAGE-MEAT down the center of each rectangle of pastry. Fold one long side over the top of the meat and brush it with beaten egg. Flap the other side over and press it down on top of the egg-coated side, turn the roll over, then brush the top with more egg. Make diagonal slashes through to the meat along the length of the roll. Cut the length up into small sausage rolls. Bake for 25 minutes at 400°F.

Cookies and biscuits

The methods used for cookies and biscuits are the same as those for rubbed-in pastry mixtures like shortcrust, or for creaming large cakes. Time the baking carefully (cookies burn fast).

Pasta

The flour used in pasta-making is hard wheat—or strong—flour. Semolina flour is sometimes used, but should not be confused with the coarser meal sold simply as semolina, which is too granular for the home cook to manage.

Commercial pasta is often made without eggs, but the easiest and most delicious pasta can be made at home as follows:

**1 lb strong flour
4 large eggs
1 tsp salt**

1 Sieve the flour and salt directly on a smooth table-top.
2 Push the flour into a ring with a central well.
3 Break the eggs into the well.
4 Using the fingertips of one hand only (or first a fork and then the fingertips), mix the eggs together, while slowly introducing the flour. The action is one of slapping and stirring, and, as the dough gets stiffer, pinching, as for *pâte à pâté*. Use a pastry scraper or the other hand to prevent the ring of flour from spreading all over the work surface. Finally gather the mass into a ball.
5 Using a palette knife or pastry scraper, scrape every morsel of dough from the hands. Wash and dry the hands.
6 Flour the hands lightly and knead the dough for 10 minutes or until it is smooth and elastic and has lost its stickiness. If the dough, far from being sticky, is too dry and crumbly or tough, work in a spoonful of olive oil.
7 Once the dough is well kneaded, wrap it up in a piece of plastic foil or a cloth wrung out in warm water. Leave it to rest for half an hour.

8 Divide the dough into manageable pieces (perhaps three or four). Rewrap all but one of them.
9 Roll out the unwrapped dough with a lightly-floured rolling pin on the floured work surface. Working as firmly and as fast as possible, so that the pasta doesn't dry out and crack, roll the dough into paper-thin sheets, frequently flouring lightly to prevent sticking.
10 Once the dough is uniformly thin, allow it to dry out by hanging it over a chair back or rail for 30 minutes, then cut it into the desired shape or strips. Drying is not strictly necessary but the pasta is easier to handle when a little drier. (For pasta that is to be stuffed, such as ravioli or cannelloni, put the stuffing in immediately, then leave the pasta to dry.)
11 Repeat the rolling and cutting process with the other pieces of dough.

Once cut to shape, pasta may be hung in a cool, airy place and kept for a week or more before cooking. Or it may be kept frozen almost indefinitely. If it is stuffed, however, it must not be kept longer than 24 hours in a refrigerator or 12 hours in a cool room or the stuffing deteriorates.

Green pasta may be made by incorporating cooked, well drained and liquefied spinach purée into the dough in place of one or two of the eggs.

Pink pasta is made by incorporating a tomato purée into the dough. Two or three tablespoons replace one egg.

Strands of two or three different colored pastas, mixed on a plate, look quite beautiful; the tastes differ little.

Whole wheat pasta is, of course, made using wholewheat flour and is made exactly as white pasta, although it may be necessary to use one more egg or a little water to obtain the correct consistency of dough, whole meal flour being more absorbent than white flour. The pasta is marginally heavier, but what it loses in texture it gains in flavor.

Pasta machines

A pasta machine takes the effort out of the kneading, rolling and cutting. Prevent sticking by keeping the pasta dough fairly firm and the machine rollers and the dough lightly floured. Dry pasta after cutting.

Cooking pasta

The most usual method of cooking pasta is boiling. It is then tossed in butter, in oil and/or cheese. Pasta is usually served with a small amount of sauce or some other seasoning ingredient, such as strips of ham, fried mushrooms, cooked mussels or clams. For this sort of dish pasta is cooked as follows:
1 Bring a large pan of well-salted water (one heaping tablespoon for every five or 6 pints to the boil. Pasta swells up during cooking, so a large, fast-moving body of water is necessary to stop the pieces sticking together.
2 Add a tablespoon of oil to the water to prevent sticking. To further lessen the chances of lasagne strips sticking, drop them in one by one.
3 Sprinkle or push the pasta into the water. Stir it vigorously with a wooden spoon to prevent sticking until the water is boiling again.

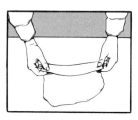

Making tagliatelle Fold up floured pasta in a loose roll.

2 Cut across the roll to make strips. Open out each of the strips.

Stuffing ravioli Brush a sheet of pasta with beaten egg. Put teaspoons of filling in rows on top of it.

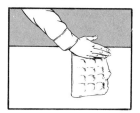

2 Put a second sheet of pasta on top. Press between each row to seal all the pockets of filling.

3 Use a pasta wheel, knife or pastry-cutter to separate the ravioli.

Hot boiled pasta dishes

	Pasta	Other ingredients	Method
Alla carbonara (with ham, eggs and cheese)	Rigatoni Lumache Linguine Spaghetti Tagliatelle	Butter Diced cooked ham Crushed garlic Heavy cream Beaten eggs or egg yolks Salt and pepper	Heat butter. Add ham and garlic. Cook for 1 minute, add eggs, cream and salt and pepper. Stir to heat without scrambling eggs. Toss with pasta.
Con tonno (with tuna)	Fettuccine Tagliatelle Trenette	Cooked tuna Olive oil Crushed garlic Canned tomatoes Chopped parsley Salt and pepper	Fry garlic in oil. Add tomatoes, their juice and parsley. Simmer until thick. Add tuna, salt and pepper. Simmer for 5 minutes.
All'Amatriciana (with onion and bacon)	Fettuccine Tagliatelle Trenette Bucatini	Unsmoked diced bacon Chopped onion Diced sweet red pepper Oil Crushed garlic Skinned chopped tomatoes (optional) Salt and pepper	Fry bacon until crisp. Sweat onion and sweet red pepper in oil. Add garlic and any tomatoes. Cook for 1 minute. Add salt and pepper and crisp bacon.
Paglia et fieno alla ghiotto "straw and hay"—with mushroom)	Fettuccine Tagliatelle, both green and plain	Chopped shallots Unsmoked diced ham Butter Sliced white mushrooms Heavy cream Salt and pepper	Sweat shallots and ham in butter. Add mushrooms. Cook for 3 minutes. Add cream. Boil up. Add seasoning. Toss with pasta.
Con fegatini (with chicken livers)	Pappardelle Tagliatelle	Chopped shallots Butter Diced unsmoked bacon Olive oil Lean ground beef Crushed garlic Dry vermouth Tomato purée Salt and pepper Sage Ground chicken livers	Sweat shallots in butter. Fry bacon and beef in oil in another pan. Add garlic. Cook for 1 minute. Moisten with vermouth and purée. Add seasonings. Cook for 8 minutes. Add livers to shallot pan. Sauté briefly. Add to beef mixture.

4 Boil the pasta until, when tested, it is *just* tender, neither raw-tasting and tough nor soft, flabby and slimy. Dried commercial pasta takes from 3 minutes for thin vermicelli to 17 minutes for thick, shell shapes or large macaroni. Small homemade pasta may cook in as little as 1 minute, the larger pasta in about 3 minutes if it is very fresh.

Test the pasta once a minute when it is nearly ready to be sure to obtain the perfect *al dente* texture.

5 Drain in a colander, moving the pasta around with a spoon to allow steam to escape and thus prevent further cooking. If it cannot be served immediately, put some butter or oil on it, or mix it with a little sauce, to prevent sticking. Serve with freshly grated Parmesan or Pecorino cheese to be sprinkled over it.

Pasta salads
Toss well-drained and cooled boiled pasta with green salad ingredients, tomatoes, cold fish, strips of ham or poultry.

Layered pasta dishes
Pasta may be turned into a homely pie or an impressive and grand baked dish.

Cook the pasta (usually the flat lasagne) as described above, then layer it in a buttered pie dish, along with other ingredients, top with cheese sauce or grated cheese and bake. The secondary ingredients may be as simple as slices of cheese and tomato or cooked spinach and cheese sauce, or as exotic and delicate as crayfish and truffles in a rich sauce.

Stuffed pasta dishes
Pasta can be stuffed with savory or sweet ingredients.

Ravioli and tortellini are stuffed while fresh, dried slightly, then cooked in stock or water and served with butter, cheese or a sauce. Cannelloni is generally pre-boiled, stuffed, then baked in sauce. If the cannelloni is made from squares of fresh pasta, they may be stuffed and baked in sauce without pre-cooking.

The stuffings for pasta need to be smooth and finely ground to reduce the risk of their bursting their pasta envelopes.

To make tortellini roll softish pasta dough out thinly, stamp or cut into circles with a pastry-cutter or glass. Put a spoonful of filling on each round of pasta, fold them over in half to enclose the filling, and press the open edges together.

Make ravioli as shown or line a ravioli mold, pressing the pasta dough into each indentation, using a small ball of dough to push it well into all the corners. Brush with beaten egg, add in the stuffing and cover with a second piece of rolled-out dough.

Fillings for stuffed pasta:
Ricotta fillings Blend, liquefy or chop and mix ricotta cheese, Parmesan cheese, parsley, a little butter, salt, pepper and nutmeg and enough cold milk to make a soft paste. *Chicken and mortadella filling* Fry in butter finely diced onion, mortadella sausage and white poultry meat. Pound or liquefy with beaten egg and grated Parmesan. Season well.

Pancakes, waffles and scones

Crêpes *Pour a thin layer of pancake batter into a greased pan, tipping to spread it evenly over base.*

2 Pour excess batter back into bowl. Fry crêpe, *turning once.*

The French *crêpe* is one of the most versatile of the many things made using BATTERS (page 114).

Dishes using French crêpes

Pancake pie In a deep flan dish place layers of thin *crêpes* with a thin spreading of BOLOGNAISE SAUCE between them. Cover with MORNAY SAUCE, sprinkle with grated cheese and breadcrumbs, and bake.

Crêpes Suzette Melt a few tablespoons of butter in a large frying pan. Add an equal amount of sugar, the juice and grated rind of two oranges (and perhaps a little lemon juice and rind for a sharper taste). Simmer to a thick syrup. Lay the pancakes, one at a time, in the sauce, soaking them well, then folding them in half and then in half again to quarters. Stack them overlapping at the edge of the frying pan to leave room for soaking and folding other pancakes. When all are thus treated re-arrange them so that they are laid evenly over the pan's surface. Add good measures of brandy and orange Curaçao (or Grand Marnier, or any other citrus-based sweet liqueur). The total amount of liquor should be about 5 to 8 tablespoons. Shake the pan over heat, and FLAME it—put a match to the alcoholic contents, and burn off the alcohol.

Serve the pancakes, boiling the remaining liquid down to a bubbling syrup, and pouring it over them.

Filled pancakes Roll thin French *crêpes* round any flavorful mixture and lay them in a buttered dish. Cover with a suitable sauce.

Waffles

In waffle-making, the special cooking iron contains the batter in a thin flat, indented shape, ensuring that it is light, just soft inside and crisp on the outside. Waffles must be eaten as they are cooked or they quickly become limp. Serve with plenty of butter and maple syrup, golden syrup, honey or jam.

Prepare the waffle-iron by greasing it and heating it well, then grease again before cooking. New waffle-irons sometimes stick badly. Keep greasing and heating them (never washing them or scraping with anything rough) until a non-stick surface is gradually built up. Once the waffle-iron is well "seasoned" it may be washed (though this is strictly unnecessary as the intense heat of the cooking process sterilizes the implement). Waffle-irons coated with non-stick material are available, but take care not to scratch the surface or the effectiveness of the non-stick coating will be impaired.

Some recipes recommend using the waffle-iron ungreased. This is really only feasible if the iron is non-stick or well seasoned.

Dry mixture:
$1\frac{1}{2}$ cups all-purpose flour
$\frac{1}{4}$ tsp salt
3 tsp (level) baking powder
2 tbs sugar
Liquid mixture:
2 eggs (separated)
$1\frac{1}{4}$ cups milk
$\frac{1}{4}$ cup butter
$\frac{1}{2}$ tsp vanilla extract

Follow the stages in batter making, omitting the egg whites. Beat these separately until fairly stiff and fold into batter. Grease and heat the iron, pour out any excess fat and put in a little butter. Pour a thin layer of batter into one side only, just enough to fill the grooves. Close the iron and cook over high heat for 1 minute per side. Do not open the iron before time is up, as the waffle will stick until cooked.

Stuffed pancakes		
Filling	Sauce	Garnish
Cooked diced chicken and Gruyère cheese in MORNAY SAUCE	Chicken VELOUTÉ or MORNAY	Breadcrumbs and cheese GRATINÉE
Cooked mussels in thick TOMATO SAUCE flavored with garlic	TOMATO and WHITE SAUCE spooned in stripes across dish	None
Herbed ground beef	TOMATO or DEMI-GLACE	Grated Parmesan
Cooked shredded leek, strips of ham and blanched beensprouts	BÉCHAMEL	Lattice of fine ham strips
Cooked mushrooms and sweetbreads in light MADEIRA SAUCE	MADEIRA SAUCE or brush with butter	Few sliced cooked mushrooms, chopped chervil or parsley

Sweet stuffed pancakes
Filling
Mincemeat preserve
Sweetened cream cheese with cinnamon
Lemon juice and brown sugar (sprinkle pancakes, then roll them up)
CRÈME PÂTISSIÈRE flavored with orange

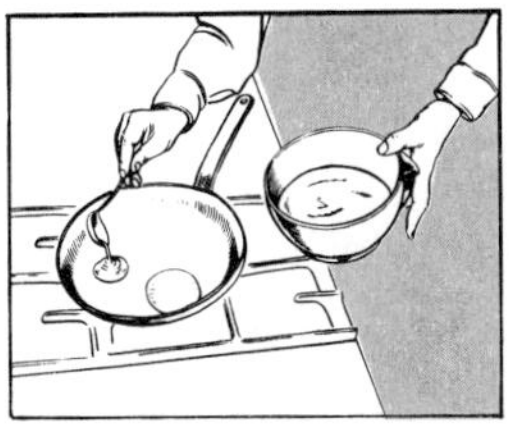

Griddle scones Put spoonfuls of batter well apart on a greased heavy pan, or griddle.

2 *When bubbles appear on the surface, the underside is browned. Turn over to brown the second side.*

Thicker pancakes—sometimes called griddle cakes or dropped scones—are yeasted, or aerated with raising agent, and cooked on a lightly greased griddle, or thick skillet or frying pan, as shown above.

Serve:

Hot with vanilla ice cream

With APRICOT SAUCE or cream

With sugar, lemon juice and, possibly cinnamon, on top. Glaze under broiler.

Reheated, then sifted heavily with confectioner's sugar and glazed with a SALAMANDER or under broiler. Soak with Grand Marnier and FLAME.

Batter pancakes (using raising agent)		
Batter ingredients	Method	To serve
Scotch pancakes Dry mixture: 3 cups all-purpose flour ¼ tsp salt 1 tsp cream of tartar ½ tsp baking soda 1½ tbs sugar Liquid mixture: 1 egg ⅔ cup milk	Follow the stages in batter making (see page 114). Drop mix in spoonfuls on to a hot, lightly greased frying pan or griddle. Cook slowly. When first bubbles burst on surface turn over and brown the other side.	Keep warm in loose cloth. Serve warm with butter and preserves.
Wholewheat griddle scones Dry mixture: 1¼ cups wholewheat flour ¾ cup plain flour ½ tsp salt ½ tsp baking soda Liquid mixture: 2 tbs butter 1½ tbs soft brown sugar 1¼ cups milk 1 egg	Warm the sugar, butter and milk together until just blended. Mix with the egg. Then follow the stages in batter making. (see page 114). Cook as for Scotch pancakes.	As above
English crumpets Dry mixture: 2 cups all-purpose flour 1 tsp (level) salt Liquid mixture: 1½ tbs (level) dried yeast 2 tsp (level) sugar 1¼ cups milk ⅓ cup water	Warm milk and water to blood-heat. Add yeast and sugar. Allow to stand for 10 minutes, then follow the stages in batter making (see page 114). Cover pan for 30–50 minutes. When mixture is frothy, grease crumpet rings or egg-poaching or large round pastry cutters. Put on a greased griddle or skillet and pour mixture into rings. Cook slowly for 4 minutes or until bubbles	Toast briefly on both sides and spread butter and honey on the side with holes
Blinis Dry mixture: 1 cup all-purpose flour 1 cup buckwheat flour ¼ tsp salt Liquid mixture: 1 scant tbs (level) dried yeast 1 tsp sugar 1½ cups milk 2 small eggs	Warm milk to blood-heat. Sprinkle in sugar and yeast. Allow to stand for 10 minutes. Add eggs. Then follow the stages in batter making (see page 114). Prove (leave covered in a warm place to rise) for 1 or 2 hours or until frothy and well risen. Cook as for Scotch pancakes.	Serve hot, well buttered. Each guest spreads his *blini* with plenty of sour cream, and with smoked salmon, caviar, or herring fillets.

Cakes

Many would-be bakers are put off by the disappointing results of their first efforts—usually attempts at rather difficult techniques. No one can really expect to make a perfect *Genoise* without some baking experience, but anyone can make a good gingerbread at the first attempt. MERINGUE cakes and cakes based on pastries are also easy for the inexperienced.

Knowledgeable cakemakers can confidently adapt or alter recipes. The less experienced cook, however, should stick strictly to the recipe, measuring ingredients exactly, making sure that the oven temperature is accurate and timing with care.

Ingredients in cake making
Eggs:
Most recipes assume a medium-size egg weighing about 2 oz. Use eggs at room temperature. Very cold eggs tend to curdle, giving the resulting cake a tough texture. When separating eggs, make sure there are no flecks of yolk in the whites—they will not beat into peaks if there are. For the same reason, bowl and beaters must be absolutely grease-free.

Sugars:
Superfine granulated sugar with its small crystals is most suitable for cakes. Very coarse granulated sugar gives a speckled appearance to a finished cake. Coarse sugar can be ground finer in a food processor or blender.

Soft brown sugar gives color and flavor to dark cakes like gingerbread and chocolate cake, but gives a drab look to pale cakes.

Honey, molasses and golden syrup are used in many "melting method" cakes. These cakes are usually cooked slowly as syrup burns easily.

Flours:
The word "flour" in a recipe means, unless otherwise specified, plain white wheat flour. The most suitable flour for cakes comes from soft wheat and is known as "weak flour," "household flour" or "cake flour."

"All-purpose" flour in Europe is generally suitable, but in North America such flour is too "strong" (or "hard") and "cake flour" must be used.

"Self-raising flour" has baking powder added to it and should only be used if specified in the recipe.

Fats:
Butter gives the best flavor to cakes. Margarine, particularly soft or tub, has less flavor but is quick to beat or to cream.

Vegetable shortenings are flavorless but give good light cakes. As butter and margarine contain some water, when substituting vegetable shortening for them use 15% less *weight* of fat.

Oils are rarely used in cakes as they do not hold air when creamed or beaten.

Raising agents:
Cakes are made by mixing flour to a paste with eggs and liquids, flavoring the mixture and incorporating air or gas to make it rise while cooking.

As the mixture cooks the strands of mixture harden in their risen positions, to give the light, open texture of cake. Gas is incorporated into the mixture in various ways. In breadmaking, yeast produces gas, but the flavor of yeast is undesirable in cakes. Other raising agents are used instead:

Air Air instilled into a mixture expands as it is heated and the mixture rises. The most efficient way of trapping air in a mixture is by folding in beaten egg whites. Well-beaten whole eggs also contain bubbles of air and some air is also incorporated into the mixture by the sifting of the flour and the creaming of the fat and sugar together until they have roughly the consistency of a mousse.

Steam Flour mixtures with a high proportion of liquid in them will rise in a hot oven since, as the water vaporizes, the steam rises, taking the uncooked flour mixture with it. Rising, however, is generally uneven and the resulting dough has large air-pockets (like a Yorkshire pudding or choux pastry). This method is, therefore, not used on its own in the making of cakes, but rising steam is a contributing factor in the rising of wet-mixture cakes such as gingerbread.

Baking soda Mixed with liquid and heated, this substance gives off the gas carbon dioxide (CO_2) which will puff up the mixture as it forms. The residue of the "bicarb" remains in the cooked mixture as carbonate of soda and has a mildly acid taste and a yellow color. This method of raising is, therefore, most suitable for strong-tasting cakes such as gingerbread or chocolate cake, and cakes flavored with molasses, lemon, orange or dried fruit in which the taste of the carbonate of soda will be masked.

The carbon dioxide trapped in the cake will gradually escape and be replaced by air.

Acid substances (vinegar, sour milk, cream of tartar, tartaric acid, yogurt, even marmalade or jam) are often added to speed up the chemical reaction which liberates the carbon dioxide from the bicarbonate of soda.

Baking powder (raising powder, rising powder) is a mixture of bicarbonate of soda and an acid powder (usually cream of tartar) stabilized with a filler. One level teaspoon of baking soda has approximately the same raising power as that of three to four level teaspoons of baking powder.

Cake-making

There are three basic cake-making techniques:

The melting method

(as for gingerbread). The raising agent is always baking soda.

1 In a heavy saucepan gently heat the fat and sugar with all the liquid ingredients, except the eggs, until the mix is melted and smooth. Cool it slightly.

2 Beat the eggs and then beat them well into the mixture.

3 Sift all the dry ingredients into a large bowl. Use a whisk or wooden spoon to make a well in the center. Gradually pour the liquids into the well, slowly beating in the surrounding flour, as in the making of BATTER.

4 Turn into prepared loaf or cake pans.

5 Bake in cool oven (to prevent the high syrup and sugar content from burning).

6 Allow to cool for 10 minutes in the pan before turning it out on a cake rack to finish cooling.

The creaming method

(as for Madeira cake, Victoria sandwich and fruit cake). Generally a little chemical raising agent is added, or self-raising flour used, but the creaming of fat and sugar to a mousse-like consistency is the secret of lightness in this type of cake.

1 First beat the fat until sloppy. Do not *melt* it. Add the sugar by degrees and continue creaming until the mixture is pale and mousse-like. The aim is to incorporate as much air as possible.

2 Beat the eggs and add them a little at a time, beating well between each addition. If the mixture shows signs of curdling, stir in a tablespoon of the sifted flour. Chilled eggs are the most likely cause of curdling. Curdled mixtures make acceptable cakes but they have a less delicate texture.

3 Add any solid, dry ingredients like dried fruit.

4 Fold in the well-sifted flour (and any baking powder), with as little mixing and stirring as possible. Use the classic FOLDING technique to ensure minimum loss of the carefully incorporated air.

5 Turn the mixture into a prepared pan, then smooth the top.

6 Bake in a moderate oven until the sides of the cake shrink slightly and the top feels springy. (Fruit cakes should feel firm and a skewer inserted into their center should emerge clean.)

7 Turn out on a cake rack to cool before splitting, filling or icing.

To stop the bowl bumping around while beating, stand it on a damp cloth · To keep cake soft and fresh store it in an airtight box along with a cut apple · To disguise a cake with a sunken middle, cut out middle and ice cake as a ring mold · Use a medicinal dropper or skewer tip to add food coloring and extracts.

Melting-method cakes		
	Ingredients	Method
Dark ginger-bread	$\frac{1}{2}$ cup butter $\frac{1}{3}$ cup molasses $\frac{2}{3}$ cup soft brown sugar $\frac{2}{3}$ cup milk 2 eggs $1\frac{1}{2}$ cups flour $\frac{1}{4}$ tsp salt 2 level tsp powdered ginger 1 level tsp baking soda	Follow the stages in the melting method. Bake for 1 hour at 325°F.
Orange cake	$\frac{1}{2}$ cup butter 1 cup sugar 1 cup orange juice 2 beaten eggs 2 cups plain flour 4 level tsp baking powder $\frac{1}{4}$ tsp salt	Follow the stages in the melting method. Bake for $1\frac{1}{4}$ hours at 350°F. Ice with orange GLACÉ ICING when cold.

Creaming-method cakes		
	Ingredients	Method
Victoria sandwich	$\frac{3}{4}$ cup soft margarine $\frac{3}{4}$ cup sugar $1\frac{1}{2}$ cups self-raising flour 3 large eggs	Follow the stages in the creaming method. Bake at 375°F for 20 to 25 minutes. Fill with whipped cream and/or jam or lemon curd. Dust the top with confectioner's sugar or coat with GLACÉ or FONDANT ICING or frosting.
Madeira cake	$\frac{3}{4}$ cup unsalted butter $\frac{3}{4}$ cup superfine granulated sugar $\frac{1}{3}$ cup lemon juice Pinch ground cinnamon 4 eggs $\frac{1}{3}$ cup rice flour 2 cups flour 1 level tsp baking soda	Follow the stages in the creaming method, folding in the sifted rice flour with the cinnamon, flour and baking soda, and the lemon juice last. Bake at 325°F for $1\frac{1}{4}$ to $1\frac{1}{2}$ hours.

Cakes/2

Beaten cakes *Beat eggs and sugar in electric mixer, or in bowl set over simmering water, to "ribbon trail."*

2 Sift in flour, folding in with large metal spoon. Use a lifting and turning, rather than stirring, action.

3 Add just-liquid butter (or other liquid) by dribbling it down side of bowl and folding in lightly.

The beating method
In all beaten cakes the trapped air, rising as it expands in the heat of the oven, is the raising agent. It is, therefore, essential to keep as much air in the cake mixture as possible at every stage.

Basic sponge
The simplest whisked cake is the basic sponge, containing no fat. It is light and springy but does not keep well.

Basic sponge
The simplest beaten
Basic sponge-making
saucepan of almost-simmering water. Beat steadily until the mixture is pale and mousse-like and will leave a "ribbon trail" when the beaters are lifted. The gentle heat speeds up the process by melting the sugar and slightly thickening the eggs. Remove from the heat and continue beating until cool. (If an electric mixer is used the heating process is not necessary.)
2 Add flavorings.

3 Fold (do not stir) in the well-sifted flour.
4 Pour in prepared pan.
5 Bake in a cool oven 350°F until the cake feels slightly springy, usually about 25 to 35 minutes, and the sides are just beginning to shrink.
6 Cool for 5 minutes in the cake pan, then turn over onto a cooling rack. Lift off the pan and peel off the backing paper. Cool completely before storing in an airtight container.

Génoise (A rich sponge, containing butter.)
1 Beat eggs and sugar as for the basic sponge.
2 Fold in half the flour as for the basic sponge.
3 Cream the butter to a sloppy, but not totally liquid, consistency and trickle it around the edge of the bowl, folding it in with the minimum of stirring. (Pouring on the top would require too much folding and consequent loss of air.)
4 Fold in rest of flour.
5 Proceed as for the basic sponge.

What went wrong?
Too dry and crumbly
Not enough liquid.
Too much raising agent.
Cooked too long.
Hard outside but not cooked in the middle
Baked too high in oven.
Oven over-hot.
Too wet a mixture.
Close-textured, heavy and doughy
Too much liquid.
Too little raising agent.
Insufficient creaming.
Sinking in the middle
Insufficient creaming.
Too hot an oven.
Fruit sinking to the bottom
Mixture too light.
Fruit wet when added (toss in flour if moist).
Fruit too large and heavy (chop up cherries and dates).
Cracking
Mixture too dry.
Too much raising agent.
Too small pan.
Oven too hot.
Uneven texture with large, uneven pockets
Uneven folding-in of the flour.
Too much raising agent.
Domed top
Oven too hot.
Too much raising agent.

The whisked cake and variations				
	Ingredients	Method	Filling	Decoration
Basic sponge (fatless)	3 eggs Half the total weight of the eggs (in the shell) in both plain flour and superfine sugar Pinch of salt	Follow the stages in basic sponge making	Jams or jellies and/or whipped cream	None, or a dusting of confectioner's sugar
Génoise	4 eggs $\frac{1}{2}$ cup sugar $\frac{3}{4}$ cup plain flour $\frac{1}{4}$ cup unsalted butter	Follow the stages in génoise making	Jam or whipped cream	Dust with confectioner's sugar
Coffee génoise	As above, and: 2 tsp instant coffee powder	Follow the stages in génoise making, adding powdered coffee to flour	Coffee BUTTER CREAM	Chocolate or coffee icing and CARAQUE

Swiss roll Bake sponge in paper-lined, shallow tray. Turn out on paper. Peel off baking paper.

2 Lay paper back on. Roll cake and papers up together while warm. When cold, unroll. Fill and re-roll.

Small cakes

Almost all cake mixtures can be baked in small cupcake pans or in individual paper cases; usually for 8 to 15 minutes at higher temperatures 400°F.

Preparing cake pans

To prevent cake mixtures sticking, the cake pan (unless it is a good new non-stick one) will need some preparation. For most cakes greasing or greasing and lightly dusting over with flour is sufficient. If the cake is to be in the oven for a long time, however, several layers of greased paper are also used to insulate the cake from the heat of the pan.

Buns and cakes where the pan is lined with a pastry or biscuit crust (like cheesecake): Grease the pan by lightly brushing it with any flavorless melted fat or oil.

Melting or creaming method cakes: As above, then line the base with wax paper cut to fit, and grease again. (To cut the paper accurately stand the pan on the paper, draw a pencil line around it and cut just inside the line.)

Cakes made by the beating method: As above, then sprinkle on a fine layer of flour, shake to distribute it evenly over the whole greased surface, then shake out the excess.

Preparing shallow cake pan for cakes Line with paper cut 2 in larger than pan. Snip corners.

2 Overlap corner papers and pin in place to create upstanding paper edge.

Combination method cakes

(The fat and sugar for these cakes are creamed, but the egg whites are beaten)

	Ingredients	Method
Chocolate layer (Devil's food) cake	½ cup butter 2 eggs 2 cups flour 1 level tsp baking soda 2 cups brown sugar 1¼ cups milk 1 tsp vanilla extract ⅔ cup bittersweet chocolate (grated)	Put the grated chocolate, half the sugar and half the milk on gentle heat to melt. Stir till smooth, add vanilla and cool. Cream the butter and remaining sugar. Beat in the yolks and the chocolate mixture. Fold in the sifted flour, baking soda, milk, and finally the beaten egg whites. Turn into 4 prepared layer-cake pans. Cook at 350°F for 35 minutes. Fill and coat with GANACHE soufflé.
Frosted white pecan layer cake	⅓ cup butter 1 cup sugar ½ tsp vanilla extract 2 large eggs ¾ cup pecan nuts (or walnuts) 2 cups flour ½ cup milk 2 level tsp baking powder	Cream butter and sugar, add vanilla. When fluffy, add yolks, chopped nuts, then fold in flour, baking powder and milk alternately by degrees. Whip whites until stiff, but not dry, and fold in. Bake in 2 prepared layer pans at 375°F for 25 to 35 minutes. Cool on rack, then fill and ice with VANILLA FROSTING and ice with white GLACÉ icing.
Pain de Genes (rich almond cake)	½ cup unsalted butter ¾ cup superfine sugar 3 eggs 1 cup ground almonds ½ cup cornstarch or plain flour ½ tsp baking powder 2 drops almond extract 2 drops vanilla extract	Beat the eggs with half the sugar to the ribbon trail consistency. Add the extracts. Cream the butter with the rest of the sugar until light and fluffy. Sift the flour, baking powder and ground almonds together. Gently mix egg and butter mixtures together. Fold in the flour and almonds. Bake at 350°F for 45 minutes. Serve plain.

Lining fruit cake pan Brush with oil. Line base with paper circle cut to size. Fold band of paper for sides.

2 Snip along outer edge so that it fits snugly (flanges overlap). Brush with oil. Fit another circle in base.

3 For large cakes, add another upright band and base. Brush with oil.

Sugar

There are several types of sugar and syrup, mostly extracted from sugar beet or sugar cane. Cane sugar "loaf sugar" used to be regarded as the purest and best for cooking, but all commercial sugars are now so well refined that there is little to choose between them. Indeed, they are exactly the same sugars with a different crystal size.

White sugars

Loaf sugar: Seldom available today, it used to be sold in brick-like cones called sugar loaves.
Cube or lump sugar: Sold in conveniently-sized cubes for sweetening tea, coffee and so on.
Preserving sugar: White sugar sold specifically for home-preserving. The extra-large size crystals allow liquid to circulate freely, making constant stirring unnecessary.
Granulated sugar: Fairly coarse white crystals. A general all-purpose sugar that is suitable for all types of cooking, including preserving. May be ground finer in a blender or food processor as a substitute for superfine sugar.
Fine granulated sugar: As above, but with slightly finer crystals. Use if superfine sugar is not available. Superfine sugar: Very fine white crystalline sugar, perfect for cake, sweet and dessert making because the fine grains are quickly dissolved when beaten or heated, leaving no gritty texture in the mixture.
Confectioner's sugar: So finely pulverized it resembles fine flour. Used for dusting cake tops, or in uncooked icings or fruit sauces (like MELBA SAUCE) where gritty sugars are undesirable.

Brown sugars

Natural (raw) brown sugars (Barbados, muscavado) are unrefined. Refining extracts the color with the molasses. Most brown sugars are just refined white sugars which have been tossed in cane molasses to color and flavor them. They may, however, simply be artificially colored white sugar.
Dark soft brown sugar: A soft sugar which creams and dissolves easily. Used for gingerbreads, and so on, which need the rich molasses flavor and dark color.
Pale (or light) soft brown sugar: As above, but paler, and of finer texture. Creams easily.
Natural demerara sugar: The most expensive of the brown sugars, it is unrefined large-grained cane sugar with a soft, almost "damp" texture and molasses taste (from the residue of molasses not refined out of the sugar). Served with coffee and used to provide a crunchy topping to cakes or puddings. Seldom used in mixtures as the large grains give a speckly appearance and do not cream well.
Molasses: The natural syrup that is extracted from sugar cane. Black molasses: Reduced, extremely strong-flavored and refined molasses, used in small quantities mainly in marmalade and dark fruit cakes.
Golden syrup: Heavy syrup made from refined white sugar.
Maple syrup: Extracted from the sugar maple. Has a very distinctive flavor.

Boiling sugar

Sugar dissolves readily in water. At room temperature water is able to dissolve twice its own weight of sugar, producing a syrup containing about 67% sugar. The warmer the water, the more sugar will dissolve in it (pure sugar may be melted directly over heat, though this, when cold, will set hard).

The more water a sugar solution contains, the lighter and more liquid will be the syrup.

When making sugar syrups there is no need to weigh sugar and measure water too accurately as, providing there is a little too much rather than too little water, the syrup may always be boiled down to the correct consistency. But obviously starting with too much water requires longer boiling, so it is costly in time and fuel. The approximate proportions measured in a pitcher or cup are: For a light syrup (for fruit salad) 1 part sugar to 3 parts water; for a medium syrup (for soaking cakes like Baba or Savarin) 2 parts sugar to 3 parts water; for a heavy syrup (for bottling rhubarb or peaches) equal parts sugar to water.

Bring the sugar and water to the boil very slowly so that the sugar dissolves before boiling. (Boiling of undissolved sugar may cause crystallization of the syrup.) Once all the sugar is dissolved, boil the solution rapidly for a minute or two until the syrup is clear.

For cake icing and confectionery cook the sugar syrups to thicker consistencies than those above. Put the sugar in a heavy pan, just cover it with water, dissolve it gently and then boil the solution rapidly. Thick syrups do tend to recrystallize, but this may be avoided by adding a pinch of CREAM OF TARTAR or a squeeze of lemon juice. These acids convert some of the sugar to "invert" sugar, which does not crystallize at all easily. Alternatively, 20% glucose (which is invert) or glucose syrup may be added but this is not suitable for sugar to be cooked beyond the hard ball stage (see opposite), as the glucose tends to give a sticky, rather than dry, caramel.

1 Put the sugar into a spotlessly clean, heavy saucepan.
2 Just cover the sugar with water. Get everything else (greased trays, skimmer, testing cup, and so on) ready as, once it is boiling, sugar will require constant attention.
3 Bring the sugar slowly to the boil so that it dissolves before boiling. If using large quantities, stir gently. If sugar crystals stick to the sides of the pan, wash them down assiduously with a clean pastry brush dipped in water. Otherwise they may cause re-crystalization of the syrup.
4 If for some reason the syrup produces a scum (perhaps the pan has been badly washed), skim carefully with a perforated spoon or skimmer.
5 Once the syrup is clear, boil it rapidly to the correct degree. At first progress is slow, with each stage taking several minutes, but, once at hard ball stage, progress is quick, with only seconds between each stage.

Angels' hair (spun sugar) *Boil sugar with a pinch of* CREAM OF TARTAR. *Stand pan in hot water to arrest cooking but keep syrup hot. Hold two forks as shown. Dip them into the caramel and wave them boldly in the air, jerking the arms to fling off the strands of sugar. Collect the strands and use to decorate cakes. The operation is made easier by standing on a stool to gain height and laying newspaper on the floor which also keeps the floor clean.*

Caramel *Boil sugar gently until bubbly, clear and pale brown. Pour on a lightly oiled baking sheet.*

2 When cold and brittle, break it up with a rolling pin or meat pounder.

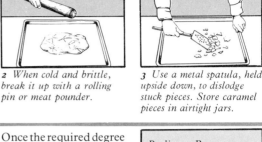

3 Use a metal spatula, held upside down, to dislodge stuck pieces. Store caramel pieces in airtight jars.

Stages in sugar boiling

Professional chefs test the consistency of sugar syrup by dipping a finger first into cold water, then into the syrup and then immediately into the cold water again. Use a teaspoon as there is less chance of being burned. (A sugar thermometer saves constant testing.)

First stage
(small thread, short thread, or gloss)
217 F
Dip a teaspoon into the boiling syrup. Cool slightly, then pinch the syrup between finger and thumb, and draw apart. Little threads, about $\frac{1}{2}$ in, form.

Second stage
(Large thread, long thread or large gloss)
230°F
After a few minutes the same test will produce longer, stronger threads, about 1 to 2 in long before they snap.

Third stage
(Small ball, soft ball)
240°F
Use a wet teaspoon to take a little of the syrup and drop it into a cupful of cold water. It forms a soft glue which can be rolled into a squashy ball between finger and thumb.

Fourth stage
(Large ball, hard ball)
250°F
The same test will now produce a firmer, more resilient ball.

Fifth stage
(Small crack, soft crack)
270°F
The cooled sugar is now very tough and, if chewed, will stick to the teeth. The sugar may be twisted and, when cold, will crack, but it is still a little pliable and sticky.

Sixth stage
(Hard crack, large crack) 300°F
The cooled sugar will now crack like glass, be dry to the touch, but as yet colorless.

Seventh stage
(Pale caramel)
310°F
After the sixth stage the sugar rapidly boils, first to pale then to medium then to dark caramel. Dark caramel is known as blackjack. After this it smokes, burns and decomposes.

Once the required degree of sugar density has been reached it is vital that cooking is stopped, especially in the latter crack and caramel stages when the heat of the pan will continue to cook the sugar after removal from the heat. To stop the cooking, dip the base of the pan into cold water for a few seconds. Take care no water splashes into the sugar as it will make it splatter dangerously. If the caramel needs to be kept liquid and hot, say for dipping PROFITEROLES or SPINNING SUGAR, stop the cooking, then stand the pan in hot water.

To coat a dish with caramel, first warm the dish. If this is not done, the hot caramel may crack it and will also become too thick, as it cools on the dish, to manoeuvre with ease. Pour the liquid caramel into the dish. If it is a metal dish, hold it with a cloth (the heat transfers rapidly and may burn the hands). Tip and tilt the dish slowly so that the caramel runs evenly all over the base and sides.

Caramel coloring
Use dark caramel (blackjack) to give color to sauces for meats which were inadequately browned. (Commercial gravy browning is colored with caramel.)

Praline Roast some almonds until lightly browned. Mix in with a caramel syrup and proceed as above. Eat as a confection, or grind finely to flavor and top soufflés, ice creams and other desserts (most other nuts can also be used as can mixed nuts).

Crème brûlée Bake custard long enough to form a skin. Cool. Next day, sift $\frac{1}{4}$ in superfine sugar over it.

2 Heat a salamander over flame for 10 minutes. Brown sugar coating evenly with it (or broil fiercely).

3 To cover blister holes, swirl caramel with teaspoon handle while still hot. Chill.

Sugar/2

Cooked icings and frostings			
	Ingredients	Method	Uses
7-minute frosting (meringue icing or vanilla frosting)	2 egg whites $1\frac{1}{3}$ cups confectioner's sugar $\frac{1}{4}$ tsp cream of tartar 6 tbs water 1 tsp vanilla extract Pinch of salt	In the top of a double boiler over simmering water, beat everything with an electric mixer until the mixture will form STIFF PEAKS. Allow to cool.	Fill and cover cake with thick layer. Leave until dry to the touch. Or put whole cake in hot oven and brown meringue (3 to 4 minutes). Good with filled sponge cake.
Crème au beurre meringuée	Half quantity of above, plus equal amount of butter cream (simple toppings, 5)	Mix cooled, 7-minute frosting with BUTTER CREAM.	Good with light cakes. For a less sweet icing, use soft, unsalted butter in place of butter cream.
Crème au beurre mousseline	$\frac{1}{4}$ cup granulated sugar 6 tbs water 2 egg yolks $\frac{1}{2}$ cup unsalted butter	Beat yolks. Boil sugar and water to LONG THREAD. Pour on whirling yolks and beat until cool and thick. Soften butter, beat in by degrees.	The richest of French frostings, used for rich gâteaux. Flavor as desired.
Chocolate icing (ganache)	$1\frac{1}{3}$ cups chopped plain chocolate $\frac{1}{2}$ cup butter $1\frac{1}{2}$ tbs golden syrup	Melt all ingredients together over very gentle heat. Remove from heat. Beat until thick enough to spread.	Use for any chocolate, coffee, or plain sponge cake
Ganache soufflée (Chocolate mousseline icing)	1 cup heavy cream 8 squares chocolate 1 tbs rum	Melt chocolate in the cream. Bring to the boil, then cool, stirring occasionally. When beginning to thicken, beat until fluffy and thick.	Chocolate or coffee cakes (use before it sets too hard).
Marshmallow icing	4 oz marshmallows 3 tbsp milk 2 egg whites 1 tbs superfine sugar	Melt marshmallows slowly in milk. Cool. Beat egg whites and sugar to a stiff meringue. Mix.	If very soft, chill briefly before using, or leave to set more solidly. Marshmallows may also be sliced, put on cake and melted under the grill.
Butterscotch frosting	$\frac{1}{2}$ cup butter 1 cup brown sugar $\frac{1}{4}$ cup milk $2\frac{1}{2}$ cups confectioner's sugar	Stir butter and brown sugar over heat until melted (2 minutes). Add milk and stir to boil. Pour on to sifted confectioner's sugar and beat well.	Good for spicy ginger cakes.
Coffee fudge icing	1 cup granulated sugar $\frac{2}{3}$ cup water $\frac{1}{4}$ cup butter $1\frac{1}{2}$ tbs instant coffee powder	Boil sugar and water to soft ball stage. Remove from heat. Add butter and beat in coffee powder. Beat until thick. Spread, while still warm.	For a softer fudge, beat in more butter, bit by bit. Best for icing layer cakes.
Cooked marzipan (almond paste)	2 eggs $\frac{3}{4}$ cup superfine sugar $1\frac{1}{4}$ cup confectioner's sugar 3 cups ground almonds $\frac{1}{2}$ tsp vanilla extract 1 tsp lemon juice	Beat eggs. Add sugars. Beat over pan of simmering water until light, thick and creamy. Remove from heat. Add remaining ingredients. Mix to a paste. Knead smooth on board dusted with confectioner's sugar.	This softer, malleable paste is easier to handle than the classic almond paste. Use for fruit cakes (see illustration opposite for molding).
Classic almond paste	1 cup superfine sugar 1 cup confectioner's sugar 4 cups ground almonds 2 egg yolks 2 whole eggs 2 tsp lemon juice $\frac{1}{2}$ tsp vanilla extract	Beat the liquids together. Add the rest of the ingredients and mix and knead (on a sugared board) to a paste.	As above.

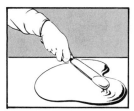

Fondant icing *Boil granulated sugar with a little water and a pinch of cream of tartar to the "soft-ball" stage (240°F). Dip the base of the pan carefully into cold water to arrest the cooking. Pour the syrup on a marble or enamel surface. Leave it until a skin has formed and it is cool enough to touch.*

2 Work the sugar with two scrapers or spatulas, twisting it and stirring it constantly until it is opaque. Keep working until it is white and stiff. Then divide it into small pieces and work each piece with the hands, squeezing and kneading until smooth, malleable and shiny. (If it becomes hard to work, leave it covered with a damp cloth for half an hour.)

3 Roll it into small balls and store in airtight jars. When it is needed, heat it in a double boiler until it is liquid. Use for icing cakes, to make flavored "fondant creams" and coat grapes, strawberries and other fruit by dipping them in it.

Royal icing *Beat 1 egg white, a drop of food coloring, 1 tsp lemon juice and ½ tsp glycerine slowly into each 1½ cups of confectioner's sugar. Beat steadily until smooth and shiny. Adjust texture by adding more egg white or sugar. Allow to stand, covered, for 30 minutes to get rid of air bubbles. For a marzipan-covered cake (as below) use fairly stiff as a first coat. Spread it evenly, using a spatula dipped in hot water. Allow to dry. Repeat with thinner icing for second coat.*

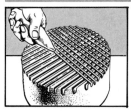

Trellis baskets *Use oiled molds. Pipe trellis with writing nozzle. Let dry.*

Sugar flowers *Use a drop of stiff icing to stick a small square oiled piece of foil on a flower icing nail.*

2 Use a flower nozzle with the pipe held almost flat to make open flowers. Allow to dry and pull off foil.

2 For perfect third coat, pipe thin line round top edge of cake. Let set. Pour in thin lake of runny icing.

2 For a higher trellis, pipe further layers of lines across each other, each at right angles to the other.

3 Use flower nozzle held on edge to make rose-buds.

4 To make bud into full flower put outer petals around it, again holding the nozzle flat.

Marzipan on fruit cake *Turn cake over. Brush with melted jam. Fit circle of marzipan on top. Roll flat.*

Piping lines or writing *Hold bag slightly above. Guide or lay—do not drag.*

Trellis baskets *Use oiled moulds. Pipe trellis with writing nozzle. Let dry.*

Cake designs *Draw pattern on paper. Fix on cake. Transfer with pin pricks.*

2 Cut strips to fit sides. Use jam-jar to roll smooth. Leave 3 days before icing.

Sugar/3

Tiered cakes Place a small cake board in center of iced bottom tier to take weight of upper layers.

2 Sift confectioner's sugar heavily over the cake. Carefully lift off the paper strips to reveal stripes.

Striped effect Lay strips of paper on top of any dark cake.

2 Sift icing sugar heavily over the cake. Carefully lift off the paper strips to reveal stripes.

Coating with butter icing Hold cake by its base so that it can be tilted to spread icing on the sides.

Feathering Stand cake on a rack in a baking tray and coat it with melted chocolate or icing. (Tray catches drips.)

2 While icing is still wet, put cake on revolving stand and pipe thin parallel lines of contrasting icing on top.

3 Drag knife point across lines every 2 inches. Turn cake around. Repeat dragging between first drag lines.

Cake icings

In uncooked icing mixtures, confectioner's sugar is generally used for its smooth texture. In cooked icings superfine sugar is more commonly used.

Simple toppings

1 Evenly sifted confectioner's sugar.
2 Melted chocolate.
3 As 1 or 2 with grated chocolate sprinkled over.
4 Use paper strips to make a pattern of sifted icing on top (see illustrations). Or use paper cut-outs as stencils for initials, flowers or patterns.
5 Butter cream: Beat icing sugar into unsalted butter in the proportions of 3 cups to 1 cup until light and fluffy, and then flavor with orange juice, grated rind, lemon juice, melted chocolate and so on.
6 Glacé icing: Beat $\frac{2}{3}$ cup of boiling water into 3 cups sugar. Beat well. The consistency should be just runny. Flavor as desired.

Marrons glacés (crystallized chestnuts), generally bottled in syrup, are used as desserts or sweetmeats. Because the chestnuts are harder than fruit, they may be candied in the pan.

On day one:
1 Peel the chestnuts.
2 Simmer carefully in water until cooked (about 15 minutes). Peel off the fibrous inner skins.
3 Make a syrup of two parts sugar, one part glucose and one part water.
4 Once the sugars are dissolved, bring the syrup to the boil and add the drained chestnuts.
5 Bring back to the boil, remove from heat and leave, covered over, for 24 hours.

On day two:
6 Boil the chestnuts in syrup again, remove from the heat, cover and leave for 24 hours.

On day three:
7 Repeat the process, adding vanilla extract (6 drops for every 1 lb of nuts).
8 Bottle the chestnuts in hot syrup by the COOKED PACK method, processing for 10 minutes in a boiling water bath or for 1 minute in a pressure cooker or CANNER; or lift the chestnuts from the syrup and dry on a rack for two to three days. To give a *glacé* finish, see *glacé* fruits (opposite).

Candying citrus peel

Cook the strips of peel in four to five successive changes of water until they are clear and tender. Then proceed as for *marrons glacés*.

Crystallizing flowers

(for decorating desserts and cakes)
Whole violet flowers and separate rose petals are the most fragrant flowers. Crystallized borage flowers are good looking but less perfumed.
1 Pick perfect, deep colored, fragrant blooms when they are absolutely dry. Pick off long stalks of violets and borage flowers. Separate geraniums or roses into petals.
2 For a professional finish, mix a teaspoon of gum arabic crystals with 2 teaspoons of rosewater, cover over and leave overnight to make a soft glue; or beat an egg white with a fork until it is just sloppy but hardly even frothy (bubbles in the egg white give an imperfect finish).
3 Paint the petals all over with the gum arabic and rose-water or egg white, using a paint brush.
4 Sprinkle lightly and evenly with superfine sugar to coat.
5 Place on a piece of paper on a cake rack.
6 Leave in a warm, airy room for a day or two, until brittle.
7 Store in airtight jars.

The principle of candying fruit (or angelica stalks or chestnuts) is to saturate and impregnate with the maximum amount of sugar. A high concentration of sugar prevents the growth of microorganisms (and, thus, acts as a preservative) as well as creating a delicious confection.

First poach the fruit, then give it frequent soakings in hot syrup. Good-quality canned fruits may be used, omitting stages 1 and 2 below. Large pieces (half pears or whole apricots) may need the full two-week treatment. Small fruit, such as red currants, will be firm and clear in four days and dry in six.

Stages in candying fruit
On day one:
1 Cut up, peel and core the fruit (fresh stem ginger, angelica stems, chestnuts and so on).
2 Poach them in water until just tender but not broken up. Peel pith from chestnuts and thick skin from angelica stems.
3 Make a syrup of one part water (the cooking water, if clear) to three parts sugar (measured in volume, not weight) in a pan. (For each 1 lb of prepared fruit use about $1\frac{1}{4}$ cup of water.) Dissolve the sugar in the water over a gentle heat, stirring continuously.

4 When dissolved, bring to the boil and pour over the prepared fruit. Leave it to soak for 24 hours.

On day two:
5 Drain the syrup back into the pan and add $\frac{1}{4}$ cup more sugar for each 1 lb of fruit. Dissolve, bring to the boil and pour back on the fruit. Soak for 24 hours.

On days three, four and five:
6 Repeat stage 5 above. The fruit may now be ready. If it is shiny, transparent and solid to the touch when cold the process has gone far enough. If satisfied, proceed to stage 9. If a more sugary product, with a slightly opaque crystallized coating, is wanted, continue as follows.

On day six:
7 Repeat stage 5 but increase the added sugar to $\frac{1}{3}$ cup. Leave for 48 hours.
8 Repeat the process, adding $\frac{1}{3}$ cup of sugar. Leave for 4 days.

On day twelve:
9 Place the fruit on a tray or cooling rack in a warm kitchen for two to three days until dry, turning the fruit every day.

Crystallizing fruit
Follow the stages in candying fruit. Then dip each piece of candied fruit briefly in boiling water, drain well and roll in superfine sugar.

Glacé fruits
1 Follow the stages in candying fruit.
2 Make a small quantity of fresh syrup using four parts sugar and one part water. Boil for one minute. (The candying syrup may be used if there is enough left and it is still quite clear and uncrystallized.)
3 Keep the syrup hot by standing it in a BAIN MARIE of simmering water (keeping it on direct heat will cook it to toffee).
4 Ladle a tablespoon or so of syrup into a cup. Dip each piece of fruit into boiling water for 20 seconds, drain, then turn it in the syrup.
5 Dry it on a wire rack.

Sweet sauces
Made in much the same way as savory ones, they are seldom thickened with flour, but more frequently with arrowroot or cornstarch. Commercial custard powder is cornstarch flavored with vanilla and colored artificially. Sweet fruit purées or syrups may be thickened with arrowroot. Purées of uncooked fruit, such as the raspberry purée used for the MELBA SAUCE, are sweetened and thickened with confectioner's sugar.

Sauces may be thickened by reduction as in JAM SAUCES where jam, sugar, water and lemon juice are simply boiled down to the required consistency.

Egg custards
These are thickened by a liaison of egg yolks. Add a vanilla bean to a pint of milk and heat to scalding point. Beat 4 to 8 egg yolks (depending on how thick and rich the custard is to be) with 2 to 4 tablespoons of sugar. Pour on scalding milk, mix well and return the custard to the pan or, if possible, to the top of a double boiler. Stir over gentle heat until the custard will coat the back of the spoon, taking care not to let the liquid come near boiling point, which would curdle the yolks. As soon as the sauce thickens, pour at once into a cold bowl to prevent further cooking.

Cheat's egg custard
Add $1\frac{1}{2}$ tablespoons of cornstarch to the egg yolks and whisk while reheating. As soon as lumps form at the edge of the pan, remove from the heat and whisk until smooth. Pour into a cold bowl.

Sabayon
An interesting and unusual sauce, well worth the trouble of making. There are two types: One warm, of which the Italian *zabaglione*, made with Marsala, is an example; the other chilled.

Warm *sabayon* (*zabaglione*)
For each person, combine
1 egg yolk
$1\frac{1}{2}$ tbs sugar
$1\frac{1}{2}$ tbs Marsala,
    Madeira, rum, port
    or sweet sherry
in the top of a double boiler set over simmering water. Take care not to let the bottom of the pan come into contact with the water. Whisk until thick and mousse-like. Serve at once either as a sauce on cake or fruit desserts or by itself in a glass.

Iced *sabayon*
Proceed as for warm *sabayon* but whisk the mixture, once thickened, until cool. (Setting the pan in ice or icy water will speed up the process.) Fold softly whipped cream into it and chill.

Ice creams and sorbets

Ice creams
The modern electric ice-cream churn or *sorbetière* has ended the tiresome business of making ice cream by hand.

Ice cream may be made without a churn, but it is difficult to get a really satin-smooth texture if the mixture is not beaten as it freezes. In the absence of a churn, ice creams are generally beaten one or more times during the freezing process, or made like mousses or meringues, with the air incorporated in them before freezing. Churning stops large ice crystals forming and also beats in air.

Ice-cream machines vary considerably. The main advantage of the bucket churn, which is cooled by ice and salt, is that it makes more ice cream than the machines sold for use in the freezer. It is, however, tedious obtaining the ice and salt and packing it into the churn. Follow the manufacturer's operating instructions.

Ice-cream freezer
(*sorbetière*)
This is a container for the ice-cream mixture with paddles to churn as it freezes. It is put into the freezer, which should be set at its lowest temperature (highest setting). Again, follow the manufacturer's instructions.

Beat-and-freeze method, requiring no special equipment
Do not attempt to make large quantities of ice cream by this method. The contents need to fit in a loaf pan or small roasting pan, and into a bowl or food processor for beating.
1 Make sure everything to be used—loaf pan, bowl, beaters, spoon—is well chilled and that the freezer is set to its lowest temperature.
2 Start freezing the mixture in the loaf pan.
3 When it has frozen round the edge (but not in the middle) take it out and beat until smooth. (If using a food processer the mixture can be frozen solid, then broken up into chunks and beaten piece by piece into a smooth creamy mousse.)
4 Refreeze.
5 If the ice cream still looks granular or streaky around the edges, repeat the beating procedure when half-frozen.

Cream
The more butterfat (in the form of cream) the mixture contains, then the easier it is to make smoothly by hand. In fact, a simple ice cream may be made with stiffly whipped cream, sweetened and flavored. Non-fat ices made with yogurt or milk, and water-ices, are best made by machine.

Bombe Spread soft but solid ice cream in an even layer on bottom and sides of a bombe mold. Chill.

3 Put mold on a plate and hold a hot wet cloth around it to melt the outer surface.

Eggs give richness, flavor and, when beaten, a mousse-like texture, to ice cream. Beaten egg whites are generally added toward the end of the process to lighten the mixture.

Sugar and flavorings
Always marginally over-flavor and over-sweeten ices before they are frozen. This offsets the masking effect which freezing has on the taste. If the flavoring requires the addition of only small quantities (vanilla extract or coffee flavoring) it will not thin down the consistency of the basic mousse or custard. If, however, the flavor is, say, orange, add it in concentrated form—grated rind with very little juice, or concentrated frozen orange juice—to keep the mixture thick and creamy. A very runny liquid is more likely to freeze into icy shards. Sorbets/sherbets are often unavoidably runny and for this reason may be made with the addition of a little gelatin, or with stiffly beaten egg white beaten into them.

Bombes are ice creams frozen in a mold, consisting of an outer layer of ice cream and contrasting inner layer (or layers) of ice cream, whipped cream and crushed meringue filling, sorbet or mousse. (Sorbet is not suitable for the outer layer of a bombe, as it melts fast and does not hold a shape well.)

Storage
Ice creams eaten within a few hours of being made are wonderfully creamy and smooth. Keeping ice creams for weeks in the freezer does little harm other than causing a slight deterioration in texture.

Take ice creams from the freezer and put them to "ripen," and to soften slightly so that they are easier to scoop, in the refrigerator one hour before serving.

There are three main types of ice cream:

Custard-based ice creams
Making a custard-based ice cream:
1 Heat the milk and/or cream with sugar.
2 Pour onto beaten egg yolks and beat. If the mixture does not thicken immediately, put back over the heat (preferably in a double boiler or bowl over hot water) until it is thick enough to coat the back of the spoon (see CUSTARD MAKING).
3 Add in the flavoring ingredient (vanilla extract, melted chocolate or fruit purée).
4 Freeze, churning, or use the freeze-and-beat method.

2 Fill with sorbet or mousse. Cover and freeze. Prick right through to release vacuum base.

4 Lift off the mold and freeze again immediately until needed. Slice bombe and serve like a cake.

Mousse-based ice creams (parfaits)

Making mousse-based ice creams:

1 Make a syrup with water and sugar. Boil to 230°F or LARGE THREAD (see page 161).

2 Beat the yolks. Pour the boiling syrup on the yolks and then beat TO THE RIBBON. Then beat until cool.

3 Add flavoring (cool melted chocolate, fruit purée, vanilla extract or ground nuts).

4 Whip cream and fold into the mousse.

5 Freeze without churning or beating again.

Meringue-based ice creams

This less-rich ice cream is best made with fruit flavoring as the sweetness of the meringue is balanced by the fruit's acidity.

Making meringue-based ice cream:

1 Beat egg whites to soft peaks.

2 Boil sugar and liquid to "large thread," beating continuously, onto the whites and continue beating until the meringue stiffens. (This method, which produces ITALIAN MERINGUE, is less arduous with an electric mixer. Or omit the liquid and put whites and sugar in a bowl over a pan of simmering water and beat with a rotary beater to make a thick MERINGUE CUITE.)

3 Fold in flavoring.

4 Fold in the whipped cream.

5 Freeze but do not churn or beat again.

Water ices and sorbets

Many terms are used to define types of water ice, some of which have become rather confused.

Classically a **sorbet** is a **sherbet** made without the addition of egg whites, depending for its creaminess on constant churning or beating while freezing. In Italy a **granita** is a water ice made without any egg whites, the grainy texture of the ice shards deliberately preserved. A **spoom** is an alcoholic sherbet, with egg whites added in the form of *meringue cuite*.

Opinions also differ about the correct consistency for sorbets. Escoffier says they should be so soft as to be almost drinkable. Other chefs insist they should be firm enough to scoop into a ball.

Below is a recipe for a granular *granita*. Recipes for a creamy sherbet containing egg whites, and one containing gelatin and *meringue cuite* are to be found on page 169.

Berry-fruit granita

¾ cup sugar
2 cups water
Pared rind and juice of 1 lemon
1 cup sieved fruit (raspberries, strawberries, loganberries or blueberries) cooked or raw, sweetened

Put sugar, water and lemon juice and rind in a heavy-bottomed pan and bring slowly to the boil, stirring. Boil rapidly for 5 minutes to produce a sticky syrup, not yet at the thread stage (about 213°F). Strain off and cool. Mix with the fruit purée and freeze, churning, or beat-and-freeze (the latter produces a more granular ice).

Custard, mousse, & meringue-based ice creams		
	Ingredients	Method
Chocolate	1¼ cups cream 2½ cups milk 1 cup sugar 8 egg yolks 4 oz chocolate	Follow stages in custard-based ice-cream making, melting the chocolate in the milk
Peach	1¼ cups cream ⅔ cup sugar 4 egg yolks 1¼ cups heavy cream 3 or 4 ripe peaches, puréed	Follow stages in custard-based ice-cream making, using the first three ingredients and adding the whipped cream and peaches to the cold custard
Apricot parfait	⅔ cup water ⅔ cup sugar 3 egg yolks 1¼ cups sweetened apricot purée ⅔ cup heavy cream, whipped	Follow stages in mousse-based ice-cream making
Rich coffee parfait	⅔ cup water ½ cup sugar 4 egg yolks 3 tbs instant coffee powder 2 cups heavy cream, whipped	Follow stages in mousse-based ice-cream making
Rhubarb and ginger ice cream	4 egg whites 1 cup sugar ⅔ cup water 1 cup sweetened thick rhubarb purée ¼ cup preserved ginger, chopped 1¼ cups heavy cream	Follow the stages in meringue-based ice-cream making, adding the ginger and rhubarb to the meringue before folding in the cream
Blackcurrant ice-cream	4 egg whites 1 cup sugar ⅓ cup water 1 cup sweetened black currant purée 1¼ cups heavy cream	Follow the stages in meringue-based ice-cream making

Egg whites and meringues

Skillful beating of an egg white can increase its volume by about eight times.

This phenomenon is useful to the cook for three reasons. Firstly, the apparent amount of a mixture may be increased without changing its flavor (egg whites themselves being almost tasteless). Secondly, the minute bubbles of air trapped in the beaten egg white provide a light and airy texture to any finished dish into which they have been incorporated. Thirdly, if the mixture is baked, the trapped air will expand and cause the mixture to rise, as in SOUFFLÉS.

A hand-operated rotary beater, electric mixer or hand whisk will do the job satisfactorily. The greatest volume is produced by whisking in a copper bowl (the copper acts as a catalyst, causing long tunnels of trapped air to be formed in the egg white) with a large balloon whisk. But this method requires a strong arm, patience and time.

Whisking in a copper bowl: First, clean the bowl by rubbing with a lemon half and coarse salt. This prevents the egg whites from acquiring a greeny-gray hue from the top layer of oxidized copper. Salt and vinegar applied with a cloth also works well, but do not use copper cleaner as this will impart an unpleasant flavor to the egg white.

Once egg whites are whisked they should be used quickly, otherwise they liquefy. This may be delayed if the bowl is turned upside down (the white will not fall if properly beaten) or covered with plastic wrap to exclude the air. Beat egg white with sugar to get a mixture which will last much longer, especially if some heat is applied during the beating to thicken the whites slightly and dissolve the sugar, as in Italian meringue and *meringue cuite*.

Swiss meringue

Perhaps the best of the meringues, it is beaten without heat. This produces a light, sometimes hollow, often slightly toffee-ish meringue. The quickest to make, it is the usual meringue for home cooks.

For every small egg white, $\frac{1}{4}$ cup sugar, and sometimes $\frac{1}{2}$ teaspoon of vinegar or 1 or 2 drops of vanilla extract, are added. Use superfine sugar for the best results. (When using large eggs, add a teaspoon more sugar per egg.)
1 Beat the whites (plus any vinegar or vanilla extract to STIFF PEAK.
2 Add in about three-quarters of the sugar.
3 Continue beating until the meringue will once again stand in stiff peaks. This time it will be shiny. It must not flow or move at all after the beater is lifted from it, but stay solidly in position.
4 Fold in rest of sugar.
5 Pipe or use as required without any delay. (The mixture gradually liquefies and if then baked it may subsequently stick to the baking sheet.)

Italian meringue is more laborious to make by hand than Swiss meringue but less can go wrong. It is impossible to over-beat; the mixture does not need to be cooked at once, and it swells very little in baking, making it ideal for VACHERINS.

This mixture cooks faster than Swiss meringue and produces very white meringue which is powdery when crushed.

The ingredients for Italian meringue are the same as for Swiss meringue (2 small whites to $\frac{1}{2}$ cup sugar), but the sugar is boiled to a SYRUP in water, then beaten in with the egg whites. (A pinch of cream of tartar or a teaspoon of lemon juice or vinegar helps to prevent crystallization of the syrup.)
1 Put the sugar in a heavy pan and just wet it with a few tablespoons of water for $\frac{1}{2}$ cup of sugar. Heat slowly, moving the pan gently to dissolve the sugar, but do not stir. If sugar crystals get stuck on the sides of the pan, brush them down with a clean, wet pastry brush.
2 Beat the egg whites to STIFF PEAK. (If using an electric machine on a stand, leave the whites beating at a moderate speed while making the sugar syrup. Aim to have the syrup at SOFT BALL (240°F) when the whites are ready.
3 Boil the syrup to soft ball. Then pour slowly onto the beating whites and keep beating. If beating in a copper bowl by hand, add a little syrup, beat to incorporate it, then a bit more, and so on, working fast. All the sugar syrup should go into the meringue while it is bubbling hot, but not thicker than soft ball.
4 Beat until the meringue is shiny and stiff enough not to move or flow at all if the beater is removed from it.
5 If not needed at once cover with a damp cloth or plastic wrap.

Meringue cuite is a meringue used mainly by professional chefs. It is a very stable, white, crisp meringue, similar to the Italian, crushing to a chalky powder. It requires lengthy beating but is easy with a portable, electric hand mixer.

Once again, the proportions of ingredients are 2 small egg whites to $\frac{1}{4}$ cup sugar, but the sugar used is confectioner's sugar, or a mixture of equal parts confectioner's sugar and superfine sugar. The proportion of sugar is often increased considerably if the meringue is for cake fillings or FROSTING.
1 Put the egg whites into a bowl that will fit over a

Meringues Use two spoons to mold into egg shapes. Bake in cool oven until crisp. Cool on rack.

Vacherin Use large bag and fluted nozzle. Pipe from center, spiraling out. Bake. Cover with fruit and cream.

2 For high-sided vacherin, pipe one more ring on top of outside edge. Fill center with fruit and cream.

large pan of water without the bottom of the bowl touching the water.
2 Beat the whites stiff.
3 Set the pan over gentle heat until the mixture simmers. Add the sugar.
4 Beat steadily until the meringue is shiny and will hold its shape without flowing or moving when the beater is withdrawn. Remove from the heat and beat until cool.
5 Keep covered with a damp cloth or with plastic wrap.

To bake meringue
Meringue can be baked until just set and yet still soft (as in baked Alaska, below) or until crisp but toffee-ish, as in Pavlova. But generally meringues are not so much baked as dried out. Indeed, Italian meringue and *meringue cuite* can be dried out satisfactorily on a shelf in a warm place near a source of heat, but Swiss meringue would start to run before drying.
1 Use a baking sheet lined with wax paper or foil. Brush with oil and dust with flour.
2 Pipe or spoon the meringue mixture on the paper or foil.
3 Set in a low oven (generally 200°F, but this varies for each recipe).
4 Bake (usually about 1 hour for tiny meringues and up to 3 hours for large *vacherin* cases) until the meringue feels light and dry to the touch (and the baking paper or foil can easily be peeled off).
5 Allow it to cool.
6 Store at once in an airtight container.

Croquembouche
Dip small baked meringues in liquid CARAMEL and pile into a pyramid; start with a circle of meringues, fill the middle, then continue working towards the apex. The smaller the meringues, the easier this is. Serve with whipped cream.

Baked Alaska
Cover an ovenproof plate with a round of sponge cake. Shape softened ice cream (vanilla or nut-flavored) into a dome on the cake, leaving a narrow border of uncovered cake. Freeze until firm. Spread a half-inch layer of meringue (Italian or *cuite* are best) all over the ice cream, covering it evenly and completely. Fork into rough swirls or ridges. Bake in a hot oven until brown on the ridges. Serve at once.

Daquoise

Meringue (any kind), 6-egg-white quantity
1¼ cups hazel nuts, toasted and skinned
1 tbs cornstarch
GANACHE filling

The meringue sometimes sticks to the baking sheets, so bake on edible rice paper if possible. Mix the nuts and cornstarch into the meringue and spread or pipe into two flat 10- to 25-inch rounds on baking sheets which have been brushed with oil and well floured. Bake at 350°F for 45 minutes. Cool for 10 minutes. Ease off the baking sheets and allow to cool completely. Sandwich and coat with *ganache*.

Pavlova
Add ½ teaspoon vanilla extract and 2 level teaspoons cornstarch to a 3-egg white quantity Swiss meringue. Bake in a dinner-plate-sized disc on oiled and floured foil or on wet wax paper for 50 minutes at 275°F. Turn over, peel off the baking paper, cool, then spread liberally with whipped cream and fresh fruit (or fruit and nuts). The meringue texture is crisp outside, squashy inside.

Gâteau Diane
Bake four thin discs of Swiss meringue on oiled and well-floured foil. Peel off the foil while still warm. When cool, pile them one on another, with layers of chocolate BUTTERCREAM or *ganache* soufflé in between. Dust with confectioner's sugar and chill, or cover with *ganache* and decorate.

Soufflé glacé
This is a frozen mousse, a cross between a PARFAIT and a mousse. The addition of egg whites (most *parfaits* contain yolks only) beaten to SOFT PEAKS, folded into the whipped cream and added before freezing, gives an ice-cream with a light, mousse-like texture. It should be eaten when recently frozen, and is best made only a few hours in advance.
A truly characteristic soufflé glacé is frozen in a soufflé dish, with a paper collar tied around it so that the filling comes slightly above the level of the dish, giving the illusion that the soufflé has risen, as if baked. Remove the collar and press chilled, finely-chopped, browned nuts round the edge.

Sorbet made with egg whites
Proceed as for *soufflé glacé*, but beat in 2 egg whites when the sorbet is almost frozen. Then churn for 10 minutes in an electric machine, or freeze for 20 minutes, beat again and refreeze.

Orange sorbet made with gelatin and meringue cuite

1¼ cups water
2 level tsp powdered gelatin
6 fluid oz (1 carton) concentrated frozen orange juice at room temperature
¼ cup sugar
1 egg white

Put the water into a small pan, sprinkle on the gelatin, leave to soak 10 minutes and then warm gently until runny and clear. Add to the orange juice and freeze. When almost frozen put the sugar and the egg white in a bowl set over a pan of simmering water and beat until thick (as *meringue cuite*). Fold into the sorbet and refreeze.

Floating islands
(oeufs à la neige) Poach spoonfuls of meringue as shown below. Drain well and smother in caramel or Grand Marnier and orange zest. Chill.

Floating islands (oeufs à la neige) Poach spoonfuls of meringue 1 to 2 min each side in milk and water.

Creams and custards

Sweetened milk or cream forms the base of many desserts, from the exquisite and luxurious *Bavarois* to the homely English baked custard.

The base used for many cream desserts is the rich, velvety *crème Anglaise*. Bake this with added egg whites until just firm, as in English baked custard; cook to thick but not set cream, as in *crème brûlée*; and mix with gelatin to set to quivering solidity, as in the *Bavarois*. Or leave unset and mix with whipped cream and fruit, as in a fool.

Basic *crème Anglaise*
2½ cups milk
6 egg yolks
3 to 4 tbs sugar

Beat the yolks and sugar well. Heat the milk. Pour into the yolks. Return to the pan and stir until thickened, without boiling.

Variations
1 Substitute cream for some or all of the milk.
2 Add extra yolks for richness.
3 Omit 2 yolks for a less rich custard.
4 Flavor with cassia, nutmeg, cinnamon, almond extract or vanilla extract.

Cream is usually served with desserts just as it is, but it can be flavored or thickened to great effect. The simplest way to thicken cream is by whipping it, but this can only be done with heavy, or whipping cream. Light cream does not contain enough butterfat to thicken on beating.

To whip cream:
1 The cream should be fresh and cold, preferably chilled. Cream that is warm or less than fresh easily turns to butter and, even if whipped successfully, it is likely to separate later.
2 Using any type of beater and bowl, go carefully. Once the cream starts to thicken it moves more quickly from "half-whipped" (thick enough to leave a ribbon trail when the beaters are lifted) to "softly whipped" (meaning it will *just* hold its shape) to "stiffly whipped" (when it is solid, but smooth, not grainy). Overwhipped cream is yellower in color and not smooth. Extreme overwhipping causes the butter to separate from the milky liquids (whey).

Crème Chantilly
Whip well-chilled cream until stiff, then fold in confectioner's or superfine sugar to taste.

Crème meringuée
Whip cream and sweeten and increase the volume with a spoonful or two of MERINGUE mixture. The usual proportions are 1¼ cups of cream to 1 egg white and ¼ cup sugar.

Flavoring creams and custards
If the cream or milk is to be heated, infuse it with the flavoring (vanilla pod, cassia, mace or cinnamon stick) and allow them to heat together. If it is not to be heated, simply add directly to the cream.

Molds and creams thickened with starch
Use semolina, farina, cornstarch or rice to thicken sweetened milk so that it will set on cooling. Such a pudding may be dull without the addition of cream or egg yolks for richness, beaten egg whites for a light texture, and flavoring.

Molds and cream puddings

Ingredients

Rice condé
2½ cups milk
¼ cup pudding rice
2 tbs sugar
¼ tsp vanilla extract
3 to 4 heaping tbs whipped cream
3 to 4 tbs warm, sieved apricot jam

Italian chocolate pudding
8 oz unsweetened chocolate
⅓ cup sugar
2½ cups milk
¼ cup cornstarch
2 drops vanilla extract
Heavy cream
Confectioner's sugar

Cinnamon milk tart
Pie shell or flan case, baked
¼ cup butter
¼ cup sugar
1 cup milk
3 tbs maize flour (or any white flour)
2 egg whites
2 to 3 drops vanilla extract
½ tsp cinnamon

Cold soufflés and mousses

If air is incorporated into the mixture (usually by beating eggs and sugar, or beaten egg whites), the texture of an otherwise smooth solid mixture becomes aerated and mousse-like. Such mixtures are generally called soufflés if they are set in a soufflé dish with a paper band tied around it so that the mixture may be poured in to come above the rim. Once set, the mousse has the risen look of a cooked soufflé. Beat main ingredients TO THE RIBBON then stir in the flavorings and the dissolved gelatin until thickening occurs. Stir in cream and fold in the egg whites.

Main ingredients	Flavoring ingredients	Setting agent	Enriching and lightening ingredients
Praline soufflé 3 egg yolks ⅔ cup superfine sugar	3 tbs crushed PRALINE Juice of 1 lemon	1 level tsp gelatin, dissolved in 3 tbs water	3 egg whites, ⅔ cup heavy cream, half-whipped
Raspberry soufflé 5 egg yolks ⅔ cup superfine sugar	⅔ cup sieved raspberry purée	2 level tsp gelatin, dissolved in 3 tbs water	3 egg whites ⅔ cup heavy cream, half-whipped
Orange and lemon mousse 4 egg yolks ¾ cup superfine sugar Juice of 1 lemon	Finely grated rind of 1 orange and 1 lemon	2 level tsp gelatin, dissolved in juice of 1 large orange	5 egg whites ⅔ cup heavy cream, half-whipped

Method

Cook the rice slowly in the milk with the sugar (in the oven or in a pan), stirring occasionally until the rice is soft and the milk absorbed. Cool. Beat to a paste. Add a few drops of vanilla, and fold in whipped cream. Spread flat in dish and spoon jam over it.

SLAKE flour with a little milk in a bowl. Heat chocolate, sugar and milk. Pour onto flour, mix, return to pan, and stir until smooth, thick and boiling. Add extract. Beat well. Set in an oiled mold. Turn out and cover with whipped cream sweetened with confectioner's sugar.

Melt butter. Add sugar and flour. Stir. Add milk. Stir till boiling. Cool slightly. Add vanilla extract. Beat whites till stiff. Fold in. Fill flan case. Bake for approx. 20 minutes in moderate oven until *just* set. Sprinkle with cinnamon.

Sweet set molds

Most set desserts are made on a custard base or with milk thickened with starch or with beaten eggs set with gelatin. Occasionally, however, butter or chocolate (if used in sufficient quantities and well chilled) will thicken the mixture sufficiently to hold its shape.

Basic ingredients	Flavoring ingredients	Lightening ingredients	Method
Chocolate mousse 3 egg yolks 3 tbs sugar 4 squares dark, sweetened cooking chocolate	1 tbs brandy, *or* Grated orange rind, 1 level tsp ginger, *or* 1 level tsp coffee powder	3 egg whites	Beat yolks and sugar until thick and mousse-like (see BEATEN CAKES). Melt grated chocolate with 2 tablespoons of water in a pan AU BAIN MARIE or in a double boiler. When smooth and thick add to the yolks. Beat whites until stiff. Fold in and set in glasses or RAMEKIN dishes.
Raspberry Malakoff $\frac{3}{4}$ cup superfine sugar $\frac{3}{4}$ cup unsalted butter 1 package *langues de chat* or lady fingers	$1\frac{1}{2}$ cups ground almonds 2 tbs kirsch 2 cups fresh raspberries	$1\frac{1}{4}$ cups whipped cream	Beat sugar and butter until soft and fluffy. Stir in the flavoring ingredients and the cream. Line an oiled, straight-sided cake pan with a round of wax paper and oil again. Stand biscuits up around the edge, good-looking sides out. Spoon in the mixture. Press down and spread flat. Chill to set. Cut biscuit tops in line with mixture. Turn out.

The *crème Anglaise* (English egg custard) family

Baked to set

Petits pots de crème
Use 8 yolks for $2\frac{1}{2}$ cups creamy milk. Flavor with vanilla, coffee or chocolate. Bake AU BAIN MARIE in small pots or RAMEKINS (325°F) for 35 to 40 min until just set.

English baked custard
Use 2 whole eggs plus 3 yolks to make custard. Bake AU BAIN MARIE (325°F) for 50 to 60 min or until just set.

Not set solidly

Crème brûlée
Use cream, not milk, in proportions $2\frac{1}{2}$ cups to 8 yolks. Pour, hot, into a shallow dish. Cook as shown on page 161.

Fruit fools
Mix with equal parts thick fruit purée and whipped cream.

Set with gelatin

Bavarois
Add whipped cream and set with gelatin. Chill. Turn out. (Variations: Flavor with coffee, chocolate, vanilla or PRALINE.)

Crème caramel
Coat baked mold with caramel before filling with custard. Bake. Cool to tepid. Turn out.

Baked Charlotte
Line mold with sponge fingers or slices of cake. Bake. Turn out while warm.

Cheat's crème brûlée
Bake custard made with half cream, half milk. Cool. Pour liquid caramel on top. Chill.

Mousse
Fold beaten egg whites into the setting custard with the cream.

Charlotte
Line mold with sponge fingers. Fill with *Bavarois* mixture. Chill. Turn out.

Bavarois aux meringues, aux fruits, au caraque
Surround with tiny meringues. Or decorate with whipped cream and fruits, or CARAQUE.

Jellied Charlotte
Decorate base of mold with banana slices, grape halves, crystallized fruit or angelica suspended in clear lemon jelly. Then proceed as for Charlotte.

Microwave ovens

A microwave oven is an extremely useful adjunct to a conventional oven and stove. Apart from reheating cooked food, thawing frozen food and cooking some raw foods (if not to perfection, at least adequately) it is invaluable as a cook's mate, softening the butter, heating the sauce, and giving a final warm-up to food about to go to table.

A microwave oven contains a magnetron (electron tube) which sends high-frequency electromagnetic microwaves into the oven, directly into the food. They pass through the container (bowl, dish or plastic box) and agitate the molecules of moisture in the food producing heat by friction. All the food within the range of the microwaves will therefore be heated very quickly. Objects without moisture content (like the container) do not absorb any of the microwaves and will therefore not be heated at all.

Food, providing it contains water, fat or sugar, *absorbs* the waves, and is heated by them. Glass, paper, china and most plastics *transmit* microwaves allowing them to pass through to the food. Metal *reflects* microwaves. Deep metal containers and foil must not be used in the oven because they will prevent the waves reaching the food and may so reflect them as to damage the magnetron (which is costly to replace). Foil may be used sometimes, in small pieces, to cover portions of food in danger of becoming overcooked, but most manufacturers do not recommend metal in the oven. TV-dinners, how-ever, in shallow foil trays may be heated in some microwave ovens, the food being shallow enough to be heated by microwaves from the top

The simplest ovens have only one setting, with full-power micro-waves in action. The disadvantage of this is that large items of food will cook on the outside before the inside is warm (because the microwaves do not penetrate the food very deeply, and the center must rely on or-dinary heat conduction). Cooks with this type of oven must allow rest-ing periods between bursts of microwaving to give the center time to heat up by conduction before the outside is cooked. Some cookers have programmed rest-periods; others have a variable power selection dial.

All microwave ovens come with booklets giving times and settings for a wide range of foods. Recipes for one brand of oven will not necess-arily apply to another. Some guidelines, how-ever, are universal:

1 Timing is critical. If at all unsure, stand by the machine and check the food frequently.

2 Dense-textured food (large pieces of meat, for example) heat more slowly than the same weight or volume of open-textured food (ground meat, bread).

3 Except for liquids, foods should be covered while processing. This prevents drying out and splashing (especially of fat) and contains the hot steam, which speeds up the cooking process. Foods with a crisp tex-ture (such as toast or fried potatoes) may be re-heated uncovered but will quickly become limp.

4 Foods must be moved about during cooking. The center of the dish gets less heat than the edges, and so food in the center should be moved to the outside half-way through cooking. This is not necessary for small items, shallow foods being reheated, or liquids, but is essential for portions of, say, raw chicken, and large casser-oles. Thicker or slower-cooking parts of food, such as the thick ends of asparagus or the stalks of broccoli, should be pointed toward the edge of the dish.

5 Anything with a hard skin (like a whole raw egg or a chestnut) can not be microwaved. The rapid expansion of the contents will explode the shell. Whole apples and po-tatoes for baking must have skins split or prick-ed all over before pro-cessing.

6 Eggs, cream, sour cream, custard, and cheese are "critical" in-gredients, liable to sep-arate or splatter if micro-waved on a high setting without stirring or rest periods.

7 Foods which require dry heat to drive off steam or to provide a crisp crust, like bread, soufflés and pastry, do not micro-wave successfully.

8 Because the dish or bowl used to heat food in a microwave does not get hot except as a result of contact with the hot food, microwave-cooked food cools down fast.

9 Cakes will not brown in a microwave, but because they do not form a top crust, they rise more and are fluffier. Use a recipe designed for mi-crowave cookery. The best are cakes with chocolate or molasses to give color. Cakes look wet and uncooked when the time is up. But do not be tempted to over-cook—the mixture will dry off as it cools.

$\frac{1}{3}$ cup golden syrup
$\frac{2}{3}$ cup soft brown sugar
$\frac{1}{2}$ cup butter
$\frac{2}{3}$ cup milk
1 large egg, beaten
$1\frac{1}{4}$ level tsp baking soda
$1\frac{1}{2}$ cups plain flour
$\frac{1}{2}$ cup cocoa powder

Grease and line an 8-in deep soufflé dish with greased paper. (Or line it with ungreased plastic wrap.) In a large mixing bowl microwave the syrup, sugar and butter together for 3 minutes on maximum setting to melt them. Add the milk, let it cool a little, then add the beaten egg, and baking soda. Sift in the flour and cocoa and mix well. Pour into the soufflé dish and microwave on maximum setting for 6 minutes or on "simmer" setting for $8\frac{1}{2}$ minutes. Remove the cake (it will still look uncooked), allow it to stand for 5 minutes, then turn it out on a cake rack to cool. (Cooking such a cake in a conventional oven takes at least 1 hour at 325°F.)

Preserving food

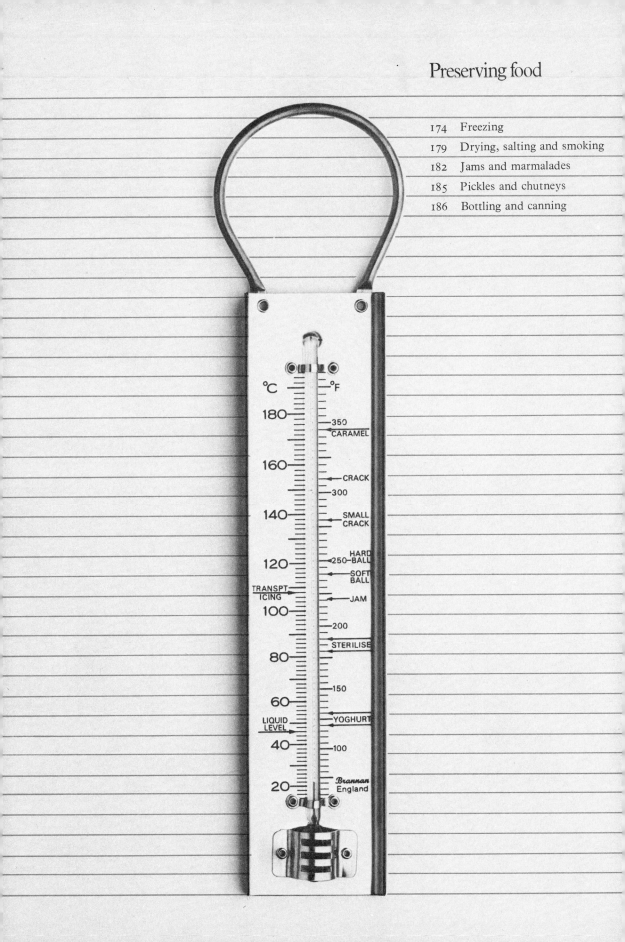

Freezing

In the past preserving food was vital to any household. If vegetables were not dried or salted, bacon not cured, fruit not bottled or turned into preserves when they were available, winter fare would have been bleak indeed.

Today, home preserving is more a matter of gastronomy than survival. Good canned fruits are readily available from every supermarket, and vacuum-packed bacon is convenient, reliable and much less trouble than home-cured pork.

Food preservation is a pleasurable and satisfying aspect of cooking, not just because it is an elegant answer to a glut of tomatoes or a crop of apples, but because the products can be varied according to the taste of the cook—pickles made extra-fierce, fresh trout smoked over beech, or bacon cured in juniper and sugar.

The freshest of food contains some microorganisms, but in concentrations so small as to be non-toxic. In time they multiply to dangerous levels and cause the decomposition of the food.

To prevent this, the activity of these molds, yeasts and bacteria must be halted.

1 By sterilizing the food, and then keeping it in this condition (as in bottling), where food is heated and sealed in airtight jars, allowing no new microorganisms to enter it.

2 By the addition of some substance which discourages the growth of any microorganisms, such as salt (as in curing bacon), vinegar (as in pickles), smoke (as in smoked salmon), sugar (as in candied fruit).

3 By rendering the food too dry (such as drying apples or apricots) to attract microorganisms, which require moisture to survive.

4 By holding the food at such low temperatures that any organisms are unable to multiply, as in freezing food.

Freezing

Freezing does not destroy microorganisms, but it does prevent their breeding. Once food is thawed, they multiply with renewed energy.

Manufacturers frequently put a "do not refreeze once thawed" label on their products. It is, in fact, often perfectly safe to refreeze thawed food, but it is not recommended because:

1 The cook might forget how long the food was unfrozen between periods in the freezer and therefore have no idea how close to going bad it is or how great the build-up of bacteria.

2 Freezing results in the loss of some juices (due to the expansion of the water-content of the food, which leads to the rupture of the moisture-containing tissues). Obviously, the more times the food is frozen and thawed the more juices will escape.

3 Some foods, like ice creams and mousses, which have had air beaten into them, lose their volume as the air escapes on thawing.

If food is to be thawed, then refrozen, give it as little time as possible in a warm kitchen. For example, if a frozen turkey is to be boned and stuffed two weeks in advance:

1 Thaw the bird as slowly as possible, preferably in the refrigerator.

2 Make the stuffing. Cool it fast if cooked. Chill it whether cooked or raw.

3 Bone the bird in a cool room, working as quickly as possible. Stuff it, wrap it and refreeze it fast.

4 Thaw it slowly again.

5 Roast it in a moderately hot oven (this will quickly kill any bacteria; a cool oven allows the stuffing to remain at incubating temperatures dangerously long).

Raw food generally freezes much more satisfactorily than cooked food. A raw PAIN DE POISSON will keep satisfactorily in a freezer for three or four months and when thawed and cooked will taste fresh and good. A cooked *pain de poisson* will not have quite such a creamy texture when thawed, being more crumbly and likely to break up, although still tasty. But gastronomy cannot always take precedence over convenience, and many cooked dishes in fact freeze perfectly adequately if they are prepared and wrapped with care.

"Storage life" in the freezer does vary for different foods. Also, food does not suddenly go bad if kept longer than the recommended storage life. There is, however, a slow deterioration in quality of all food in the freezer which, while almost or completely undetectable after a short period, gradually becomes apparent in the change of texture, color and flavor. The times given in the chart on page 178 are the limits beyond which deterioration, even though slight, is likely to be detectable.

The freezer has advantages other than that of storing food safely. It enables the cook to prepare foods well in advance, to prepare food in quantity (some to eat immediately, some later), and it makes possible numerous FROZEN DESSERTS and ICE CREAMS.

The freezing process
Rapid freezing

Freeze everything as quickly as possible. The faster food is frozen, the smaller the ice crystals formed in it will be, causing less damage to the cell walls of the food and resulting in less loss of juices on thawing.

Turn the freezer to maximum or the "fast freeze" setting 12 hours before putting food in.

Packing the freezer

Freeze small amounts at a time. Large quantities slow down the process. Use the fast freeze compartment if there is one.

Pack food in small quantities (again to speed up freezing, but also to ease thawing and to have food in convenient sizes).

Shallower blocks of food will freeze faster, thaw quicker and are more easily broken apart. For example, a thin rectangle of spinach is easier to break up to put in a pan than a block.

Once food is frozen, stack the packages as tightly as possible. A full freezer costs less to run than a half-empty one.

Wrapping

The most usual cause of deterioration of frozen foods is inadequate wrapping. Direct contact with air causes "freezer burn" (dry, discolored patches) on some foods.

Cooked meat, especially chicken, becomes shreddy and stringy if frozen badly wrapped.

Freezing/2

Containers

Heavyweight plastic bags are the cheapest and best. But they must be freezer gauge or they will burst or be torn and spill their contents.

Foil, plastic containers, old yogurt cartons, bowls or dishes may also be used as long as they are able to withstand freezing, are robust enough to survive some bumping and shoving in the freezer, and can be covered securely and labeled clearly.

Freezing food in casseroles or pie dishes freezes the food in convenient amounts but locks up the utensils for weeks at a time and can give awkward-shaped, unstackable packages in the freezer. Instead:

1 Freeze the food in the dish or casserole.

2 Once frozen, run hot water over the base to dislodge the block of food.

3 Wrap the food, or put it in a freezer bag and label it.

4 When needed, unwrap it, put it back in its dish, and allow it to thaw before cooking.

To freeze liquids, line a square box with a plastic bag, pour in the liquid and freeze until solid. Lift the bag out of the container, tie the top, label and store.

If using plastic containers or tubs for freezing liquids, leave 10% headroom to allow for expansion.

Good freezer tape will stick plastic wrap around awkward-shaped packages or keep plastic wrapping on pies. But ordinary Scotch tape will not survive freezing.

Buy labels made for the freezer. All-purpose stationer's labels come unstuck when frozen.

Some ballpoint pens will write on plastic but many will not. A china-graph pencil or "freezer pen" is best. Felt-tipped pens are no use. They write well but the ink rubs off in the freezer.

"Free-flow" freezing

Wet foods, frozen in a mass, emerge from the freezer in a solid block and need time and patience to thaw. To avoid this, put food to be frozen out on trays in a single layer. It does not matter if the peas, broad-beans, or whatever, are touching but they must not be piled one on the other. Freeze on the open tray. Once frozen, break up and pack in plastic bags. (More delicate foods, like raspberries, should be frozen without allowing the berries to touch each other—they will retain their shape better.)

Use this method for sausages (which again should *not* touch each other, otherwise the skins tear when they are taken apart), hamburgers, bread rolls, almost all fruit and vegetables. Open-freeze whenever possible. Open-freeze decorated cakes. Once the decoration is hard enough to withstand wrapping, wrap well and label.

Freezing in a block

Some foods cannot be open-frozen. Freeze casseroles in a shallow layer, with just enough sauce to submerge the food completely.

Freeze any mixtures which do not have sufficient sauce to cover them, like pie filling, under a layer of insulating mashed potatoes or pastry. Alternatively, double-wrap tightly.

Pack vegetables such as beans, peas or broad-beans, in shallow layers in plastic bags and freeze directly, without pre-freezing by the open method. They will emerge from the freezer in a solid piece but drop them on the table top several times and they will break up into a fairly free-flow pack.

Thawing

If food is thawed rapidly more moisture is lost. Almost all food is best thawed before cooking, including most green vegetables, because the center of food cooked from frozen is unlikely to be tender before the outside is overcooked or discolored.

If thawing must be done in a hurry, put the food into a hole-free plastic bag and submerge it in cold water. Do not use hot water; it does not work much faster and tends to cook the outside surface of the food.

Alternatively, use the defrost cycle on a microwave oven.

Hamburgers can be cooked from frozen, but not if they are to be rare, otherwise the rare middle will still be cold when the outside is cooked.

Small items of egg-and-breadcrumbed food may be cooked from frozen.

Foods that do not freeze successfully

1 EMULSIONS, such as MAYONNAISE or HOLLANDAISE, separate on thawing.

2 Yogurt, milk and cream will not be smooth when thawed. If yogurt must be frozen, churn it in an ice-cream maker to keep it smooth; heavy cream will freeze satisfactorily if it is whipped before freezing. Cheese loses some of its texture on freezing but keeps better if very well wrapped. (Butter on the other hand freezes well.)

3 Eggs cannot be frozen in the shell, as they burst. Freeze whites and yolks separately.

4 Jelly and aspic lose their texture if frozen and have to be melted and re-set before being served.

5 Foods with a high water-content do not retain a sufficiently crisp texture after thawing to be good eaten raw. Frozen vegetables and fruit are better served cooked. Some vegetables, notably tomatoes, marrow, cucumber and salad leaves such as watercress or lettuce, become too mushy to serve whole—even when cooked they can only be used for PURÉES or soups.

6 Meats and fish with a high fat content do not freeze as well as lean flesh, and sometimes develop a slightly rancid flavor if stored for as long as a year.

7 Foods with a high salt content do not keep well frozen.

How to freeze

Vegetables (use only the best, freshest produce)

Most vegetables must be blanched before freezing to halt enzyme activity which would otherwise continue in the freezer affecting color and flavor. They may be frozen un-blanched but their storage time would then be greatly reduced.

Filling and sealing freezer bags Press all the air out of the bag. Seal as near the top as possible.

2 *Leave plenty of room in the bag and shake to spread evenly for a flat, loose pack.*

Blanching (or heat-treating) vegetables

1 Wash carefully.

2 Examine each vegetable and discard any less than perfect.

3 Trim or cut to size, or sort to size (small beans in one batch, large ones in another).

4 Bring a large saucepan of water to the boil. A small volume will be cooled too much by the cold vegetables, which will then lose color before they are done.

5 Lower a basket of vegetables (not more than 2 lbs) into 8 pints of water or drop them in loose. Bring the water back to the boil. The times in the table overleaf assume the heat source is powerful enough to bring the water back to the boil almost immediately. If it is not, slightly longer times are necessary. To tell if the vegetables have been adequately blanched, break one open and put the exposed surface briefly against the tongue: It should feel unpleasantly hot, not just warm.

6 Lift the vegetables out immediately and dunk them into a sinkful of cold water, running in a continuous supply of fresh cold water to cool them rapidly. Cooling time is about the same as heat-treatment time. Do not leave them to soak longer than necessary or they lose taste and nutrients to the water.

7 Drain and dry well. Then open-freeze if feasible, otherwise pack into bags, exclude air, label and freeze.

Vegetable purées

(storage life, six months) Most vegetables may be frozen successfully if cooked and puréed.

Fruit purées (storage life, six months)

All fruit may be puréed and frozen. Purée raw, cooked or cooked-and-sweetened fruit, and freeze. (Sweetened fruit thaws more rapidly.)

Dry sugar packs (storage life, six months)

Raw fruit may be frozen by the open method, then packed and frozen with dry sugar. It will thaw more quickly but more "wetly" than unsweetened fruit.

Discoloration

Some fruits, such as apples, plums and pears, discolor on thawing. Add ascorbic acid (vitamin C) or citric acid in powder or tablet form to the syrup, juice or purée before freezing to reduce discoloration. Use the fruit as quickly as possible on thawing or cook while still slightly icy. Such fruits are better preserved by BOTTLING.

Supermarket "charcuterie" packages

(storage life, two months) Freeze sausages, small roasts of ham, sliced bacon, salami and liver-wurst in their plastic wrappers. To thaw them quickly, put the whole packabe under cold water.

Raw meat and poultry

(storage life, nine months for small items; 12 months for large) Wrap securely and label manageable-sized cuts and freeze fast. Wrap chicken portions, steaks or chops individually, or at least with double sheets of plastic between them so that they may be separated easily if the whole pack is not needed at once. Do not salt hamburgers before freezing as this draws the juices from the flesh. Open-freeze or pack with double sheets of plastic between the layers.

Breads and other flour-based products

(storage life, 12 months) Freeze perfectly. For short-term there is no need to wrap cooked breads, cakes and pastries as they do not dry much, but wrap and label if they are to be stored more than a few days. Wrap raw doughs and pastries.

Herbs (storage life, four months)

Freeze dry leaves in small polythene bags or packets, or chop finely, put into ice-trays and just cover with water. The frozen cubes can be transferred to labeled bags. On thawing, herbs are too wet to sprinkle over dishes as a garnish, but use for sauces and soups. Crumble or chop leaves while frozen.

Fish (storage life, 12 months for white fish; six months for oily fish; three months for cooked fish dishes)

Fish may be frozen exactly as meat, wrapped as tightly as possible to exclude air. Or, one of the following methods may be used:

Breadcrumb coating

Prepare thin fillets of fish in egg and breadcrumbs. Open-freeze. Cook from frozen.

Icepack Lay fillets of fish in a shallow metal or plastic container. Add very cold water just to cover, and freeze. Loosen the frozen block from the container by running under cold water, then wrap and freeze.

Ice-glaze Freeze the fish fillets or whole fish, skinned or unskinned, until solid. (Make sure the freezer is at its coldest —the fish needs to be well below freezing point.) Dip the fish briefly in very cold water. A thin film of ice will form on the surface of the fish. Refreeze, then repeat until a thin ice-glaze is built up.

Seafood

may be frozen raw, either by the breadcrumb, icepack or ice-glaze methods. The best method for cooking and freezing seafood is to poach it gently in a COURT BOUILLON. Put the pan in a sinkful of cold water to cool it rapidly and so prevent over-cooking. Freeze the whole pan. When solid, unmold the block by standing the pan in water. Wrap, label and freeze.

Freezing /3

Cooked farinaceous dishes (storage life, nine months)
Cooked pasta, polenta, rice and mashed potatoes freeze quite satisfactorily.

Sauces (storage life, three months)
Sauces thickened with flour or containing cream may be frozen but might separate if thawed too rapidly or over-heated. Thaw gradually. If the sauce curdles, beat well or process in a blender, then sieve.

Puddings and desserts
Gelatin-based mousses (storage life, three months), flans, pies, fruit crumbles and cakes (storage life, six months), steamed or baked puddings (storage life, 12 months), all freeze well. The exceptions are gelatins, fruit salads and custards, which do not.

Defrosting a freezer
Follow the manufacturer's instructions precisely. Keep the frozen food wrapped in newspaper or a blanket so it will not thaw, and transfer rapid-thawing foods like ice cream to the refrigerator while you work. Work as fast as possible, melting the ice in the freezer by standing trays or bowls of hot water inside it, scraping the ice carefully with a *blunt* instrument which will not damage the freezer. Use the opportunity to sort things out and re-label foods if necessary.
   Most freezers need defrosting once a year, and late spring, before fresh garden vegetables arrive, is a good time to do it.

Blanching vegetables			
	Preparation	Blanching (minutes)	Storage (months)
Artichokes (globe)	Remove stalks and outer tough leaves.	7	6
Artichokes (Jerusalem)	Freeze cooked into a purée.		6
Asparagus	Do not tie in bunches.	3–4	12
Beans, French or runner	French: Trim the ends. Runner: Slice thickly.	2–3 $1\frac{1}{2}$–2	12 6
Beets	Freeze completely cooked and skinned. Slice if large.		6
Broadbeans	Sort by size.	3	12
Broccoli	Trim stalks.	$2\frac{1}{2}$–4	12
Brussels sprouts	Choose small, firm sprouts. Remove outer leaves.	4–6	12
Cabbage (green or red)	Shred. (As cabbage is available all year, freezing is not usual.)	$1\frac{1}{2}$	6
Carrots	Choose small, young, strongly-colored ones. Scrape. Freeze whole.	5–6	12
Cauliflower	Break heads into florets.	3–4	6
Celery	Will be soft when thawed, but good for soups and stews.	3	12
Corn on the cob	Remove husks and silks.	6–10	9
Kale	Remove stalks.	1	6
Leeks	Finely slice, chop in chunks or leave whole.	1–3	12
Mushrooms	Do not peel. Freeze unblanched for up to one month For longer storage, cook in butter.		4
Onions	Unblanched onions, sliced or chopped. Sliced or chopped onions can be blanched in water or oil. Pearl or Spring onions can be blanched whole.	1–3 1–3	5 5
Peas	Choose young, very fresh peas.	1–2	12
Peppers	Remove seeds, slice or cut in half.	2–3	12
Potatoes	French fries: Blanch in oil. Boiled or mashed: Freeze cooked.	2–4	6
Root vegetables	Cut into chunks and blanch or cook completely.	3	12
Spinach	Move about in water to separate leaves.	1	12
Tomatoes	Do not blanch. Freeze whole, in slices, or as juice or purée, cooked or raw. (Skin frozen whole tomatoes under running hot water.)		12
Zucchini	Use only finger-sized small ones. Do not peel. Cut in chunks.	1	12

Drying, smoking and salting

Drying

Fruit and vegetables may be preserved by drying them in the sun, but it is more practical to use artificial heat for the dehydration process. The loss of nutrients in dehydration is minimal and food dried at home is the perfect "health food," containing no added preservatives.

Equipment

No specially designed cabinet is necessary if a space over a boiler, solid-fuel kitchen range or an electric fan-heater (set on low heat) is available. What is necessary is a current of mildly warm air, preferably between 90°F and 105°F.

If a constantly warm position in a current of air is available, a dehydrator can be set up by fixing or suspending open trays, one above the other, over the source of heat. If built or hung over the kitchen range or refrigerator (which can give out good heat) it may be necessary to arrange sides to the device to prevent the current of air dispersing sideways instead of rising straight up through the food trays.

Trays must allow the free passage of air, so they usually consist of a wooden frame with a stainless steel wire mesh stretched across it (a cake cooling rack will suffice).

Line wire trays with muslin to prevent the imprint of the wire mesh marking the food being dried. If the muslin is new, wash it to remove any coating.

Dry green vegetables and herbs in the dark, as light causes gradual loss of color.

Stages in dehydration

1 Cut the fruit, vegetables, meat or fish into small thin pieces of even size. Leave small plums and cherries whole. Fruit such as pears, peaches and apricots need not necessarily be peeled. Fruits which discolor easily should be dipped in lemon juice or in water containing vitamin C (ascorbic acid)—1 teaspoon for each 2 pints of water. Season fish fillets by sprinkling them with lemon juice and salt or by dipping them in soy sauce. Beef and venison, which are very lean, are the best meats for drying. Cut thin pieces across the grain for tender jerky (dried meat), with the grain for chewier meat. Season both with salt or soy sauce.

2 Lay the pieces, not touching each other, on the trays. Allow plenty of space for air circulation.

3 Allow to dry, moving the trays around to ensure even processing. (The tray nearest the heat source will be dried first, then the others can be moved down one place. Do not put the top tray, which will be the dampest, at the bottom otherwise the rising moisture from this will prevent the food above drying satisfactorily.)

4 If drying for preserving, fruit must feel stiff and leathery—harder than commercially dried fruit which contains preservatives that make hard drying unnecessary. Vegetables such as carrots and onions should be bone dry. Fish should be rigid and stiff, like Bombay duck. Leaf vegetables and herbs must be brittle. Jerky (dried meat) must be hard, almost black, and difficult to cut. If, however, fruit is to be eaten within a week or two it may be dried until pleasantly pliable—with the feel of chamois leather. Underdried jerky, which is softer to chew and cut, should be kept refrigerated and eaten within two weeks. Fish is always dried completely and there is little point in under-drying vegetables, long storage being the only reason for drying them. When the food feels dried to the right degree, remove it.

5 Keep hard-dried food in an airtight container, between sheets of parchment or wax paper, in a cool place, away from light. Pack in small convenient quantities so that if, by some mishap, one bag becomes moldy, it will not affect the others. Lay half-dried fruit between sheets of parchment or wax paper and keep in a non-airtight box. Tightly sealed, it may start to "sweat."

Drying herbs

Dry small bunches of herbs in any warm airy place by tying a few sprigs together by the stalks and suspending the bunch. Once brittle, strip the leaves from the stalks, crush them roughly or sieve them to a powder, according to preference, and store in clean, dry, airtight jars.

Smoking

Not-too-dry hard wood, traditionally oak or hickory, in the form of chippings or sawdust, smolders slowly, giving off vapor which rises, carrying with it chemicals released from the burning wood. These chemicals (aldehydes and phenols, ketones and acetic acid) are the preservatives. Given long enough, the moisture in the food allows the chemicals to penetrate deeply. They kill microorganisms present in the food and make it inhospitable to new ones. They also flavor the food with the characteristic smoky taste. In addition, the gentle heat causes partial dehydration of the meat, which is in itself a preservative and means the food becomes denser and more concentrated in flavor.

Smoking equipment

Whatever the type of smoker used, the object is the same—partially to trap the smoke so that it does not rush past the food too quickly to be absorbed by it. The usual hot-smoker consists of a container in the bottom of which is a small spirit or charcoal briquette fire or a heating element. (Wood is unsuitable as it is too bulky and burns too fast.) Over this is a pan or tray of sawdust or wood chippings which, as it heats, will smoke without bursting into flame, and over this, at a little distance, the food is suspended or laid on an open rack. Holes or a gap near the bottom allow the fire a supply of oxygen, and exit holes at the top allow the slow escape of smoke, which, if trapped, gives the food a bitter flavor.

Drying, smoking and salting /2

A cold-smoker has the source of heat and smoke far removed from the smoke-box (connected, say, by a length of piping) so that the smoke cools before it comes into contact with the food.

To maintain a smoker, wipe it to remove food grease from the interior and, more importantly, the gummy smoke residue which, if allowed to build up, can impart a bitter taste to the food.

The smoking process
Food may be cured by salting in brine or in dry salt before being smoked. The curing is done to add flavor and to ensure preservation. The curing time will depend on how salty the food is to be,

varying perhaps from an hour for a fish fillet to three weeks for a whole ham. Most commercially sold smoked foods are first cured. At home, if a fresh-tasting product to be eaten almost at once is required, dispense with the salt-cure, or flavor the fresh food with a marinade.

Suspending the food in smoke below 100°F is known as cold-smoking and is a longer process than hot-smoking, when the temperature of the smoke might be anything from 100°F to 225°F. Cold-smoking is used for products intended to be eaten raw (like smoked salmon) or to be cooked by conventional methods, such as kippers or

hams that will later be poached, or bacon to be fried. Hot-smoking cooks the food gently at the same time as smoking it, and is used for food to be eaten without further cooking, such as smoked trout, smoked mackerel, and many kinds of European sausage. However, sometimes hot-smoked foods, such as pork chops, are fried briefly to brown them attractively.

What to smoke?
Any fish or shell fish may be smoked, and, though it is true that the oilier salmon and herring yield an exceptionally moist and delicate product, even the soft-fleshed carp and uninteresting

ling or sucker improve greatly.

All poultry smokes well, though the drier birds need to have their breasts covered with bacon or strips of pork back fat to prevent over-drying. They are generally hot-smoked, then eaten cold.

Game and red meats smoke well, the more tender cuts being good cold-smoked, to be eaten thinly sliced and raw, the tougher cuts needing subsequent slow cooking.

Hard cheeses may be smoked, though not soft creamy cheeses. Smoked cheeses are expensive to buy and it is easy to smoke plain cheeses at home.

Some cold-smoked foods Monitor temperatures frequently when smoking over long periods.

	Preparation	Curing	Smoking
Whole small haddock	Remove heads. Split fish carefully from the belly and clean. Open flat.	Sprinkle with salt and leave for 15 minutes.	Smoke at 80°F for 8 hours. They should lose 12% weight.
Whole chicken	Clean, wash and dry well. Prick deeply with needle.	Cure for 2½ hours in brine. Hang to dry for 24 hours in a cool place.	Cold-smoke for 48 hours at 60°F then hot-smoke 2 hours at 220°F.
Fillet of beef (whole)	Trim meat well. Weigh.	Cure for 2½ hours in brine. Hang for 2 hours to dry.	Smoke at 80°F for 5 days or until weight loss is 22%. Outside will turn black.
Raw salami-type sausage	Make up salami (p140). Hang in refrigerator for 2 days.		Smoke at 9°F for 15 hours Then refrigerate for 14 days before eating raw.
Hard cheese	Remove any rind, wax or cheesecloth. Cut into bars 1 in thick.		Smoke at 60°F for 2 to 4 hours, according to taste. Wrap with foil and refrigerate.
Nuts	Blanch almonds, skin hazel nuts if liked. Place on wire mesh.		Smoke at 80°F for 2 to 12 hours according to taste.
Whole trout (one portion size)	Clean fish, taking care to remove all blood. Do not remove heads. Weigh gutted fish.	Cure for 1 hour in brine, then hang up to dry for 2 hours. Or salt, inside and out, and leave for 15 minutes. Or do not cure.	Use small pieces of wood (like headless matches) to hold belly flaps apart. Smoke at 180°F for 2 hours until the skin is slightly brown and wrinkled.
Duck	Clean. Prick well all over.	Cure for 2½ to 3½ hours in brine. Hang to dry for 24 hours in a cool place.	Smoke at 80°F for 36 hours, then hot-smoke at 200°F for 3 to 4 hours or until firm, cooked and with a red-gold skin. Draw off all fat and juices. Dry thoroughly.

Gravlax Lay boned, unskinned raw salmon side, flesh up, on foil. Rub with olive oil. Cover with salt

2 and fine sugar. Sprinkle liberally with chopped dill and crushed white or green peppercorns.

3 Cover with second salmon side, skin side up. Wrap the foil up around it and chill for 6 hours on each side.

4 Unwrap. Slice thinly at an angle. Serve with brown bread and butter and oil, mustard and basil dressing.

Salting

Preserving food by impregnating it with salt is known as curing. Today curing is done mainly for the flavor it imparts.

Fish, meat and some vegetables may be cured. Curing may be done in dry salt or in salt solution (brine). Dry salting is used for short cures, such as for fish (gravlax), preserving green beans and for making SALAMI.

The brine or dry salt is generally mixed with sugar (frequently brown sugar) for flavor, and perhaps with spices or herbs. Saltpetre (potassium nitrate) may be added in small quantities to give a pink tinge to the cured meat, which otherwise looks dull and gray.

Stages in hard-curing using brine:

If not following a specific recipe, make brine as follows. The solution is for an all-purpose (about 80%) brine. The instructions are for curing for preservation rather than simply for flavor.

1 In a large pan put roughly the amount of liquid needed to submerge the food to be cured. (Do *not* put in the food.)

2 Warm the water up: The salt will dissolve faster.

3 Add a raw, not-too-old potato, washed but not peeled. It will sink to the bottom.

4 Stir in enough pure common salt (not table salt, which has additives in it which will cloud the brine) by degrees until the potato is just floating and then remove the potato. One part salt, measured by volume, to five parts water is usually about right.

5 Stir in any other ingredients such as spices, sugar, saltpetre (about $\frac{3}{4}$ cup sugar and $1\frac{1}{2}$ tsp saltpetre for each 4 cups salt).

6 Let it cool, then chill.

7 If curing pork, beat, squeeze and press it to get out trapped blood.

8 Put the meat or fish in a deep non-metal or stainless steel container. Pour the brine over the food to cover it. To keep it submerged, weight the food down, using a heavy plate, board or a stainless steel cake rack with a water-filled jar on top. Weight birds by putting a scrubbed stone in them.

9 Leave the food for the required time: 20 days for a leg of pork or a thick rolled cut of beef. Seven days brining will suffice for cuts 1 in thick. Keep the brine bath in a cold place, or in a refrigerator. Stir the brine and move the pieces of food about in it every day to ensure even brining. If it starts to smell sour, drain it off and discard it, rinse the flesh and rub it with vinegar, then continue in a fresh solution.

10 Once the curing time is up, remove the meat, rinse it and hang it up to drip dry. Large cuts need about six days drying in a cool current of air in a place out of the sunlight and free of flies. Smaller pieces and thin, flat cuts need only three days.

11 Wrap the meat up tightly in cheesecloth or muslin. Hang it in a cool (below 50°F) airy place, or keep refrigerated; or bury in a box of wood ash (which serves as an insect repellent and imparts a pleasant smoky flavor to the meat).

Do not rinse meat or fish destined for smoking, but lift them straight from the brine and let them drip dry.

Foods cured for more than a week, as above, will need to be soaked in cold fresh water in a cool place before cooking, otherwise they will be too salty.

Before soaking, wash cuts of meat and poultry in lukewarm water to remove any "bloom." If the soaking time exceeds 10 hours, change the water two or three times a day to prevent the salt being re-absorbed.

Soaking times vary: Two hours for a thin fillet of fish; six hours for a thin pork belly (streaky bacon); overnight for a 2-in thin beef roast; 48 hours for a ham or large rolled beef roast.

Sauerkraut

Shred dry white cabbage finely. Pack it into a wide deep crock, to a depth of 4 in. Press down hard, pounding the cabbage to bruise it. Scatter a peeled, chopped cooking apple and a good handful of salt (at least 6 tablespoons) over it. Then repeat alternate layers of cabbage and apple and salt. Continue until the container is two-thirds full. Cover with a thick layer of salt, then a double layer of clean muslin and finally with a weighted round wooden board or plate. Put in a room at 65°F to ferment. If nothing happens within 36 hours, add enough cold boiled water to just wet the cabbage. After a week, lift the lid and skim off any scum. Scrub the lid, replace the cloth with clean muslin and leave for a further week in a cool place. By now the cabbage will be fermenting well, and more scum may be skimmed off. Remove the sauerkraut and any juice to clean buckets, and wash and scrub the lid and crock. Replace the sauerkraut, cover with clean muslin, and replace the weighted lid. Allow the fermenting to continue until the bubbling and fizzing stops.

Cook sauerkraut with a little white wine or sauté it lightly in butter or oil.

Jams and marmalades

The names of preserves can be confusing, especially as they are used in cookbooks and in ordinary speech, with "jelly" used for "jam," "marmalade" for "fruit butter" and so on. To define them:

Preserves Anything preserved, but here used to cover the items below.

Jellies Made from clear fruit juice and sugar. They should be "set" sufficiently thick to hold their shape, but only *just* solid.

Jams Made from crushed or cut-up fruit, or whole berries which break up during cooking. They are not usually set as solidly as jellies.

Marmalades Jams made exclusively from citrus fruit.

Butters (Sometimes called curds or cheeses). Fruit purées cooked with sugar until thick. (They usually do not keep well.)

Pickles Fruit or vegetables preserved in vinegar, with or without other seasonings.

Chutneys Cooked mixtures of fruit and/or vegetables which contain both sugar and vinegar.

Relishes Similar to chutneys but the vegetables or fruits are sieved, or minced or chopped fine, giving a sauce-like consistency.

Jams, jellies and marmalades

These preserves depend on four factors to prevent them from deteriorating during storage:

1 *Pectin* A substance found in fruit which, when combined with acid and sugar and heated, will cause the mixture to "set" (thicken or congeal into a near-solid form once cold). Not all fruits have enough pectin to obtain a set. If jam is to be made from such fruits, commercial pectin, or juice or pulp from a high-pectin fruit, must be included. Fruit contains most pectin when perfectly ripe or *just* under-ripe, not when over-ripe. High-pectin fruits include lemons, apples, quinces, damson plums, sour plums and red currants. Low-pectin fruits include rhubarb, strawberries, mulberries and pears. Test for pectin content in the following way. Put a teaspoon of the simmered fruit juice (before adding the sugar) into a glass. When cold, cover it with methylated spirits (denatured alcohol). After a minute or so a jelly will have formed. If it is in one or two firm clots there is adequate pectin in the fruit. If the jelly clots are numerous and soft, the jam will not set without more pectin.

2 *Sugar* A high concentration of sugar is necessary to react with the acid and pectin to obtain a set. The sugar is also itself a preservative.

3 *Acid* The presence of fruit acid is vital. Like sugar, it reacts with the pectin. Without acid, a set will not occur. Acid also discourages the growth of bacteria and helps to prevent crystallization of the jam during storage. If the fruit used is low in acid, tartaric acid, citric acid or lemon juice must be added.

4 *The destruction and exclusion of molds and yeasts* The jam itself is sterilized by the rapid boiling it undergoes. Generally, jars, jam funnels and other equipment are not sterilized as contact with the boiling jam is sufficient to kill most microorganisms. Sometimes, however, molds do grow on the jar rim and they can spread to the surface of the jam. Sterilizing equipment and jars helps to prevent this. It can be done by any of the following methods:

a) Put jars, lids and ladles into a deep pan, cover with hot, not boiling, water. Bring slowly to the boil and simmer for 20 minutes. Dry on a freshly laundered cloth or in a cool oven.

b) Immerse the equipment in a weak bleach solution (any household bleach will do). Then pour boiling water over and into everything to get rid of any lingering smell and taste of chlorine.

c) Use a patent sterilizing agent such as the tablets or powder sold to sterilize babies' feeding bottles.

Wooden spoons and skimmers need not be sterilized as the boiling jam will do it. Jelly bags and cloths, or buckets and bowls, need not be sterilized as the juice is reboiled after filtering.

Once the sterilized jam is put into the clean jars, ensure, by proper sealing, that no new mold spores can enter.

Sealing jam jars

1 *Paper covers and wax discs* These are sold in speciality or gourmet shops. The packages usually contain cellophane covers, small rubber bands and wax discs of a size suitable for large or small jam jars. Buy the right size. Over-large discs on the surface of jam in small pots ruckle the surface and do not provide a proper seal. Discs that are too small leave too much jam uncovered.

Fill the hot, dry, clean jam jars with hot jam. Fill each jar to within $\frac{1}{2}$ in of the brim. Immediately lay a disc, wax side down, on the surface of the jam. Then wet one side only of the cellophane cover and stretch it, wet side up, over the top of the jar, pulling it tight and smooth. Secure with a rubber band. As the cellophane dries, it shrinks tightly round the jar. Plastic wrap, stretched tightly, also provides a good seal.

2 *Paraffin wax* Fill the jars with hot jam to *just* below the rim. Leave to cool and set. Melt paraffin wax (or plain white candles) in a pot standing in hot water or in the oven. Pour or brush a thin layer of melted wax all over the surface of the jam. Leave to cool and set. Repeat the process, filling up any cracks around the edge that may have developed as the wax cooled. Wax provides an excellent seal, but ensure that the jam jar is full. If the wax runs under the shoulders of the jar, getting it out will be frustrating and messy.

3 *Screw-tops* Fill the jars, leaving at least $\frac{1}{2}$ in headroom. Seal immediately with a metal screw-top. This is un-

doubtedly the best method if commercial jam pots with screw-lids are available. The lid must be rust-free, well-fitting, very clean and preferably with a plasticized or laminated underside. If the seal is perfect the cooling air in the neck of the jar creates a partial vacuum. (Plastic screw-tops do not give a good seal.)

4 *Preserving jars* If the storage place is damp and, in spite of all precautions, mold always appears, then use preserving jars. This is the one method of ensuring an absolutely reliable seal. Preserving jars are, however, expensive and most cooks make do with one of the above methods, resigning themselves to scraping a layer of moldy jam from one or two jars. The mold is harmless and the jam underneath will be perfectly good. It should, however, be eaten promptly before more spores, which will certainly be present, develop.

Yield

Most jelly and jam mixtures will yield between $1\frac{1}{2}$ times and twice the weight of sugar used in the recipe, but a given weight of fruit used for whole fruit jam will give twice as much as the same weight of fruit simmered and strained to provide juice for a jelly. Always overestimate the amount of jars needed. A few jars left over are much less trouble than having to wash, dry, and warm more jars at the last minute.

Stages in jam-making

1 Choose ripe or barely-ripe fruit.
2 Chill a few saucers to use later in the test for setting.
3 Examine the fruit, and wash or wipe. Weigh it and calculate sugar quantity (usually equal to weight of fruit).
4 Sterilize or wash the jam jars. Dry and warm them in a cool oven (overheated jars cause the jam to sizzle and bubble when potted).
5 Put the fruit and water in the preserving pan and set to simmer. If the fruit is quick-cooking, soft and juicy (like berries) allow enough water to come barely a quarter way up the fruit. If the fruit is hard (like quinces or pears) add enough water to float the fruit.
6 Warm the sugar gently in the oven (otherwise it lowers the temperature of the fruit which then takes longer to reboil and cook, and may lose its bright color).
7 Test the fruit juice for pectin, as described above. If low in pectin add lemon juice or high-pectin fruit, simmer and re-test.
8 Bring to a good boil and tip in the sugar. Stir without boiling until the sugar is dissolved, then boil fast (if the fruit is very fragile, boil gently).

9 Once it begins to look and smell like jam, test it for setting. Jams reach setting point at 220°F, and marmalades at 222°F. To test, put a teaspoon of the jam on a cold dish and return it briefly to the refrigerator. Using the tip of a finger, push the surface of the jam in the dish to see if a skin, which wrinkles in tiny waves when pushed, has formed. If it has, setting point has been reached.
10 Take the pan from the heat and skim carefully, removing any scum and floating pips or stones. If it contains large pieces of fruit or rind, which will float if the jam is potted while still hot, cool first for 20 minutes.
11 Put the hot, dry jars close together on a board and use a pitcher or jam funnel to fill them.
12 Seal them.
13 Wipe with a clean, hot, damp cloth to remove any drips while liquid.
14 Leave overnight.
15 Label with the type of jam and the date.
16 Store in a cool, dark, dry, airy place. Too much light may cause loss of color, and a warm, close or damp atmosphere will encourage the growth of micro-organisms and rot paper covers.

Stages in marmalade-making

As jam-making, but because the tough rind of the fruit is included in the preserve, soaking the rind and longer cooking is necessary.
1 Squeeze the fruit, reserving the juice. Tie the pips in a loosely-packed muslin bag (they contain pectin and should be simmered with the fruit).
2 Chop up pith and rind finely or coarsely as desired.
3 Cover the rinds (and pip bag) generously with water. Leave to soak in a plastic bucket or china or plastic bowl.
4 Transfer the rind and pip bag to a preserving pan and simmer slowly for at least two hours or until soft.
5 Remove the pip bag but squeeze it well over the pan to extract any pectin.
6 Add the juice.
7 Proceed as for jam, adding sugar (usually twice the weight of sugar to that of the original fruit).
8 Test for setting at 222°F.
9 Cool for 20 minutes before potting so that the pieces of fruit will not float to the top of the too-liquid syrup.

Jams	
Damson plum	Slit each damson from top to stalk—this will allow the stone to float out. Follow the stages in jam-making, using water to half cover the fruit and 50% more weight of sugar than fruit. Skim off the stones before potting.
Plum	Remove stones. Weigh fruit. Follow the stages in jam-making, using water to come a quarter way up the fruit and same weight of sugar as prepared fruit.
Strawberry	Use 25% less sugar than fruit. Make syrup with the sugar, the juice of 1 lemon for every 2 lbs fruit and very little water. When dissolved, add the berries. Stir gently and boil slowly to set.

Jams and marmalades/2

Stages in jelly-making

Jellies are similar to jams but they are made with the simmered fruit juice only, the whole fruit being discarded. The juice is filtered to clarify it.

1 Cook a little fruit until pulpy and test for pectin content. Add lemon juice or high-pectin fruit if necessary.
2 Simmer the fruit (chopped up, but including skins, cores and pips) with sufficient water to cover barely.
3 Suspend a clean jelly bag over a large bowl or bucket so that the cloth does not touch the bowl. It must be *over*, not in, the bowl. In the absence of a jelly bag lay a thick flannel cloth in a stainless steel or nylon sieve and put that over the bucket or bowl.
4 Pour the fruit and juice into the bag and leave to drip overnight. Do not attempt to hurry the process—squeezing the bag will produce cloudy jelly.
5 Next day, measure the juice in the bowl or bucket and bring it to the boil in the preserving pan.
6 Add the sugar (usually 1 lb sugar to each 2½ cups liquid).
7 Stir until dissolved, then boil to set. Setting point is 220°F.
Test as for jam, or dip the skimmer or spoon into the jelly and hold it up over the pan at eye level: If the drips run off in a steady single stream, the jelly is not ready, but if they start (especially as they cool slightly) to drip from two or three places, forming a wavy curtain of dripping jelly, reluctant to leave the spoon, it is ready to pot.
8 Pot, seal and store as for jams.

Stages in the making of fruit butter

1 Cook the fruit with sufficient water to prevent it sticking to the pan and burning. Stir until soft and pulpy.
2 Push through a sieve, or liquefy and then sieve to remove skins and pips.
3 Return the pulp to the preserving pan with ¾ cup sugar for each 1 cup. Stir continuously over gentle heat until the sugar has dissolved.
4 Boil fast, stirring until thick enough to draw the spoon through the pulp exposing the bottom of the pan without it running immediately back into the channel. (Wear rubber gloves and long sleeves as the boiling fruit splatters.)
5 Pack into hot, sterile jars, seal and keep cool.

Lemon curd

Put the strained juice and very finely grated rind of 2 small lemons with ¼ cup butter, ½ cup sugar and 3 beaten eggs, into a pan and bring slowly to the boil, stirring briskly all the time. Cook until thick (the lemon juice will prevent the eggs scrambling). Strain if preferred, or pot as it is. It keeps, refrigerated, for three weeks.

What went wrong?

Mildew on the surface of the preserve:
1 Wet jars.
2 Covering the jam when lukewarm (if sealed while hot, the heat trapped under the seal will kill any newly-arrived mildew spores. If sealed lukewarm, ideal incubating conditions are created. Sealing cold, though not as safe as sealing while hot, is less conducive to mold growth).
3 Imperfect sealing.
4 Damp or warm storage place.
5 Equipment that was not properly sterilized.

Crystallization of the preserve:
1 Insufficient acid in the fruit.
2 Boiling the jam before the sugar is dissolved.
3 Too much sugar.
4 Leaving the jam uncovered.
5 Storing in too cold a place, such as the refrigerator.

Fermentation of the preserve:
1 Insufficient boiling, leading to non-setting.
2 Insufficient acid, pectin or sugar, leading to non-setting.
3 Storing in too warm a place.
4 Jars that were not properly sterilized.

Marmalades		
	Ingredients	Method
Clear grapefruit marmalade	2 large grapefruit 2 medium lemons 13 cups water 7 cups sugar	Follow the stages in marmalade-making, but put the chopped pith and rind into a loosely-packed muslin bag with the pips. Squeeze well to extract liquid after simmering, then discard. Add the juice and boil fast to set.
Dark Seville marmalade	2 lb Seville oranges 2 medium lemons 13 cups water 8 cups sugar 6 tbs molasses	Follow the stages in marmalade-making, adding the molasses with the sugar.

Jellies	
Quince	Follow the stages in jelly-making, boiling chopped fruit in sufficient water to float the fruit. Strain when pulpy.
Tomato and mint	Use equal parts tomatoes and sour apples (or apple skins and cores). Follow the stages in jelly-making, adding fresh chopped mint before potting.

Pickles and chutneys

Pickles and chutneys depend for their preservation on a high concentration of acid, usually in the form of vinegar, which prevents the growth of bacteria.

Raw pickles

Vegetables are frequently pickled raw but they are first salted or "brined" to draw the juices from them, otherwise these would seep into the vinegar during storage and so weaken it as to impair its effectiveness as a preservative. Salt is itself an effective preservative and its penetration into food helps to prevent spoilage (see BRINING). In pickling its role is secondary.

Making raw pickles

1 Cut the vegetables up into the desired size.
2 Salt them. If they are "wet," like squash or cucumber, layer them in a bowl, sprinkling pure rock salt (not table salt which produces a cloudy pickle) liberally between the layers. Leave for 24 hours in a cool place.

If they are firm vegetables such as shallots or carrots, slice them or prick them deeply with a needle in several places to allow the brine to penetrate. Dissolve salt in 8 times its volume of water, bring the solution slowly to the boil, then allow it to cool. Soak the prepared vegetables for 24 hours in the brine, keeping them well submerged with a weighted plate or a wooden board.
3 Rinse well and pat dry with a clean cloth.
4 Commercial pickling vinegar may be used, or spice plain vinegar as follows:
a Put the vinegar (which must contain at least 5% acetic acid)

into a large pan (not made of unlined copper, brass or iron as these metals react with the vinegar, impairing the flavor). Add (for every 5 cups):

1 tbsp blades of mace
2 cinnamon sticks
2 tsp allspice berries
2 tsp black peppercorns
2 tsp mustard seed
4 cloves
1 chili pepper, split
10 slices ginger root

b Bring, covered, slowly to simmering point, then remove from the heat. Leave for 3 hours.
c Strain, or, if preferred, leave spices in the vinegar—they look good in glass jars.
5 Pack the vegetables, without bruising, into wide-necked jars.
6 Top up jars with cold spiced vinegar. If the jars have metal lids, leave a little headroom to prevent the vinegar corroding the metal which in turn affects the vinegar's flavor. Cork-stoppered or glass-stoppered jars can be filled to the brim.
7 Seal tightly. If using metal lids or slightly ill-fitting stoppers, cover the jar with plastic wrap or wax paper before putting on the lid. Do not use jam covers as they are too insubstantial for a liquid preserve. Pickles will not go moldy if exposed to the air, but the vinegar will evaporate quickly.
8 Store for 6 months, if possible, before using.

Baby onions, shallots

Follow the stages in raw pickle-making, pricking the whole, peeled vegetables well.

Dill cucumber

Follow the stages in raw pickle making, using dry salt on the sliced or whole cucumbers. (If whole, prick well before salting.) Make the spiced vinegar with the addition of 2 sliced cloves of garlic, 1 fresh dill head (or 1 tbs dill seeds) and $\frac{3}{4}$ cup sugar for 5 cups of vinegar. Pack the dill head in the jar with the cucumbers.

Cooked pickles

Occasionally, tough vegetables are pickled after cooking, in which case they do not need salting. For instance, beets are drained after boiling in water and are then packed in salted vinegar.

If a less strong pickle is required than one in pure vinegar (say, equal parts vinegar and water), then the pickle must be processed in a preserving jar (see BOTTLING).

Chutneys

These are the easiest preserves to make. They are mixtures of cooked fruit and vegetables, usually highly spiced, resembling jam in texture but depending for preservation on their vinegar content.

Endless combinations of flavors are possible and almost any glut of garden produce can be made into chutney.

Chutney-making

1 Cut up fruit and vegetables roughly (except onions which should be chopped or sliced finely).
2 Put all the ingredients except the sugar and vinegar into a thick-bottomed pan (but, as in PICKLING, not an unlined iron, copper or brass one). Tie any spices to be extracted later into a small cloth bag.

3 Cover the ingredients with vinegar. Cook slowly until the ingredients are soft and most of the vinegar has evaporated. Stir frequently to prevent sticking and burning.
4 Add the sugar and the rest of the vinegar. Stir till dissolved.
5 Boil rapidly, stirring often, until thick and just syrupy.
6 Put into clean, dry, hot jars.
7 Seal and label. (If the chutney is to be eaten within 6 months, jam covers are adequate. Use screw-tops, cork stoppers or a few tough layers of plastic if storing for longer.)
8 Store, if possible, for 6 months to allow time for the harshness of the vinegar to mellow.

Green tomato and apple chutney

2 lb apples
3 lb green tomatoes
2 medium onions, sliced
$\frac{1}{2}$ cup golden raisins
2 tsp salt (rock or sea, not table)
Few slices ginger root
1 tsp white peppercorns
5 to 6 allspice berries
$3\frac{3}{4}$ cups pickling vinegar
$1\frac{1}{2}$ cups sugar

Put the spices in a small cloth bag and put to boil with everything except a cupful of the vinegar and the sugar. Follow the stages as in chutney-making, extracting the spices before potting.

Bottling and canning

Any microorganisms present in bottled or canned food are destroyed by heat. Further contamination of the sterilized food inside the jars or cans is prevented by the specially designed lids which provide an absolutely airtight seal.

The procedure described here is for fruit and tomatoes only. It is possible to bottle vegetables, fish and meat, but the practice is not recommended, because they contain little or no acid and are thus liable to contain bacteria. Some bacteria are able to survive astonishingly high temperatures and, unless the food is processed for a very long time, there still remains the risk of food poisoning. If meat and vegetables are processed sufficiently long to ensure safety, the quality of the food is impaired—vegetables become soggy, meat shreddy—which explains the usually poor quality of canned meat and vegetables. The prolonged processing also alters the taste of the original food radically. Canned sardines and peas bear little relation to their fresh counterparts.

Fruit, because of its high acid content, will be bacteria-free, and the harmless yeasts and molds are more easily destroyed by heat. Figs, sweet tomatoes and pears are relatively low in acid, so add 2 teaspoons of lemon juice (or a pinch of citric or ascorbic acid) to each 1 lb.

Canned or bottling?

No home cook needs to invest in canning *and* bottling equipment, as both methods produce the same preserves. Sometimes there is no choice—at the time of writing home-canning equipment is simply not available in Britain. But if there is a choice the cook should consider the advantages and disadvantages of both.

1 New cans (supplied with lids) must be bought for every operation. Jars, though expensive, may be re-used until broken or chipped, but they do need new lids or seals for each operation. Jars are generally more easily available, but are often re-designed by the manufacturer, and replacing old-style lids can be difficult.

2 Cans are less bulky and easier to stack. (But they do not look as good on the shelf.)

3 If the label comes off the can the contents become a mystery; not a problem with glass jars.

4 Jars must be stored in the dark if the contents are not to discolor.

5 The canning process requires one more step than bottling, "exhausting" (see page 188).

Cans

Buy R-enamel, or "fruit" cans, lined to prevent the acid in the food reacting with the metal causing food discoloration. Use the domestic sizes (up to 2 lb only).

The sealer or seamer

Cans cannot be sealed except with a seamer which crimps the edges of can and lid together. This adjusts to various sizes of can. When sealing a batch of cans, seal all the cans of one size together. Before sealing the first can, half fill it with water, seal it and hold it under water. If air bubbles rise, it is imperfectly sealed and the sealer must be adjusted.

Jars

There are two basic designs of preserving jar on the market, though many manufacturers produce them, and shapes vary slightly.

Some, like the Mason and Kilner jars, have screw-top glass or ceramic lids; others like the Le Parfait or Lightening jars have glass lids held in place by one or two wire clamps.

Older versions of both have separate rubber sealing rings (which have to be replaced each time) and have to be processed with the lid held only loosely in place to allow air to escape. They are tightly screwed on, or the second clamp put in place, after processing and before cooling.

More modern screw-type jars usually have the rubber seal bonded to the lid or have a ring of rubber sealing compound round the edge of the lid. These and the more modern clamp-type jars can be processed fully tightened as the seals allow the air to escape but not to re-enter.

In each case, read the manufacturer's instructions carefully.

Testing for a good seal

To test for a perfect seal (when the jar is stone cold) remove the screw band or metal clips and carefully pick up the jar by the lid only. If the seal remains unbroken, the seal is perfect. If the lid comes off, start again with a new seal, or eat the contents within a day or two.

Methods of canning and bottling fruit

There are two basic methods:

The raw pack
Fruit is cooked and sterilized in a single process. The raw prepared fruit is packed into the can or jar and the hot syrup or water is poured over it. The jar is then processed for long enough to cook and sterilize the contents. Most suitable for soft berry fruits, for tomatoes and other easily pulped items.

The cooked pack (also sometimes called hot-pack, but as hot liquid is used for both methods this can be confusing)

The fruit is cooked in syrup in a pan before packing into jars with the hot liquid. More cooked fruit can be got into a jar than raw. Most suitable for whole pears, dessert apples and other firm items which can be checked for tenderness before bottling. The cans or jars need only be processed long enough to sterilize the contents.

Sterilization

The filled jars or cans may be sterilized in various ways:

The boiling water bath
This is the most common home method of sterilization, requiring only a deep pan or preserving kettle. The water level should come over the top of the lids and the water should always be at a good rolling boil. If jars are too tall to be submerged, cover the tops over with dish towels and foil to prevent the escape of steam; the water must, however, at least reach the necks of the jars. Process for 20% longer than the recommended times, and expect a greater failure rate.

Bottling fruits and tomatoes

Fruits are usually bottled in sugar syrup, made by dissolving sugar in water. The more sugar, the heavier the syrup. Equal volume measures of sugar and water heated together will give a thick syrup suitable for peaches or sour plums; half as much sugar as water will give a light, thin syrup. Use whatever kind of syrup suits the fruit. The sugar is not necessary as a preservative but for flavor. Tomatoes are bottled in salted water.

Fruit	Preparation	Method	Syrup	Time in boiling water bath	Time in pressure cooker
Whole dessert apples	Peel, core, quarter. Keep in acidulated water containing a teaspoon of vitamin C powder to prevent discoloration until ready.	Poach in thin syrup until tender.	Pack in hot jars/cans with hot syrup and added lemon juice.	2 lb 10 min 4 lb 15 min	2 lb 1 min 4 lb 2 min
Slices of cooking apple	Peel and slice. Keep in acidulated water until ready.	Pack raw slices tightly. Fill up to neck.	Cover with hot thin syrup.	2 lb 20 min 4 lb 30 min	2 lb 1 min 4 lb 2 min
Soft berries and currants	Wash only if sandy or muddy. Pick over carefully.	Pack raw, to neck, sprinkle liberally with sugar and leave overnight.	Do not add any more liquid. The juice will be enough.	2 lb 10 min 4 lb 15 min	2 lb 1 min 4 lb 2 min
Cherries	Wash, de-stalk and prick each cherry with a needle (to prevent bursting).	Pack raw, shaking down firmly, to neck.	Cover with hot heavy syrup for sour cherries, hot medium syrup for sweet.	2 lb 20 min 4 lb 30 min	2 lb 1 min 4 lb 2 min
Gooseberries and rhubarb	Wash and prepare as for stewing.	Pack raw, filling to neck.	Cover with hot thick syrup.	2 lb 10 min 4 lb 15 min	2 lb 1 min 4 lb 2 min
Peaches (halved)	Boil in water for 10 seconds, or until skin will come off easily. Peel, halve and pit.	Pack raw, filling to neck.	Cover with hot medium or heavy syrup.	2 lb 25 min 4 lb 30 min	2 lb 2 min 4 lb 3 min
Ripe pears	Peel, halve and core.	Pack raw, filling to neck.	Cover with hot medium syrup, with added lemon juice.	2 lb 30 min 4 lb 40 min	2 lb 3 min 4 lb 4 min
Whole hard pears	Peel. Keep in acidulated water until ready.	Poach in medium syrup.	Pack in hot jars/cans with hot syrup and lemon juice.	2 lb 10 min 4 lb 15 min	2 lb 1 min 4 lb 2 min
Plums	Wash, de-stalk and prick with large needle.	Pack raw, filling to neck.	Cover with hot medium syrup	2 lb 20 min 4 lb 25 min	2 lb 1 min 4 lb 2 min
Tomatoes	Dip into boiling water for 5 seconds. Skin and quarter or slice.	Pack raw, sprinkling salt and sugar between layers, filling to neck.	Do not add any liquid. The juice will be enough. Add lemon juice if tomatoes lack acid.	2 lb 35 min 4 lb 40 min	2 lb 3 min 4 lb 4 min

Bottling and canning /2

The pressure cooker

Because pressure cookers are tight-closed in operation, the trapped steam and air inside the cooker reaches temperatures greater than in an unpressurized pan. This means that sterilization can safely be done in steam rather than under water, and the process is quicker.

Process all fruits at low pressure (about 5 lbs): Too much pressure may cause the jars to shake about too vigorously and crack, or force the contents of the jars to bubble up to the lids, spoiling the chances of a good seal. Check the manufacturer's instruction booklet.

The pressure-canner

Like a giant pressure cooker, and designed for sterilizing jars and cans in steam. Very expensive but easy to use and useful for the home cook regularly canning or bottling large quantities. Follow the manufacturer's instructions exactly.

Stages in canning and bottling

1 Check that cans or jars, and lids (plus screw bands, rubber seals, wire clips where appropriate) are in perfect condition. Rubber parts cannot be used more than once and should not be kept for more than a year before use. If they are that old, check to ensure they are not perished by stretching them fairly hard. It should take some pressure to close wire clasps with the rubber seal in place. If they have lost all their spring, replace them or buy new jars. Make sure all jars and cans are clean and dust-free. They need not be sterilized, as the processing of the fruit will do this.

2 Make the syrup.

3 Prepare the fruit: peel, remove blemishes, cut to even size, de-stalk and wash as appropriate.

4 If using the cooked pack method, cook the fruit in the syrup.

5 If using jars, warm them so they will not crack when the syrup is poured into them.

6 Pack the fruit. If using raw pack method, pack the fruit into the jars or cans, shaking down well but without bruising. Pour the hot syrup over it. If using the cooked-pack method, spoon the cooked fruit into the jars and cover with hot syrup.

(Fill cans to the brim with fruit and syrup. If using jars, make sure the fruit is covered with syrup but that the neck space of the jar is left empty. This gives an air space to become a partial vacuum on cooling.)

7 "Exhausting" This applies only to processing in cans, not jars. Stand the cans in a deep pan and fill with boiling water up to within 1 in of the rim. Cover with a lid or foil. Simmer gently until the temperature of the food in the open cans has reached 170°F. (As cans must be sealed before processing, there is no escape route for any air trapped inside the can. Even with cans filled to the brim, some air may be trapped inside food if it is cold. For this reason food to be canned is always heated. Hot air rises, and in this case it rises safely out of the can.

8 Put on the lids. If cans, seal by machine. If screw-type jars, screw closed loosely (spin the lid until just closed, but do not tighten). If old-style wire-clasp jars, close loosely; if modern, tighten completely.

9 Process for the required time. If using a pressure-cooker, heat the cooker with an inch or two of water in the bottom and the lid on, but without the indicator weight or pressure-cock in place, until a steady stream of steam rises from the vent. Then close the vent with the weight or cock, and time the processing from the time the gauge registers the desired pressure.

10 Cool. If bottling in jars, leave the cooker to depressurize at room temperature. Do not cool hastily (the sudden release of pressure may cause the fruit in the jars to bubble up under the jar lid). If using cans, release the pressure as fast as possible by standing the pan in cold water, by removing the indicator weight or releasing the pressure-cock, but do not attempt to remove the lid until the pressure registers zero. Once it does, unclamp the lid and remove it so that the steam will rise away from you. Remove the cans and dunk them at once into a sinkful of cold water, running in more water to cool them.

If using a boiling water bath, time the processing from the moment the water is at a rolling boil. When the time is up, lift out the jars and stand them on a wooden board, or, if using cans, dunk them at once in a sinkful of cold water and run more cold water in to cool them.

11 Tighten the seals if possible.

12 Leave overnight, or until stone cold.

13 Test for a good seal as described above.

14 Label with the date and type of fruit. (Use wrap-around labels for cans to minimize loss.)

Serving food

Meat

Carving rib roast *Make a deep cut against the rib bones.*

2 Slice meat toward the bones to meet the first cut.

For good carving the first requirements are a razor-sharp knife, a carving fork and a large board or plate sitting firmly on a non-slip surface. If the table-top is slippery and the serving plate is china, put a cloth mat or folded napkin under it to keep it from moving about. The dish or board should be almost flat (carving in a deep-lipped dish is virtually impossible).

It does not really matter if you do not know the correct angle at which to slice the meat. There are many different methods of carving almost any cut and few people will notice what the carver is doing if the carving actions are not clumsy or awkward and the carver is not obviously flustered. As far as possible make sure the cuts go against the meat grain. Cutting with the grain gives shreddy, "stringy" slices. Carve slices as thick or as thin as personal preference dictates. Cold meat is generally sliced more thinly than hot meat and American and French chefs carve most meat, particularly beef, in thicker slices than the British, who prefer to serve several paper-thin slices.

Carving ham *Make a cut down to the bone near to the knuckle.*

2 Carve shallow flat slices toward the first cut (the wedge acts as a guard for the hands).

Carving shoulder of lamb *Carve slices in a "V" out of the central fleshy section.*

Saddle of lamb *Cut down to the bone across chump end and down each side of the backbone.*

Carving leg of pork *Starting at the fat end, carve down to the bone in thin slices.*

Carving pork with crackling *Slide knife under crackling to loosen and remove it in one piece.*

Carving leg of lamb *Cut slices toward the bone.*

2 Cut long vertical, thin slices parallel to the backbone; or, if the meat is well done,

It may look attractive to put the potatoes and other vegetables around the roast, but it does make carving awkward and messy · If carving meat to serve as cold cuts wait until the meat is quite cold; otherwise the slices lose their juices, colour and taste. It is also easier to carve thin even slices from a cold joint · When carving undersides of roasts, like sirloins of beef or legs of lamb, it is easier to cut more thickly and with the grain of the meat · Whenever possible cut away from the hand holding the fork.

2 Lift crackling off and cut it into strips along the scoring lines.

2 Work from alternate sides of first cut. Turn over. Carve underside flat against bone.

3 ease the butt off the bone. Slice across. Cut chump end at an angle from each side.

3 Then carve the pork in thin slices.

Poultry

Chicken Lay the bird on its side. Cut under the thigh, lifting the whole leg up with the fork.

2 Cut through the shoulder.

Use a short flexible carving knife and a table fork or a small carving fork. As with meat, make sure the plate on which the bird is served is almost flat and will not slip on the table-top. Again, avoid the clutter of vegetables or unnecessary garnish on the plate. If the bird is large, try to give diners both breast and dark meat. If the bird is small, it is easier to cut it apart than to carve it. Use a heavy, sharp knife or chef's shears to cut straight through small bones (for example, when splitting a chicken in two). If uncertain of the correct cuts, aim for the articulated joints, cutting through flesh, and the tendons between the bones. Trim off unsightly ends of skin or projecting bone; the aim is to present an attractive neat portion on the diner's plate.

Make sure the diners' plates are hot and all the vegetables, sauces and garnishes are close at hand. If there is more than one vegetable to be dished up from the carver's end get someone to help; they can add vegetables and sauces to the plate and pass them around, or carry the vegetables around so guests can help themselves.

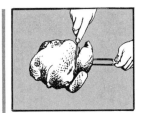

Turkey Cut between the body and the thigh all around, and cut through the connecting sinews.

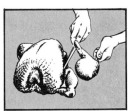

2 Pull the leg away. Carve the flesh of a large leg in small slices parallel to the bone.

3 Cut around to remove the shoulder, wing and a long strip of breast all in one piece.

Duck Put a long wooden spoon into the body cavity and use it to lift the bird. Hold, tilted, to drain juices.

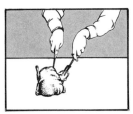

2 Lay the duck on its back and remove the thigh and leg by cutting with a knife and pulling with a fork.

3 If the leg is small, split it in two, cutting through the tendons at the joint.

4 Lift this piece with the fork, holding body down with the knife. Repeat for second leg and wing and breast.

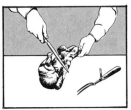

3 If it will not come away easily, tip the bird on its side to cut right around the leg joint.

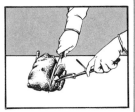

4 Cut through the shoulder joint parallel to the breast-bone (almost vertically) to remove shoulder and wing.

4 Cut through the shoulder joint, removing a small piece of breast with the shoulder and wing.

5 Finally, cut the central breast portion off the carcass.

It is much easier to carve a bird at the table if the wishbone is removed before cooking (see BONING, page 87) · Carve pheasant in the same way as chicken; smaller game birds are simply cut in half.

5 Slice the breast at the same angle, in long, thin slices.

5 Repeat for other leg and shoulder. Slice the breast in large, thin slices.

Seafood

Boning cooked sole *Run a fork down the backbone line to separate the two top fillets.*

2 Then run fork under each fillet, against backbone, to loosen fillets. Push them off sideways. Remove backbone.

Serving large whole fish is made much easier by using fish servers (a wide-bladed knife and broad fork designed both to cut and lift portions of cooked fish). A knife to split the flesh into fillets or portions, and a spoon and fork to lift them will suffice. Do not try to lift pieces of fish with a carving knife and fork; they break up and fall off the fork.

Make sure the serving platter is large enough in which to manoeuvre. Too narrow a dish is frustrating for the carver and will inevitably mean spilt juices on the table. Have a large second platter for the bones, head and other debris, allowing the carver to leave the rest of the fish looking attractive for second helpings.

Most shellfish are removed from the shell and cut up by the diners, initial preparation having been done in the kitchen beforehand. Provide large finger-bowls (about two-thirds full of warm water) and good-sized cloth napkins as they will almost certainly need to rinse their fingers.

Carving smoked salmon *Run the fingertips down the flesh to find bones. Extract them with pliers or tweezers.*

2 Cut almost horizontally to produce flat slices as large and thin as possible.

3 Place the two bottom fillets on a plate. Carefully lay the two top fillets on top of the bottom ones.

Shelling cooked crab *Twist off the legs. Crack them to extract their meat. Break off the claws.*

2 Turn the crab over. With the thumbs, force up the "apron" to remove it with the body flesh attached.

Specialist equipment is a great help. Snail tongs prevent burnt fingers; lobster picks make feasible the removal of leg meat; oyster dishes prevent oysters tipping and losing their juices. As diners' hands are likely to be messy (making passing things at the table difficult) it is wise to provide individual condiments, like tiny bowls of mayonnaise, in front of each place setting.

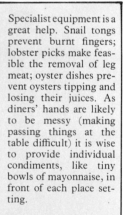

4 Once the fish is restored to its original shape, pour the pan juices over it.

3 Stomach complex remains near mouth. Discard. Use teaspoon handle to get out all the meat.

4 Crack the shell with a meat pounder to enlarge the opening evenly, making it like a lipped dish.

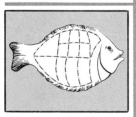

Carving turbot *Cut down middle, then into neat rectangles. Repeat other side.*

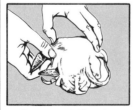

5 Remove and discard spongy gills (dead man's fingers) from each side.

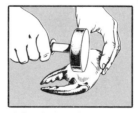

6 Break open the claws with a meat pounder and extract the meat.

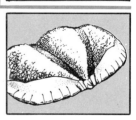

7 Mix brown flesh with mayonnaise, white with lemon juice. Arrange in shell.

Salads and vegetables

Salads
In salad-making, almost anything goes—the variety of combinations and dressings, colors and textures being almost limitless. There are a few basic guidelines:

1 Whether ingredients are to be used cooked or raw in a salad, use them as soon as possible. Cooked vegetables lose their flavor and texture just as quickly as raw salad ingredients.

2 Do not be too ambitious. The best salads are sometimes made of only two, or perhaps three, ingredients with a straightforward dressing. Cooked green beans, cooked lima beans and fried almonds are delicious dressed with a plain vinaigrette. However, the strong flavor of the fried almonds would be lost if the vinaigrette contained, say, garlic and savory—either of which would be excellent with the beans on their own. Unless the combinations are tried and true, keep them simple.

3 Think about texture. If serving two salads, make one of them crisp and crunchy (say, celery, apple and cabbage) if the other is soft (say, cooked zucchini and raw tomato). Color is also important, but the colors need not necessarily be contrasting. An all-green salad containing the subtle shades of green cucumber, endive, chicory, lettuce, spinach and watercress will look fresh and elegant. The brilliant Mediterranean colors of tomato, eggplant and zucchini on the other hand, seem to demand even *more* color—try serving them with black olives, hard-boiled egg and red peppers, in a garlic vinaigrette.

4 If serving more than one salad, make one light and fresh (served, say, with a lemon vinaigrette) one rich and creamy with a mustard mayonnaise).

Before scattering any chopped herbs over a salad, check first that the flavor will be good, by testing on a small amount. Chopped chives are good on potatoes, less so on salads with fruit.

5 Don't make salads more than a few hours in advance, and keep them covered in plastic wrap even if they must wait as little as an hour. Do not dress delicate leaves (like spinach, lettuce or sorrel) until the last minute, or they will go limp. Even cooked leeks or beans will discolor slightly if left soaking in a vinaigrette.

6 Do not *over*-refrigerate salads. They will stay crisper in a cooler atmosphere, but too much chilling masks flavor. If they are in a refrigerator more than two hours, remove them 20 minutes before serving.

Salades tièdes
Salads served at room temperature, or even mixed with warm or hot food, have recently become popular first courses. Arrange some crisp green salad lightly tossed in a minimum of dressing on individual plates. Just before serving add the fried or poached principal ingredient, hot or warm. Serve the salad, looking fresh and exquisitely arranged, promptly.

Vegetable terrines
Cook the contrasting brightly-colored vegetables fast until tender. Drain well and PURÉE them separately. Add butter to taste, and plenty of seasoning. Add cream. Bind with 3 eggs or 6 yolks per $1\frac{1}{4}$ cups of purée. Mix the lightly-beaten eggs into the hot purées. They should thicken sufficiently to be spooned in layers without merging. If purée is very liquid (like tomatoes) allow the rest to cook until set before pouring it on top. Bake AU BAIN MARIE in a moderate oven until just set. Allow to cool. Turn out and serve in slices with or without a sauce (TOMATO or HOLLANDAISE).

Vegetable terrines		
Purées	**Other ingredients**	**Method**
Celeriac purée seasoned with nutmeg Green bean purée seasoned with garlic	Small whole cooked carrots Strips of blanched green pepper	Spoon the purées in alternate layers in a buttered loaf tin, laying the carrots and pepper lengthwise on the mixture when half full
Cauliflower purée mixed with 20% cream Carrot purée seasoned with ground ginger	Whole small French beans	As above, substituting beans for carrots
Spinach purée seasoned with nutmeg Fish MOUSSELINE or QUENELLE mixture	Whole or sliced fried mushrooms, well drained	Butter a mold and line with blanched spinach leaves. Spoon in layers of purée and MOUSSELINE mixed with the mushrooms

Salades tièdes		
Basic salad	**Dressing**	**Main ingredient(s)**
Frilly endive, chicory, watercress	Vinaigrette with lemon and fennel	Scallops lightly poached in COURT BOUILLON and halved horizontally
Cooked snow peas, watercress	Vinaigrette with a few green peppercorns	Duck breasts grilled, then skinned and sliced thinly and fried almonds
Spinach or beet leaves	Sour cream and oil, seasoned with garlic	Bacon pieces crisply fried and small bread CROÛTONS
Small freshly cooked green beans, shredded lettuce	Yogurt and MAYONNAISE mixed in equal quantities	Chicken or duck livers fried in olive oil

Garnishing and presentation

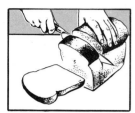

Croustade *Cut a square loaf into 2-in slices.*

2 Cut off the crusts to make a block. Cut a slice just in from each side to form an inner square.

3 Using the cuts as "walls," scrape out a cavity with a "floor." Deep fry and/or fill with savory mixtures.

Savory cornets *Line oiled metal mold with thin slices of ham, tongue or smoked salmon. Fill appropriately.*

2 Trim off edges. Chill well. Tap and shake to unmold, easing cornet out.

The diner looks before tasting and if the presentation of food is attractive, will be predisposed to like its taste. Conversely, clumsy or sloppy presentation so prejudices the diner against the dish that even excellent flavor may not appease. The diner remains unimpressed with both appearance *and* taste.

Therefore, always take great care with dishing-up and garnishing. This does not mean that elaborate or time-consuming efforts are necessary. Indeed, simply presented food, looking fresh and uncluttered, is perhaps the most pleasing of all to the eye. Take care to remove unsightly bone-ends from chicken pieces in a sauté, turn broiled food best side up, keep back a few good-looking mushrooms, carrots or baby onions to put on top of the stew, spoon shiny sauces over a dish only seconds before serving, and choose the plate to complement the food. Elaborate dishes look best on plain plates; simple one-color dishes look pretty on patterned plates. Small items look ridiculous and rather stingy on large plates; over-laden plates look clumsy and gross.

Much of presentation is instinctive: The cook knows that a mousse looks dull and could do with some color, or that the meringues will look good piled in a pyramid, that the fruit salad will be best in a clear glass bowl. The difficulty is knowing when to stop. A cake, needing some form of decoration, is piped with cream. It still looks dull, so it gets a dusting of nuts. Still not satisfied, the cook gradually adds

angelica, candied cherries, grated chocolate, and so on, until the cake is now as over-garnished as previously it was dreary-looking.

Garnishes should be appropriate. Chopped parsley on everything has become a catering cliché. Lemon slices or segments are good with food that needs the tang of lemon juice (fried fish, for example) but pointless with chicken mayonnaise. Sprigs of watercress look good with broiled foods, but large roasts do not need them. Paper frills are useful on a ham-bone, to give the carver a better grip, as well as looking festive; but frills around sponge cakes make the cake look "store-bought" and get in the way of the server, who has to remove them first anyway.

Radishes, painstakingly and perfectly cut into roses, can be exquisite, but unless they are done expertly they are best just topped and tailed and left to speak for themselves. A shiny, young, white-tipped radish is a good-looking thing and does not need to masquerade as a rose. Radishes are useful for adding color to a tray of cocktail canapés or a green salad.

Aspic is good in small amounts, either chopped and served with cold meat or fish, or used to give a thin shiny glaze to food. Use it *carefully*. Any decoration underneath it must be fine, delicate and elegant, not clumsy or garish; and the aspic layer itself must be thin (thick aspic looks like a coating of plastic).

Olives look good in Mediterranean dishes such as *salade niçoise*, or served in a pile, with

clumps of CRUDITÉS, to accompany drinks, but they are superfluous with pâtés and fish pastes.

Croûtons, either small, crisp dice, or carefully cut triangles, are pretty in salad, scattered on soup or used to top or to surround rich-sauced dishes.

The most important factor in presentation is care. Food that has been cooked and dished carefully and with thought "sells" itself. Any garnish (none is *really* necessary) should be edible, appropriate, and above all should play a secondary role. The leading role should still be left to the dish itself.

Celery frills *Cut celery into short chunks. Make parallel cuts 1 in deep into one end of each chunk.*

2 Flatten the cut section and cut across it carefully to split each "tooth" in half, producing two rows.

3 Repeat at the other end. Chill in iced water to encourage curling.

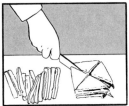

Stacking sandwiches Saw with a sharp knife, using the minimum of pressure to de-crust and quarter.

Melba toast Cut the crusts from fresh toast and split each slice in half horizontally.

2 Bake the halves in a hot oven until well browned, crisp and curled.

Deep-fried parsley Hold sprig by a length of string. Lower into hot fat. Fry until brilliant green and crisp.

2 Stand the quarters on their ends to display the fillings attractively.

Asparagus rolls Roll crustless thin brown bread slices gently to flatten them.

Cucumber twists Cut a cucumber into blocks. Split each block down its length from the center to the edge.

Cocktail eggs Split hard-boiled eggs in half across their equator. Keep nozzle close to egg to pipe evenly.

Catherine wheels Cut long, thin horizontal slices from the top of loaf. Spread with butter and filling.

2 Butter well, right to the edges. Lay well-drained asparagus on it. Add salt and pepper and roll up.

2 Slice the block into thin rings. Twist each slice so it will stand up steadily.

Cream rosettes Pipe generous swirls, not tiny ones. Odd numbers of rosettes look better.

2 Roll up. Keep rolls wrapped and chilled for 1 to 2 hours. Then slice into small rounds.

3 Once the roll overlaps sufficiently to stick, trim off excess bread.

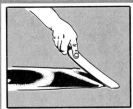

Chocolate caraque Spread melted chocolate on a smooth cool surface.

Making croûtons First trim the crusts from slices of bread. Dice or cut slices into decorative shapes (dice with diagonal cuts to make diamonds, cut plain dice in half to make triangles). Either sauté or deep-fry the pieces gently in clarified butter or good oil until light brown. Drain well. For extra flavor, first rub the bread with crushed garlic or cook in flavored butter. Alternatively, butter the bread first and bake the pieces in a cool oven, or toast slices of buttered bread lightly and then cut into dice.

Liquorice all-sorts Sandwich multi-layer rye with colored fillings. Cube.

4 Wrap. Chill for 1 to 2 hours. Cut into blocks. Stand on their ends on a plate.

2 Drag a heavy rigid knife with both hands across the chocolate to shave off curls.

Garnishing and presentation /2

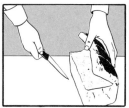

Bread box *(for displaying small sandwiches). Slice top almost through but leave it attached along one side.*

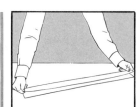

Ham frill *Fold a long strip of paper in half, lengthwise, but* do not *press the fold.*

2 Cut parallel cuts in from folded side. Open out paper and fold again the opposite way to make frills billow out.

Tomato tongues *Cut the pale core from quartered, peeled tomatoes.*

2 Slice off the bottom completely.

3 Roll the band up around the fingers.

4 Secure with a pin around the ham bone.

2 Press out the seeds and juice with the thumbs.

3 Cut out the soft bread from the center in one big block.

Radish roses *Trim off root from tip of radish. Make small cuts just under skin to create petals.*

2 Make these cuts all around the top. Then cut another row of petals further down.

2 Split the quarters into narrower "tongues".

4 Remove it from the underside and use it to make the small sandwiches.

3 If the radish is large, cut a third and even a fourth row of petals. Pry the petals open gently.

4 Soak in ice-cold water and the roses will open out.

4 Use these tongues to garnish the edge of dishes.

5 Place sandwiches in box, lid slightly open. Use several different breads for effect.

Muslin-wrapped lemon halves *Cut around flesh with a grapefruit knife.*

2 Wrap each lemon half in fine muslin. This prevents uneven squirting of juice.

3 Twist to tighten and tie securely with thread.

Turned (fluted) mushrooms *Use only firm, white mushrooms. Hold a short, sharp knife as shown.*

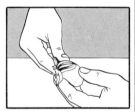

2 Use thumb as a pivot on mushroom top behind knife. Keep mushroom still, push blade forward and down.

Serving in rows *Neat lines of cocktail savories, petits fours or biscuits look attractive and professional.*

Terrines and galantines *look best served whole and should be sliced at the table.*

Serving two foods on one plate *Keep it simple; try to use contrasting colors.*

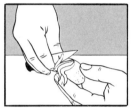

3 The blade should shave off even strips. Repeat all around the mushroom.

Formal radiating arrangement *Make neat. Use alternating garnish (here watercress and sliced aspic).*

Bread-lined pudding *Cut and arrange bread carefully, as, when turned out, this gives final design.*

Overlapping strips *(for bread-and-butter and similar puddings). Pattern enlivens a plain dish.*

4 Or, for easier carved mushrooms, cut a slice off top of mushroom. Then cut three "spokes" across flat top.

Pastry-lattice top *looks attractive and uses less pastry than a full-top crust, giving a lighter dish.*

Uneven numbers *are easier to arrange on a round plate and look better.*

Concentric circles *Use with particular effect with round slices (especially if they are stuffed).*

5 Follow cuts shown. Make eyes and scales. Remove layer to leave "fish" in relief.

Central height *gives a generous look—particularly to sautés. Do not pile too high.*

Soufflés *Those baked without a collar develop a "crown" (as one on left).*

Serving sliced bread *Arrange triangles to overlap alternately.*

Menu planning

Menu planning

1 Choose a menu that will not need much time and attention at the last moment. If there are last-minute green vegetables to be cooked, make sure the sauce, main dish and the first courses and desserts can all be prepared in advance.

2 Check that the oven is not going to be overcrowded. If a soufflé is to be the last course, the oven cannot be used for warming plates or keeping casseroles hot. If the main dish needs to go in the oven, make sure that little else does.

3 Aim for overall balance. If one course has cream and brandy in it, make sure the others are light, clean and comparatively plain. Avoid too much butter, cream, starch, eggs and alcohol —all of which leave the diner feeling over-fed.

4 Think about the color of the food: Do not follow a white soup with a pale-sauced main course and a cream-colored pudding. Make sure the vegetables and main course are of contrasting color so they will not look drab on the plate.

5 Check the textures of the proposed menu. Contrast in texture is preferable to, say, a totally soft and moist meal such as mousse followed by fish in a cream sauce, with a soufflé for dessert (or, conversely, an entirely crisp and crunchy meal).

6 Check the feasibility of serving the menu without fuss and panic. It must fit on the table or sideboard, leaving room for dinner plates and ample elbow room for the server.

It must be simple enough to dispense fairly quickly. Having boned the turkey before cooking, for example, can mean that carving is as easy as slicing bread, and as quick.

Mixing two or three vegetables—say, tiny carrots, peas and broadbeans—up in one dish and using a large serving spoon can drastically reduce serving time.

7 When inviting guests for a meal, do not hesitate to ask them whether or not they have any special dietary restrictions, food allergies, or plain hearty dislikes. This avoids any potential embarrassment and panic remedial action later.

Try to plan a menu around any such guests' needs. This avoids the extra work involved in cooking them separate dishes (which can make the guests feel uncomfortably conspicuous).

Gaining such early reassurance gives the cook absolute *carte blanche*— and the chance to plan an adventurous menu, rather than the usual "playing safe" and avoiding things like seafood and heavily spiced dishes.

Presentation

Tableware

The presentation of a meal has a distinct influence on its overall success. It is a matter of "packaging" or "framing." As with dish presentation and garnishing, tableware and its arrangement can enhance diners' enjoyment of their food and also set the tone of the occasion as either casual or elegant. The cook who has spent much time and money on a delicious dinner usually wishes to do it justice at the end.

Tableware

Bone china The finest and most delicate material used for tableware. Its name and its characteristic pink-white translucent appearance come from the calcined animal bone which it contains. The remainder of its composition is the same as ordinary porcelain.

Porcelain is a mixture of china stone and kaolin, the pure white china clay. Porcelain is also translucent, with a slight gray or bluish cast. Both bone china and porcelain, despite their delicate appearance, are surprisingly tough. Each piece is fired twice, the second time at intense heat, thus producing a vitreous surface resistant to chipping and crazing. Bone china and porcelain can be identified easily by the characteristic "ring" they make when flicked with the forefinger (like good crystal glasses).

Earthenware is made of more common clays and fired at lower temperatures. It is thus more porous and more likely to chip.

Stoneware is a hefty type of pottery with a silicious or flint content, impervious to liquids even before firing. Because so much earthenware and stoneware are made individually by craftsmen, pieces are not necessarily absolutely identical.

In buying and using any sort of tableware, be sure to check any label or underside markings for specific uses. Only those designated *flameproof* can withstand direct heat. They are more likely to be *ovenproof*, a useful feature in handsome pots that go straight from oven to table. *Shockproof* means that the item can survive extreme changes of temperature, *not* that it can be dropped on a hard floor with impunity.

If buying with a view to collecting more in future, be sure the design is likely to remain one of the manufacturer's lines for some time. Wash, or at least rinse, good china as soon as possible after use, as acid-containing foods may attack any decoration. Pieces with metallic or hand-painted decoration should be washed by hand to avoid the scratching that can occur in dishwashers. Never use abrasive powdered detergent on them. Remove tea and coffee stains with a damp cloth dipped in baking soda or borax. Ideally, plates should be stored upright in wooden, rubber (or plastic) aerated racks to minimize damage by abrasion. The most common cause of breakage is uneven application of heat, so always warm items gradually before use.

Basic tableware

Coffee pot

Dinner plate

Soup plate

Dessert plate

Side plate

Tea pot

Cup and saucer

Milk pitcher

Sugar bowl

Creamer

Serving dishes

Table settings

A formal occasion calls for table linen—a tablecloth, perhaps, and linen napkins—which must be crisp and fresh. Paper table-cloths and napkins are excellent for informal parties and buffets.

Napkins can be folded in many elaborately decorative ways, and yet a simple flat folded cloth napkin, which does not look as if it has been handled too much, looks most appealing.

Plans for table decoration must take into account the size of the table, the number of guests, and the space consumed by place settings, serving dishes, wine bottles and so on. Decoration should enhance, not overpower, the meal, and guests' comfort should be the first consideration.

Never have any decoration, including flowers and candles, so large or high that diners cannot easily see one another.

Etiquette dictates that the most senior woman present or the guest of honor should sit on the right hand of the host and be served first, followed by the other women, excluding the hostess. The most senior man is seated on the hostess's right and is the first man to be served. The host and hostess are served last. If the hostess sees to the food, and the host to the wine, each should be seated with easy access to their respective responsibilities.

Such rules are now interpreted much more freely in an era when the host might well be doing the cooking, when single people entertain at home, and the ladies no longer "withdraw."

A more informal attitude must be adopted, following more relaxed and pragmatic rules.

Informal entertaining, almost by definition, has no set rules. Serve food either family-style, at the table, or from a buffet.

When setting out a buffet, put napkins, cutlery and then plates at one end of the table, followed by the food. For a large party, have items ranked at both ends of the table with the food in the middle. Above all, at buffet parties where guests have to eat standing up, serve food that does not need cutting up.

Other, less basic, items of tableware:

1 Gras-maigre gravy boat *Ingenious design has one lip which pours fatty gravy straight from the top and another lip which brings fat-free gravy up from the bottom via a spout.*

2 Egg cup *Ceramic ones are better. (Wooden ones can be very difficult to clean.) Always rinse them before the egg has time to dry.*

3 Mustard pot and spoon *Lid keeps the mustard from drying out and has a notch to allow the spoon to be left in the pot.*

4 Toast rack *Only of use if the toast is going to be consumed almost immediately; otherwise the toast cools rapidly and dries out. If delay is inevitable, serve toast on a plate wrapped in a linen napkin.*

5 Corn on the cob holders and dish *The holders keep the fingers cleaner and the shaped dish enables the corn to be turned in melted butter more effectively.*

6 Artichoke plate *With a wide lip to hold discarded leaves which also incorporates a recess to hold dressing.*

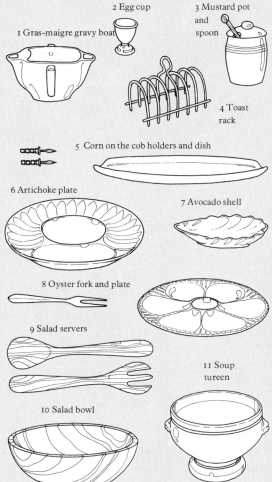

1 Gras-maigre gravy boat

2 Egg cup

3 Mustard pot and spoon

4 Toast rack

5 Corn on the cob holders and dish

6 Artichoke plate

7 Avocado shell

8 Oyster fork and plate

9 Salad servers

10 Salad bowl

11 Soup tureen

7 Avocado shell *Shaped to hold a half avocado in a stable position. This makes it easier for the diner and helps keep vinaigrette and other dressings in the avocado.*

8 Oyster fork and shell *Essential if oysters are to be served at all frequently. They keep the oysters steady and prevent any spilling of their juices. There are conventionally six indentations to hold one oyster each and a recess in the center to hold any sauce.*

9 Salad servers *Preferably made of wood (sycamore or maple) to match the salad bowl.*

10 Salad bowl *Wooden and as large as possible. Contrary to kitchen myth, salad bowls should be washed regularly, (see pages 28/9) not just wiped down with an oiled cloth. The oil in the wood can become rancid. Re-season after each wash.*

11 Soup tureen *Ceramic, heavy and thick to keep in heat. Must be very stable, even when brim-full.*

Cutlery

Sterling silver cutlery is made of an alloy that is, officially, 92.5% silver and 7.5% copper. In addition to its renowned beauty and value, it has pleasing weight and balance in the hand.

Silver plate is made of a base metal alloy composed of copper, zinc and nickel, and covered with a layer of silver. The quality of the plate varies with the amount of silver used. Both sterling and plate will not taint food in the way that a carbon steel knife might react with fruit, but they do tarnish readily when in contact with anything sulphurous, notably egg.

Do not leave silver or silver-plate cutlery out to drain or to remain un-washed overnight as salt or fatty food can corrode and pit the surface. Because silver is a soft metal it eventually acquires an attractive dulled patina from the countless tiny scratches it inevitably receives. Silver certified as "dishwasher-safe" by the manufacturer may be washed in a dishwasher, but this will abrade it more than is desirable unless the machine is loaded so that the items do not touch one another. Ideally, wash silver by hand after use and dry it with a clean, soft cloth. Polish it regularly to remove the tarnish that develops as it oxidizes. Use a soft toothbrush to clean awkward crevices.

Inhibit tarnishing by storing silver and silver-plate inside an airtight compartment lined with tarnish-preventing cloth, usually baize, or wrapping the pieces in flannel rolls.

Stainless steel is the most widely-used metal for cutlery because it is reasonably priced and so easy to look after. Although it is essentially non-corrosive, it may mark or pit in certain circumstances. For instance, proprietary dip-solutions for silver etch and dull stainless steel; wet fragments of steel wool left lying on it leave marks; and hard water leaves stains if not dried off immediately. Remove such hard-water stains by wiping with a dilute solution of vinegar.

Knife handles require special attention. Those not made of metal (wood, bone, ivory and porcelain) should not be left to soak. Wipe them with a hot, damp cloth and dry them immediately. Rub them (all bar the porcelain) with a little linseed oil occasionally to prevent any cracking or splitting.

Silver knife handles, especially on antique pieces, require particular care, because the steel blade may corrode near the joint due to the old soldering techniques. Modern methods have reduced this risk, but no piece should be immersed in water for long.

Most antique knives have a weighted handle filled with sealing wax or pitch; modern ones are weighted with cement. Hollow handles are obviously lighter in weight, but not necessarily inferior in quality of silver.

To set a place for a formal meal lay the cutlery in the order in which it will be used, working inwards to the plate—knife blades to the left.

Place glasses in a line above the right-hand cutlery, again with the order of use working inward to the plate.

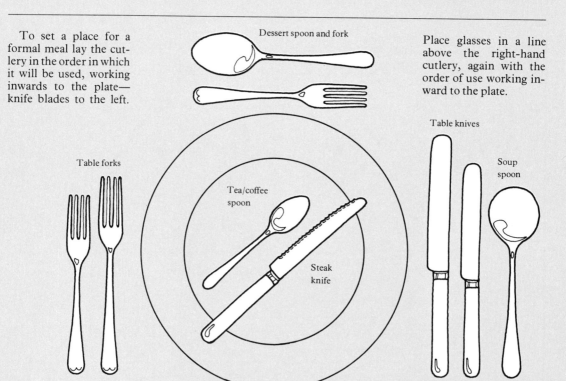

Dessert spoon and fork

Table knives

Table forks

Soup spoon

Tea/coffee spoon

Steak knife

Glass

Lead crystal is the most highly regarded glassware. Whereas ordinary glass or crystal is composed of silica (sand), alkali and lime alone, lead crystal contains at least 30% lead oxide, which gives it exceptional clarity, weight and great strength. The finest lead crystal gives slightly to the pressure of the hand, and the goblet will sway, barely perceptibly, on its stem. Although much lead crystal glassware is decoratively cut, many wine experts prefer a totally plain glass.

Wine glasses of any quality should be capacious in order to let the *bouquet* or scent gather appreciably. (Never fill a wine glass more than half full.) They should also be clear, rather than tinted, so that the true color of the wine may be seen— part of the total appreciation of the wine. Both tulip-shaped glasses and the rounder-bowled and wider-mouthed "Paris" goblet are suitable for general use with any wine.

White wine and cocktail glasses have longer stems to prevent the hand from coming into contact with the bowl and warming the contents. Conversely, the shorter stem for red wines and brandies deliberately encourages this warming.

Sherry, port and liqueur glasses are similar to the basic shapes of wine and claret glasses, but are proportionately smaller.

Brandy glasses should have comparatively big bowls to develop and contain the bouquet but they need not be the exaggerated balloon shape.

Cleaning glassware
Clean glassware separately from other dishes in warm water with a mild liquid detergent. Rinse well as any residue can be ruinous to the taste of the wine subsequently poured into it. Use a plastic basin and rubber guards on the taps to avoid chipping and breakage. Add a few drops of ammonia to the water to remove ingrained grime. Clean the crevices of cut glass with a soapy, soft-bristled toothbrush. Do not immerse (or use ammonia on) glass decorated with enamel or gilt. Instead use a soft cloth moistened with water and detergent. In both the washing and drying of glassware avoid undue pressure in handling and extreme changes of temperature which might cause breakage.

Dry glassware with clean, soft cloths used only for that purpose. Linen is preferable to cotton as it leaves no lint.

Wine glass

Tumbler

Carafes

Water jugs

Dry using two cloths, one in each hand, drying the inside and outside at the same time.

Remove mild stains, particularly any water stains, by polishing with jeweller's rouge, dishwasher "rinse-aid" or a fine metal polish applied with a soft rag.

Do not use a bottle brush on decanters as it may scratch or break them. If simple washing with warm soapy water fails, add a few drops of ammonia to the cleaning water or leave a solution of denture-cleaner soaking in it overnight.

Decanters have two specific functions. They aerate or oxidize a young wine, giving it a more mature taste; and they allow older wines to be served with the sediment already discarded. In both cases, a decanter with a wide, flat bottom (traditional ship's decanter shape) is ideal because the wider liquid surface area produced ensures greater aeration. As with glasses, decanters should not be filled to the top, so buy one which is big enough to hold at least a bottle of wine with space to spare. Reserve tall rectilinear decanters for spirits and sherries.

Glass stoppers must be completely dry before they are replaced in decanters, or else they may become stuck fast. Do *not* attempt to wrest a stuck stopper from the decanter—it will inevitably cause breakage. Apply a mixture of glycerin, alcohol and salt, or of denatured alcohol and cooking oil around the join and leave it to soak in for a day. Then use a very gentle, side-to-side movement to ease it out.

Spirit decanter

Wine decanter

Brandy glass

Liqueur glass

Cocktail glass

Sherry glass

Champagne glass

White wine glass

Scheduling

When cooking for several guests organization is essential, and ten minutes' careful planning can save a lot of time and temper. Everyday meals are frequently so simple that no exceptional organization is required, but few people can cope even with dinner for six without some pre-planning.

There are a few obvious but nonetheless vital rules:

1 Plan the menu (see Menu planning, page 198) and make a shopping list. Plan alternatives to each dish, in case it is impossible to obtain any vital ingredient. Include a list of the ingredients for these dishes as a postscript to the shopping list.

2 Order anything for which the retailer may need advance notice.

3 Do the shopping. Stick rigidly to the list. (Being inspired by the sight of some particularly good produce in the supermarket and deciding on avocado, mozzarella and tomato salad instead of the fish pâté planned for the first course can unbalance the entire menu.)

4 Make a list of the things that can be done in advance, and do them, ticking them off the list as they are done. Carry this to extremes. The more that is out of the way before the guests arrive, the better. If the table is laid; fresh towels are in the bathroom; drinks and ice are on the sideboard; the parsley is chopped and the bread ready in the toaster, last-minute work will be very fast.

5 Ideally, every last item used in the cooking should be washed up and put way so there is a minimum of clutter in the kitchen—nothing but clear surfaces for dishing up and for putting down the dirty dishes as they come out of the dining room.

6 Do not disappear into the kitchen the minute friends arrive. More than anything, they have come to be sociable and enjoy themselves, not to judge anyone's kitchen accomplishments. If their host or hostess is relaxed and happy, not dashing about flapping oven cloths, they are more likely to enjoy the meal.

7 With really large festivities the scheduling is even more important. Shopping, preparation and planning start days, if not weeks, in advance, and a time plan for the hours leading up to Christmas day, for instance, is essential. A time plan that has everything, followed to the letter, prevents constant fretting that something might have been forgotten.

Drinks

Drinking and dining

Drink may be taken before the meal to stimulate the appetite, with the meal to complement the food, and after the meal to aid digestion.

Alcoholic drinks are made by two principal methods—by distillation or fermentation.

Distillation produces high-alcohol spirits such as gin, vodka or whisky, generally served as pre-dinner drinks, or dry brandies, such as cognac, slivovitz or kirsch, which are served after dinner. They are usually served in small quantities, diluted with water, soda or mineral waters before meals, and/or served neat after meals.

Fermentation produces low-alcohol drinks like wines, beers and ciders, which are served in generous measures as aperitifs or for consumption during meals.

In addition there are the "fortified" wines, such as sherry, Madeira, port and vermouth (which are grape-wines to which alcoholic spirit is added during manufacture) and liqueurs which are sweet fruit syrups, also fortified with brandy. Fortified wines are usually served as pre-dinner drinks, although port, especially in Britain, is traditionally served after the meal. Liqueurs are served undiluted as after-dinner drinks, and they are used as the alcoholic base for cocktails.

Before the meal

The pre-dinner drink may be plain or mixed, short or tall, sweet or dry or even interestingly bitter. Its purpose is threefold: To whet the diners' appetites; to keep them occupied until dinner; and to put them in a convivial mood.

Sometimes wine is taken on its own before the meal. A cold, dry white wine is good for this purpose in summer, and even light fruity red, especially served chilled, makes an acceptable aperitif. Any substantial red, however, is better served with food. Kir (chilled dry white wine with a few drops of CRÈME DE CASSIS to turn it faint pink), Buck's fizz (chilled champagne mixed with fresh orange juice) and spritzer (wine topped up with carbonated water) are all light summer aperitifs without a high alcoholic content which can dull the palate. Sparkling drinks do have a livening effect, giving a quick lift, and an aperitif like *kir royale* (made with sparkling white wine) combines beauty, lightness, vivacity and fast action.

Before the meal is a good time to drink champagne. It is incomparably stimulating and never fails to confer a sense of occasion. When there are large numbers to be served, a punch can provide a festive feeling more economically. Punches can be as individual as cocktails, and are the ideal way to get mileage and pleasure out of the inexpensive wines. Punches are generally a blend of wine and spirit with fruit juice and/or carbonated water, often sweetened with sugar or cordial. A bowl of punch

generally contains a lot of ice cubes, and, perhaps, some mint leaves or lemon slices.

An aperitif is by definition an alcoholic appetizer—hence any drink taken before the meal. In addition to that general meaning it is used more specifically for the family of fortified wines, including all the sherries and the range of vermouths and such patent aperitifs as Campari and Dubonnet.

Sherries are wines fortified with brandy. Depending on the base wine, they run from very sweet to very dry. Sherry is usually served straight; the sweeter ones at room temperature or just below; and the drier ones moderately chilled (increasingly, sherry is even served with ice).

Sherries fall into three principal categories: dry, pale-colored *fino* (including the almost salty *manzanilla*); the medium *amontillado*; and the richly-colored, sweet, *oloroso* (including *amoroso*, cream, golden and brown). All are best served on their own and are too substantial to accompany food except, perhaps, soup or nuts.

Vermouths are fortified with pure alcohol. The array of patent potions, such as *Cinzano, Martini, Dubonnet, Campari, Punt è Mes, Pernod* and so on, depend for their distinctive flavors on the addition of herbs and extracts to the wine during manufacture. (Originally these ingredients were intended to preserve the wine, or to mask any unpleasant taste, but today house recipes are closely guarded secrets.) The name "vermouth" comes from the German word for wormwood, one of the most widely-used flavoring agents. These drinks are best served cold, with ice, or as the base for long cocktails.

Cocktails afford great freedom of expression. Whereas wine with dinner and, perhaps, some brandy to follow are almost universally served, mixed drinks are much more likely to reflect geographical or seasonal differences—like gin and tonic inseparable from the English summer, or a Marguerita as being synonymous with the American Southwest.

Each of the principal spirits is used as the base for cocktails: Gin for martinis; whisky for Manhattans; rum for the daiquiris; vodka for Bloody Marys; and countless others, both known and waiting to be invented.

The well-stocked bar needs a generous quota of the above-mentioned spirits, plus fruit juices and mixers (soda water, tonic water, bitter lemon, ginger ale) and bitters. For garnishes, provide oranges, lemons, limes, olives, tiny onions and maraschino cherries.

Cocktails call for a

steady supply of ice and the means, when required, to crush it. Apart from all this, the basic equipment for domestic bartending is a glass pitcher and long bar spoon, a cocktail shaker and strainer, an ice bucket and tongs, a sharp knife and cutting board, a drinks measure, a fruit squeezer, a lemon peeler, and a reliable corkscrew and bottle-opener. The glasses used vary with the drinks, but a stem or a heavy base serves to keep hand heat away from the cool contents.

Whatever the choice of before-the-meal drinks, do not let too much drinking go on for too long, dulling the palate.

With the meal

The overall success of a meal will be determined to a great extent by the drinks chosen to accompany it.

Wine is the most important accompaniment to food, and a spectacular range is available. Wine, however, is not obligatory. Beer suits those dishes cooked with it, such as CARBONNADE, as it does numerous informal foods, like PIZZA or HAMBURGERS. Beer or lager is often preferred to accompany spicy dishes, such as CURRY, which can overpower wine.

Another pleasing and economical drink to go with some meals is dry cider. The French Normandy cider and the best quality English ciders are excellent with savory CRÊPES, or dishes such as ham cooked in cider, or some oily fish (the strong taste of which can affect the flavor of wines).

For those who are happiest with no alcohol at all, as well as those who hope to ameliorate its effects, there is a choice of increasingly popular bottled waters in numerous still and sparkling varieties. These should be served with ice and a twist of lemon.

The taste of wine, assessed at its most basic, is a balance between sweet and sour—just as grapes themselves contain sugar and acid. Beyond the simple classifications of sweet or dry, wines may be considered light or heavy, young or mature, with increasingly subtle distinctions as to color and nose or bouquet (smell).

While the rules about which wine to serve with what dish are infinitely flexible, some conventions have established themselves over the years, not without reason. Each wine has characteristics which make it more, or sometimess less, appropriate with certain foods (see overleaf).

The conventions of the lighter, dry white wine with delicate white meats and seafood and stronger red wines with hearty red meats and full-flavored cheese are well justified. Richer food calls for a heavier, full-bodied wine that will not be swamped by the flavor of the dish.

If a dish has been cooked with wine, that wine or a more refined relative from the same family is appropriate with it. Generally, when more than one wine is being served: Red should follow white; old should follow young; sweet follows dry. In short, strong or "big" should follow delicate or "little."

Serving wine

The custom of serving red wine at "room temperature" was established before the age of central heating. Room temperature should be interpreted as around 62°F. A young Beaujolais could even be slightly chilled. If the wine is too cold, never heat it directly, but pour it into a warmed decanter. It will also warm by standing in the glass. If wine is too warm, it becomes flabby (diminished in taste and aroma). A young red wine needs more time to breathe (to become aerated to develop its full flavor) than an older one. If possible, open it an hour or more before use.

White wine should be chilled. Quite how chilled is a matter of taste (but over-chilling subdues the flavor drastically). Bottles may be refrigerated for two hours or set for half an hour in a tub of ice and water. Champagne and sparkling wine should be served colder than other white table wines.

When opening wine, take care not to shake up the sediment. Have a clean napkin on hand to wipe the mouth of the bottle and clear it of any bits of cork or capsule. Try not to pierce the cork all the way through with the corkscrew, as bits of cork may fall into the wine. If the cork itself is bad, the wine may be undrinkably musty.

The trick to opening champagne or sparkling wine is to twist the bottle rather than the cork. Use a napkin to hold the cork and do not let it go (flying corks can cause damage and injury). Point the neck out of harm's way so any spurting champagne will not douse the company. Have the glasses lined up ready for pouring. Apart from reasons of taste, champagne must be well chilled to prevent too explosive an opening. If a cork sticks, hold the neck of the bottle under hot running water for a minute or so.

Drinking and dining /2

Buying wine

When studying a wine merchant's list, or surveying the stock on display, most buyers have a notion of what they are prepared to spend, and make their selections first according to cost, modified by personal preference and with regard to the food the wine will accompany. Since the quality of wines can vary profoundly within a particular price range, it pays to sample as many as possible over a period of time—and to take notice of what friends serve, in the hope of making useful discoveries.

There is everything to be said for buying known and trusted wine by the case whenever possible. Apart from being more economical, it means the wine is on hand well before it is needed so that it may have time to be at its best when served. Try to get to know a local shipper or merchant to ensure consistent quality of supply.

Examine the label. It gives the name of the wine, where it was bottled, the vintage, quality or style, and the name of the shipper. Regulations governing labeling vary; usually, the more information, the better the wine. There are certain terms that may be used only to describe specific wines: "Champagne" refers exclusively to the product of the Champagne area of northern France; "port" to the product of the *Alto Douro* region of northern Portugal. AC or AOC (*Appellation d'Origine Controlée*) is a symbol of French quality control, ensuring that a wine labeled with a place name actually comes from there and meets certain standards.

The own-brand wines sold by supermarkets and shops are blends which generally provide a drinkable *vin ordinaire*, or table wine, at an economic price.

Be sure before buying these (or any wines) that they have not been stored upright (letting the corks dry out, which then lets air in) or exposed to direct sunlight in shop windows (causing deterioration).

Suggested wine and food combinations	
Hors d'oeuvres, salads, cold meats	Strong white wine: *Traminer*, the medium-sweet German wines, white *Burgundy* or Rosé: *Cabernet, Rosé d'Anjou*
Soups	*Sherry* or a light *Madeira* with *consommé* or Any dry white wine
Shellfish (served in rich sauce or garnishes)	Dry white: *Graves, Chablis*, white *Burgundy* or *Champagne*, or Rhine wine or *Moselle*. Mellow white, like *Sauternes*, for sweeter sauces
Shellfish (plain or broiled)	Dry, light white: *Chablis* (traditional with oysters), *Riesling*, especially *Moselles*, young white *Burgundy Aligoté*
Fish (plain)	Light dry white as above
Fish (with cream or wine-based sauces)	Fairly fruity, robust white: *Traminer*, white *Bordeaux*, *Valpolicella, Riesling, Hermitage blanc*
Broiled and roasted dark meats	Medium, not-too-heavy reds: Any good *Bordeaux*, or *Burgundy, Californian Cabernet Sauvignon*
Casseroles and stews (dark meats)	Heavy, full-bodied reds: *Burgundy, Rhône, Beaujolais, Chianti*
Poultry (plain cooked or roasted)	Heavy white: White *Burgundy, Alsation* or *Hungarian Riesling, Traminer*
Poultry (with rich garnish or stuffing)	Light, dry red: *Beaujolais, Barolo, Bardolino* (particularly good with fatty birds like duck and goose)
White meat	Full-bodied dry or medium-dry white wine: white *Rioja, Graves*, white *Burgundy* or Light-bodied red: *Entre-Deux-Mers, Côtes du Rhône*, or *Rosé* (for pork and ham): *Côtes de Provence, Tavel*
Game birds	Full-bodied red: *Chianti*, red *Burgundy, Bordeaux, Rhône*
Game	Strong, robust red: Mature red *Rhône, Rioja, Burgundy*
Soft cheese, like Brie	Fine, light red: *Bordeaux*
Hard and medium cheese, like Cheddar	Light, fruity red: *Beaujolais*, or Strong white: *Soave, Alsace, Loire*
Veined cheese, like Stilton	Medium light white: *Sauternes*, white *Burgundy*, or Light red: *Bardolino, Cabernet Sauvignon*
Desserts	Sweet white: *Sauternes, Barsac, Muscat*, sweet German dessert wines or *Champagne* or other sparkling wine

Storage

Any closet or spare space which is dark, remains at a constant (preferably cool—50° to 54°F) temperature, and is comparatively free of vibration may be fitted with wine racks. Bottles are stored horizontally so that the corks are kept moist. If they are allowed to dry out, air can enter the bottle and the wine spoils. Any wine which is to be kept more than about a fortnight should be stored in a rack.

Finer wines bought young for laying down and maturing should be disturbed as little as possible. When they are ready for drinking, they should be stood upright at least a week before opening to allow the sediment to settle, and then decanted.

After the meal

Many people prefer to stay with a good sweet wine, particularly a rich *Sauternes*, like *Château d'Yquem*, a fine fragrant *Muscat*, like *Beaumes-de-Venise* or *Sétubal*, or a champagne. These provide the sweet rich rounding off required after a meal, without the high alcohol content of a brandy or a liqueur.

Brandy is a distillation of fermented fresh grapes. The designations *Cognac* and *Armagnac* are strictly reserved for the brandies produced in those regions. Both are blends of the different vines in their respective districts and are matured in wooden casks.

Brandies are made in many other areas, particularly in the border region where France, Switzerland and Germany join. They are generally made from fruits other than the grape. Perhaps the best known is *Kirsch*, which is made from cherries.

Lesser known, but increasingly popular, brandies include *poire* (pear), *mirabelle* (plum), *framboise* (raspberry) and *fraise de bois* (wild strawberry).

Brandy glasses should be big enough to swirl the brandy in, leaving ample room for the scent to develop. Brandy need not be artificially warmed. Cupping the bowl of the glass with the hands raises the temperature sufficiently.

Some liqueurs and their key ingredients	
Amaretto	Almonds
Anis	Aniseed
Benedictine	Herbs, brandy, citrus fruit peel
Chartreuse	Balm, hyssop, angelica, cinnamon, mace, saffron
Calvados	Apples
Cointreau	Oranges
Crème de cacao	Cocoa and vanilla beans
Crème de cassis	Black currants
Crème de menthe	Mint
Curaçao	Orange peel
Drambuie	Herbs, honey, Scotch whisky
Grand Marnier	Oranges and mature brandy
Maraschino	Maraschino cherries
Tia Maria	Rum, coffee and Jamaican spices
Van der Hum	Tangerines, rum and Cape brandy

Port is a fortified wine which comes only from the *Alto Douro* district of northern Portugal. Its production is limited and its shipment carefully controlled. Its fortification takes place during the last stage of fermentation, when it is pumped into vats containing grape brandy. This halts fermentation, ensuring the port remains sweet. Port takes time to mature and lose the harsh edge of the brandy. Most is matured in casks; some in bottles.

The cask-aged ports are known variously as: Ruby, the youngest and cheapest port with color to match its name; tawny, a golden-colored port aged eight to 40 years; white, a pale port made from white grapes; vintage character, superior-quality aged ruby; and late-bottled, which is of almost vintage quality.

The bottle-aged ports are called crusted (port bottled after three or four years in the cask forms a deposit of crust in the bottle); and vintage, declared only during exceptional years, and not blended. Vintage port is bottled after two or three years in the cask, and drunk when between 14 and 30 years of age, depending on the vintage.

Decanting port

Port matured in casks leaves its crust (sediment) in the cask, and so may be poured straight from the bottle to the glass.

Bottle-aged port must be decanted in order to get rid of the deposit, and to refresh the port by contact with the air.

Decanting requires a delicate touch. Have ready a piece of clean muslin, a lighted candle and a funnel, preferably with a hooked end so that the port runs gently down the side of the decanter and not straight into the center, which could cause frothing. Take the bottle carefully from the rack, retaining the horizontal position so as to disturb it as little as possible, and lay it on the table with the neck over the edge. The decanter rests just beneath, with the funnel inside covered with muslin. Gently remove the wax seal from the bottle neck, then the cork. As the bottle empties, raise the end of it slightly to ensure that all the port is decanted without disturbing the crust. Finally, hold the decanted port to the candlelight, to check that it is free of sediment.

Liqueurs are short and sweet. Their colors and flavors come from fruits, herbs, seeds and kernels. Many trace their origins through the early church, from the days when monks concocted them to make medicines palatable. They may be of a single flavor, such as *crème de menthe*, or a combination such as *Drambuie* (herbs, honey and Scotch whisky). They are usually served straight, and in tiny quantities, at room temperature or just below. Many combine well with coffee. (Simply pour black coffee over a measure of liqueur, add some sugar to taste and top with cream.)

Coffees and teas

Coffee and tea

Coffee and tea are an indispensable part of life for most people. The stimulants they contain work morning and night to galvanize the just-risen or revitalize the sated diner. Whatever the characteristics of the different brews, the quality of the water used distinctly affects their taste. Fresh water, not previously boiled, is essential.

Coffee

A cup of coffee may be anything from a benign milky bowl of *café au lait* to a startlingly intense *espresso*. The differences in coffee depend on where it is grown, how it is roasted, how it is brewed and how it is served.

Coffee shops stock a selection of beans from different countries, such as pure Colombian or Jamaican Blue Mountain, as well as their own special blends for morning or after dinner. The beans are normally sold already roasted, and, thus, are rarely seen in their raw green state; their varying shades of brown indicate how strongly roasted they are.

Those with no coffee grinder at home have the beans ground in the shop, but grinding does release the flavor and ground coffee has a far shorter life than beans. Fresh grinding makes a great deal of difference to the taste, so it is inadvisable to have more ground than will be used immediately. Store any leftover ground coffee or beans in an airtight container in the refrigerator. Meanwhile, a home grinder is essential for those who love good coffee.

The degree of grind is mostly determined by the method chosen for brewing. Percolators require a regular, gritty grind. Regular to fine grind is required for steeped, drip or filter method coffee. True Italian *espresso* can only be made with the steam-pressure *espresso* machine and an especially dark, powdery grind. No conventional grind is fine enough to make Turkish coffee; the beans must actually be pulverized (this can be done in an electric blender). Turkish coffee-pots are narrow at the top so as to contain the brew's characteristic froth, although it can be made in an ordinary pan. For the standard brewing methods, allow two tablespoons of ground coffee per cup ane never re-use the grounds. Drip or filter coffee may have cooled too much while brewing and should be gently heated (but not boiled) before serving.

Tea

The many kinds of tea available all derive from the same plant. Growing conditions, age and blending of leaves, and, in some cases, additional ingredients account for the different types. The two broad categories for tea are: Black, which has been fermented during the curing process; and green, which is not fermented. "Oolong" is semi-fermented.

Black teas—including Assam, Ceylon, Darjeeling, English and Irish Breakfast, Orange Pekoe, bergamot-flavored Earl Grey and smoky Lapsang Souchong—are preferred in the West, as are the jasmine, orange or lemon-flavored oolongs.

In Britain it is usual to add milk (with or without sugar) to black tea, particularly that designated Indian (Assam blends) as opposed to the more fragrant China (Earl Grey, Lapsang Souchong), which some feel must be served on its own. Among some tea-drinkers feeling runs high as to when the milk should be added. There are those who insist it should be poured in the cup first, which causes it to blend better with the tea and makes stirring unnecessary. Others like adding it afterwards, when it is easier to control the amount. Whatever the pros and cons may be, the two techniques produce quite different tastes: The former cooks the milk slightly, giving a caramelized flavor; the latter does not, leaving a much stronger, truer tea taste. Many Americans prefer tea with a squeeze of lemon.

Except in Scotland, cream is considered too rich to add to tea. Green tea is taken absolutely plain.

Rituals aside, there are a few basic rules for making good tea. Start with a kettle of freshly-drawn cold water. Warm the teapot by rinsing it with hot water so that when the boiling tea water is added, it will stay hot. Then dry the pot and put in the tea. Allow a teaspoon of tea, or one teabag, per person and "one for the pot". Above all, be sure the water is still boiling when it is poured into the teapot. Let the brew infuse for a good four minutes; the subtler teas need longer than the strong ones to develop. Stir before serving to distribute the essential oil evenly.

Herbal teas, or tisanes, are becoming increasingly popular as people become more health-conscious. These natural sedatives—good for the digestion and the nervous system—may be infused from specific single plants or combinations. Herbal teas sometimes use the flower and root as well as the leaves. The mild soporifics, such as camomile, are recommended as nightcaps; peppermint aids the digestive system. Both make excellent after-dinner alternatives to coffee, especially for those who are caffeine-sensitive. Elderflower makes a fragrant tisane which may be enjoyed hot or cold and also makes a good mixer (once cooled) for vodka or gin.

Herbal teas are brewed in the same way as ordinary teas, although some require longer to infuse. They are generally served plain, or with lemon and/or honey.

Weights and measures

Careful weighing and measuring is not all that important when making soups, stews and sauces; and the cook may jump from measuring in grams to measuring in ounces, cups or liters, with impunity.

However, if following a recipe for the first time and *certainly* when making cakes, soufflés and desserts, it is quite inadvisable to jump from one system of measurements to another.

Cookery writers, when testing a recipe and faced with an awkward equivalent (like 28.35 grams for an ounce) will round down (1oz = 25g) or up (1oz = 30g), depending on the ingredient. This means that the metric, imperial and American proportions will each work individually. But using, say, imperial quantities for half the cake and metric quantities for the other half might be disastrous.

Weights

Metric	Imperial
8g	$\frac{1}{4}$oz
15	$\frac{1}{2}$
20	$\frac{3}{4}$
25	1
30	1
45	$1\frac{1}{2}$
50	2
55	2
75	$2\frac{1}{2}$
85	3
100	$3\frac{1}{2}$
115	4
125	$4\frac{1}{2}$
140	5
150	$5\frac{1}{2}$
170	6
175	$6\frac{1}{2}$
200	7
210	$7\frac{1}{2}$
225	8
250	$8\frac{1}{2}$
255	9
275	$9\frac{1}{2}$
285	10
300	$10\frac{1}{2}$
325	11
350	12
375	13
400	14
425	15
450	16 (1lb)
550	$1\frac{1}{4}$lb
675	$1\frac{1}{2}$lb
700	$1\frac{5}{8}$lb
800	$1\frac{3}{4}$lb
900	2lb
1 kilo	$2\frac{1}{4}$lb
1.35k	3lb
1.5k	$3\frac{1}{2}$lb
1.8k	4lb
2k	$4\frac{1}{2}$lb
2.3k	5lb
2.5k	$5\frac{1}{2}$lb
2.7k	6lb
3k	$6\frac{1}{2}$lb
3.2k	7lb
3.5k	8lb
4k	9lb
4.5k	10lb
5k	11lb

Approximate weight and volume equivalents

Commodity	Metric	Imperial	American
Butter (also margarine and lard)	115g	4oz	$\frac{1}{2}$C
	225g	8oz	1C
	450g	1 lb	2C
Breadcrumbs (dry)	90g	$3\frac{1}{4}$oz	1C
	175g	$6\frac{1}{2}$oz	2C
Cheese (hard fresh, like Cheddar, grated coarsely; Parmesan, grated)	55g	2oz	1C
	100g	$3\frac{1}{2}$oz	1C
Dried fruit (like raisins and apricots)	110g	4oz	$\frac{1}{2}$C
	225g	8oz	1C
	450g	1 lb	2C
Flours (finely ground, including cornstarch, wholewheat, and rice flour)	115g	4oz	1C
	170g	6oz	$1\frac{1}{2}$C
	225g	8oz	2C
Coarse meals (including semolina, coarse oatmeal, coarse cornmeal)	115g	4oz	$\frac{3}{4}$C
	140g	5oz	1C
	225g	8oz	$1\frac{1}{2}$C
Nuts (almonds, hazel-nuts, walnuts)	75g	$2\frac{1}{2}$oz	$\frac{1}{2}$C
	150g	$5\frac{1}{2}$oz	1C
Ground nuts	50g	2oz	$\frac{1}{2}$C
	115g	4oz	1C
	225g	8oz	2C
Rice (uncooked)	55g	2oz	$\frac{1}{4}$C
	115g	4oz	$\frac{1}{2}$C
	225g	8oz	1C
Sugars (granulated and superfine)	115g	4oz	$\frac{1}{2}$C
	170g	6oz	$\frac{3}{4}$C
	225g	8oz	1C
	350g	12oz	$1\frac{1}{2}$C
Brown	115g	4oz	$\frac{2}{3}$C
	170g	6oz	1C
	225g	8oz	$1\frac{1}{3}$C
	350g	12oz	2C
Confectioner's	140g	5oz	1C
	170g	6oz	$1\frac{1}{4}$C
	225g	8oz	$1\frac{1}{2}$C
Molasses or corn syrup	85g	3oz	$\frac{1}{4}$C
	170g	6oz	$1\frac{1}{4}$C
	350g	12oz	1C
Fish, meat, vegetables (and other ingredients, when accuracy is not vital)	250g	$\frac{1}{2}$lb	$\frac{1}{2}$lb
	$\frac{1}{2}$ kilo	1lb	1lb
	1 kilo	2lb	2lb
	2 kilo	4lb	4lb
	$3\frac{1}{2}$ kilo	8lb	8lb
	$4\frac{1}{2}$ kilo	10lb	10lb
	5 kilo	11lb	11lb

Note: Similarly, the equivalents given below are not strictly accurate, but are rounded-up or down for convenience.)

In American recipe books, when dry measures are given in spoonfuls, level spoonfuls are menat. British recipes call for "heaped" or "rounded" spoonfuls unless otherwise stated. This means, effectively, that for dry measures 2 US tablespoons are equal to one British tablespoonful.

Volume

Metric	Imperial		American
5ml	—	1 tsp	1 tsp
10ml	—	2 tsp	2 tsp
20ml	—	1 tbsp	$1\frac{1}{2}$ tbsp
30ml	1 fl oz	$1\frac{1}{2}$ tbsp	2tbsp
50ml	2 fl oz	3 tbsp	$\frac{1}{4}$ Cup
60ml	$2\frac{1}{2}$ fl oz ($\frac{1}{2}$ gill)	$3\frac{1}{2}$ tbsp	$\frac{1}{4}$C + 2 tsp
75ml	3 fl oz	4 tbsp	$\frac{1}{3}$C (6 tbsp)
100ml	4 fl oz	$\frac{1}{5}$ pint	$\frac{1}{2}$C ($\frac{1}{4}$ pint)
150ml	5 fl oz (1 gill)	$\frac{1}{4}$ pint	$\frac{2}{3}$C
175ml	6 fl oz	—	$\frac{3}{4}$C
200ml	7 fl oz	—	—
250ml	8 fl oz	$\frac{1}{3}$ pint	1C ($\frac{1}{2}$ pint)
300ml	10 fl oz (2 gills)	$\frac{1}{2}$ pint	$1\frac{1}{4}$C
350ml	12 fl oz	—	$1\frac{1}{2}$C
400ml	14 fl oz	$\frac{2}{3}$ pint	$1\frac{3}{4}$C
450ml	15 fl oz	$\frac{3}{4}$ pint	—
500ml	16 fl oz	—	2C (1 pint)
550ml	18 fl oz	—	$2\frac{1}{4}$C
575ml	20 fl oz	1 pint	$2\frac{1}{2}$C
600ml	21 fl oz	—	$2\frac{3}{4}$C
700ml	25 fl oz	$1\frac{1}{4}$ pint	3C
750ml	27 fl oz	—	$3\frac{1}{2}$C
800ml	28 fl oz	—	$3\frac{1}{3}$C
850ml	30 fl oz	$1\frac{1}{2}$ pints	$3\frac{3}{4}$C
900ml	32 fl oz	$1\frac{3}{5}$ pints	4C
1 litre	35 fl oz	$1\frac{3}{4}$ pints	$4\frac{1}{2}$C
1.1 liter	40 fl oz	2 pints	5C
1.3 liter	48 fl oz	—	6C
1.5 liter	50 fl oz	$2\frac{1}{2}$ pints	$6\frac{1}{4}$C
1.66 liter	56 fl oz	$2\frac{3}{4}$ pints	7C
1.75 liter	60 fl oz	3 pints	$7\frac{1}{2}$C
1.8 liter	64 fl oz	$3\frac{1}{4}$ pints	8C
2 liter	72 fl oz	$3\frac{1}{2}$ pints	9C
2.1 liter	76 fl oz	$3\frac{2}{5}$ pints	$9\frac{1}{2}$C
2.2 liter	80 fl oz	$3\frac{3}{4}$ pints	10C
2.25 liter	84 fl oz	2 quarts	$10\frac{1}{2}$C

Length

Metric (cms)	Imperial (ins)
0.3	$\frac{1}{8}$
0.6	$\frac{1}{4}$
1	$\frac{1}{2}$
2	$\frac{3}{4}$
2.5	1
5	2
15	6
30	12 (1ft)
46	18
92	36 (1yd)
100 (1m)	39

Temperature

°C	°F	Gas mark
3	37	
10	50	
16	60	
21	70	
24	75	
27	80	
29	85	
38	100	
41	105	
43	110	
46	115	
49	120	
54	130	
57	135	
60	140	
66	150	
71	160	
77	170	
82	180	
88	190	
93	200	
96	205	
100	212	
107	225	$\frac{1}{4}$ (vc)
110	228	
115	238	
120	250	$\frac{1}{2}$
130	275	1
140	285	
150	300	2 (c)
160	325	3 (w)
180	350	4
190	375	5 (m)
205	400	6 (fh)
220	425	7
230	450	8 (h)
250	475	9 (vh)
260	500	

Oven terminology

vc = very cool	
c = cool	
w = warm	
m = moderate	
fh = fairly hot	
h = hot	
vh = very hot	

Glossary

al dente Italian term used to describe food, such as pasta, which has been cooked until it is just firm to the bite.
apéritif alcoholic appetizer particularly a fortified wine.
arrowroot very fine starch or flour made from the root of a tropical plant; used to thicken soups and sauces.
aspic clear savory jelly made from clarified meat stock.

bain marie pan or dish in which water is kept hot; to hold a container of a delicate mixture such as a sauce or custard that requires gentle indirect heat to cook.
bake blind to bake a pastry shell without a filling; usually weighted down to prevent the shell rising during baking.
ballotine meat which has been boned, stuffed and rolled before cooking; normally served hot.
bard to tie bacon or pork fat over part or all of a piece of meat, poultry or game before roasting. This keeps the flesh from drying out and makes basting unnecessary.
baste to spoon or brush liquid or fat over food during cooking to prevent it drying out.
bavarois creamy custard dessert set with gelatin.
beurre manié (kneaded butter) equal parts butter and flour worked together to a smooth paste; used to thicken liquids such as sauces.
beurre noisette (brown butter sauce) butter cooked until dark brown (hazel-nut color; finely chopped parsley, capers and vinegar may also be added to it.
blanch to plunge food into boiling water for a specified short period of time. Meats such as sweetbreads are blanched to make the flesh firm and preserve their whiteness; bacon may be blanched to remove excess saltiness; some vegetables are blanched to remove pungency. Most vegetables are blanched to prepare them for freezing.
blanquette white stew made with lamb, chicken or veal. The sauce is made from the liquid in which the meat is cooked, thickened with an egg yolk and cream liaison.
bouquet garni bunch of herbs, classically parsley, thyme and bay leaf, tied together or wrapped in muslin for easy removal from the dish it has seasoned before serving. Other herbs may be added according to taste.
breathe, let to allow wine to become aerated by opening the bottle or decanting it so

that its full flavor can develop.
butter preserve made from fruit purée cooked with sugar until thick.
buttercream cake icing and filling made by beating icing sugar into unsalted butter; may be colored and flavored to taste.

caramelize to boil sugar, or sugar syrup, until it is a brown toffee; this caramel is used to coat molds for puddings. Also, to sprinkle sugar over a pudding and broil until it is melted to a caramel topping.
carbonnade Flemish dish of beef stewed or braised with beer.
casserole method of cooking meat, poultry and game in a covered container, very slowly, usually in the oven. Also, the cooking vessel used.
caul fatty membrane from the lower portion of pig's or sheep's bowel which is used to wrap and bard meat and fish dishes which are dry and are to be given long cooking.
chine to remove the backbone from a rib roast or rack of lamb before cooking, to make carving easier.
chutney a condiment of Indian origin. Strictly speaking, a chutney is either a spicy or a cooling side-dish to a curry, but the term is generally applied to a cooked mixture of fruit and/or vegetables containing sugar and vinegar.
clarify to remove all impurities. Butter is clarified by being heated until it foams, then being skimmed or strained through muslin. Stock for *consommé* or aspic is clarified by being beaten with egg whites and shells over heat and strained similarly.
consommé clear soup made from clarified stock; it may be set to a jelly and served cold.
court bouillon slightly acidulated, aromatic liquid used for poaching, usually fish and seafood, but also some meat and vegetables.
crackling scored crisp skin of a roast of pork.
cream to mix ingredients such as fat and sugar to a mousse-like consistency.
crème anglaise English egg custard which forms the base for many creamy desserts, both baked and set with gelatin. Can also be served as a hot or cold sauce.
crème pâtissière (confectioner's custard) thick custard used as a filling for cakes and pastries.
crêpe large, wafer-thin

French pancake which may be filled with a sweet or savoury mixture.
croquette chilled savory mixture rolled into a cylinder, coated with egg and breadcrumbs and deep-fried.
croustade fried bread case or baked pastry crust, in which hot savory mixtures are served.
croûte pastry case in which food is cooked (such as beef *en croûte*); or toasted bread base on which it is served.
croûton fried bread dice used to garnish soups or other dishes.
crystallize to dip candied fruit or flowers into boiling water and then coat with superfine sugar.
curry powder/paste blend of powdered spices generally containing turmeric, fenugreek, coriander, cumin, cardamom and chili. The more chili used, the hotter the curry.

decant to pour wine from its bottle into a decanter, leaving any sediment behind.
deglaze to dilute the sediment and concentrated juices left in a pan after cooking (particularly sautéing) usually with wine or stock, to make a gravy or sauce.
dégorger to draw out excess or strong juice from vegetables, such as aubergine (and some meats) generally by salting.
dripping melted meat fat.
dropping consistency when a mixture is thick enough to fall only reluctantly from the back of a spoon.
duxelles mixture of very finely chopped mushrooms, shallots (and sometimes ham), butter and seasonings: used to flavor soups and sauces or as a stuffing.

emulsion liquid like mayonnaise, containing tiny drops of oil or fat distributed through it in a stable suspension.

farce French term for stuffing or forcemeat.
fines herbes classic combination of chives, chervil, parsley and tarragon.
flamber (**flame**) to set alight a spirit such as brandy and pour it, flaming, over food. The alcohol is burned off leaving just the flavor of the spirit.
fold to incorporate a light airy mixture, such as beaten egg whites, into a heavier one without a stirring action which might result in loss of air.

fraiser to work pastry dough with the heel of the hand, to make it smooth and distribute the fat evenly.
freezer burn grayish-white patches on frozen food caused by dehydration (on exposure to the air) during storage.
fricassee stew made from poultry or white meat.
frosting American term for icing, usually made with egg white and confectioner's sugar.

galantine meat which has been boned, stuffed and rolled, wrapped in muslin and poached; served cold.
garam masala mixture of spices, ground or pounded together, which is used extensively in Indian cooking. The spices usually include cinnamon, cloves, coriander, cardamom, cumin and black peppercorns.
gelatin colorless, odorless substance containing protein, produced by boiling beef bones, cartilage and tendons; used to gel (set) soups, and stocks, because it melts on warming and sets on cooling. Gelatin is available in powdered or sheet form.
glace de viande/de poisson brown or fish stock simmered until reduced to an almost solid consistency.
glaze to give food a shiny or glossy finish.
gluten a mixture of two proteins found in cereal grains produced when water is added to flour. Gluten helps all leavened breads, cakes and other foods containing flour to rise and hold their shape once risen.
goujon small strip of white fish, coated with egg and breadcrumbs and deep-fried.
gratiner to form a crust on the surface of a dish by sprinkling it with breadcrumbs, dotting with butter and browning under the broiler.

julienne thin matchstick slices or very fine shreds of meat or vegetables.

knead to mix yeast through a dough by pressing, stretching and folding it with the hands.

lard to thread narrow strips of bacon or pork back-fat through lean meat before cooking; these 'lardons' give the meat flavor and keep it moist and succulent.
lard leaves thin slices of pork back fat used for lining pans to keep terrines from drying out.
lardons narrow strips of larding fat. Also, fried bacon

strips or cubes used as a garnish.

liaison thickening agent, such as *beurre manié*, roux, egg yolk and cream, or blood; for soups, sauces and other liquids.

macerate to soak food in the syrup or liquid in which it will be served.

marinade seasoned acidulated liquid, cooked or uncooked, in which foods are soaked to be preserved, tenderized and/or seasoned before cooking. The verb marinate describes the soaking.

marmalade jam made exclusively from citrus fruit.

médaillon small round of meat or sometimes vegetable; also, a small round biscuit.

meringue egg whites beaten with sugar until thick or stiff, and, sometimes, baked.

mincemeat a preserve containing dried fruits, apple, sugar, suet, spices and (usually) brandy. Medieval recipes also included meat, hence the name. Mincemeat is used as a filling for pies and tarts.

mirepoix bed of mixed diced vegetables such as that used for braising.

moule à manqué French cake baked in a pan with sloping sides.

mousse sweet or savory, lightly-set cold dish; with an airy texture, usually due to stiffly-beaten egg whites which have been folded in.

mousseline generally, a mixture which has had whipped cream added to it. Also, little molds made from poultry or fish, enriched with cream and served hot or cold.

noisette (hazel-nut) browned to a hazel-nut color. Rolled lamb chop cut from a rack which has been boned rolled and tied.

nouvelle cuisine style of cooking that promotes light and delicate dishes using unusual combinations of very fresh ingredients.

oyster small piece of meat, shaped like an oyster, found on either side of the backbone of a chicken or other bird.

panade/panada very thick mixture such as a white sauce used as the base for dishes such as soufflés and *quenelles*.

papillote, en fish or poultry cooked in a parcel of oiled greaseproof paper.

parboil partially cook food in boiling water or stock.

pâte pastry

pâté seasoned and flavored mixture of finely ground meats, game, liver and so on, sometimes baked.

paupiette thin slice of meat, such as veal scallop, rolled around a stuffing and tied before cooking.

peak to denote the stiffness of a beaten mixture. Soft peak—thick but not stiff; medium peak—when the peaks flop over slightly at the top and don't stay rigidly in place; stiff peak—when the peaks stay pointed.

pecorino generic term for Italian cheeses made from sheep's milk.

petits fours bite-sized cakes and sweetmeats, usually served with coffee after dinner.

pickle fruit or vegetables preserved in vinegar with or without other flavorings.

pilau, pilaff light, fluffy rice dish, prepared with or without other ingredients.

poppadum crisp, thin savory Indian pastry made from lentil flour; may be plain or spiced.

praline sugar and almonds cooked until brown and caramelized, then cooled and pounded to a powder. Used as a flavoring or as a decoration.

pressure cooker pan with airtight lid that locks in place; in this pan food is cooked quickly in steam under pressure at which it may reach very high temperatures.

pulses dried seeds of leguminous plants such as beans and peas.

purée mashed, sieved or liquefied food.

quenelle dumpling, usually oval, made from finely ground fish, chicken or meat, bound with eggs and poached. *Quenelles* are used as a garnish or served in a sauce as a light dish.

reduce to thicken a liquid like a sauce by boiling it down and evaporating the more volatile content.

refresh to rinse freshly-cooked vegetables briefly under cold water before serving; this prevents further cooking and "sets" the color.

relish cooked mixture of fruit and/or vegetables, similar to a chutney but the ingredients are sieved, ground or finely chopped to give a sauce-like consistency.

render to melt fat down to dripping.

ribbon, to the to beat ingredients, usually egg yolks and sugar, together until the mixture is very thick and will

make a ribbon trail on itself when the beaters are lifted.

risotto Italian method of cooking rice in which all the cooking liquid is absorbed and none left to drain off.

roux mixture of butter and flour which forms the base, and thickening agent, for a sauce.

sherbet originally a cooling drink, today the term is used for a frozen dessert made from fruit juice or purée, sugar and egg whites.

shuck to shell crustaceans such as clams and oysters.

slake to dissolve thickening agents, such as cornstarch, in a little cold liquid before adding it to the hot liquid which is to be thickened.

sorbet sweet, fresh iced dessert, like a sherbet but made without egg whites. The creamy texture is produced by constant churning or frequent beating while freezing.

soufflé sweet or savory dish made from a purée or sauce thickened with egg yolks and lightened with stiffly beaten egg whites. May be baked and served hot or set with gelatin and chilled.

souse to marinate and cook fish, usually oily, in a pickling mixture of vinegar, spices and seasonings.

spun sugar (angel's hair) sugar syrup boiled to the crack stage, then worked to give fine glass-like threads; used to decorate desserts and confectionery.

strudel pastry rich dough rolled and stretched until paper thin, to be rolled around a sweet or savory filling before baking. Filo pastry is similar, and is usually layered in sheets with a filling.

suprême breast of poultry.

sweat to cook food, usually vegetables, gently in butter or oil until the flavoring juices are exuded but the food is not browned.

syrup sugar syrup is sugar and water boiled until thick; the more sugar, the heavier and thicker the syrup. It may be flavored with fruit juices.

tabasco sauce proprietary brandy of hot red pepper sauce.

terrine seasoned and flavored mixture of finely ground meats, game or liver (the same as for a pâté), baked in a dish lined with pork fat or bacon.

tomalley creamy, greenish liver of a lobster.

tournedos thick slice from the narrower end of a beef fillet.

vacherin dessert made from baked meringue rounds usually sandwiched together with Chantilly cream.

vinaigrette French dressing, of oil, vinegar and seasoning.

vintage a particular year's wine produce.

waffle thin batter, sometimes made with yeast, baked in a special iron with characteristic indentations, until puffed up, crisp and golden brown.

yogurt milk flavored and set to a solid with a bacterial culture; the creamy curd produced may be sweetened and flavored with fruit or other ingredients.

zest thinly pared or grated colored skin of an orange or lemon, without any of the bitter white pith.

Index

Bibliography

Androuet, J. *Guide du Fromage* A. Ellis 1973

Ayrton, E. *Cookery of England* Deutsch 1975; Penguin 1977

Beard, J. *Beard on Bread* Michael Joseph 1976

Beck, S., Bertholle, L. and Child, J. *Mastering the Art of French Cooking* Michael Joseph 1977; Penguin 1978

Beck, S. and J. M. *New Menus from Simca's Cuisine* John Murray 1980

Beeton, Mrs Isabella *Book of Household Management* Jonathan Cape 1978

Bocuse, P. *New Cuisine* Hart-Davis 1978

Boxer, A. *Garden Cook Book* Weidenfeld and Nicolson 1975; Sphere 1977

Boyd, L. *British Cookery* Croom Helm 1976

Buonassisi, V. *Classic Book of Pasta* Macdonald and Jane's 1977

Carrier, R. *Cookery Course* W.H. Allen 1974; Sphere 1976

Child, J. *From Julia Child's Kitchen* Jonathan Cape 1978

Claiborne, C. and Lee, V. *Chinese Cook Book* Deutsch 1973; Sphere 1974

Cradock, F. and J. *A Cook's Essential Alphabet* W.H. Allen 1979

Composition of Foods Medical Research Council HMSO 1978

Conran, T. *Kitchen Book* Mitchell Beazley 1977

Cookery Encyclopedia Octopus Books 1978

Cookery Year Reader's Digest 1976

Costa, M. *Four Seasons Cookery Book* Nelson 1970; Sphere 1972

David, E. *English Bread and Yeast Cookery* Allen Lane 1977

David, E. *French Provincial Cooking* Penguin 1970; Michael Joseph 1975

David, E. *Spices, Salts and Aromatics in the English Kitchen* Penguin 1970

Davidson, A. *Mediterranean Seafood* Penguin 1972

Davidson, A. *North Atlantic Seafood* Macmillan 1979

Deighton, L. *Basic French Cooking* Jonathan Cape 1979

Dictionary of Classical and Modern Cookery (Hering) Virtue 1974

Dubbs, C. and Heberte, D. *The Easy Art of Smoking Food* Winchester Press 1977 (US)

Erlandson, K. *Home Smoking and Curing* Barrie and Jenkins 1977

Escoffier, G. *Complete Guide to the Art of Modern Cookery (Le Guide Culinaire)* Heinemann 1979

Fawcett, H. and Strang, J. *Good Cook's Guide* David and Charles 1974

Grieve, M. *Modern Herbal* Penguin 1976

Grigson, J. *Charcuterie and French Pork Cookery* Michael Joseph 1967; Penguin 1970

Grigson, J. *English Food* Macmillan 1974; Penguin 1977

Good Cook Series Time Life Books 1979

Guérard, M. *Cuisine Gourmande* Macmillan 1978

Guérard, M. *Cuisine Minceur* Macmillan 1977

Hammond, B. *Cooking Explained* Longman 1974

Hazan, M. *Classic Italian Cook Book* Macmillan 1980

Hertzberg, R., Greene, J. and Vaughan, B. *Putting Food By* Stephen Greene Press 1973; Bantam Books 1976

Home Preservation of Fruit and Vegetables Ministry of Agriculture, Fisheries and Food Bulletin 21 HMSO

Howe, R. *Poultry and Game* International Wine and Food Society 1970

Howe, R. *Regional Italian Cookery* International Wine and Food Society 1972

Johnson, H. *World Atlas of Wine* Mitchell Beazley 1977

Larousse Gastronomique Hamlyn 1965 (*New Larousse Gastronomique* Hamlyn 1977)

Lees, H., Lovell, M. *New Iris Syrett Cookery Book* Faber 1978

Leith, P. and Waldegrave, C. *Leith's Cookery Course* Fontana 1979

Lenôtre, G. *Lenôtre's Desserts and Pastries* Barron's Educational Series 1977

Lo, K. *Cooking the Chinese Way* Mayflower 1972

Lyon, N. and Benton, P. *Eggs, Milk and Cheese* Faber 1971

Mace, H. *Storing, Preserving and Pickling* Adam and Charles Black 1940

MacManiman, G. *Dry It—You'll Like It* MacManiman 1974

Mawson, M. *Cooking with Herbs and Spices* Hamlyn 1978

McNeill, M. *Scots Kitchen: Recipes* Blackie 1974; Mayflower 1974

Morgan, J. *The Big Book of Chocolates, Sweets and Toffees* Ward Lock 1979

Ogilvy, S. *Making Cheeses* Batsford 1976

Pépin, J. *La Technique* Hamlyn 1978

Perkins, W.L. *Fannie Farmer Cook Book* Little, Brown and Company 1965 (US)

Reingold, C.B. *Cuisinart Food Processor Cooking* Dell 1976 (US)

Robyns, G. *Blender Cook Book* Elm Tree Books 1971

Rockwell, F.F. *Save it for Winter* Frederick A. Stokes 1918 (US)

Rombauer, I. and Becker, M. *The Joy of Cooking* Dent 1974

Rosier, A. *Toshiba Book of Microwave Cookery* Woodhead-Faulkner 1978

Saulnier, L. *Le Répertoire de la Cuisine* Florian Press 1950

Simon, A. and Howe, R. *Dictionary of Gastronomy* Nelson 1970

Smith, H. *Master Book of Fish* Practical Press 1949

Spry, C. and Hume, R. *The Constance Spry Cookery Book* Pan 1972; Dent 1978

Tovey, J. *Entertaining with Tovey* Macdonald 1979

Vergé, R. *Cuisine of the Sun* Macmillan 1979

Wood, B. *Let's Preserve It* Souvenir Press 1970; Mayflower 1972

Acknowledgements

Illustrators
Bill le Fever (Linda Rogers Associates)
Jonathan Newdick (Anglo-Continental Artists)
Ivan Ripley (Anglo-Continental Artists)
Fred St Ward (John Martin Ltd)

Photographer
Phillip Dowell

Typesetting
Servis Filmsetting Ltd, Manchester

Origination
Acolortone Ltd, Ipswich

**The Author and Publishers gratefully
acknowledge invaluable assistance from the
following people and organizations:**

Elizabeth David, Ltd
Kate Duffield
Mannie Franks (and the staff of Wainwright &
    Daughter)
Seemah Joshuah
Mr Kelly (Fruit and Vegetable Department,
    Fortnum and Mason, Ltd)
Ann Kramer
Annie Langford
Ruth Lewis (American Meat Export Federation,
    Inc)
David Mellor, Ltd
Susan Mitchell
John Prizeman ARIBA
Jean Reynaud
Alison Tomlinson
Caroline Waldegrave (and the staff and students of
    Leith's School of Food and Wine)
Jazz Wilson